The Seven Last Words of Christ Explained

Archbishop Fulton J. Sheen

Cover design by Janicka Barman www.twitter.com/barman_janika
Artwork inside the book: Jesus and the Two Thieves (2008) painting by Michael D. O'Brien © Michael D. O'Brien.

Scripture quotations are taken from the Douay-Rheims edition of the Old and New Testaments.

Bishop Sheen Today
280 John Street
Midland, Ontario, Canada
L4R 2J5
www.bishopsheentoday.com

Library of Congress Cataloging-in-Publication Data
Names: Sheen, Fulton J. (Fulton John), 1895-1979, author. | Smith, Al (Allan J.), editor. | Sheen, Fulton J. (Fulton John), 1895-1979. Cross and the Beatitudes. | Sheen, Fulton J. (Fulton John), 1895-1979. Rainbow of sorrow. | Sheen, Fulton J. (Fulton John), 1895-1979. Seven last words. | Sheen, Fulton J. (Fulton John), 1895-1979. Seven virtues. | Sheen, Fulton J. (Fulton John), 1895-1979. Seven Words of Jesus and Mary. | Sheen, Fulton J. (Fulton John), 1895-1979. Seven Words to the Cross. | Sheen, Fulton J. (Fulton John), 1895-1979. Victory Over Vice. | Sheen, Fulton J. (Fulton John), 1895-1979. Cross and the Beatitudes.

Title: The Seven Last Words of Christ Explained. / Archbishop Fulton J. Sheen: compiled by Al Smith.

Description: Midland, Ontario: Bishop Sheen Today Publishing, 2021. | Includes bibliographical references.

Identifiers: paperback ISBN 978-1-990427-24-4 / e-Book ISBN 978-1-990427-25-1 / Hardcover ISBN 978-990427-72-5 /
Subjects: LCSH: Jesus Christ — Seven last words.

J.M.J.

To Our Lady, Seat of Wisdom,
In Humble Petition That,
Through The Immaculate Heart Of Mary,
The World May Find Its Way Back To
The Sacred Heart of Jesus

The Seven Last Words of Christ

The First Word

"Father, Forgive Them For They Know Not What They Do."

The Second Word

"This Day Thou Shalt Be With Me In Paradise."

The Third Word

"Woman, Behold Thy Son; Behold Thy Mother."

The Fourth Word

"My God! My God! Why Hast Thou Forsaken Me?"

The Fifth Word

"I Thirst."

The Sixth Word

"It Is Finished."

The Seventh Word

"Father, Into Thy Hands I Commend My Spirit."

Contents

Introduction

I have learned more from the crucifix than from any book.

St. Thomas Aquinas

Archbishop Fulton J. Sheen was a man for all seasons. Over his lifetime, he spent himself for souls, transforming lives with the clear teaching of the truths of Christ and His Church through his books, his radio addresses, his lectures, his television series, and his many newspaper columns.

The topics of this much-sought-after lecturer ranged from the social concerns of the day to matters of faith and morals. With an easy and personable manner, Sheen could strike up a conversation on just about any subject, making numerous friends as well as converts.

During the 1930s and '40s, Fulton Sheen was the featured speaker on The Catholic Hour radio broadcast, and millions of listeners heard his radio addresses each week. His topics ranged from politics and the economy to philosophy and man's eternal pursuit of happiness.

Along with his weekly radio program, Sheen wrote dozens of books and pamphlets. One can safely say that through his writings, thousands of people changed their perspective about God and the Church. Sheen was quoted as saying, "There are not one hundred people in the United States who hate the Catholic Church, but there are millions who hate what they wrongly perceive the Catholic Church to be."

Possessing a burning zeal to dispel the myths about Our Lord and His Church, Sheen gave a series of powerful presentations on Christ's Passion and His seven last words from the Cross. As a Scripture scholar, Archbishop Sheen knew full well the power contained in preaching Christ crucified. With St. Paul, he could say, "For I decided to know nothing among you except Jesus Christ and him crucified" (1 Cor. 2:2).

During his last recorded Good Friday address in 1979, Archbishop Sheen spoke of having given this type of reflection on the subject of Christ's seven last words from the cross "for the fifty-eighth consecutive time." Whether from the young priest in Peoria, Illinois, the university professor in Washington, D.C., or the bishop in New York, Sheen's messages were sure to make an indelible mark on his listeners.

Given their importance and the impact they had on society, it seemed appropriate to bring together in this anthology some of Archbishop Sheen's meditations on the Seven Last Words Our Blessed Lord spoke from the Cross on Calvary.

The meditations contained in this book are taken from several books and articles written by Sheen between 1933 and 1945.

The Seven Last Words
(New York: Century, 1933)

The Seven Last Words and the Our Father
(Huntington, Indiana: Our Sunday Visitor, 1935)

Calvary and the Mass
(New York: P. J. Kenedy and Sons, 1936)

The Cross and the Beatitudes
(New York: P. J. Kenedy and Sons, 1937)

The Rainbow of Sorrow
(New York: P. J. Kenedy and Sons, 1938)

Victory over Vice
(New York: P. J. Kenedy and Sons, 1939)

The Seven Virtues
(New York: P. J. Kenedy and Sons, 1940)

Seven Words to the Cross
(New York: P. J. Kenedy and Sons, 1944)

The Seven Words of Jesus and Mary
(New York: P. J. Kenedy and Sons, 1945)

These mediations have been selected to provide nine unique reflections for study and meditation on the Seven Last Words.

The first meditation of each chapter begins with a reflection on the words spoken by Christ from the cross, while the second meditation presents a reflection on a passage from the Lord's Prayer.

The third meditation contains a reflection on the Mass while the fourth meditation presents a reflection on one of the Beatitudes.

The fifth meditation represents reflections on why there is sorrow and suffering in the world, while the sixth meditation offers the reader advice on overcoming the seven deadly sins.

The seventh meditation offer a reflection on the virtues, followed by the eighth meditation will provide some timely insights on how to deal with individuals who reject the Church and Christ's teachings.

Each chapter in this treasury of writings concludes with a ninth meditation that looks at the seven recorded times in sacred scripture that the Blessed Virgin Mary spoke and how her words are connected to the Seven Last Words Our Blessed Lord spoke from the Cross.

As the reader ponders these reflections, they might have to pause for a moment or two over a sentence that is full of deep meaning that stirs the heart. He might also find that Archbishop Sheen has repeated certain lines throughout these reflections to drive home a point or an important theme, as any good teacher would do.

On October 2, 1979, when visiting St. Patrick's Cathedral in New York City, Pope John Paul II embraced Fulton Sheen and spoke into his ear a blessing and an affirmation. He said: "You have written and spoken well of the Lord Jesus Christ. You are a loyal son of the Church."

On the day Archbishop Sheen died (December 9, 1979), he was found in his private chapel before the Eucharist in the shadow of the cross. Archbishop Sheen was a man purified in the fires of love and by the wood of the Cross.

It is hoped that, upon reading these reflections, the reader will concur with the heartfelt affirmation given by St. John Paul II and countless others of Sheen's wisdom and fidelity. May these writings by Archbishop Fulton J. Sheen evoke a greater love and appreciation for the Church, the Passion of Lord Jesus Christ, and the need for us to look into our souls each day.

Archbishop Sheen's dynamic personality combined with his brilliant mind, tireless pen, and eloquent voice has made him one of the best-known figures in the world. His radio and television appearances have been phenomenally successful and are still viewed today. His books and magazine articles continue to gratify and attract a boundless circle of readers. This collection of meditations gives still another example of why this continues to be so today.

FATHER, FORGIVE THEM FOR THEY KNOW NOT WHAT THEY DO
Meditations on the First Word from the Cross
Archbishop Fulton J. Sheen

First Meditation

FATHER, FORGIVE THEM, FOR THEY KNOW NOT WHAT THEY DO.

It seems to be a fact of human psychology that when death approaches, the human heart speaks its words of love to those whom it holds closest and dearest. There is no reason to suspect that it is otherwise in the case of the Heart of hearts. If He spoke in a graduated order to those whom He loved most, then we may expect to find in His first three words the order of His love and affection. His first words went out to enemies: "Father, forgive them," His second to sinners: "This day you will be with Me in Paradise," and His third to saints: "Woman, behold your son." Enemies, sinners, and saints -- such is the order of Divine Love and Thoughtfulness.

The congregation anxiously awaited His first word. The executioners expected Him to cry, for everyone pinned on the gibbet of the Cross had done it before Him. Seneca tells us that those who were crucified cursed the day of their birth, the executioners, their mothers, and even spat on those who looked upon them. Cicero tells us that at times it was necessary to cut out the tongues of those who were crucified, to stop their terrible blasphemies. Hence the executioners expected a cry but not the kind of cry that they heard. The scribes and Pharisees expected a cry, too, and they were quite sure that He who had preached "Love your enemies," and "Do good to them that hate you," would now forget that Gospel with the piercing of feet and hands. They felt that the excruciating and agonizing pains would scatter to the winds any resolution He might have taken to keep up appearances. Everyone expected a cry, but no one with the exception of the three at the foot of the Cross expected the cry they did hear. Like some fragrant trees which bathe in perfume the very axe which gnashes them, the great Heart on the Tree of Love poured out from its depths something less a cry than a prayer, the soft, sweet, low prayer of pardon and forgiveness: "Father, forgive them, for they know not what they do."

Forgive whom? Forgive enemies? The soldier in the court-room of Caiaphas who struck Him with a mailed fist; Pilate, the politician, who condemned a God to retain the friendship of Caesar; Herod, who robed Wisdom in the garment of a fool; the soldiers who swung the King of Kings on a tree between heaven and earth -- forgive them? Forgive them, why? Because they know what they do? No, because they know not what they do. If they knew what they were doing and still went on doing it; if they knew what a terrible crime they were committing by sentencing Life to death; if they knew what a perversion of justice it was to choose Barabbas to Christ; if they knew what cruelty it was to take the feet that trod everlasting hills and pinion them to the limb of a tree; if they knew what they were doing and still went on doing it, unmindful of the fact that the very blood which they shed was capable of redeeming them, they would never be saved! Why, they would be damned if it were not for the fact that they were ignorant of the terrible thing they did when they crucified Christ! It was only the ignorance of their great sin that brought them within the pale of the hearing of that cry from the Cross. It is not wisdom that saves; it is ignorance!

There is no redemption for the fallen angels. Those great spirits headed by the Bearer of Light, Lucifer, endowed with an intelligence compared with which ours is but that of a child, saw the consequences of each of their decisions just as clearly as we see that two and two make four. Having made a decision, they made it irrevocably; there was no taking it back, and hence there was no future redemption. It is because they knew what they were doing that they were excluded from the hearing of that cry that went forth from the Cross. It is not wisdom that saves; it is ignorance!

In like manner, if we knew what a terrible thing sin was and went on sinning; if we knew how much love there was in the Incarnation and still refused to nourish ourselves with the Bread of Life; if we knew how much sacrificial love there was in the Sacrifice of the Cross and still refused to fill the chalice of our heart with that love; if we knew how much mercy there was in the Sacrament of Penance, and still refused to bend a humble knee to a hand that had the power to loose both in heaven and on earth; if we knew how much life there was in the Eucharist and still refused to take of the Bread which makes life everlasting and still refused to drink of that Wine that produces and enriches virgins; if we knew all the truth there is in the Church as the mystical body of Christ and still turned our backs to it like other Pilates; if we knew all these things and still stayed away from Christ and His Church, we should be lost! It is not wisdom that saves; it is ignorance! It is only our ignorance of how good God is that excuses us for not being saints!

PRAYER

Dear Jesus! I do not want to know the wisdom of the world; I do not want to know on whose anvil snow-flakes are hammered or the hiding-place of darkness or from whose womb came the ice, or why the gold falls to the earth earthly, and fire climbs to the heavens heavenly; I do not want to know literature and science, or the four-dimensional universe in which we live; I do not want to know the length of the universe in terms of light years; I do not want to know the breadth of the earth as it dances about the chariot of the sun; I do not want to know the heights of the stars, chaste candles of the night; I do not want to know the depths of the sea or the secrets of its watery palace. I want to be ignorant of all these things. I want only to know the length, the breadth, the height and the depth of Thy redeeming Love on the Cross, Sweet Saviour of Men. I want to be ignorant of everything in the world -- everything but You, dear Jesus. And then, by the strangest of strange paradoxes, I shall be wise!

The Seven Last Words, 1933

Second Meditation

OUR FATHER WHO ART IN HEAVEN

"Our Father Who art in heaven."

"Father, forgive them for they know not what they do."

The first petition of the Our Father Our Lord taught us was the prayer of priestly intercession: "Our Father Who art in heaven." The first word from the Cross was the intercessory prayer of the perfect Priest: "Father forgive them for they know not what they do."

The Priest whence all priesthood is derived once asked us to look up to our Father Who is in Heaven. Now He begs that same Father to blot out the sins of those who crucify Him and to forgive them "for they know not what they do." He was finding an excuse for sins. He was telling His Father that we crucified Him only because of our ignorance. If we knew what we were doing, we would never have denied the Father in Heaven. Salvation is possible only because of our ignorance of how good God the Father is to send His only begotten Son into the world that we might have life in His name.

When our enemies crucify us, we say: "They should have known better." When we crucified Him, He said: "Forgive them, for they know not what they do." We love those who love us and honor those who flatter us; He loved those who hated Him and forgave even the hands that drove the nails. He loves not only the lovable, as we do – He also loves the hateful, which we are. That is why there is hope for us! Our Father Who art in heaven, forgive us for we know not what we do".

The Seven Last Words and the Our Father, 1935

Third Meditation

THE CONFITEOR

"Father, forgive them, for they know not what they do."

The Mass begins with the Confiteor. The Confiteor is a prayer in which we confess our sins and ask the Blessed Mother and the saints to intercede to God for our forgiveness, for only the clean of heart can see God. Our Blessed Lord too begins His Mass with the Confiteor. But His Confiteor differs from ours in this: He has no sins to confess. He is God and therefore is sinless. "Which of you shall convince me of sin?" His Confiteor then cannot be a prayer for the forgiveness of *His* sins; but it can be a prayer for the forgiveness of *our* sins.

Others would have screamed, cursed, wrestled, as the nails pierced their hands and feet. But no vindictiveness finds place in the Saviour's breast; no appeal comes from His lips for vengeance on His murderers; He breathes no prayer for strength to bear His pain. Incarnate Love forgets injury, forgets pain, and in that moment of concentrated agony reveals something of the height, the depth, and the breadth of the wonderful love of God, as He says His Confiteor: "Father, forgive them, for they know not what they do."

He did not say "Forgive Me," but "Forgive them." The moment of death was certainly the one most likely to produce confession of sin, for conscience in the last solemn hours does assert its authority; and yet not a single sigh of penitence escaped His lips. He was associated with sinners, but never associated with sin. In death as well as life, He was unconscious of a single unfulfilled duty to His heavenly Father. And why? Because a sinless Man is not just a man; He is more than mere man. He is sinless, because He is God -- and there is the difference. We draw our prayers from the depths of our consciousness of sin: He drew His silence from

His own intrinsic sinlessness. That one word "Forgive" proves Him to be the Son of God.

Notice the grounds on which He asked His heavenly Father to forgive us -- "Because they know not what they do." When anyone injures us, or blames us wrongly, we say: "They should have known better." But when we sin against God, He finds an excuse for forgiveness -- our ignorance.

There is no redemption for the fallen angels. The blood drops that fell from the cross on Good Friday in that Mass of Christ did not touch the spirits of the fallen angels. Why? Because they knew what they were doing? They saw all the consequences of their acts, just as clearly as we see that two and two make four, or that a thing cannot exist and not exist at the same time. Truths of this kind when understood cannot be taken back; they are irrevocable and eternal. Hence when they decided to rebel against Almighty God, there was no taking back the decision. They *knew* what they were doing!

But with us it is different. We do not see the consequences of our acts as clearly as the angels; we are weaker, we are ignorant. But if we did know that every sin of pride wove a crown of thorns for the head of Christ; if we knew that every contradiction of His divine command made for Him the sign of contradiction, the Cross; if we knew that every grasping avaricious act nailed His hands, and every journey into the byways of sin dug His feet; if we knew how good God is and still went on sinning, we would never be saved. It is only our ignorance of the infinite love of the Sacred Heart that brings us within the hearing of His Confiteor from the Cross: "Father, forgive them, for they know not what they do."

These words, let it be deeply graven on our souls, do not constitute an *excuse* for continued sin, but a *motive* for contrition and penance. Forgiveness is not a denial of sin. Our Lord does not *deny* the horrible fact of sin, and that is where the modern world is wrong. It explains sin away: it ascribes it to a fall in the evolutionary process, to a survival of ancient taboos; it identifies it with psychological verbiage.

In a word, the modern world *denies* sin. Our Lord reminds us that it is the most terrible of all realities. Otherwise why does it give Sinlessness a cross? Why does it shed innocent blood? Why does it have such awful associations: blindness, compromise, cowardice, hatred, and cruelty? Why does it now lift itself out of the realm of the impersonal and assert itself as personal by nailing Innocence to a gibbet? An abstraction cannot do that. But sinful man can.

Hence He, who loved men unto death, allowed sin to wreak its vengeance upon Him, in order that they might forever understand its horror as the crucifixion of Him who loved them most.

There is no denial of sin here -- and yet, with all its horror, the Victim forgives. In that one and the same event, there is the sign of sin's utter depravity and the seal of divine forgiveness. From that point on, no man can look upon a crucifix and say that sin is not serious, nor can he ever say that it cannot be forgiven. By the way He suffered, He revealed the reality of sin; by the way He bore it, He shows His mercy toward the sinner.

It is the Victim who has suffered that forgives: and in that combination of a Victim so humanly beautiful, so divinely loving, so wholly innocent, does one find a Great Crime and a Greater Forgiveness. Under the shelter of the Blood of Christ the worst sinners may take their stand; for there is a power in that Blood to turn back the tides of vengeance which threaten to drown the world.

The world will give you sin explained away, but only on Calvary do you experience the divine contradiction of sin forgiven. On the Cross, supreme self-giving and divine love transforms sin's worst act in the noblest deed and sweetest prayer the world has ever seen or heard, the Confiteor of

Christ: “Father, forgive them, for they know not what they do."

That word "Forgive," which rang out from the Cross that day when sin rose to its full strength and then fell defeated by Love, did not die with its echo. Not long before, that same merciful Saviour had taken means to prolong forgiveness through space and time, even to the consummation of the world. Gathering the nucleus of His Church round about Him, He said to His Apostles: "Whose sins you shall forgive, they are forgiven."

Somewhere in the world today then, the successors of the Apostles have the power to forgive. It is not for us to ask: But how can man forgive sins? -- for man cannot forgive sins. But God can forgive sins *through* man, for is not that the way God forgave His executioners on the cross, namely through the instrumentality of His human nature?

Why then is it not reasonable to expect Him still to forgive sins through other human natures to whom He gave that power? And where find those human natures?

You know the story of the box, which was long ignored and even ridiculed as worthless; and one day it was opened and found to contain the great heart of a giant. In every Catholic Church that box exists. We call it the confessional box. It is ignored and ridiculed by many, but in it is to be found the Sacred Heart of the forgiving Christ forgiving sinners through the uplifted hand of His priest as He once forgave through His own uplifted hands on the Cross. There is only one forgiveness -- the Forgiveness of God. There is only one "Forgive" -- the "Forgive" of an eternal Divine Act in which we come in contact at various moments of time.

As the air is always filled with symphony and speech, but we do not hear it unless we tune it in on our radios, so neither do souls feel the joy of that eternal and divine "Forgive" unless they are attuned to it in time; and the confessional box is the place where we tune in to that cry from the Cross.

Would to God that our modern mind instead of denying the guilt, would look to the Cross, admit its guilt, and seek forgiveness; would that those who have uneasy consciences that worry them in the light, and haunt them in the darkness, would seek relief, not on the plane of medicine but on the plane of Divine Justice; would that they who tell the dark secrets of their minds, would do so not for the sake of sublimation, but for the sake of purgation; would that those poor mortals who shed tears in silence would find an absolving hand to wipe them away.

Must it be forever true that the greatest tragedy of life is not what happens to souls, but rather what souls miss. And what greater tragedy is there than to miss the peace of sin forgiven? The Confiteor is at the foot of the altar our cry of unworthiness: the Confiteor from the Cross is our hope of pardon and absolution. The wounds of the Saviour were terrible, but the worst wound of all would be to be unmindful that we caused it all. The Confiteor can save us from that, for it is an admission that there is something to be forgiven -- and more than we shall ever know.

There is a story told of a nun who was one day dusting a small image of our Blessed Lord in the chapel. In the course of her duty, she let it slip to the floor. She picked it up undamaged, she kissed it, and put it back again in its place, saying, "If you had never fallen, you never would have received that." I wonder if our Blessed Lord does not feel the same way about us, for if we had never sinned, we never could call Him "Saviour."

Calvary and the Mass, 1936

Fourth Meditation

BLESSED ARE THE MEEK

"Blessed are the meek: for they shall possess the land."

"Father, forgive them, for they know not what they do."

Our Blessed Lord began His public life on the Mount of the Beatitudes, by preaching: "Blessed are the meek: for they shall possess the land." He finished his public life on the Hill of Calvary by practicing that meekness: "Father, forgive them, for they know not what they do."

How different this is from the beatitude of the world! The world blesses not the meek, but the vindictive; it praises not the one who turns the other cheek, but the one who renders evil for evil; it exalts not the humble, but the aggressive. Communism has carried that spirit of violence, class-struggle, and the clenched fist to an extreme the like of which the world before has never seen.

To correct such a war-like attitude of the clenched fist, Our Lord both *preached* and *practiced* meekness.

He preached it in those memorable words that continue the Beatitudes: "You have heard that it hath been said: An eye for an eye, and a tooth for a tooth. But I say to you not to resist evil: but if one strike thee on thy right cheek, turn to him also the other: and if a man will contend with thee in judgment, and take away thy coat, let go thy cloak also unto him. And whosoever shall force thee one mile, go with him other two. ... You have heard that it hath been said: Thou shalt love your neighbor, and hate thy enemy. But I say to you: Love your enemies: do good to them that hate you: and pray for them that persecute and calumniate you that you may be the children of your Father who is in heaven, who maketh His sun to rise upon the good and bad, and raineth upon the just and the unjust. For if you love them that love you, what reward shall you have? do not even the publicans do this? And if you salute your brethren only, what do you more? do not also the heathens this? Be you therefore perfect, as also your heavenly Father is perfect."

But He not only preached meekness; He *practiced* it. When His own people picked up stones to throw at Him, He threw none back in return; when His fellow townsmen brought Him to the brow of the hill to cast Him over the precipice, He walked through their midst unharmed; when the soldier struck Him with a mailed fist, and made the Saviour feel by anticipation the clenched fist of Communism He answered meekly: "If I have spoken evil, give testimony of the evil: but if well, why strikest thou me."

When they swore to kill Him, He did not use His power to strike dead even a single enemy; and now on the Cross, meekness reaches its peak, when to those who dig the Hands which feed the world, and to those who pierce the Feet which shepherd souls, He pleads: "Father, forgive them, for they know not what they do."

Which is right -- the violence of Communism or the meekness of Christ? Communism says meekness is weakness. But that is because it does not understand the meaning of Christian meekness. Meekness is not cowardice; meekness is not an easy-going temperament, sluggish and hard to arouse; meekness is not a spineless passivity which allows everyone to walk over us. No! Meekness is self-possession. That is why the reward of meekness is possession.

A weak person can never be meek, because he is never self-possessed; meekness is that virtue which controls the combative, violent, and pugnacious powers of our nature, and is therefore the best and noblest road to self-realization.

The meek man is not a man who refuses to fight, nor is he a man who will never become angry. A meek man is a man who will never do one thing: he will never fight when his conceit is attacked, but only when a principle is at stake. And there is the keynote to the difference of the anger of the Communist and the anger of the meek man.

Communism begins at the moment conceit is attacked; fist clenched and rise as soon as the ego is challenged; cheeks flush as soon as self-love is wounded, and blood boils and flows at that split second when pride is humbled.

The anger of the Communist is based on selfishness; he hates the rich not because he loves the poor in spirit, but because he wants to be rich himself. Every Communist is really a capitalist without any cash in his pockets. Selfishness is the world's greatest sin; that is why the world hates those who hate it, why it is jealous of those who have more; why it is envious of those who do more; why it dislikes those who refuse to flatter, and why it scorns those who tell us the truth about ourselves; its whole life is inspired by the egotistical, and the personal, and its wrath is born of that self-love.

Now consider the anger of the meek man. For the meek man, not selfishness but righteousness is his guiding principle. He is so possessed, he never allows his fists to go up for an unholy purpose, or in defense of his pride or vanity, or conceit, or because he wants the wealth of another. Only the principles of God's righteousness arouse a meek man. Moses was a meek man, but he broke the tablets of stone when he found his people were disobeying God.

Our Lord is Meekness itself, and yet He drove the buyers and sellers from the Temple when they prostituted His Father's House; but when He came to the doves, He was so self-possessed He gently released them from the cages. He is so much master of Himself, that He is angry only when holiness is attacked, but never when His Person is attacked.

That is why when the Gerasenes besought Our Lord to leave their coasts, without a single retort, "entering into a boat, He passed over the water and came into His own city."

That is why when men laughed Him to scorn He said nothing but approached the dead daughter of Jairus, and went on His work of mercy, oblivious to their insults, and restored her to life. That is why He addressed Judas as "Friend" when he blistered his lips with a kiss. That is why Our Lord from the Cross prays for the forgiveness of His enemies. Their wrath directed against His Body He would not return, though He might have smitten them all dead by the power of His Divinity. Rather, He forgave them, for "they know not what they do."

If ever innocence had a right to protest against injustice, it was in the case of Our Lord. And yet he extends pardon. Their insults to His Person, He ignores. Had He not preached meekness? Now must He not practice it?

And how could He practice it better than to pray for those who were crucifying him? And what greater meekness could there be than to excuse them because they knew not what they did. What a lesson for us to remember: that those who do us harm, may, too, be of the same type of misguided consciences as those who crucified Christ?

From that dread day on, there have been two motives for withdrawing from battle: either because we are afraid or because we are husbanding our energies for a more important battle. The second kind is the meekness of Our Lord.

Be not angry, then, when your conceit is attacked. It will do no harm. As Our Lord reminds us: "Blessed are they that suffer persecution for justice's sake; for theirs is the kingdom of heaven."

In contrast to this Christian philosophy of forgiveness, there exist for the first time in the history of the world a philosophy and a political and social system based not on love, but on hate, and that is Communism. Communism believes that the only way it can establish itself is by inciting revolution, class-struggle, and violence. Hence its regime is characterized by a hatred of those who believe the family is the basic unit of society. The very Communistic gesture of the clenched fist is a token of its pugnacious and destructive spirit, and a striking contrast indeed to the nailed hand of the Saviour pleading forgiveness for the clenched-fisted generation who sent Him to the Cross.

It is startling indeed to recall that we followers of Our Lord believe in violence just as much as do the Communists. Has not Our Lord said: "the kingdom of heaven suffereth violence, and the violent bear it away." But here is the difference: Communists believe in violence to one's neighbor; we believe in violence to ourselves. Communists struggle against all who refuse to have the same hate; we struggle against ourselves, our lower passions, our concupiscence, our selfishness, our egotism, our sensuality, and our meanness -- in a word, against all that prevents us from realizing the best and highest things in our nature. Communism crucifies its enemies; we crucify that which makes us think anyone is our enemy. Communism hates the love of Christians; we hate that which makes us hate Communists. If Communists used as much violence on their selfishness as they use on others, they would all be saints!

Their hatred is weakness, for it refuses to see that collective selfishness is just as wrong as individual selfishness; it is the weakness of the man who is not self-possessed, who uses his fist instead of his mind, who resorts to violence for the same reason the ignorant man resorts to blasphemy; namely, because he has not sufficient intellectual strength to express himself otherwise.

What, then, must be our attitude toward the hatred Communists bear to us? It must be the attitude of the Holy

Father who asked us to pray for the *Communists*. It must be the attitude of those Spanish priests who before being shot by the Communists asked them to kneel down and receive their blessing and their forgiveness. And what is this but a reflection of Our Lord's attitude on the Cross: meekness, love, and forgiveness?

What must be our attitude toward *Communism*? We must possess a strength, a force, and a daring which exposes its errors and goes down to death on the Cross rather than accept the least of its principles of hate.

They will not love us for our meekness, and it will be hard for us not to be angry when our conceit and our pride, and possibly our possessions, are attacked; but there is no escaping the Divine injunction: Blessed are ye when they shall revile you, and persecute you, and speak all that is evil against you, untruly, for my sake: Be glad and rejoice for your reward is very great in heaven". "If the world hate you, know ye that it has hated me before you. If you had been of the world, the world would love its own; but because you are not of the world, but I have chosen you out of the world, therefore the world hateth you". "The hour cometh that whosoever killeth you will think that he doth a service to God."

If then we have enemies, let us forgive them. If we suffer unjustly, then we can practice the virtue of charity. If we suffer justly, and we probably do, for we have sins to atone for, then we can practice the virtue of justice.

What right have we to hate others, since our own selfishness is often the cause of their hatred? The first word from the Cross and the Beatitude of meekness both demand that we tear up self-love by the roots; love our executioners; forgive them, for they know not what they do; do a favor for those who insult us; be kind to the thieves who accuse us of theft; be forgiving to liars who denounce us for lying; be charitable to the adulterers who charge us with impurity.

Be glad and rejoice for their hate. It will only harm our pride, but not our character; it will cauterize our conceit, but not blemish our soul -- for the very insult of the world is the consecration of our goodness.

We know it is not the worldly thing to do -- to pray for those who nail us to a cross. But that is just the point: Christianity is not worldliness; it is turning the world upside down. We know it is not "common sense" to love our enemies, for to love our enemies means hating ourselves; but that is the meaning of Christianity -- hating that which is hateful in us. And in reference to Communism let me say: I hate communism because it is destructive of civilization as Russia and Spain so well prove, but *I love the Communists.* I love them because they are the potential children of God.

Our enemy is often our saviour; our persecutor is often our redeemer; our executioners are often our allies, our crucifiers are often our benefactors -- for they reveal what is selfish, base, conceited, and ignoble in us. But we must not hate them for that. To hate them for hating us is weakness.

If we go on answering hate with hate, how will hate ever end? The violent answer to violence is the propagation of further violence; strife increases the sum of bitterness, regardless of who triumphs. Hate is like a seed: if we sow it we reap more hate. If hatred is to be overcome, the sting must be taken out of it; it must not be nourished, or cultivated, or propagated. But how can this be, except by returning good for evil?

How else can we banish hatred from the earth? Suppose 5,000 men are in line and before them is a Communist propagandist telling them that the only way they can overthrow governments and property is by violence, revolution, and the clenched fist. Suppose the first man in line, inspired by that Communist's hatred, strikes the second man in line on the right cheek; the second raises his clenched fist to strike the third; the third wishes to strike the right cheek of the fourth, and on and on clenched fists fly -- because their Gospel is hate.

Is there any way at all to stop that hatred and violence? Yes, on one condition, and that is if one man in that line who is struck on his right cheek, instead of striking his neighbor, turns and offers to the one who struck him his left cheek. He would kill hatred, because he refused to sow it.

Hatred would no longer have soil on which it could grow, for hatred can grow on a right cheek but never on a left cheek: "If any man strikes thee on the right cheek, turn the other cheek."

That is not weakness; it is strength, the strength that makes man master of himself and the conqueror of hate.

If you doubt it, try it sometime to see how much strength it takes. It took so much strength that only Divinity's cry of forgiveness could overcome the hatred of those who crucify.

If you have enemies, if they hate you, if they revile you, and persecute you and say all manner of evil things against you, and you wish to stop their hatred, to release the hatred in their clenched fists, drive them off the face of the earth -- then there is but one way to do it -- *Love them!*

The Cross and the Beatitudes, 1937

Fifth Meditation

UNJUST SUFFERING

"Father, forgive them, for they know not what they do."

The world is full of those who suffer unjustly and who through no fault of their own bear the "slings and arrows of outrageous fortune." What should be our attitude to those who speak untruly of us, who malign our good names, who steal our reputations, and who sneer at our acts of kindness?

The answer is to be found in the first word from the Cross: *forgive.* If there was ever anyone who had a right to protest against injustice it was He Who is Divine Justice; if ever there was anyone who was entitled to reproach those who dug His hands and feet with steel, it was Our Lord on the Cross.

And yet, at that very moment when a tree turns against Him and becomes a cross, when iron turns against Him and becomes nails, when roses turn against Him and become thorns, when men turn against Him and become executioners, He lets fall from His lips for the first time in the history of the world a prayer for enemies: "Father, forgive them, for they know not what they do" *(Luke 23:34).*

Dwell for a moment on what He did not say. He did not say: "I am innocent," and yet who else could have better claimed innocence? Many times before this Good Friday and many times since, men have been sent to a cross, a guillotine, or a scaffold, for a crime they never committed; but not one of them has ever failed to cry: "I am innocent."

But Our Lord made no such protest, for it would have been to have falsely assumed that man is the Judge of God. Now if Our Lord, Who was Innocence, refrained from asserting His Innocence, then we who are not without sin should not forever be crying our innocence.

To do this is wrongly to admit that man, and not God, is our Judge. Our souls are to be judged not before the tribunal of men, but before the throne of the God of Love; and He "who sees in secret will reward in secret." Our eternal salvation does not depend on how the world judges us, but on how God judges us.

It matters little if our fellow citizens condemn us even when we are right, for Truth always finds its contradictors; that is why Truth is now nailed to a Cross. What does matter is that we be found right in God's judgment, for in that our eternal happiness depends. There is every chance in the world that the two judgments will differ, for man sees only the face, but God reads the heart. We can fool men, but we cannot fool God.

There was another thing Our Blessed Lord did not say to the representatives of Caesar and the Temple who sent Him to the Cross, namely, “You are unjust.” The Father gave all judgment unto Him and yet He does not judge man and say: “You will suffer for this.” He knew, being God as well as man, that while there is life there is hope, and His patient suffering before death might purchase the souls of many who now condemn.

Why judge them before the time for judgment? Longinus of the Roman army and Joseph of the Sanhedrin would come to His saving embrace and forgiveness even before He was taken down from the Cross. The sinner of this hour might be the saint of the next.

One reason for a long life is penance. Time is given us not just to accumulate that which we cannot take with us, but to make reparation for our sins.

That is why in the parable of the fig tree which had not borne fruit for three years and which the owner wished to cut down because it "cumbereth the ground", the dresser of the vineyard said: "Let it alone this year also, until I dig about it, and dung it. And if happily it bear fruit" *(Luke 13:6-9).*

So the Lord is with the wicked. He gives them another month, another year of life that they may dig their soul with penance and dung it with mortification, and happily save their souls.

If then the Lord did not judge His executioners before the hour of their judgment, why should we, who really know nothing about them anyway, judge them even when they do us wrong? While they live, may not our refraining from judgment be the very means of their conversion? In any case, judgment has not been given to us, and the world may be thankful that it has not, for God is a more merciful judge than man. "Judge not that you may not be judged" *(Matthew 7:1).*

What Our Lord did say on the Cross was, *forgive.* Forgive your Pilates, who are too weak to defend your justice; forgive your Herods, who are too sensual to perceive your spirituality; forgive your Judases, who think worth is to be measured in terms of silver. "Forgive them -- for they know not what they do."

In that sentence is packed the united love of Father and Son, whereby the holy love of God met the sin of man, and remained innocent. This first word of forgiveness is the strongest evidence of Our Lord's absolute sinlessness. The rest of us at our death must witness the great parade of our sins, and the sight of them is so awful that we dare not go before God without a prayer for pardon.

Yet Jesus, on dying, craved no forgiveness, for He had no sin. The forgiveness He asked was for those who accused Him of sin. And the reason He asked for pardon was that "they know not what they do."

He is God as well as man, which means He knows all the secrets of every human heart. Because He knows all, He can find an excuse: "they know not what they do." But we know so little of our enemies' hearts and so little of the circumstances of their acts and the good faith mingled with their evil deeds, that we are less likely to find an excuse. Because we are ignorant of their hearts, we are apt to be less excusing.

In order to judge others, we must be inside them and outside them, but only God can do this. Our neighbors are just as impenetrable to us as we are to them. Judgment on our part, then, would be wrong, for to judge without a mandate is unjust. Our Lord alone has a mandate to judge; we have not.

If possessing that mandate, and knowing all, He still found reason to forgive, then we who have no jurisdiction and who cannot possibly with our puny minds know our neighbors' hearts, have only one thing left to do; that is, to pray: "Father, forgive ... for they know not what they do."

Our Lord used the word, *forgive*, because He was innocent and knew all, but we must use it for other reasons. Firstly, because we have been forgiven greater sins by God. Secondly, because only by forgiving can hate be banished from the world. And thirdly, because our own pardon is conditioned by the pardon we extend to others.

Firstly, we must forgive others because God has forgiven us. There is no injustice any human being has ever committed against us which is comparable to the injustice we commit against God by our sins. It is this idea Our Lord suggests in the parable of the unmerciful servant *(Matthew 18:21-35)* who was forgiven a debt of ten thousand talents by his master, and immediately afterwards went out and choked a fellow-servant who owed him only a hundred pence.

The debt which the master forgave the servant was 1,250,000 times greater than the debt owed by the fellow servant. In this great disproportion is revealed how much greater are man's sins against God than are the sins of our fellowmen against us. We must therefore forgive our enemies, because we have been forgiven the greater sin of treating God as an enemy.

And if we do not forgive the sins of our enemies, it is very likely because we have never cast up our accounts with God. Herein is to be found the secret of so much of the violence and bitterness of some men in our modern world; they refuse to think of themselves as ever having offended God and therefore never think of themselves as needing pardon.

They think they need no pardon, hence no one else should ever have it. The man who knows not his own guilt before God is apt to be most unforgiving to others, as David at the time of his worst sin.

Our condemnation is often the veil for our own weakness: we cover up our own nakedness with the mantle of criticism; we see the mote in our brother's eye, but never the beam in our own. We carry all our neighbor's faults on a sack in front of us, and all our own on a sack behind us.

The cruelest master is the man who never learned to obey, and the severest judge is the man who never examines his own conscience. The man who is conscious of his need of absolution is the one who is most likely to be indulgent to others.

Such was Paul, who, writing to Titus, finds a reason for being merciful to men: "For we ourselves also were some time unwise, incredulous, erring, slaves to divers desires and pleasures, living in malice and envy, hateful, and hating one another" *(Titus 3:3).*

It is the forgetfulness of its own sins which makes modern hate so deep and bitter. Men throttle their neighbor for a penny because they forget God forgave them a debt of ten thousand talents. Let them only think of how good God has been to them, and they will begin to be good to others.

A second reason for forgiving those who make us suffer unjustly is that if we do not forgive, hate will multiply until the whole world is hateful. Hate is extremely fertile; it reproduces itself with amazing rapidity.

Communism knows hate can disrupt society more quickly than armies, that is why it never speaks of charity. That too is why it sows hatred in labor against capital; hatred in atheists against religion; hatred in themselves against all who oppose them.

How can all this hatred be stopped when one man is slapping another on the cheek? There is only one way, and that is by turning the other cheek, which means: "I forgive; I refuse to hate you. If I hate you, I will add my quota to the sum total of hate. This I refuse to do. I will kill your hate; I will drive it from the earth. I will love you."

That was the way Stephen conquered the hate of those who killed him; namely, by praying: "Lord, lay not this sin to their charge" *(Acts 7:59).* He was practically repeating the first word from the Cross.

And that prayer of forgiveness won over the heart of a young man named Saul who stood nearby, holding the garments of those who stoned him, and "consenting to his death." If Stephen had cursed Saul, Saul might never have become St. Paul. What a loss that would have been! But hate lost the day because Stephen forgave.

In our day love is still winning victories over hate. When Father Pro of Mexico, a few years ago was shot by the Mexican revolutionists, he turned to them and said: "I forgive you; kneel and I will give you my blessing." And every soldier in the firing line fell on his knees for the blessing.

It was a beautiful spectacle indeed to see a man forgiving those who are about to kill him! Only the Captain refused to kneel, and it was he who did what to Father Pro was an act of great kindness -- ushered him, by a blow through the heart, into the company of Stephen, a martyr of the Church of God.

During the Civil War in Spain when the Reds were slaughtering hundreds of priests, one of them was lined up before the firing squad with his arms tightly bound by ropes. Facing the firing squad, he said: "Untie these ropes and let me give you my blessing before I die." The Communists untied the ropes, but they cut off his hands. Then sarcastically they said: "All right, see if you can give us your blessing now." And the priest raised the stumps of his arms as crimson rags and with blood dripping from them like beads forming on the earth the red rosary of redemption, he moved them about in the form of a cross. Thus hate was defeated, for he refused to nourish it. Hate died as he forgave and the world has been better for it.

Finally, we must forgive others, for on no other condition will our own sins be forgiven. In fact, it is almost a moral impossibility for God to forgive us unless we in turn forgive. Has He not said: "Blessed are the merciful: for they shall obtain mercy" *(Matthew 5:7)*. "Forgive, and you shall be forgiven. Give, and it shall be given unto you . . . For with the same measure that you shall mete withal, it shall be measured to you again" *(Luke 6:37-38)*.

The law is inescapable. Unless we sow, we shall not reap; unless we show mercy to our fellowmen, God will revoke His mercy toward us. As in the parable, the master cancelled the forgiveness of the servant because he refused to show a smaller mercy to his fellowman, "so also shall my heavenly Father do to you, if you forgive not every one, his brother from your hearts" *(Matthew 18:35).*

If a box is filled with salt it cannot be filled with sand, and if our hearts are filled with hatred of our neighbor, how can God fill them with His love? It is just as simple as that. There can be and there will be no mercy toward us unless we ourselves are merciful. The real test of the Christian then is not how much he loves his friends, but how much he loves his enemies.

The divine command is clear: "Love your enemies: do good to them that hate you: and pray for them that persecute and calumniate you: that you may be the children of your Father who is in heaven, who maketh his sun to rise upon the good, and bad, and raineth upon the just and the unjust.

"For if you love them that love you, what reward shall you have? Do not even the publicans this? And if you salute your brethren only, what do you more? Do not also the heathens this?" *(Matthew 5:44-47).*

Forgive, then! Forgive even seventy times seven! Soften the pillow of death by forgiving your enemies their little sins against you, that you may be forgiven your great sins against God. Forgive those who hate you, that you may conquer them by love. Forgive those who injure you, that you may be forgiven your offenses. Our world is so full of hate!

The race of the clenched fists is multiplying like the race of Cain. The struggle for existence has become existence for struggle. There are even those who talk about peace only because they want the world to wait until they are strong enough for war.

"Dear Lord, what can we, thy followers, do to bring peace to the world? How can we stop brother rising up against brother and class against class, blurring the very sky with their cross-covered Golgothas? Thy First Word on the Cross gives the answer: We must see in the body of every man who hates, a soul that was made to love. If we are too easily offended by their hate, it is because we have forgotten either the destiny of their souls or our own sins. Forgive us our trespasses as we forgive those who trespass against us. Forgive us for ever having been offended. Then we, like Thee, may find among our executioners another Longinus, who had forgotten there was love in a heart until he opened it with a lance."

The Rainbow of Sorrow, 1938

Sixth Meditation

ANGER

"Father, forgive them, for they know not what they do."

The one passion in man that has deeper roots in his rational nature than any other is the passion of anger. Anger and reason are capable of great compatibility, because anger is based upon reason, which weighs the injury done and the satisfaction to be demanded. We are never angry unless someone has injured us in some way -- or we think he has.

But not all anger is sinful, for there is such a thing as just anger. The most perfect expression of just anger we find in Our Blessed Lord's cleansing of the Temple. Passing through its shadowed doorways at the festival of the Pasch, He found greedy traders, victimizing at every turn the worshippers who needed lambs and doves for the temple sacrifices.

Making a scourge of little cords He moved through their midst with a calm dignity and beautiful self-control even more compelling than the whip. The oxen and sheep He drove out with His scourge; with His Hands, He upset the tables of the money changers who scrambled on the floor after their rolling coins; with His finger He pointed to the vendors of doves and bade them leave the outer court; to all He said: "Take these things hence, and make not the house of my Father a house of traffic."

Here was fulfilled the injunction of the Scriptures, "Be angry, and sin not," for anger is no sin under three conditions: 1 -- If the cause of anger be just, for example, defense of God's honor; 2 -- If it is no greater than the cause demands, that is, if it is kept under control; and 3 -- If it is quickly subdued: "Let not the sun go down upon your anger."

Here we are not concerned with just anger, but with unjust anger, namely, that which has no rightful cause -- anger which is excessive, revengeful, and enduring; the kind of anger and hatred against God that has destroyed religion on one sixth of the earth's surface; and which recently in Spain burned 25,000 churches and chapels and murdered 12,000 servants of God: the kind of hatred which is not only directed against God, but also against fellowman, and is fanned by the disciples of class conflict who talk peace but glory in war; the red anger which rushes the blood to the surface, and the white anger which pushes it to the depths and bleaches the face; the anger that seeks to “get even”, to repay in kind, bump for bump, punch for punch, eye for eye, lie for lie; the anger of the clenched fist prepared to strike, not in defense of that which is loved but in offense against that which is hated; in a word, the kind of anger that will destroy our civilization unless we smother it by love.

Our Blessed Lord came to make reparation for the sin of anger, first by teaching us a prayer: "Forgive us our trespasses as we forgive those who trespass against us"; and then by giving us a precept: "Love your enemies; do good to them that hate you." More concretely still, He added, "Whosoever will force thee one mile, go with him another two ... if a man ... take away thy coat, let go thy cloak also unto him."

Revenge and retaliation were forbidden: "You have heard that it has been said: an eye for an eye, and a tooth for a tooth. But I say unto you, Love your enemies." These precepts were made all the more striking because He practiced them.

When the Gerasenes became angry at Him because He put a higher value on an afflicted man than on a herd of swine, Scripture records no retort: "And entering into the boat, He passed over the water." To the soldier who struck Him with a mailed fist, He meekly responded: "If I have spoken evil, give testimony of the evil, but if well, why strikest thou me?"

The perfect reparation for anger was made on Calvary. We might also say that anger and hate led Him up that hill. His own people hated Him, for they asked for His crucifixion; the law hated Him, for it forsook justice to condemn Justice; the Gentiles hated Him for they consented to His death; the forests hated Him for one of its trees bore the burden of His weight; the flowers hated Him as they wove thorns for His brow; the bowels of the earth hated Him as it gave its steel as hammer and nails.

Then as if to personalize all that hatred, the first generation of clenched fists in the history of the world stood beneath the Cross and shook them in the face of God. That day they tore His body to shreds as in this day they smash His tabernacle to bits. Their sons and daughters have shattered crucifixes in Spain and Russia as they once smote the Crucified on Calvary.

Let no one think the clenched fist is a phenomenon of the twentieth century; they whose hearts freeze into fists today are but the lineal descendants of those who stood beneath the Cross with hands lifted like clubs against Love as they hoarsely sang the first International of hate.

As one contemplates those clenched fists, one cannot help but feel that if ever anger would have been justified, if ever Justice might have fittingly judged, if ever Power might have rightfully struck, if ever Innocence might have lawfully protested, if ever God might have justly revenged Himself against man -- it was at that moment.

And yet, just at that second when a sickle and a hammer combined to cut down the grass on Calvary's hill to erect a cross, and drive nails through hands to render impotent the blessings of Love incarnate, He, like a tree which bathes in perfume the axe which kills it, let's fall from His lips for the earth's first hearing the perfect reparation for anger and hate -- a prayer for the army of clenched fists, the first Word from the Cross: "Father, forgive them, for they know not what they do."

The greatest sinner may now be saved; the blackest sin may now be blotted out; the clenched fist may now be opened; the unforgivable may now be forgiven. While they were most certain that they knew what they were doing, He seizes upon the only possible palliation of their crime and urges it upon His Heavenly Father with all the ardor of a merciful Heart: ignorance -- "they know not what they do." If they did know what they were doing as they fastened Love to a tree, and still went on doing it, they would never be saved. They would be *damned.*

It is only because fists are clenched in ignorance that they may yet be opened into folded hands; it is only because tongues blaspheme in ignorance that they may yet speak in prayer. It is not their conscious wisdom that saves them; it is their unconscious ignorance.

This Word from the Cross teaches us two lessons: 1 -- The reason for forgiving is ignorance; and 2 -- There are no limits to forgiveness.

The reason for forgiving is ignorance. Divine Innocence found such a reason for pardon; certainly guilt can do no less. St. Peter's first Pentecostal sermon used this very excuse of ignorance for the Crucifixion so fresh in his mind: "The author of life you killed . . . and now, brethren, I know that you did it through ignorance, as did also your rulers."

If there were full consciousness of the evil, perfect deliberation, perfect understanding of the consequences of acts, there would be no room for forgiveness. That is why there is no redemption for the fallen angels. They knew what they were doing. We do not. We are very ignorant -- ignorant of ourselves and ignorant of others.

Ignorant of others! How little we know of their motives, their good faith, the circumstances surrounding their actions. When others visit violence upon us we too often forget how little we know about their hearts and say: "I cannot see that they have the slightest excuse; they knew very well what they were doing." And yet in exactly the same circumstances, Jesus found an excuse: "They know not what they do."

We know nothing about the inside of our neighbor's heart and hence we refuse to forgive. He knew the heart inside out, and because He did know, He forgave. Take any scene of action, let five people look upon it, and you will get five different stories of what happened. No one of them sees all sides. Our Lord does, and that is why He forgives.

Why is it that we can find excuses for our anger against our neighbor, and yet we refuse to admit the same excuses when our neighbor is angry with us? We say others would forgive us if they understood us perfectly, and that the only reason they are angry with us is because "they do not understand."

Why is not that ignorance reversible? Can we not be as ignorant of their motives, as we say they are ignorant of ours? Does not our refusal to find an excuse for their hatred tacitly mean that under similar circumstances, we ourselves will be unfit to be forgiven?

Ignorance of ourselves is another reason for forgiving others. Unfortunately, it is ourselves we know least; our neighbor's sins, weaknesses and failures we know a thousand times better than our own. Criticism of others may be bad, but it is want of self-criticism, which is worse.

It would be less wrong to criticize others if we first criticized ourselves, for if we first turned the searchlight into our own souls, we would never feel we had a right to turn it on the soul of anyone else. It is only because we are ignorant of our true condition that we fail to realize how badly we stand in need of pardon.

Have we ever offended God? Has He any right to be angry with us? Then why should we, who need pardon so badly, strive not to purchase it by pardoning others? The answer is because we never examine our own consciences.

We are so ignorant of our true condition that we know little more of ourselves than our name and address and how much we have; of our selfishness, our envy, our detraction, our sin, we know absolutely nothing. In fact, in order that we may never know ourselves, we hate silence and solitariness. Lest our conscience should carry on with us an unbearable repartee, we drown out its voice in amusements, distractions, and noise. If we met ourselves in others, we would hate them.

If we knew ourselves better, we would be more forgiving of others. The harder we are on ourselves, the easier we will be on others; the man who has never learned to obey knows not how to command; and the man who has never disciplined himself knows not how to be merciful.

It is always the selfish who are unkind to others, and those who are hardest on themselves are the kindest to others, as the teacher who knows the least is always the most intolerant to his pupils.

Only a Lord who thought so little of Himself as to become man and die like a criminal could ever forgive the weakness of those who crucified Him.

It is not hatred that is wrong; it is hating the wrong thing that is wrong. It is not anger that is wrong, it is being angry at the wrong thing that is wrong. Tell me your enemy, and I will tell you what you are. Tell me your hatred, and I will tell you your character.

Do you hate religion? Then your conscience bothers you. Do you hate the capitalists? Then you are avaricious, and you want to be a capitalist. Do you hate the laborer? Then you are selfish and a snob. Do you hate sin? Then you love God. Do you hate your hate, your selfishness, your quick temper, and your wickedness? Then you are a good soul, for "If any man come to me . . . and hate not his own life, he cannot be my disciple."

The second lesson to be derived from this First Word from the Cross is that there is no limit to pardon. Our Lord forgave when He was innocent and not because He Himself had been forgiven. Hence we must forgive not only when we have been forgiven, but even when we are innocent.

The problem of the limits of pardon once troubled Peter, and He asked our Lord: "How often shall my brother offend against me, and I forgive him till seven times?" Peter thought he was stretching forgiveness by saying "seven times," for it was four more than the Jewish Masters enjoined.

Peter proposed a limit beyond which there was to be no forgiveness. Peter assumed the right to be forgiven is automatically renounced after seven offenses. It is equivalent to saying, "I renounce my right to collect debts from you if you never owe me more than seven dollars, but if you exceed that sum, then my duty of further cancellation ceases. I can throttle you for eight dollars."

Our Lord, in answering Peter says that forgiveness has no limits; forgiveness is the surrender of all rights and the denial of limits. "I say not to thee till seven times but till seventy times seven." That does not mean 490 literally, but infinitely. The Saviour then proceeded to tell the parable of the unjust steward who immediately after being forgiven by his lord a debt of 10,000 talents, choked a fellow servant who owed him a hundred pence. The unmerciful steward by refusing to be merciful to his debtor had his own mercy revoked. His guilt was not that, needing mercy he refused to show it, but having received mercy, he was unmerciful still. "So also shall my heavenly Father do to you if you forgive not every one his brother."

Forgive then, and we will be forgiven; remit our anger against others and God will remit His anger against us.

Judgment is a harvest where we sow what we reap. If we sowed anger against our brethren during life, we will reap the just anger of God. Judge not, and we shall not be judged.

If, during life, we forgive others from our hearts, on Judgment Day the All Wise God will permit something very unusual to Himself: He will forget how to add and will know only how to subtract. He who has a memory from all eternity will no longer remember our sins. Thus, we will be saved once again through Divine "Ignorance."

By forgiving others on the ground that they know not what they do, Our Lord will forgive us on the ground that He no longer remembers what we did. It may well be that if He looks on a hand that, now after hearing the first Word on the Cross gives a kindly blessing to an enemy, He will even forget that it was once a clenched fist red with the blood of Christendom.

"And dars't thou venture still to live in sin,
And crucify thy dying Lord again?
Were not His pangs sufficient? Must he bleed
Yet more? O, must our sinful pleasures feed
Upon his torments, and augment the story
Of the sad passion of the Lord of glory!
Is there no pity? Is there no remorse
In human breasts? Is there a firm divorce
Betwixt all mercy and the hearts of men?
Parted forever – ne'er to meet again?

No Mercy bides with us: 'tis thou alone,
Hast it, sweet Jesu, for us, that have none
For thee: thou hast forestall'd our markets so
That all's above, and we have none below:
Nay, blessed Lord, we have not wherewithal
To serve our shiftless selves: unless we call

To thee, thou art our Saviour, and hast power
To give, and whom we crucify each hour:
We are cruel, Lord, to thee and ourselves too;
Jesu forgive us; we know not what we do."

(Francis Quarles)

Victory Over Vice, 1939

Seventh Meditation

FORTITUDE

"Father, forgive them, for they know not what they do."

There is entirely too much psycho-analysis in the world; what is needed is a little more psycho-synthesis. Hearts and minds have been analyzed to a point where they are nothing more than a chaotic mass of unrelated nerve impulses. There is need for someone to pull them together, to give them a pattern of life and above all, peace. The pattern around which we shall psycho-synthesize all these soul-states will be the Cross.

Here we are interested in three types of souls: a) Those who suffer and mourn, saying "What have I done to deserve this?"; b) those who possess faith, but who through a love of the world deny their faith or hide it; c) and those who do not possess the faith, but are convinced of its truth and yet refuse to pay the price.

There is a virtue, which these three types of souls need for their peace, and that is the virtue of Fortitude.

Fortitude may be defined as that virtue which enables us to face undismayed and fearlessly the difficulties and dangers which stand in the way of duty and goodness. It stands midway between foolhardiness, which rushes into danger heedlessly, and cowardice, which flees from it recreantly. Because fortitude is related to bravery, it must not be thought that bravery is devoid of fear; rather it is control of fear. Fortitude is of two kinds, depending upon whether it is directed to a natural good or a supernatural good.

A soldier, for example, who braves the dangers of battle for love of country practices natural fortitude. But the saint who overcomes all difficulties and dangers for the sake of the glory of God and the salvation of his soul, practices supernatural fortitude.

It is in the presence of the fear of death that Fortitude reaches its peak; that is why the highest peak of supernatural fortitude is martyrdom. We are here concerned only with supernatural fortitude.

This virtue reaches its peak in practice in the life of Our Divine Lord: He was primarily a Redeemer -- God in the form of man saving men of whom He was King and Captain. "For God sent not his Son into the world, to judge the world, but that the world may be saved by him" *(John 3:17)*.

His baptism was death and He was "straitened until it be accomplished" *(Luke 12:50)*. Being truly a man, He felt the fear every normal man feels in the face of danger. "If it be possible, let this chalice pass from Me" *(Matthew 26:39)*; but resigned to the Father's business, He added: "Nevertheless not as I will, but as thou wilt" *(Matthew 26:39)*.

No difficulty, however great, would deter Him from the Divine purpose of laying down His life for the redemption of many. Not even "twelve legions of Angels" *(Matthew 26:53)* would He permit to solace Him in His darkest hour, and not even a drug would He touch to His lips to deaden the pains of the Cross.

Solomon of old had said: "Give strong drink to them that are sad, and wine to them that are grieved in mind: Let them drink and forget their want, and remember their sorrow no more" *(Proverbs 31:6,7)*.

The Talmud says it was the custom to put a grain of incense in the draft of those who were being led to death, to deaden the sense of pain.

This intoxicating draft which was given Him as His hands and feet were nailed to a tree of His own creation, He refused to drink *(Matthew 27:34)*. He strides forth boldly to the high things of God. He will meet death in the full possession of His faculties -- fearlessly.

But not in this was His fortitude greatest: when death is upon Him by His own submission, for "no man taketh it away from me: but I lay it down of myself" *(John 10:18)*, His first word from the Cross is not in self-defence, not a protestation of His own innocence, not a fear of death nor a plea for deliverance, nor even fear of enemies.

Fear of death makes most men turn away from doing good. It makes even innocent men thoughtful of themselves as they proclaim their innocence to their executioners. Not so with Him. Fortitude reaches the peak of self-forgetfulness. On the Cross He thinks only of others and their salvation.

For His first word is not about death, but about the good it will accomplish; it is directed not to His friends, His Apostles, or His believers who will proclaim His gospel, but to those who hate Him and His Apostles and His Church: "Father, forgive them, for they know not what they do" *(Luke 23:34)*.

Often during His life, He preached: "Love your enemies: do good to them that hate you" *(Matthew 5:44)*. Now that He is strong enough to ignore death, He the Conqueror bestows on His momentary conquerors the very thing they had forfeited by their sins -- forgiveness.

Why is it that He appeals to His Father to forgive, and does not Himself forgive directly? Because He is looking at the crucifixion not from the human point of view, but from the Divine. They were wronging the Father by killing His Divine Son. The crucifixion is not murder; it is *deicide*.

Murder is a sin against God Who gave human life to human care. Deicide is a sin against God Who entrusted Divine Life to human love. It was not the candle of a man's life the executioners were snuffing out; it was the sun they were trying to extinguish.

The noon-day sun never darkened on murder, but it hid its face in shame as the Light of the World went into the momentary eclipse of death.

No stronger proclamation of His Divinity could have been uttered than for the Divine Son to ask the Divine Father to forgive the sons of men for their Golgothas, their swastikas, and their hammers and sickles. If He were only a man He would have asked His own forgiveness, but being God He asked His Father for the pardon of men.

Scripture does not record that anyone except the Thief on the right, within the hearing of that cry, repented or even regretted driving the nails and unfurling the flag of the Cross to the four winds of the world. There is not a single record that anyone else expressed a desire to follow Him or that they were touched by His calmness under fire.

Thus the world's greatest act of bravery when He who was thoughtless of self became thoughtful of others, went momentarily barren. They were apparently satisfied to sit and watch.

But it was for a bigger world than Calvary that He died, and for greater harvests than Jerusalem that He suffered. "And not for them only do I pray, but for them also who through their word shall believe in me" *(John 17:20).*

Now that the Divine Physician has prepared the medicine, apply it to the first of our three types of souls, namely, those who suffer and mourn saying: "What have I done to deserve this? "

There are many good men and women tossing on beds of pain, their bodies wasted by long sickness, their hearts broken with woe and sorrow, or their minds tortured by irreparable loss of friends and fortune. If these souls want peace they must recognize that in this world there is no intrinsic connection between personal sin and suffering.

One day "Jesus passing by, saw a man, who was blind from his birth: And his disciples asked him: Rabbi, who hath sinned, this man, or his parents, that he should be born blind? Jesus answered: Neither hath this man sinned, nor his parents" *(John 9:1-3).*

That brings us face to face with the inscrutable will of God which we cannot understand, any more than a mouse in a piano can understand why a musician disturbs him by playing. Our puny minds cannot understand the mysteries of God. But there are two basic truths which such burdened souls must never surrender, otherwise they will never find peace. First, God is love.

Hence anything He does to me deserves my gratitude and I will say "thank you." God is still good even though He does not give me whatever I *want* in this world. He gives me only what I *need* for the next.

Parents do not give five-year-old boys guns to play with, though there is hardly a boy of five who does not want a gun. As Job put it: "If we have received good things at the hand of God, why should we not receive evil?" *(Job 2:10).*

Second, the final reward for virtue comes not in this life, but in the next. As tapestries are woven not from the front but from the back, so too in this life we see only the underside of God's plan.

"My life is but a weaving
Between my God and me.
I may but choose the colors
He worketh skilfully.

Full oft He chooses sorrow,
And I, in foolish pride,
Forget He sees the upper,
And I the under, side."

(Father Tabb)

We are not to have our moods made by the world; the world should revolve about us; not us about the world. Like the earth in its revolution about the sun we will carry our own atmosphere with us -- resignation to the will of God. Then nothing can ever happen against our will, because our will is the will of God.

This is not fatalism, which is subjection to blind necessity; it is patience, which is resignation to the will of the Divine Love who in the end can desire nothing but the eternal happiness and perfection of the one loved.

Fatalism is nonsense as the man walking precariously on the railing of a ship in a stormy sea proved when he said to the worried onlookers: "I'm a fatalist."

But patient resignation is exemplified by the child who said to her father: "Daddy, I do not know why you want me to go to the hospital for that operation. It hurts. I know only that you love me."

The shock of sorrow comes only to those who think this world is fixed and absolute, that there is nothing beyond. They think everything here below should be perfect. Hence they ask questions: "Why should I suffer? What have I done to deserve this?" Maybe you did nothing to deserve it. Certainly Our Lord did nothing to deserve His Cross. But it came and through it He went to His glory.

The virtue to be cultivated then by such souls is what is known as Patience. Patience and Fortitude are related as the convex and concave sides of a saucer. Fortitude is exercised in the active struggle with dangers and difficulties, while Patience is the passive acceptance of what is hard to bear.

Our Lord on the Cross practiced Fortitude by freely and fearlessly meeting death to purchase our forgiveness; He practiced Patience by passively accepting the Father's will.

Being God, He could have stepped down from the Cross. Twelve legions of angels could have ministered to His wounds, the earth could have been His footstool, the seas as healing balm, the sun as His chariot, the planets His cortège, and the Cross His triumphal throne. But He willed to accept death to give us an example: "Not my will, but thine be done" *(Luke 22:42).*

Passive acceptance of God's will is Patience. Patience, other things being equal, is nobler than Fortitude; for in active works we may choose what pleases us and thereby sometimes deceive ourselves, but in resignation to the crosses of life it is always God's will that we do.

"In your patience," He said, "you shall possess your souls" *(Luke 21:19).* In His Patience, He possesses His, for He did not choose His Cross, it was made for Him. He was fitted and patterned to it; we might almost say cut to fit it.

To take the Cross God sends us as He took the one given to Him, even though we do not deserve it, is the shortest way to identification with God's will which is the beginning of Power and Peace: Power because we are one with Him who can do all things; Peace because we are tranquil in the love of Him who is just.

Dare we call ourselves Christian and expect another road to heaven than that which Christ Himself travelled? Love leads the way -- it is enough for us to follow the Beloved knowing that He loves and cares. Then instead of seeking to have a road free of obstacles to attain God, we shall, like hurdles in the race of life, make a race out of obstacles.

Embracing the crosses of life because given to us by Love on the Cross, does not mean that any of us ever reach the stage where our nature is willing to suffer. On the contrary our nature rebels against it, because it is contrary to nature. But we can will *supernaturally* what nature rejects, just as our reason can accept what the senses reject.

My eyes tell me I should not let the doctor lance the festering boil, for it will hurt. But my reason tells me that my senses must momentarily submit to the pain for the sake of a future good. So too we can will to bear the unavoidable ills of life for *supernatural* reasons. The First Word from the Cross suggests doing so for the sake of the *remission* of sins: "Forgive them."

In the business world, we contract debts and recognize our obligation and duty to acquit them. Why should we think that in the same moral universe we can sin with impunity? If then we bear the imprints of the Cross, instead of complaining against God let us occasionally think of offering them up to God for our own sins, or for the sins of our neighbors.

Of all the nonsense our modern world has invented, nothing surpasses the catchwords or claptrap we give the unfortunate or the sick: "Keep your chin up" or "Forget it." This is not solace, but a drug. Consolation is in explaining suffering, not forgetting it; in relating it to Love, not ignoring it; in making it an expiation for sin, not another sin. But who shall understand this unless he looks at a Cross and loves the Crucified?

The second type of soul who can be helped by this First Word from the Cross is he who, possessing the great gift of Faith, out of love of the world either hides it or denies it. This applies to those lukewarm Catholics who say: "Of course I ate meat at the party on Friday. Did you think I was going to have everyone laughing at me?" "Yes, I sent my son to a non-Catholic college. They are more social you know, and I don't want my boy to meet policemen's sons." Or, "When that chap at the office ridiculed the Mass, I did not say I was a Catholic, for the boss is anti-Catholic and I might lose my job."

Doubtlessly such spineless Catholics would fit the spirit of the world better if they gave up their faith. Business men could then meet the challenge of chiseling competitors;

the passion of youth could have its fling; husbands could have second wives; wives could have third husbands; both husbands and wives could find an alternative to self-restraint and thus escape the comparative poverty attendant upon raising a family; politicians could improve their chances for election if they were less Catholic; lawyers could be richer if they did not have to confess their sins and make amends; doctors could be wealthier if they were less conscientious and ceased to believe in Divine Justice. There is no challenging the fact that Catholics could get on better with the world if they were less Catholic.

Not a single sentence can be found in the words of our Divine Lord promising you the love of the world because of your faith. But you can find a golden string of texts warning you that the world will hate you because you are His: "If you had been of the world, the world would love its own: but because you are not of the world, but I have chosen you out of the world, therefore the world hateth you" *(John 15:19).*

"Every one therefore that shall confess me before men, I will also confess him before my Father who is in heaven. But he that shall deny me before men, I will also deny him before my Father who is in heaven . . . And he that taketh not up his cross, and followeth me, is not worthy of me. He that findeth his life, shall lose it and he that shall lose his life for me, shall find it" *(Matthew 10:32-33, 38-39).*

"How narrow is the gate, and strait is the way that leadeth to life: and few there are that find it" *(Matthew 7:14).*

"For he that shall be ashamed of me, and of my words, in this adulterous and sinful generation: the Son of man also will be ashamed of him, when he shall come in the glory of his Father with the holy angels" *(Mark 8:38; Cf. Luke 9:26).*

"If we suffer, we shall also reign with him. If we deny him, he will also deny us" *(2Timothy 2:12).*

"And if thy right hand scandalize thee, cut it off, and cast it from thee: for it is expedient for thee that one of thy members should perish, rather than that thy whole body go into hell" *(Matthew 5:30)*.

The true followers of Christ were meant to be at odds with the world: The pure of heart will be laughed at by the Freudians; the meek will be scorned by the Marxists; the humble will be walked on by the go-getters; the liberal Sadducees will call them reactionaries; the reactionary Pharisees will call them liberals.

And Our Lord so warned: "Blessed are ye when they shall revile you, and persecute you, and speak all that is evil against you, untruly, for my sake: Be glad and rejoice for your reward is very great in heaven. For so they persecuted the prophets that were before you" *(Matthew 5:11)*.

To all those compromising Catholics, a plea is made to practice the Fortitude of the Saviour on the Cross who, being thoughtless of death for the sake of our forgiveness, taught us to be thoughtless of the world's scorn for the sake of being forgiven.

We must not forget the word of Our Saviour: "He that shall deny me before men, I will also deny him before my Father who is in heaven" *(Matthew 10:33)*. And if Catholics will not be strong in their love of Christ because of Christ, then let them be strong out of fear of the scandal of their weakness.

The example of a bad Catholic is most often appealed to as a justification for evil. Why is it that the world is more scandalized at a bad Catholic than a bad anything else, if it be not because his fall is rightfully measured by the heights from which he has fallen.

And let this fortitude be not a muscular fortitude, or abusive fortitude, but a fortitude brave enough to declare the belief in God even among the enemies who nail us to the cross of scorn, a fortitude like unto that of Eleazar, who, when commanded by Antiochus the enemy of the Jews to eat forbidden meat and who was advised by his own friends to do so, answered: "It doth not become our age . . . to dissemble . . . Though, for the present time, I should be delivered from the punishments of men, yet should I not escape the hand of the Almighty neither alive nor dead" *(2Maccabees 6:24, 26).*

The third type of soul to whom this First Word offers Fortitude comprises those who are convinced of the truth of the faith but are unwilling to pay the price. A price does have to be paid for conversion, and that price is scorn. Many souls stand poised between an inner conviction that the Church is true and the certitude that if they embrace it they must make enemies.

Once they cross its threshold a thinly veiled hostility often takes the place of friendship. They may be accused of having lost their reason; their jobs may be endangered; their friends who believed in freedom of conscience may now turn against them because their consciences acted freely; their love of liturgy will be scorned, as superstition and their supernatural faith will be called credulity.

If they joined a crazy cult or became a sun worshipper or a Yogi follower or founded a new religion, their friends would say they acted within their constitutional rights; but when they join the Church, some will say they lost their minds, as they told Our Lord He had a devil.

Why this revolution of attitude once the threshold of the Church has been passed? Very simply because entering into the Church lifts us into another world -- the supernatural world. It gives us a new set of values, a new objective, new ways of thinking, new standards of judgment, all of which are in opposition to the spirit of the world.

The world with its hatred of discipline, its courtesy to the flesh, and its indifference to truth, cannot tolerate a life based upon the primacy of Christ and the salvation of souls. "I have chosen you out of the world, therefore the world hateth you. If you had been of the world, the world would love its own . . . [but] know ye, that it hath hated me before you" *(John 15:19, 18).*

Most people today want a religion which suits the way they live, rather than one which makes demands upon them. The result is that in order to make religion popular, too many prophets have watered down religion until it is hardly distinct from sentimental secularism. Religion thus becomes a luxury like an opera, not a responsibility like life.

There is no doubt that a religion which makes concessions to human weakness will be popular; for example, one that denies hell for those who are unjust, and is silent about divorce for those who have repudiated their vows.

But as Catholics, we may not tamper with the message of Christ; for religion is of His making not ours. Furthermore, the only religion which will help the world is one which contradicts the world.

Most Americans have been so disillusioned by a Cross-less Christ, that they are now looking back to the Cross as the only point of reference which gives meaning to life. They may not know how to phrase the conflict within, but they dimly perceive that all unhappiness is due to a conflict of wills: Family quarrels arise that way; misery of souls arises that way too when our selfish will contradicts the Divine will.

Peace, we are just discovering, is in the identity of our will with God who wills our perfection. When we disobey His will we are not asserting our independence; we are mutilating our personality as we might mutilate a razor by using it to cut a tree. Being made for God, we can be happy only with Him.

All our misery is traceable to that rebellion. All our peace is traceable to training the lower part of ourselves in service to Him. Hence the Cross, the symbol of that sacrifice inspired by love.

The Seven Virtues, 1940

Eighth Meditation

A WORD TO HUMANISTS

There are millions of souls in this great country of ours who have no religion whatsoever. Their attitudes vary from an earnest yearning for religion to an intense hatred of it. It is quite possible that all of them could be reduced to seven distinct categories.

Our Lord spoke seven times *from* the Cross -- and these are called His Seven Last Words. But those who were on Calvary's Hill that afternoon addressed seven words to Him on the Cross, thus revealing the seven different impacts the Cross makes on souls.

The seven words, which Our Lord spoke *from* the Cross were not specific answers to specific challenges, but they do reveal lessons applicable to the challenge.

The first of seven possible attitudes toward the Cross is that of Humanism, for the first group to challenge the Cross was the Humanists. The term Humanist is here understood in the modern philosophical sense, and embraces all those who want a religion without a Cross. They believe that man is naturally good, that progress is inevitable through science, and that human reason by its own effort is able to restore peace to the world and to consciences.

They regard all suggestions about faith, grace, and the supernatural order as impractical and unnecessary. They want an education of self-expression, a God without justice, a morality without religion, a Christ without a Cross, a Christianity without sacrifice, a Kingdom of God without redemption.

These Humanists of our day had their prototypes on Calvary on Good Friday. They were those whom Sacred Scripture calls the "passers-by"; a significant term indeed for it suggests those who never remain long enough with religion to know anything about it, those who think themselves wise because they have had a passing acquaintance with Christ.

It is they who speak the First Word to the Cross: "Vah, thou that destroyest the temple of God, and in three days dost rebuild it; save thy own self: if thou be the Son of God, come down from the Cross" *(Matthew 27:40).*

He is no sooner on the Cross than they ask Him *to* come down. "Come down from your belief in divinity! Come down from your teaching of hell! Come down from your belief that what God hath joined together no man may put asunder! Come down from your belief that Christ will preserve Peter from the gates of hell even to the consummation of the world! Come down from your belief in infallibility! Come down and we will believe!"

And while the mob jeers, there comes from the Cross the answer: "Father, forgive them, for they know not what they do." They said: "*If* thou be the Son of God." Humanists are certain only of humanity, not of divinity.

But He spoke of God: "Father." they said: "Come down." They judged power by deliverance from pain. He said: "Forgive." He judged power by deliverance from sin. They boasted of their knowledge and superior wisdom, and He reminded them that all their wisdom was ignorance: "They know not what they do."

Religion, the Humanists insist, must be love! And who speaks more of brotherhood than humanists? But they want Love without a Cross. And that Our Blessed Lord seems to imply is impossible, for how shall love forgive without first satisfying justice? Shall love mean, "to let the sinner go on sinning" or shall it mean "to make the sinner sinless"?

A religion without a Cross! That is the essence of Humanism. What we want to do here is not to prove the Humanists wrong, but to try to make them understand the meaning of the Cross and how much it symbolizes the love to God. I speak directly to them.

Humanists: You have humanized God, and thus you have dehumanized man. By denying man is supernatural you have not left him even *natural*. For every man wants to be more than he is.

You have tried to make all men brothers, but have you not forgotten that men cannot be brothers unless they have a common Father, and God cannot be a Father unless He has a Son -- to whom we all are patterned as brothers?

Swine are content. But you Humanists are not content with humanity, wherein, like monsters of the deep, man preys on man!

You want humanity to be humane. But if there be no model for humaneness, how shall men be modeled?

Look to your doctrines of man: Whence came that which is best in him, if it be not from the Best and Holiest?

In Godless hands man has withered like a rose without roots.

You make indeed a Republic of Kings, but you have no one to crown or anoint them.

The tragedy of your Humanism is believing that dirty things are clean, that cruel are kind, that hence there is no need of a Cross: "Come down and we will believe." To you, all men are good. There are halos even in hell.

And so on Calvary's Hill you stand and ask in wisdom for a Christ without a Cross, while He answers: "Forgive!"

Do you not know that to have a world without a Cross is in itself a cross? Do you know a mother worthy of the name who would not, out of love, take the pain of her tender babe as her very own, because she loves? Why then should not Supreme Love, in the face of evil, seek to take the penalty which sin deserves, that the evil might be innocent again?

Then why do you say: "Come down and we will believe"? If He came down, in whom would you believe?

Humanists, why are we at war if it be not because sin is in some human blood, and only in the shedding of just blood can there be remission of that sin?

Why not see then that great evils can be conquered only by a God-made-man upon a Cross? Why do you say: "Come down and we will believe"? For if He came down where would love be? "Greater love than this no man hath, that a man lay down his life for his friends" *(John 15:13).*

To avoid a war, when it alone can preserve justice, is not sanctity, you say, but vile surrender! Then to avoid a Cross which alone can redeem from sin, is not human. It is ignorance of man's great needs.

He that made your eye, shall He not see? He that made your ear, shall He not hear? He that made your soldiers, brave enough to die, may not He Himself be a Captain dying to make wrong right?

Then why do you say: "Come down and we will believe"? Do you believe that you, who out of love of neighbor can sacrifice yourself, can do that which God cannot do? Truly! You know not what you do.

Have you Humanists ever seen Love stand up against brute Force and go down because it would not cease to love? If then you bless the Sermon on the Mount, wherein love was preached, why do you curse the Sermon on the Cross, where

Love met hate and died? Is not Calvary inseparable from the Mount, for love preached to evil must be crucified.

Love without Power is destroyed by evil. But Love armed with power will die rather than surrender goodness.

God must suffer too as man suffers. Else how can Love be love if it costs not the Lover? Did not your Goethe say: "If I were God this world of sin would break my heart"? Well, that is just what it did to Christ! It broke His Heart!

Why then, if your love for man is sometimes met by sneer and scorn, do you say to a Christ whose God-love was crucified: "Come down and we will believe"? In what can you believe, if Love must love without a Cross?

Not from any talisman of ancient times, but from heaven itself, has come the Cross. For there is "the Lamb, which was slain from the beginning of the world" *(Revelation 13:8).* From that primal day when the shedding of a brother's blood cried up to the heavens, to this very hour when the race of Abel lies slain by the jealous brethren of the race of Cain, the spilling of unjust blood cries out to heaven, until God heard, and came down as man to shed His blood, that a man might be more than a man -- Aye! A very child of God!

The Cross is eternal! It cannot be dug up; it cannot be taken down! It is the core of creation! It is the root of all our lesser Calvaries! Then why do you say: "Come down and we will believe"?

It is God who gives us the Cross. And it is the Cross that gives us God.

You want the Cross but not the crucifix. The cross you wear can be a charm, but the crucifix cannot. Somehow, when you see it, you feel involved! A statue of Buddha does not stir you. Put a crucifix on your desk for three days, and see what it does to you!

Humanists! Remember the days of the French revolution, when a mob swept into the Tuilleries, through room after room it went, destroying. Then, through a closed door, and, lo and behold: a chapel! Above the tabernacle hung the crucifix. A hush fell upon the enraged mob. Someone cried: "Hats off." Every head was bowed, then every knee was bent. Indifference was impossible. Then a humanist took the crucifix down, hung it in an adjoining house, and the wild tide of destruction rolled on! They had taken the Christ down from the Cross! Now they could proceed! Religion now was comfortable!

No wonder men want Christ to come down! They want a Cross but not a crucifix. A crucifix perils your soul. You stand unmoved before the Sphinx -- but the Christ on His Cross involves you in Its guilt.

Suppose the Christ upon that Cross came down as you bade! He would have forced you then to do His will; and where then would be your freedom? One day He will come without His Cross! Bearing it rather than being borne! But that will be to judge and strike and not to heal, as now; for then the time of healing will be past!

The human never long remains the Humanist, for either beast or angel he becomes, but not just man! If you came from the beast you cannot leave the beast behind. But if you came from God then you can leave humanity behind and be a child of God! This is true Humanism, where man finds his center in his Source.

Before 'tis too late, dear Humanists, desist your plea: "Come down and we will believe." But harken: "Father! Forgive." Forgiveness is not cheap. If He offered it without a Cross, you would not take it. But from a nail-pierced hand, how could you refuse? That Cross is the price God paid to buy you from your sins. Without it, there is neither sin nor God.

As you rise in the scale of nobility, do you not choose pain and trouble rather than comfort and ease? Then why not choose Him who did just that for you?

Seven Words to the Cross, 1944

Ninth Meditation

THE VALUE OF IGNORANCE

One thousand years before Our Blessed Lord was born, there lived one of the greatest of all poets: the glorious Homer of the Greeks. Two great epics are ascribed to him: one the Iliad; the other, the Odyssey. The hero of the Iliad was not Achilles, but Hector, the leader of the enemy Trojans whom Achilles defeated and killed. The poem ends not with the glorification of Achilles but of the defeated Hector.

The other poem, the Odyssey, has as its hero, not Odysseus, but Penelope, his wife, who was faithful to him during the years of his travels. As the suitors pressed for her affections, she told them that when she finished weaving the garment they saw before her, she would listen to their courtship. But each night she unraveled what she had woven in the day, and thus remained faithful until her husband returned. "Of all women," she said, "I am the most sorrowful." Well might be applied to her the words of Shakespeare: "Sorrow sits in my soul as on a throne. Bid kings come and bow down to it."

For a thousand years before the birth of Our Blessed Lord, pagan antiquity resounded with these two stories of the poet who threw into the teeth of history the mysterious challenge of glorifying a defeated man and hailing a sorrowful woman. How, the subsequent centuries asked, could anyone be victorious in defeat and glorious in sorrow? And the answer was never given until that day when there came One Who was glorious in defeat: the Christ on His Cross and one who was magnificent in sorrow: His Blessed Mother beneath the cross.

It is interesting that Our Lord spoke seven times on Calvary and that His Mother is recorded as having spoken but seven times in Sacred Scripture. Her last recorded word was at the Marriage Feast of Cana, when her Divine Son began His Public Life. Now that the sun was out, there was no longer need of the moon to shine. Now that the Word has spoken, there was no longer need of words.

St. Luke records five of the seven words which he could have known only from her. St. John records the other two. One wonders, as Our Blessed Lord spoke each of His Seven Words, if Our Blessed Mother at the foot of the Cross did not think of each of her corresponding words. Such will be the subject of our meditation: Our Lord's Seven Words on the Cross and the Seven Words of Mary's Life.

Men cannot stand weakness. Men are, in a certain sense, the weaker sex. There is nothing that so much unnerves a man as a woman's tears. Therefore men need the strength and the inspiration of women who do not break down in a crisis. They need someone not prostrate at the foot of the cross, but standing, as Mary stood. John was there; he saw her standing, and he wrote it down in his Gospel.

Generally, when innocent men suffer at the hands of impious judges, their last words are either: "I am innocent" or "The courts are rotten." But here, for the first time in the hearing of the world, is one who asked neither for the forgiveness of His own sins, for He is God, nor proclaimed His own innocence, for men are not judges of God. Rather does He plead for those who kill him: "Father, forgive them, for they know not what they do" *(Luke 23:34).*

Mary beneath the gibbet heard Her Divine Son speak that First Word. I wonder when she heard him say, "know not" if she did not recall her own First Word. It, too, contained those words: "know not."

The occasion was the Annunciation, the first good news to reach the earth in centuries. The angel announced to her that she was to become the Mother of God: "Behold thou shalt conceive in thy womb and shalt bring forth a son: and thou shalt call his name Jesus. He shall be great and shall be called the son of the Most High. And the Lord God shall give unto him the throne of David his father: and he shall reign in the house of Jacob forever. And of his Kingdom there shall be no end. And Mary said to the Angel: How shall this be done, because I know not man?" *(Luke 1:31-34).*

These words of Jesus and Mary seem to suggest that there is sometimes wisdom in not knowing. Ignorance is here represented not as a cure, but a blessing. This rather shocks our modern sensibilities which so much glorify education, but that is because we fail to distinguish between true wisdom and false wisdom. St. Paul called the wisdom of the world "foolishness," and Our Blessed Lord thanked His Heavenly Father that He had not revealed Heavenly Wisdom to the worldly wise.

The ignorance which is here extolled is not ignorance of the truth, but ignorance of evil. Notice it first of all in the word of Our Saviour to His executioners: He implied that they could be forgiven only because they were ignorant of their terrible crime. It was not their wisdom that would save them, but their ignorance.

If they knew what they were doing as they smote the Hands of Everlasting Mercy, dug the Feet of the Good Shepherd, crowned the Head of Wisdom Incarnate, and still went on doing it, they would never have been saved. They would have been damned! It was only their ignorance which brought them within the pale of redemption and forgiveness. As St. Peter told them on Pentecost: "I know that you did it through ignorance: as did also your rulers." *(Acts 3:17).*

Why is it that you and I, for example, can sin a thousand times and be forgiven, and the angels who have sinned but once are eternally unforgiven? The reason is that the angels *knew* what they were doing. The angels see the consequences of each and every one of their decisions with the same clarity that you see that a part can never be greater than the whole. Once you make that judgment you can never take it back. It is irrevocable; it is eternal.

Now the angels saw the consequences of their choices with still greater clarity. Therefore, when they made a decision, they made it knowingly and there was no taking it back. They were lost forever. Tremendous are the responsibilities of knowing! Those who know the truth will be judged more severely than those who know it not. As Our Blessed Lord said: "If I had not come...they would not have sin" *(John 15:22)*.

The First Word Our Blessed Mother spoke at the Annunciation revealed the same lesson. She said: "I know not man." Why was there a value in not knowing man? Because she had consecrated her virginity to God. At a moment when every woman sought the privilege of being the mother of the Messiah, Mary gave up the hope and received it. She refuses to discuss with an angel any kind of compromise with her high resolve.

If the condition of becoming the Mother of God was the surrender of her vow, she would not make that surrender, knowing man would have been evil for her, though it would not have been evil in other circumstances. Not knowing man is a kind of ignorance, but here it proves to be such a blessing that in an instant the Holy Spirit overshadows her, making her a living ciborium privileged to bear within herself for nine months the Guest Who is the Host of the World.

These first words of Jesus and Mary suggest there is value in not knowing evil. You live in a world in which the worldly wise say: "You do not know life; you have never lived." They assume that you can know nothing except by experience -- experience not only of good but of evil.

It was with this kind of lie that Satan tempted our First Parents. He told them that the reason God forbade them to eat of the tree of the knowledge of good and evil was because God did not want them to be wise as He was wise. Satan did not tell them that if they came to a knowledge of good and evil, it would be very different from God's knowledge.

God knows evil only abstractly, i.e., by negation of His Goodness and Love. But man would know it concretely and experimentally, and thus would to some extent fall captive to the very evil which he experienced. God wanted our First Parents to know typhoid fever, for example, as a healthy doctor knows it; he did not want them to know it as the stricken patient knows it. And from that day of the Great Lie, down to this, no one is better because he knows evil through experience.

Examine your own life. If you know evil by experience, are you wiser because of it? Have you not despised that very evil and are you not the more tragic for having experienced it? You may even have become mastered by the evil you experienced. How often the disillusioned say: "I wish I had never tasted liquor" or "I regret the day I stole my first dollar," and "I wish I had never known that person." How much wiser you would have been had you been ignorant!

Over and over again, when you broke some law which you thought arbitrary and meaningless, you discovered the principle which dictated it. As a child, you could not understand why your parents forbade you to play with matches, but the burn convinced you of the truth of the law. So the world by violating God's moral law is finding through war, strife, and misery the wisdom of the law. How it would now like to unlearn its false learning!

Think not, then, that in order to "know life" you must "experience evil." Is a doctor wiser because he is prostrate with disease? Do we know cleanliness by living in sewers? Do we know education by experiencing stupidity? Do we know peace by fighting? Do we know the joys of vision by being blinded? Do you become a better pianist by hitting the wrong keys? You do not need to get drunk to know what drunkenness is.

Do not excuse yourself by saying, "temptations are too strong" or "good people do not know what temptation is." The good know more about the strength of temptations than those who fall. How do you know how strong the current of a river is? By swimming with the current or by swimming against it? How do you know how strong the enemy is in battle? By being captured or by conquering? How can you know the strength of a temptation unless you overcome it? Our Blessed Lord really understands the power of temptation better than anyone, because He overcame the temptations of Satan.

The great fallacy of modern education is the assumption that the reason there is evil in the world is because there is ignorance, and that if we pour more facts in the minds of the young we will make them better. If this were true, we should be the most virtuous people in the history of the world, because we are the best educated.

The facts, however, point the other way: Never before has there been so much education and never before so little coming to the knowledge of the truth. We forget that ignorance is better than error. *Scientia* is not *sapientia*. Much of modern education is making the mind sceptical about the wisdom of God. The young are not born sceptics, but a false education can make them sceptical. The modern world is dying of sceptic poisoning.

The fallacy of sex education is assuming that if children know the evil effects of certain acts, they will abstain from those acts. It is argued that if you knew there was typhoid fever in a house you would not go into that house. But what these educators forget is that sex-appeal is not at all like the typhoid fever appeal. No person has an urge to break down the doors of a typhoid patient, but the same cannot be said about sex. There is a sex-impulse, but there is no typhoid instinct.

Sex wisdom does not necessarily make one wise; it can make one desire the evil, particularly when we learn that the evil effects can be avoided. Sex Hygiene is not morality. Soap is not the same as virtue. Badness comes not from our ignorance of knowing, but from our perversity of doing. That is why in our Catholic schools, we train and discipline the will as well as inform the intellect, because we know that character is in our choices, not in our knowing. All of us already *know* enough to be good, even before we start to school. What we have to learn is how to *do better.*

If we forget the burden of our fallen nature, and the accumulated proneness to evil that comes from submitting to it, we soon become chained as Samson was and all the education in the world cannot break those chains. Education may conceivably rationalize the chains and make us believe they are charms, but only the effort of the will plus the grace of God can free us from their servitude. Without those two energies we will never do one jot or tittle beyond that which we have already done.

Train your children and yourself, then, in the true wisdom which is the knowledge of God, and in the ignorance of the things that are evil. The unknown is the undesired; to be ignorant of wickedness is not to desire it. There are no joys like Innocence.

Here on the Cross and on its shadow were the two most Innocent Persons of all history: Jesus was absolutely sinless because He is the Son of God; Mary was Immaculate because she was preserved free from original sin, in virtue of the merits of her Divine Son. It was their innocence which made their sufferings so keen.

People living in dirt hardly ever realize how dirty dirt is. Those who live in sin hardly understand the horror of sin. The one peculiar and terrifying thing about sin is that the more experience you have with it, the less you know about it. You become so identified with it that you know neither the depths to which you have sunk nor the heights from which you have fallen.

You never know you were asleep until you wake up, and you never know the horror of sin until you get out of sin. Hence, only the sinless really know what sin is. And since here on the Cross and beneath it, there is Innocence at its highest, it follows that there was also the greatest sorrow. Since there was no sin, there was the greatest understanding of its evil. It was their innocence, or their ignorance of evil, which made the agonies of Calvary.

To Jesus Who forgave those who "know not," to Mary who won God because she could say "I know not," pray that you may know not evil and thus be good.

Honestly, if you had the choice now either of learning more about the world, or of unlearning the evil you know, would you not rather unlearn than learn? Would you not be better if you were stripped of your wickedness than if you were clothed in the sheepskin of diplomas?

Would you not like to be right now, just as you came from the hands of God at the baptismal font, with no worldly wisdom yet gathered to your mind, so that like an empty chalice, you might spend your life filling it with the wine of His Love? The world would call you ignorant, saying you knew nothing about life. Do not believe it -- you would have Life! Therefore you would be one of the wisest persons in the world.

There is so much error in the world today, there are such vast areas of experienced and lived evil, that it would be a blessing if some generous soul would endow a University for Unlearning. Its purpose would be to do with error and evil exactly what doctors do with disease.

Would you be surprised to know that Our Lord did actually institute such a University for Unlearning, and to it all devout Catholics go about once a month? It is called the confessional! You will not be given a sheepskin when you walk out of that confessional, but you will feel like a lamb because Christ is your Shepherd. You will be amazed at how much you will learn by unlearning. It is easier for God to write on a blank page than on one covered with your scribblings.

Seven Words of Jesus and Mary, 1945

THIS DAY THOU SHALT BE WITH
ME IN PARADISE
Meditations on the Second Word from the Cross
Archbishop Fulton J. Sheen

First Meditation

THIS DAY THOU SHALT BE WITH ME IN PARADISE

There is a legend to the effect that when, to escape the wrath of Herod, Saint Joseph and the Blessed Virgin were fleeing into Egypt with the Divine Child, they stopped at a desert inn. The Blessed Mother asked the lady of the inn for water in which to bathe the Babe. The lady then asked if she might not bathe her own child, who was suffering from leprosy, in the same waters in which the Divine Child had been immersed. Immediately upon touching those waters baptized with the Divine Presence, the child became whole. Her child advanced in age and grew to be a thief. He is Dismas, now hanging on the Cross at the right hand of Christ!

Whether the memory of the story his mother told him now came back to the thief and made him look kindly on Christ, we know not. It might have been that his first meeting with the Saviour was on the day when his heart was filled with compunction on hearing the story of a certain man who went down from Jerusalem to Jericho and fell among robbers. Perhaps, too, his first intimation that he was suffering with the Redeemer came to him as he turned his tortured head and read an inscription which bore His name, "Jesus"; His city, "Nazareth"; His crime, "King of the Jews." At any rate, enough dry fuel of the right kind gathers on the altar of his soul, and now a spark from the central Cross falls upon it, creating in it a glorious illumination of faith. He sees a Cross and adores a Throne; he sees a condemned Man, and invokes a King: "Lord, remember me when Thou shalt come into Thy Kingdom."

Our Blessed Lord was owned at last! Amidst the clamor of the raving crowd and the dismal universal hiss of sin, in all that delirium of man's revolt against God, no voice was lifted in praise and recognition except the voice of a man condemned. It was a cry of faith in Him whom every one else had forsaken, and it was only the testimony of a thief. If the son of the widow of Nain, who had been raised from the dead, had cried out a word of faith in the Kingdom of One who was seemingly losing His Kingdom; if Peter, who on the Mount of Transfiguration had seen His face shine like the sun and His garments whiten like snow, had acknowledged Him; if the blind man of Jericho whose eyes were opened to the light of God's sunshine had been opened anew to proclaim His Divinity, we should not have been surprised. Why, if any of these had cried out, perhaps the timid disciples and friends would have rallied, perhaps the Scribes and Pharisees would have believed! But at that moment when death was upon Him, when defeat stared Him in the face, the only one outside the small group at the foot of the Cross to acknowledge Him as Lord of a Kingdom, as the Captain of Souls, was a thief at the right hand of Christ.

At the very moment when the testimony of a thief was given, Our Blessed Lord was winning a greater victory than any life can win, and was exerting a greater energy than that which harnesses waterfalls; He was losing His life and saving a soul. And on that day when Herod and his whole court could not make Him speak, nor all the power of Jerusalem make Him step down from the Cross, nor the unjust accusations of a court-room force Him to break silence, nor a mob crying, "He saved others; Himself He cannot save," bring from His burning lips a retort, He turns to a quivering life beside Him, speaks, and saves a thief: "This day thou shalt be with Me in Paradise." No one before was ever the object of such a promise, not even Moses nor John, not even Magdalen nor Mary!

It was the thief's last prayer, perhaps also his first. He knocked once, sought once, asked once, dared everything and found everything. When our spirits stand with John on Patmos, we can see the white-stoled army in Heaven riding after the conquering Christ; when we stand with Luke on Calvary, we see the one who rode first in that procession. Christ, who was poor, died rich. His hands were nailed to a Cross and yet He unlocked the keys of Paradise and won a soul. His escort into Heaven was a thief. May we not say that the thief died a thief, for he stole Paradise?

Oh, what greater assurance is there in all the world of the mercy of God? Lost sheep, prodigal sons, broken Magdalens, penitent Peters, forgiven thieves! Such is the rosary of Divine forgiveness.

God is more anxious to save us than we are to save ourselves. There is a story told to the effect that one day Our Blessed Lord appeared to Saint Jerome, saying to him, "Jerome, what will you give Me?" Jerome answered, "I will give you my writings," to which Our Lord replied that it was not enough. "Then," said Jerome, "what shall I give you? My life of penance and mortification?" But the answer was, "Even that is not enough!" "What have I left to give Thee?" cried Jerome. Our Blessed Lord answered, "Jerome, you can give Me your sins."

PRAYER

DEAR Jesus! Your kindness to the penitent thief recalls the prophetic words of the Old Testament: "If your sins be as scarlet, they shall be made as white as snow: and if they be as red as crimson, they shall be white as wool." In Your words of forgiveness to the penitent thief, I understand now the meaning of your words: "I have not come to call the just, but sinners ... They that are in health need not a physician; but they that are ill." "There shall be joy in Heaven upon one sinner that doth penance more than upon ninety-nine just who need not penance." I see now why Peter was not made Thy first vicar on earth until after he had fallen three times, in order that the Church of which he was the head might forever understand forgiveness and pardon. Jesus, I begin to see that if I had never sinned, I never could call You "Saviour." The thief is not the only sinner. Here am I! But Thou art the only Saviour.

The Seven Last Words, 1933

Second Meditation

HALLOWED BE THY NAME

"Hallowed be Thy Name"

"Amen, I say to thee, this day thou
shalt be with me in paradise."

God's name is hallowed by the recognition of His power and glory. The thief recognized God's power despite His powerlessness, and God's glory despite His defeat.

Picture two scenes as this second word is being spoken. On opposite sides of Sion, there were men hanging on trees. On one side of the hill, Judas was hanging from a tree; on the opposite side hung Our Lord between two thieves. Note the difference in attitude of Judas and the thief on the right. Both were thieves. But there was this difference. Judas thought God's glory was purely external, manifested by earthly pomp and circumstance. Hence when he saw Our Lord go down to defeat, he sold Him for thirty pieces of silver. The thief on the left of Our Lord was like Judas. He too, felt the only power worth having was the power of saving him from pain. Hence he cried in agony: "Save thyself and us." In other words, do something external. But the thief on the right moved his pain-racked head toward Our Lord, saw Him divested of every robe of royalty, and denuded of every badge of kingship. And yet he perceived the gold beneath the dust, and the kingdom through a cloud, and power to save a soul beneath the weakness of a drained body: "Lord, remember me when Thou shalt come into Thy Kingdom."

Our Blessed Saviour was so pleased to find His name hallowed amidst blasphemy, and His blessing recognized amidst curses, that He granted the humble prayer of the thief: "Amen, I say to thee, this day thou shalt be with me in Paradise."

The world is full of Judases who think the name of God is hallowed only by worldly pomp and splendor. They forget that the Kingdom of God is internal and "cometh not by observation," and that the Church, which is the Mystical Christ, manifests her greatest strength in the forgiveness of sins.

The world asks: "How can man forgive sin?" It might just as well ask how could a man whose kingdom is no wider than a beam of wood promise the kingdom of heaven to a thief.

The forgiveness of sin is a greater manifestation of the Power of God than the creation of the world. Creation makes something out of nothing. Forgiveness puts something into nothing. But the forgiveness which opens Paradise is obtained as the thief obtained his, namely by asking for it. Pardon, like all gifts of God, is conditioned. The latch on the door of divine forgiveness is on the inside of our soul – on our side, not on God's side. "Behold, I stand at the door and knock." He knocks! He does not force down the door. That would destroy human freedom. He knocks to be admitted; we alone have the power to unlatch the door to invite Him in, that He may sup with us and we with Him. Christ's greatest sorrow is to be denied admittance. "Ye will not come to me." His greatest joy is to be welcomed even by sinners, for "there is more joy in heaven for one sinner doing penance than for ninety-nine just who need not penance." There is no power as strong as the uplifted hand of an absolving priest; there is no joy like the return of a prodigal; there is no peace like the peace of sin forgiven. There is no hope like the hope the thief gives us: Paradise may still be stolen.

The Seven Last Words and the Our Father, 1935

Third Meditation

THE OFFERTORY

"Amen I say to thee, this day thou shalt be with me in paradise." -- Luke 23:43.

This is now the offertory of the Mass, for our Lord is offering Himself to His heavenly Father. But in order to remind us that He is not offered alone, but in union with us, He unites with His offertory the soul of the thief at the right. To make His ignominy more complete, in a master stroke of malice, they crucified Him between two thieves. He walked among sinners during His life, so now they let Him hang between them at death. But He changed the picture, and made the two thieves the symbols of the sheep and the goats, which will stand at His right and left hand when He comes in the clouds of heaven, with His then triumphant cross, to judge both the living and the dead.

Both thieves at first reviled and blasphemed, but one of them, whom tradition calls Dismas, turned his head to read the meekness and dignity on the face of the crucified Saviour. As a piece of coal thrown into the fire is transformed into a bright and glowing thing, so the black soul of this thief thrown into the fires of the Crucifixion glowed with love for the Sacred Heart.

While the thief on the left was saying: "If thou be Christ, save thyself and us," the repentant thief rebuked him saying: "Neither dost thou fear God, seeing thou art under the same condemnation. And we indeed justly, for we receive the due reward of our deeds; but this man hath done no evil." That same thief then emitted a plea, not for a place in the seats of the mighty, but only not to be forgotten: "Remember me, when thou shalt come into thy kingdom."

Such sorrow and faith must not go unrewarded. At a moment when the power of Rome could not make Him speak, when His friends thought all was lost and His enemies believed all was won, our Lord broke the silence. He who was the accused, became the Judge: He who was the crucified, became the Divine Assessor of souls, as to the penitent thief He trumpeted the words: "This day thou shalt be with me in paradise." This day -- when you said your first prayer and your last; this day -- thou shalt be with me -- and where I am, there is paradise.

With these words our Lord who was offering Himself to His heavenly Father as the great Host, now unites with Him on the paten of the cross the first small host ever offered in the Mass, the host of the repentant thief, a brand plucked from the burning, a sheaf torn from the earthly reapers; the wheat ground in the mill of the crucifixion and made bread for the Eucharist.

Our Lord does not suffer alone on the Cross; He suffers with us. That is why He united the sacrifice of the thief with His own. It is this St. Paul means when he says that we should fill up those things that are wanting to the sufferings of Christ. This does not mean our Lord on the cross did not suffer all He could. It means rather that the physical, historical Christ suffered all He could in His own human nature, but that the Mystical Christ, which is Christ and us, has not suffered to *our* fullness. All the other good thieves in the history of the world have not yet admitted their wrong and pleaded for remembrances. Our Lord is now in heaven. He therefore can suffer no more in His human nature but He can suffer more in our human natures.

So He reaches out to other human natures, to yours and mine, and asks us to do as the thief did, namely, to incorporate ourselves to Him on the Cross, that sharing in His Crucifixion we might also share in His Resurrection, and that made partakers of His Cross we might also be made partakers of His glory in heaven.

As our Blessed Lord on that day chose the thief as the small host of sacrifice, He chooses us today as the other small hosts united with Him on the paten of the altar. Go back in your mind's eye to a Mass, to any Mass which was celebrated in the first centuries of the Church, before civilization became completely financial and economic. If we went to the Holy Sacrifice in the early Church, we would have brought to the altar each morning some bread and some wine. The priest would have used one piece of that unleavened bread and some of that wine for the sacrifice of the Mass. The rest would have been put aside, blessed, and distributed to the poor. Today we do not bring bread and wine. We bring its equivalent; we bring that which buys bread and wine. Hence the offertory collection.

Why do we bring bread and wine or its equivalent to the Mass? We bring bread and wine because these two things, of all things in nature, most represent the substance of life. Wheat is as the very marrow of the ground, and the grapes its very blood, both of which give us the body and blood of life. In bringing those two things, which give us life, nourish us, *we are equivalently bringing ourselves to* the Sacrifice of the Mass.

We are therefore present at each and every Mass under the appearance of bread and wine, which stand as symbols of our body and blood. We are not passive spectators as we might be watching a spectacle in a theater, but we are co-offering our Mass with Christ. If any picture adequately describes our role in this drama it is this: There is a great cross before us on which is stretched the great Host, Christ. Round about the hill of Calvary are our small crosses on which we, the small hosts, are to be offered. When our Lord goes to His Cross we go to our little crosses, and offer ourselves in union with Him, as a clean oblation to the heavenly Father.

At that moment we literally fulfill to the smallest detail the Saviour's command: Take up your cross daily and follow Me. In doing so, He is not asking us to do anything He has not already done Himself. Nor is it any excuse to say: "I am a poor unworthy host." So was the thief.

Note that there were two attitudes in the soul of that thief, both of which made him acceptable to our Lord. The first was the recognition of the fact that He deserved what He was suffering, but that the sinless Christ did not deserve His Cross; in other words, he was *penitent.* The second was *faith* in Him whom men rejected, but whom the thief recognized as the very King of Kings.

Upon what conditions do we become small hosts in the Mass? How does our sacrifice become one with Christ's and as acceptable as the thief's? Only by reproducing in our souls the two attitudes in the soul of the thief: *penitence and faith.*

First of all we must be penitent with the thief and say: "I deserve punishment for my sins. I stand in need of sacrifice." Some of us do not know how wicked or how ungrateful to God we are. If we did, we would not so complain about the shocks and pains of life. Our consciences are like darkened rooms from which light has been long excluded. We draw the curtain, and lo! everywhere what we thought was cleanliness, we now find dust.

Some consciences have been so filmed over with excuses that they pray with the Pharisee: "I thank Thee, O God, that I am not as the rest of men." Others blaspheme the God of heaven for their pain and sins but repent not. The World War, for example, was meant to be a purgation of evil; it was meant to teach us that we cannot get along without God, but the world refused to learn the lesson. Like the thief on the left, it refuses to be penitent: it refuses to see any relation of justice between sin and sacrifice, between rebellion and a cross.

But the more penitent we are, the less anxious we are to escape our cross. The more we see ourselves as we are, the more we say with the good thief: "I deserved this cross."

He did not want to be excused; he did not want to have his sin explained away; he did not want to be let off; he did not ask to be taken down. He wanted only to be forgiven. He was willing even to be a small host on his own little cross -- but that was because he was penitent. Nor is there given to us any other way to become little hosts with Christ in the Mass than by breaking our hearts with sorrow; for unless we admit we are wounded how can we feel the need of healing? Unless we are sorry for our part in the Crucifixion, how could we ever ask to be forgiven its sin?

The second condition of becoming a host in the offertory of the Mass is *faith.* The thief looked above the head of our Blessed Lord and saw a sign which read: "KING." Queer king that! For a crown: thorns. For royal purple: His own blood. For a throne: a cross. For courtiers: executioners. For a coronation: a crucifixion. And yet beneath all that dross the thief saw the gold; amidst all those blasphemies he prayed.

His faith was so strong he was content to remain on his cross. The thief on the left asked to be taken down, but not the thief on the right. Why? Because he knew there were greater evils than crucifixions, and another life beyond the cross. He had faith in the Man on the central cross who could have turned thorns into garlands and nails into rosebuds if He willed; but he had faith in a Kingdom beyond the cross, knowing that the sufferings of this world are not worthy to be compared with the joys that are to come. With the Psalmist his soul cried: "Though I should walk in the midst of the shadow of death I will fear no evils, for thou art with me."

Such faith was like that of the three youths in the fiery furnace who were commanded by the king, Nebuchadnezzar, to adore the golden statue. Their answer was: "For behold our God, whom we worship, is able to save us from the furnace of burning fire, and to deliver us out of thy hands, O king. But if He will not, be it known to thee, O king, that we will not worship thy gods, nor adore the golden statue which thou hast set up." Note that they did not ask God to deliver them from the fiery furnace, though they knew God could do it, "for He is able to save us from the furnace of burning fire." They left themselves wholly in God's hands, and like Job they trusted Him.

So likewise with the good thief: He knew our Lord could deliver Him. But *he did not ask to be taken down from the cross*, for our Lord did not come down Himself even though the mob challenged Him. The thief would be a small host, if need be, unto the very end of the Mass. This did not mean the thief did not love life: He loved life as much as we love it. He wanted life, and a long life, and he found it, for what life is longer than Life Eternal. To each and every one of us in like manner it is given to discover that Eternal Life. But there is no other way to enter it than by penance and by faith which unite us to that Great Host -- the Priest and Victim Christ. Thus do we become spiritual thieves, and steal heaven once again.

Calvary and the Mass, 1936

Fourth Meditation

BLESSED ARE THE MERCIFUL

"Blessed are the merciful: for they shall obtain mercy."
"This day thou shalt be with me in paradise."

At the beginning of His Public Life, on the Hill of the Beatitudes, Our Lord preached: "Blessed are the merciful: for they shall obtain mercy." At the end of His Public Life, on the Hill of Calvary, He practiced that Beatitude as He addressed the thief: "This day you shall be with me in paradise."

The Beatitude of the world is quite different; it runs like this: "Blessed is the man who thinketh first about himself." Life for the world is a struggle for existence in which victory belongs only to the egotists. Liberality, generosity, and graciousness are rare. How often the world insists on "rights," how rarely does it emphasize "duties"; how often it uses the possessive "mine," and how rarely the generous "thine." How full it is of "courts of justice," but how few are its "courts of mercy."

Our Lord came to correct such an exaggerated justice which knew no mercy. Mercy, he reminded us, was something more than a sentimental, emotional tenderheartedness. The very word mercy is derived in Latin from *miserum cor*, a sorrowful heart. Mercy is therefore a compassionate understanding of another's unhappiness.

A person is merciful when he feels the sorrow and misery of another as if it were his own. Disliking misery and unhappiness, the merciful man seeks to dispel the misery of his neighbor just as much as he would if the misery were his own. That is why, whenever mercy is confronted not only with pain, but with sin and wrong-doing, it becomes forgiveness which not merely pardons, but even rebuilds into justice, repentance, and love.

Mercy is one of the dominant notes in the preaching of Our Lord. His parables were parables of mercy. Take for example the hundred sheep, the ten pieces of money, and the two sons. Of the hundred sheep, one was lost; of the ten pieces of money, one was lost; of the two sons, one led a life of dissipation.

It is interesting to note that the lost sheep is the one that was sought, and the shepherd finding it, places it upon his shoulders and brings it into the house rejoicing. But there is no record in the Gospels of any such attention being paid to the ninety-nine sheep who were not lost.

When the woman lost a piece of money and found it, she called in her neighbors to rejoice. But there is no record that she ever called in her neighbors to rejoice in the possession of the other nine which were never lost.

One son went into a foreign country and wasted his substance living riotously. And when he came back, he was given the fatted calf. But the brother who stayed at home was not so rewarded. All these illustrations Our Lord followed with the simple truth: "There shall be more joy in heaven upon one sinner that doth penance than upon ninety-nine just who need not penance."

One day Peter went to Him to inquire just what limitation should be placed upon mercy. And so he asked Our Lord a question about mercy and gave what he thought was rather an extravagant limit: "How often shall my brother offend against me, and I forgive him? till seven times? " And Our Lord answered, "Not till seven times, but till seventy times seven times." And that does not mean four hundred and ninety -- that means infinity.

Developing the idea of infinite mercy, Our Lord said He had come "to heal the contrite of heart"; and that "they that are in health need not a physician, but they that are ill...For I am not come to call the just, but sinners."

Some were scandalized at Him because He "dined with publicans and sinners," but He never ceased to remind us that we should be merciful because the heavenly Father was merciful. "That you may be the children of your Father who is in heaven, who maketh his sun to rise upon the good and bad, and raineth upon the just and the unjust. For if you love them that love you, what reward shall you have? Do not even the publicans do this? ... Be ye therefore perfect as also your heavenly Father is perfect."

Here He is suggesting that we must, like Our Heavenly Father, be merciful to those who according to human estimation least deserve it. That is why he was merciful to Magdalen, to the woman at the well, to Peter who denied him, to Zacchaeus, and even to Judas whom He addressed as "friend."

There was no mistaking His point of view; He was interested in sinners not because of their merits, but because of their misery. And now at the close of His Life, He fulfills the beatitude of mercy in His second word from the Cross.

There were three crosses on Calvary: the crosses of two thieves and the Cross of the Good Shepherd. Of the three who hung silhouetted against that blackened sky, one only was selfish and thought of himself, and that was the thief on the left. He was interested neither in the Saviour who suffered patiently nor in the thief who begged for mercy. He had no thought but for himself as he addressed the Man on the central cross: "If you be Christ, save thyself and us."

The thief on the right, on the contrary, thought not of himself, but about others, namely the thief on the left and Our Blessed Lord. His compassion went out to the thief on the left, because he was not turning to God in this the last hour of his life and begging for forgiveness: "Neither doest thou fear God, seeing thou art under the same condemnation." He also thought of the meek Man crucified between the two of them, who had just prayed for His executioners and was innocent and good: "We indeed (suffer) justly, for we receive the due reward of our deeds; but this man hath done no evil."

It is interesting to inquire why the Merciful Saviour not only forgave the penitent thief, but even gave him the Divine Promise: "This day thou shalt be with me in paradise." Why did not Our Lord address the same words to the thief on the left? The answer is to be found in the Beatitude of Mercy: "Blessed are the merciful: for they shall obtain mercy."

Because the thief on the right was merciful and compassionate, he received mercy and compassion. Because he was thoughtless of self, someone thought of him. There is a law about mercy just as rigid as the laws of nature. What we sow that also we reap. If we sow sparingly we reap sparingly. If we sow generously we reap an abundant harvest. Raised to a spiritual level, this means, as Our Lord has said, "For with what judgment you judge, you shall be judged; and with what measure you mete, it shall be measured to you again."

In other words, by thinking of others we get God to think of us. If the seed of the springtime thought only of self, but never of the soil, the rain, and the sun, it would never bloom and blossom into flower and fruit. But once it forgets itself and goes outside itself, and even dies to seed-life for the sake of the soil and sun and air, lo! it finds itself renewed and beautified a thousand times. If the coal in the bowels of the earth thought only of itself, it would never release its imprisoned sunlight as light and heat.

And so it is with us. Mercy is a compassion which seeks to unburden the sorrows of others as if they were our own. But if we have no such compassion, then how can compassion ever come back to us?

Unless we throw something up, nothing will come down; unless there is an action there can never be a reaction; unless we give, it shall not be given to us; unless we love, we shall not be loved; unless we pardon evil, our evil shall not be forgiven; unless we are merciful to others, God cannot be merciful to us.

If our heart is filled with the sand of our ego, how can God fill it with the fire of his Sacred Heart? If there is no "for sale" sign on the selfishness of our souls, how can God take possession of them?

If then we wish to receive mercy, we must, like the good thief, think of others, for it seems that God finds us best when we are lost in others. *Blessed are the merciful; for they shall obtain mercy.*

In a negative way, Our Lord has reminded us of this Law of Mercy in the parable of the unjust steward: “Therefore is the kingdom of heaven likened to a king, who would take an account of his servants. And when he had begun to take the account, one was brought to him that owed him ten thousand talents. And as he had not wherewith to pay it, his lord commanded that he should be sold, and his wife and children, and all that he had, and payment to be made. But that servant falling down, besought him, saying: "Have patience with me, and I will pay thee all." And the lord of that servant, being moved with pity, let him go and forgave him the debt.

But when that servant was gone out, he found one of his fellow-servants that owed him a hundred pence: and laying hold of him, he throttled him, saying: "Pay what thou owest." And his fellow-servant falling down, besought him, saying: "Have patience with me, and I will pay you all." And he would not, but went and cast him into prison, till he paid the debt.

Now his fellow-servants, seeing what was done, were very much grieved, and they came, and told their lord all that was done. Then his lord called him and said to him: "Thou wicked servant, I forgave thee all the debt, because thou besoughtest me. Shouldst not thou then have had compassion also on thy fellow-servant, even as I had compassion on thee?" And his lord being angry, delivered him to the torturers until he paid all the debt. So also shall my heavenly Father do to you, if you forgive not every one his brother from your hearts."

Be merciful then to others, if you would have God kind to you at the last day. Think of others, rather than of yourself. Our Lord has made mercy the very soul of His Church. I think that is the reason why He chose as the head of His Church, not the innocent, not the pure, not the virgin disciple John, but that impetuous, strong man called Peter -- the one who had denied Him, and who, the night of the trial, cursed and swore that he knew not the Man.

His merciful Lord passed him en route to the ignominy of that sorrowful night preceding Good Friday, and Peter, seeing him, went out and "wept bitterly." And tradition adds that Peter wept so much during his life that even his cheeks became furrowed with tears.

And so he who knew by experience the mercy and forgiveness of Our Lord was chosen the head of the Church, in order that the Church might forever practice mercy and kindness.

There is every reason in the world for mercy. There is some good in the worst of us, and there is some bad in the best of us. The good are those who try to find some good in others, and they generally do find it. The evil are those who look for the faults of others, and as a result never see their own.

It was these Our Lord rebuked: "And why seest thou the mote that is in thy brother's eye; and seest not the beam that is in thy own eye? Or how sayest thou to thy brother: Let me cast the mote out of thy eye; and behold a beam is in thy own eye! Thou hypocrite, cast out first the beam of thy own eye, and then shalt thou see to cast out the mote out of thy brother's eye."

If then on the last day we would receive a merciful judgment, we must begin here below to be merciful to others. Just as the clouds release only the moisture which they gathered from the earth, so too can Heaven release only the mercy we have sent heavenward.

By constantly thinking of ourselves, we render ourselves incapable of receiving the kindness of others. Only to the extent that we have emptied ourselves of ourselves can God fill us with Himself. And likewise, the best way to have our prayers answered is to pray for the intentions of others: for God begins to think of us when we cease to think of ourselves.

Therein probably must be sought the reason why more of our prayers are not answered. How can God answer the prayers we address to Him unless we answer the prayers others address to us? Do we answer the prayers of the poor? the maimed? the lame? the sinner? the missionary? If not, then by what right can we expect God to answer our requests?

How can God give us His gifts, if we never give others our gifts? How can God fill our coffers with His treasures, unless we empty them to others?

The law is as simple as that: sow and you reap; do not keep your seed in your barns; give it away -- scatter it over the fields; do the foolish thing; dissipate it, so that even the birds may eat of your bounty. And lo! in a short time you will find your seed increased five, ten, one hundred-fold. But keep it in your barn, and the birds starve and you have no increase.

Give and you shall receive; be merciful and you shall receive mercy. When therefore you are on a cross of pain or sorrow always think of that cross as the cross of the thief on the right.

As such, let your prayers go out to those on the left cross that they may be mindful of the expiatory value of their suffering; let your love also go out to the Good Shepherd on the Central Cross who suffers so innocently for all men, and because you never once thought of yourself but of others, or in other words, because you were merciful, you will hear the reward of Mercy from the Central Cross: "This day you shall be with me in paradise." In that way you become another Good Thief, for a Good Thief is one who steals Paradise!

The Cross and the Beatitudes, 1937

Fifth Meditation

PAIN

"This day thou shalt be with me in paradise."

The First Word from the Cross tells us what should be our attitude toward unjust suffering, but the Second Word tells us what should be our attitude toward pain. There are two ways of looking at it; one is to see it without purpose, the other to see it with purpose.

The first view regards pain as opaque, like a stone wall; the other view regards it as transparent, like a window pane. The way we will react to pain depends entirely upon our philosophy of life. As the poet has put it:

"Two men looked out through their prison bars;
The one saw mud, the other stars."

In like manner, there are those who, looking upon a rose, would say: "Isn't it a pity that those roses have thorns"; while others would say: "Isn't it consoling that those thorns have roses!' These two attitudes are manifested in the two thieves crucified on either side of Our Blessed Lord. The thief on the right is the model for those for whom pain has a meaning; the thief on the left is the symbol of unconsecrated suffering.

Consider first the thief on the left. He suffered no more than the thief on the right, but he began and ended his crucifixion with a curse. Never for a moment did he correlate his sufferings with the Man on the central cross. Our Lord's prayer of forgiveness meant no more to that thief than the flight of a bird.

He saw no more purpose in his suffering than a fly sees purpose in the window pane that floods man's habitation with God's warmth and sunlight. Because he could not assimilate his pain and make it turn to the nourishment of his soul, pain turned against him as a foreign substance taken into the stomach turns against it and infects and poisons the whole system.

That is why he became bitter, why his mouth became like a crater of hate, and why he cursed the very Lord Who could have shepherded him into peace and paradise.

The world today is full of those who, like the thief on the left, see no meaning in pain. Knowing nothing of the Redemption of Our Lord they are unable to fit pain into a pattern; it becomes just an odd patch on the crazy quilt of life. Life becomes so wholly unpredictable for them that "a troubled manhood follows their baffled youth."

Never having thought of God as anything more than a name, they are now unable to fit the stark realities of life into His Divine Plan. That is why so many who cease to believe in God become cynics, killing not only themselves but, in a certain sense, even the beauties of flowers and the faces of children for whom they refuse to live.

The lesson of the thief on the left is clear: Pain of itself does not make us better; it is very apt to make us worse. No man was ever better simply because he had an earache. Unspiritualized suffering does not improve man; it degenerates him. The thief at the left is no better for his crucifixion: it sears him, burns him, and tarnishes his soul.

Refusing to think of pain as related to anything else, he ends by thinking only of himself and who would take him down from the cross. So it is with those who have lost their faith in God. To them Our Lord on a cross is only an event in the history of the Roman Empire; He is not a message of hope or a proof of love.

They would not have a tool in their hands five minutes without discovering its purpose, but they live their lives without ever having inquired its meaning. Having no reason for living, suffering embitters them, poisons them, and finally, the great door of life's opportunity is closed in their faces, and like the thief on the left they go out into the night unblessed.

Now look at the thief on the right -- the symbol of those for whom pain has a meaning. At first he did not understand it, and therefore joined in the curses with the thief on the left. But just as sometimes a flash of lightning will illumine the path we have missed, so too the Saviour's forgiveness of His executioners illumined for the thief the road of mercy.

He began to see that if pain had no reason, Jesus would not have embraced it. If the cross had no purpose, Jesus would not have climbed it. Surely He Who claimed to be God would never have taken that badge of shame unless it could be transformed and transmuted to some holy purpose.

Pain was beginning to be comprehensible to the thief; for the present at least it meant an occasion to do penance for his life of crime. And the moment that that light came to him he rebuked the thief on the left saying: "Neither dost thou fear God, seeing thou art under the same condemnation? And we indeed suffer justly, for we receive the due reward of our deeds; but this man hath done no evil" *(Luke 23:40-41)*.

Now he saw pain as doing to his soul like to that which fire does to gold: burning away the dross. Or something like that which fever does to disease; killing the germs. Pain was dropping scales away from his eyes; and, turning toward the central cross, he no longer saw a crucified man, but a Heavenly King.

Surely, He Who can pray for pardon for His murderers will not cast off a thief: "Lord, remember me when Thou shalt come into Thy kingdom." Such great faith found its reward: "Amen I say to thee, this day thou shalt be with Me in paradise" *(Luke 23:42-43).*

Pain in itself is not unbearable; it is the failure to understand its meaning that is unbearable. If that thief did not see purpose in pain he would never have saved his soul. Pain can be the death of our soul, or it can be its life.

It all depends on whether or not we link it up with Him Who, "having joy set before him, endured the cross." One of the greatest tragedies in the world is wasted pain. Pain without relation to the cross is like an unsigned check -- without value. But once we have it countersigned with the Signature of the Saviour on the Cross, it takes on an infinite value.

A feverish brow that never throbs in unison with a Head crowned with thorns, or an aching hand never borne in patience with a Hand on the Cross, is sheer waste. The world is worse for that pain when it might have been so much the better.

All the sick-beds in the world, therefore, are either on the right side of the Cross or on the left; their position is determined by whether, like the thief on the left, they ask to be taken down, or, like the thief on the right, they ask to be taken up.

It is not so much what people suffer that makes the world mysterious; it is rather how much they miss when they suffer. They seem to forget that even as children they made obstacles in their games in order to have something to overcome.

Why, then, when they grow into man's estate, should there not be prizes won by effort and struggle? Cannot the spirit of man rise with adversity as the bird rises against the resistance of the wind? Do not the game fish swim upstream? Must not the alabaster box be broken to fill the house with ointment? Must not the chisel cut away the marble to bring out the form? Must not the seed falling to the ground die before it can spring forth into life? Must not the little streams speed into the ocean to escape their stagnant self-content? Must not grapes be crushed that there may be wine to drink, and wheat ground that there may be bread to eat?

Why then cannot pain be made redemption? Why under the alchemy of Divine Love cannot crosses be turned into crucifixes? Why cannot chastisements be regarded as penances? Why cannot we use a cross to become God-like? We cannot become like Him in His Power: we cannot become like Him in His Knowledge.

There is only one way we can become like Him, and that is in the way He bore His sorrows and His Cross. And that way was with love. "Greater love than this no man hath, that a man lay down his life for his friends." It is love that makes pain bearable.

As long as we feel it is doing good for another, or even for our own soul by increasing the glory of God, it is easier to bear. A mother keeps a vigil at the bedside of her sick child. The world calls it "fatigue" but she calls it love.

A little child was commanded by his mother not to walk the picket fence. He disobeyed and fell, maimed himself and was never able to walk again. Being told of his misfortune he said to his mother: "I know I will never walk again; I know it is my own fault; but if you will go on loving me I can stand anything." So it is with our own pains.

If we can be assured that God still loves and cares, then we shall find joy even in carrying on His redemptive work -- by being redeemers with a small "r" as He is Redeemer with a capital "R." Then will come to us the vision of the difference between Pain and Sacrifice. Pain is sacrifice without love. Sacrifice is pain with love.

When we understand this, then we shall have an answer for those who feel that God should have let us sin without pain:

"The cry of earth's anguish went up unto God, --
'Lord, take away pain, --
The shadow that darkens the world Thou hast made,
The close-coiling chain
That strangles the heart, the burden that weighs
On the wings that would soar, --
Lord, take away pain from the world Thou hast made
That it love Thee the more.'

"Then answered the Lord to the world He had made,
'Shall I take away pain?
And with it the power of the soul to endure
Made strong by the strain?
Shall I take away pity that knits heart to heart
And sacrifice high?
Will ye lose all your heroes who lift from the flame
White brows to the sky?
Shall I take away love that redeems with a price
And smiles through the loss, --
Can ye spare from the lives that would climb unto mine
The Christ on His Cross?' "

(God and Pain, by George Stewart)

And now this final lesson. You and I often ask God for many favors which are never granted. We can imagine the thief on the right during his life asking God for many favors, and very especially for wealth which was probably not granted. On the other hand, though God does not always grant our material favors, there is one prayer He always grants.

There is a favor that you and I can ask of God this very moment, if we had the courage to do it, and that favor would be granted before the day is over. That prayer which God has never refused and will never refuse is the prayer for suffering. Ask Him to send you a cross and you will receive it!

But why does He not always answer our prayers for *an increase in* salary, for larger commissions, for more money? Why did He not answer the prayer of the thief on the left to be taken down from the cross, and why did He answer the prayer of the thief on the right to forgive his sins? *Because material favors draw us away from Him, but the cross always draws us to Him. And God does not want the world to have us!*

He wants us Himself because He died for us!

The Rainbow of Sorrow, 1938

Sixth Meditation

ENVY

"This day thou shalt be with me in paradise."

Envy is sadness at another's good, and joy at another's evil. What rust is to iron, what moths are to wool, what termites are to wood, that envy is to the soul: the assassination of brotherly love.

We are not here concerned with just envy or zeal which inspires us to emulate good example and to progress with those who are our betters, for the Scriptures enjoin us to "be zealous for spiritual gifts"; rather, we here touch on that sinful envy which is a wilful grieving at another's good, either spiritual or temporal, for the reason that it seems to diminish our own good. The honor paid to another is regarded by the envious man as a reflected disgrace on himself, and he is sad in consequence. Envy manifests itself in discord, hatred, malicious joy, back-biting, detraction, imputing of evil motives, jealousy, and calumny.

A sample of this kind of envy we find in one of the two women who asked Solomon to adjudicate their dispute. The first woman said, "I and this woman dwelt in one house . . . And this woman's child died in the night: for in her sleep, she overlaid him. And rising in the dead time of the night, she took my child from my side while I thy handmaid was asleep . . . and laid her dead child in my bosom. "To which the other woman answered: "It is not so as thou sayest, but thy child is dead, and mine is alive."

Since there were no witnesses, Solomon ordered a sword to be brought to him, for he rightly judged that the motherly heart of the real mother would rather give up her child than see it killed. Brandishing the glittering sword, he said, "Divide the living child in two, and give half to the one, and half to the other." Hearing this, the woman whose child was alive cried out in terror and pity, "I beseech thee, my lord, give her the child alive, and do not kill it." But the other said, "Let it be neither mine nor thine, but divide it."

Then the king commanded the child be given to her who would rather give it up to another than have it killed, knowing that she must be the mother. The point of the story is that envy which is so jealous of the good of another may reach a point where it scruples not to take a life.

In our times, envy has taken on an economic form. The avarice of the rich is being matched by the envy of the poor. Some poor hate the rich not because they have unjustly stolen their possessions, but because they want their possessions. Certain *have-nots* are scandalized at the wealth of the *haves*, only because they are tempted by lust for their possessions.

The Communists hate the Capitalists only because they want to be Capitalists themselves; they envy the rich, not because of their need, but because of their greed.

Combined with this is social envy or snobbery which sneers at the higher position of others, because the snobs want to sit in their chairs and enjoy their applause. They assume that in not arriving at such popular favor themselves they were deprived of their due. That is why we hate those who do not pay sufficient attention to us and why we love those who flatter us.

If envy is on the increase today, as it undoubtedly is, it is because of the surrender of the belief of a future life and righteous Divine Justice. If this life is all, they think they should have all. From that point on, envy of others becomes their rule of life.

Our Lord was unceasing in His preaching against envy. To those who were envious of the mercy extended to lost sheep He pictured the angels of Heaven rejoicing more at the one sinner doing penance than at the ninety-nine just who needed not penance. To those who were envious of wealth He warned: "Lay not up to yourselves treasures on earth: where the rust and moth consume, and where thieves break through and steal. But lay up to yourselves treasures in heaven: where neither the rust nor moth consume and where thieves do not break through, nor steal."

To those who were envious of power, such as the Apostles quarreling about first place, He placed a child in the midst of them and, "putting His arms around him" reminded them that heaven was open only to those who were as simple children, for Christ is not in the great but in the little: "Whosoever shall receive one such child as this in my name, receiveth me. And whosoever shall receive me, receiveth not me, but him that sent me."

But His preaching against envy did not save Him from the envious. Pilate was envious of His power; Annas was envious of His innocence; Caiphas was envious of His popularity; Herod was envious of His moral superiority; the Scribes and Pharisees were envious of His wisdom. Each of these had built his judgment seat of mock moral superiority from which to sentence Morality to the Cross. And in order that He might no longer be a person to be envied, they reputed Him with the wicked.

Born between an ox and an ass, they now crucify Him between two criminals. That was the last insult they could give Him. To the public eye they created the impression that three thieves and not two were silhouetted against the sky. In a certain sense, it was true: two stole gold out of avarice; one stole hearts out of love. *Salvandus*, *Salvator* and *Salvatus*: The thief who could have been saved; the thief who was saved; and the Saviour who saved them. The crosses spelled out the words Envy, Mercy, and Pity.

The thief on the left envied the Power which Our Blessed Lord claimed. As the chief priests, scribes, and ancients ridiculed the Saviour, sneering: "He saved others -- himself he cannot save," the thief on the left added to their revilings: "If Thou be Christ, save thyself and us. "In other words: "If I had that power of yours, that power which you claim as the Messiah, I would use it differently than to hang helpless on a tree. I would step down from the Cross, smite my enemies, and prove what power really is."

Thus did Envy reveal that if it had the gifts which it envies in others it would misuse them, as the thief on the left would have surrendered redemption from sin for release from a nail. In like manner many in the world today who are envious of wealth would probably lose their souls if they had that wealth. Envy never thinks of responsibilities. Looking only to self it misuses every gift that comes its way.

Pity has quite a different effect on the soul. The thief on the right had no envy of the Master's Power but only pity for the Master's sufferings. Rebuking his companion on the left, the good thief said: "Neither dost thou fear God, seeing thou art under the same condemnation? And we indeed, justly, for we receive the due reward of our deeds; but this man hath done no evil."

There was not a spark of envy in him. He wanted nothing in all the world, not even to be removed from tragic companioning with his cross. He was not envious of God's Power, for God knows best what to do with His Power. He was not envious of his fellowmen, for they had nothing worth giving.

So he threw himself upon Divine Providence and asked only for forgiveness: "Lord, remember me when thou shalt come into thy kingdom." A dying man asked a dying Man for life; a man without possessions asked a Poor Man for a Kingdom; a thief at the door of death asked to die a thief and steal Paradise. And because He envied nothing, He received all: "Amen, I say to thee, this day thou shalt be with me in Paradise."

One would have thought a saint would have been the first soul purchased over the counter of Calvary by the red coins of redemption, but in the Divine plan, it is a thief who steals that privilege and marches as the escort of the King of Kings into Paradise.

Two lessons are taught us by this Second Word from the Cross. The first is that envy is the source of our wrong judgments about others. The chances are that if we are envious of others, nine times out of ten we will misjudge their characters.

Because the thief on the left was envious of the Power of Our Lord, he misjudged Him and missed both the Divinity of the Saviour and his own salvation. He falsely argued that Power should always be used the way he would have used it, namely to turn nails into rosebuds, a cross into a throne, blood into royal purple, and the blades of grass on the hillside into bayonets of offensive steel.

No one in the history of the world ever came closer to Redemption, and yet no one ever missed it so far. His envy made him ask for the wrong thing; he asked to be taken down when he should have asked to be taken up. It makes one think of how much the envy of Herod resulted in an equally false judgment: He massacred the Innocents because He thought the Infant King came to destroy an earthy kingdom, whereas He came only to announce a heavenly one.

So it is with us. Backbiting, calumny, false judgments, are all born of our envy. We say, "Oh, he is jealous," or "she is jealous"; but how do we know that he or she is jealous unless we ourselves have felt that way? How do we know others are acting proudly unless we know how pride asserts itself? Every envious word is based on a false judgment of our own moral superiority. To sit in judgment makes us feel that we are above those who are judged and more righteous and more innocent than they.

To accuse others is to say: "I am not like that." To be envious of others is to say: "You have stolen that which is mine." Envy of others' wealth has resulted in the gross misjudgment that the best way to do away with its abuse in the hands of the rich is to dispossess them violently, so that the dispossessors may in their turn, enjoy its abuse.

Envy of others' political power has given rise to the erroneous philosophy that even governments may be overthrown if organized violence is strong enough to do so.

Envy thus becomes the denial of all justice and love. In individuals it develops a cynicism that destroys all moral values, for by bankrupting others do we ourselves become bankrupt. In groups it produces a deceit that extends the glad hand of welcome to those who differ, only until they are strong enough to cut it off.

Since envy is so rampant in the world today, it is extremely good counsel to disbelieve 99/100 per cent of the wicked statements we hear about others. Think of how much the thief on the right had to discount to arrive at the truth. He had to disbelieve the judgment of four envious judges, the raillery of envious scribes and ancients, the blasphemous utterances of curious onlookers who loved murders, and the envious taunts of the thief on the left who was willing to lose his soul if only he could keep his fingers nimble for more thefts.

But if he had been envious of the Lord's power, he would never have been saved. He found peace by disbelieving the envious scandalmongers. Our peace is found in the same incredulity.

The chances are that there is a bit of jealousy, a bit of envy, behind every cutting remark and barbed whispering we hear about our neighbor. It is always well to remember that there are always more sticks under the tree that has the most apples. There should be some consolation for those who are so unjustly attacked to remember that it is a physical impossibility for any man to get ahead of us who stays behind to kick us.

A second lesson to be learned from this Word is that the only way to overcome envy is, like the thief on the right, to show pity. As Christians in good faith, we are all members of the Mystical Body of Christ and should therefore love one another as Christ has loved us.

If our arm suffers an injury our whole body feels the pain. In like manner, if the Church in any part of the world suffers martyrdom, we should feel pity toward it as part of our body, and that pity should express itself in prayer and good works. Pity should be extended not only to those outside the Church who are living as if the earth never bore a Cross, but even to the enemies of the Church who would destroy even the shadow of the Cross. God is their Judge; not we.

And as potential brothers of Christ, sons of a Heavenly Father and children of Mary, they must be worth our pity since they were worth the Saviour's Blood. Unfortunately, there are some who blame the Church for receiving great sinners into the Church on their deathbeds.

A few years ago one who was generally believed to be a racketeer and murderer met death at the hands of his fellow criminals. A few minutes before his death, he asked to be received into the Church, was baptized, received First Communion, and was anointed and given the last blessing. Some who should have known better protested against the Church. Imagine! Envy at the salvation of a soul!

Why not rather rejoice in God 's Mercy, for after all did he not belong to the same profession as the thief on the right -- and why should not Our Lord be just as anxious to save twentieth century thieves as first century thieves? They both have souls. It would seem that sinful envy of the salvation of a thief is a greater sin than thievery.

One thief was saved: therefore let no one despair. One thief was lost: therefore let no one presume. Have pity then on the miserable, and Divine Mercy will be the reward for your pity. When the Pharisees accused Our Lord of eating with publicans and sinners He retorted by reiterating the necessity of mercy: "The healthy have no need of a physician, but the sick have. Now go and learn what this means; *I will have mercy and not sacrifice.* For I am not come to call the just, but sinners."

One day a woman went to the saintly Father John Vianney, the Curé of Ars, in France, and said: "My husband has not been to the sacraments or to Mass for years. He has been unfaithful, wicked, and unjust. He has just fallen from a bridge and was drowned -- a double death of body and soul." The Curé answered: "Madam, there is a short distance between the bridge and the water, and it is that distance which forbids you to judge. "

There was just that distance between the two crosses which saved the penitent thief. If the thief on the right had been self-righteous, he would have looked down on Jesus and lost his soul. But because he was conscious of his own sin, he left room for Divine Pardon.

And the answer of the Redeemer to his request proves that to the merciful, love is blind -- for if we love God and our neighbor, who may even be our enemy, Divine Love will go blind as it did for the thief on the right. Christ will no longer be able to see our faults, and that blindness will be for us the dawn of the vision of Love.

THE PENITENT THIEF

"Say, bold but blessed thief,
That in a trice
Slipped into paradise,
And in plain day
Stol'st heaven away,
What trick couldst thou invent
To compass thy intent?
What arms?
What charms?"
"Love and belief."
"Say, bold but blessed thief,
How couldst thou read
A crown upon that head?
What text, what gloss –
A kingdom and a cross?
How couldst thou come to spy
God in a man to die?
What light?
What sight?"
"The sight of grief --"
"I sight to God his pain;
And by that sight
I saw the light,
Thus did my grief
Beget relief.
And take this rule from me,
Pity thou him he'll pity thee.
Use this,
Ne'er miss,
Heaven may be stolen again."

(Anonymous)

Victory Over Vice, 1939

Seventh Meditation

HOPE

"This day thou shalt be with me in paradise."

Our concern presently is with two kinds of souls; the despairing and the presumptuous: either those who say, "I am too wicked for God to be interested in me," or those who say, "Oh, I need not worry about my sins. God will take good care of me in the end."

Both these statements are sins of exaggeration. The first is the sin of despair, which exaggerates Divine Justice; the second is the sin of presumption, which exaggerates Divine Mercy. Somewhere there is a golden mean where "Justice and mercy kiss" as the Psalmist puts it, and that is the virtue of Hope.

The *virtue* of Hope is quite different from the *emotion* of Hope. The emotion centers in the body and is a kind of dreamy desire that we can be saved without much effort. The virtue of Hope, however, is centered in the *will* and may be defined as a divinely infused disposition of the will by which with sure confidence, thanks to the powerful help of Almighty God, we expect to pursue eternal happiness, using all the means necessary for attaining it.

The virtue of Hope lies not in the future of time, but beyond the tomb in eternity; its object is not the abundant life of earth, but the eternal love of God.

No stage was ever better set for the drama of Hope than Calvary. Seven centuries before, Isaias had prophesied that Our Divine Lord would be numbered with the wicked. In this hour the prophesy is fulfilled as two thieves, like unholy courtiers, stand unwilling guard on the King of Kings. Nothing could better reveal the contempt in which the Son of

God was held than to have crucified Him between two common thieves.

To this ridicule of unholy companionship was added the mockery of a parade that passed before the throne of the central Cross. The Evangelists note them as they pass: *rulers*, soldiers, and passersby. "And the people stood beholding, and the rulers with them derided him, saying: He saved others; let him save himself, if he be Christ, the elect of God" *(Luke 23:35)*. "And the soldiers also mocked him, coming to him, and offering him vinegar" *(Luke 23:36)*. "And they that passed by, blasphemed him, wagging their heads, and saying: Vah, thou that destroyest the temple of God, and in three days dost rebuild it; save thy own self; and if thou be the Son of God, come down from the cross" *(Matthew 27:39-40)*.

As one gazes on that spectacle of three crosses silhouetted against a black and frightened sky, one sees in prospect the future judgment of the world; the Judge in the center and the two divisions of humanity on either side: The sheep and the goats; the blessed and the lost; those who love and those who hate; for the end shall be as the beginning, except that Christ shall appear for the final judgment not on the cross of ignominy but with the cross in glory in the clouds of heaven.

The spiritual development of the thief on the right, reveals how hope is born first out of fear, then out of faith. His conversion began the moment he *feared*. Like the thief on the left he too had blasphemed that Man on the central Cross. Then suddenly turning his head he shouted across the face of Divine Mercy, to his blaspheming fellow thief: "Neither dost thou *fear* God, seeing thou art under the same condemnation? And we indeed justly, for we receive the due reward of our deeds; but this man hath done no evil" *(Luke 23:40-41)*.

The fear of God of which this robber spoke was not a *servile fear* that God would punish them for their thefts; it was rather a *filial fear* based on reverence -- a fear of displeasing Him who had done nothing to deserve such a humiliating death.

There is the first lesson: *Hope begins with fear*; hope involves fear because Hope is not certainty. We can, of course, be certain God will help us and give us sufficient strength to be saved, but we cannot be sure that we will always be faithful to His Grace.

God will not fail us; we need have no fear on that score. But we may fail God. The certitude that I am on the way to God does not exclude the fear that through some fault of mine, I may not come to His Blessed Presence.

Note the next step toward hope in the good thief as his fear led to faith, for "The fear of the Lord . . . is wisdom" *(Job 28:28)*.

In a single moment a soul with a genuine fear of God can come to a greater understanding of the purpose of life than in a lifetime spent in the study of the ephemeral philosophies of men. That is why death-bed conversions may be sincere conversions. The hardened soul disbelieves in God until that awful moment when he has no one to deceive but himself. Once the spark of salutary fear of God had jumped into the soul of the thief from the flaming furnace of that central Cross, fear gave way to faith. His next words were believing.

No longer was Christ an innocent man, nor an exiled upstart, nor a mock monarch. He was a King! Those thorns were His crown; that Cross was His throne; He had Omnipotent Power; that nail was His sceptre; He was a Saviour -- that is why He forgave His enemies.

Out from the full heart of the thief, there welled up the hopeful petition: "Remember me when thou shalt come into thy kingdom" *(Luke 23:42)*. He could not desire what he did not know; he could not hope in what he did not believe. The thief had faith in the Son of God; now he could hope.

And that hope born of fear and faith received its immediate response: "This day thou shalt be with me in paradise" *(Luke 23:43)*.

Above the blasphemous, raucous background of others shouting "Himself He cannot save," he heard: "*This* Day." He had only asked for the future, but the answer was more than he had hoped: "*This* Day." His arms were still pinioned, but he felt them loosen at the sound of "*This* Day"; his body was still racked by pain, but he felt it freshen at "*This* Day." His life was of little value -- but his soul took on eternal worth as he heard "This Day . . . Paradise." A thief had learned to call "Lord" to One whom he despised. And the Lord can forgive sins . . . Such is the beginning of Hope.

Two thieves there were: One who loved and one who hated. Each was on a cross. Neither the good nor the bad ever escape the cross. One thief was saved; therefore, let no one despair. One thief was lost; therefore, let no one presume.

The two extremes to be avoided then are presumption and despair. Presumption is an excess of hope, and despair is a defect of hope. Presumption is an inordinate trust in Divine Mercy, a hope of pardon without repentance, a heaven without merit.

A word to the presumptuous who hope for a death-bed conversion to make their peace with God, and who say: "God would not send me to hell," or "I have lived a fairly decent life, so I have nothing to worry about," or "I know I am a sinner, but no worse than my neighbor; why should I worry? God is merciful."

When you make the statement "God is good," what do you mean? Only this: "God is insensible to evil. He is good because He is unmindful of my wickedness." You forget that God is good *precisely* because He is the enemy of evil. A healthy man is not indifferent to disease; nor is a government good because it ignores crimes and injustice. Why then should you think that God will be complacent about that which you refuse to accept in others?

If you really believed that God is good, would you not be scrupulous about offending Him? Do you not do that much for your friends? The nobler a person is the more you dread offending him. Even for those whom you do not love, you show respect.

Will you then exploit Divine Goodness and deceive One in whom you repose the confidence of salvation? Will you forget that Goodness wounded by cynicism avenges itself?

If you lose your earthly friends by prostituting their generosity, will you not in like manner lose your Heavenly Friend by presuming? Will you make Divine Mercy the excuse for greater sinning? Is there not in every life a *last* pardon as there is also a *last* sin? Have we not allotted to each of us a final sin, which fills up the "bag of sin" and seals our eternity?

You may sin a thousand times and be forgiven, but like the man who threw himself into a river a hundred times, each time to be rescued by the bridge-tender, you may be told by the rescuer: "Someday you will throw yourself into the river and I may not be here to pull you out."

What we all have to realize is that when we sin we turn our back on God. He does not turn His back on us. If we are ever to see His face again we must turn around, that is, turn from sin. That is what is meant by conversion. "Turn ye to me, saith the Lord of hosts" *(Zechariah 1:3)*.

God cannot save us without that conversion; if we die in our unrepentant sin we are forever turned away from God. Where the tree falleth there it lies. There is no reversal of values after death.

We cannot love sin during life and begin to love virtue at death. The joys of heaven are the continuance of the Christ-like joys of earth. We do not develop a new set of loves with our last breath. We shall reap in eternity only what we sowed on earth. If we loved sin, we shall reap corruption; but we shall never gather grapes from thistles.

The Justice of God is not separable from His Goodness. If He were not Just, He would not be Good. Because He is Goodness, His Justice pardons; because He is Justice, His Goodness expiates. The thief on the right saw the need of Justice the moment he admitted, "We suffer justly"; that is why immediately he felt the response of Goodness: "This Day . . . Paradise."

Then let not our presuming moderns who pile sin on sin think that they can insult God until their lease on life has run out and then expect an eternal lease on one of the Father's mansions. Did He who went to Heaven by a Cross intend that you should go there by sinning?

Let us consider the other type of soul: the despairing. As presumption forgets Divine Justice, so despair forgets Divine Mercy. Modern despair is not only hopeless about eternal life, which it doubts, but even about earthly life, which it mocks. Never before in the history of Christianity has despair been so abysmal. Today there is everywhere an anticipation of catastrophe, an appalling sense of unpredictability and impending disaster.

In the past, men recovered from despair either by returning to the glories of the past or by looking forward to a crown beyond the cross; but now that minds have lost faith in God, they have only this world to give them hope.

Since that has turned against them they feel a conscious rupture with hope. They curse a meaningless existence, succumb to a continuous exasperation with uncertainty, and yield to a suicidal intent to escape the inescapable.

There are two causes for modern despair: Sensuality and sadness. It is a fact that those poets who have most ridiculed the future life and those writers who have poured the most scorn on sin and Divine Justice were themselves most abandoned to sensuality.

The singers of voluptuousness are always the singers of despair. This is because sensuality produces continuous disillusionment. Its pleasures must be repeated because of their *unsatisfyingness*; therefore, they make hungry where most they satisfy.

Being deceived so many times by the alluring promises of the flesh, its addicts feel that all life is a deceit. Having been fooled by that which promised pleasure, they conclude that nothing can give pleasure. The fruit of pessimism blossom on the tree of a dissolute life.

From another point of view sensuality begets despair because by its very nature it is directed to a sensual object, and an excessive dedication to the carnal kills the capacity for the spiritual. Delicate hands lose their skill by handling rough stones, and souls lose their appetite for the Divine by undue attachment to the flesh. The eyes that refuse to look upon the light soon lose their power to see: "Having eyes, [they] see . . . not" *(Mark 8:18).*

Hope implies love; but if love is centered in the corporal, the soul is deadened to all that is not carnal: It finds less and less satisfaction in duty, family, work, profession, and, above all else, God. There is time only for the wicked joy to which one is slave.

Naturally, the future life and heaven and the Cross cease to move such a person. There is no desire except the biological; the future begins to be disgusting. From a stage where there is no time for God, they reach another where there is no taste for God. Thus does a world, which forgot love for sex, pay its terrible penalty in the despair, which calls life meaningless because it has made its own life a wreck.

The second cause of despair is sadness. Sadness does not mean sorrow caused by a death, but rather a surrender to states of depression because of a consciousness of sin and unworthiness. Many falls produce melancholy; repeated defeats induce despair.

St. Paul speaks of carnal excesses and greed for money as the feeble compensations for the one who experiences melancholy induced by multiplied sin: "Who despairing have given themselves up to lasciviousness, unto the working of all uncleanness unto covetousness" *(Ephesians 4:19)*.

Despair, born of the loss of God, also ends in persecution. In their impiety, such souls would kill the God they left. That is why wherever you find an atheistic government in the world today, you find "purges." Not being able to tolerate their own inner sadness, they must compensate for it by killing hope in others.

Each despairing soul must decide for itself the reason for despair. Regardless however of how multiplied or grievous your sins may have been, there is still room for hope. Did not Our Lord say: "For I came not to call the just, but sinners" *(Mark 2:17)*; and on another occasion "there shall be joy in heaven upon one sinner that doth penance, more than upon ninety-nine just who need not penance" *(Luke 15:7)*.

If He forgave the thief, and Magdalene, and Peter, why not you? What makes many in old age sad is not that their joys are gone, but that their hopes are gone. Your earthly hopes may decrease with the years, but not heavenly hope. Regardless of the sinful burden of the years, God's mercy is greater than your faults.

Only when God ceases to be infinitely merciful and only when you begin to be infinitely evil, will there be reason for despair; and that will be *never*; Peter denied Our Lord, but Our Lord did not deny Peter. The thief cursed Christ, but He did not curse the thief. If we had never sinned, we could never call Christ Saviour.

The Divine Invitation has never been annulled: "Come to me, all you that labour, and are burdened, and I will refresh you" *(Matthew 11:28)*. That invitation is not only for the weary, it is also for the sinful.

If you insist that you are disgusted with yourself, remember that you can come to God even by a succession of disgusts. What does your disgust mean except that everything earthly has failed you? That is one of the ways God makes you feel hunger for the Divine. Do you not crave food most when you are hungry? Do you not want water most when you are thirsty?

Your own disgust, if you knew it, is the distant call of Divine Mercy. If then the poverty of your merits makes you shrink from the Divine Presence, then let your needs draw you to Him.

The principal reason for the increase of nervous disorders in the world is due to *hidden guilt* or unatoned sin locked on the inside until it festered. These souls are running off to psychoanalysts to have their sins explained away, when what they need is to get down on their knees and right themselves with God.

When disgusted with our sins we can go into a confessional box, become our own accuser, hear the words of absolution Our Lord Himself gave, make amends and start life all over again, for none of us want our sins explained away; we want them forgiven. That is the miracle of the Sacrament of Penance and the rekindling of Hope.

"If I had sat at supper with the Lord
And laid my head upon that saving breast
I might have turned and fled among the rest –
I might have been that one who left the board
To add the high priests' silver to his hoard.
Had our Redeemer stooped to wash my feet,
Would I have washed my neighbor's clean and sweet
Or thrice denied the Christ I had adored?

"Long have I grieved that I was not St. Paul
Who rode those seas and saw the tempest toss
The ships he sailed in when he heard the call
To preach the risen Christ and gain through loss.
Tonight I envy most among them all
That thief who hung repentant on his cross."

(Alexander Harvey)

The Seven Virtues, 1940

Eighth Meditation

A WORD TO THE SINNERS

There are two ways of coming to God: through the preservation of innocence; and through the loss of it. Some have come to God because they were good, like Mary, who was "full of grace"; like Joseph, the "just man"; like Nathaniel, "in whom there was no guile"; or like John the Baptist, "the greatest man ever born of woman."

But others have come to God who were bad like the young man of the Gerasenes "possessed of devils," like Magdalen, out of whose corrupt soul the Lord cast seven devils; and like the thief at the right who spoke the second word to the Cross.

The world loves the mediocre. The world hates the very good and the very bad. The good are a reproach to the mediocre, and the evil are a disturbance. That is why Christ was crucified with thieves. Seven hundred years before, Isaiah had prophesied that He would be "reputed with the wicked" *(Isaiah 53:12)*. Luke verified it: "And with the wicked was he reckoned" *(Luke 22: 37)*.

So it was willed by God. This is His true position: Jesus among the worthless ones. During his life He was accused of eating and drinking with sinners; now they can accuse Him of dying with them. And these companions on their crosses were not political prisoners, nor castoff capitalists from a proletarian revolution; they were just plain bandits -- pure and simple.

Here is a supreme instance of the Right Man in the right place: Christ among the bandits; the Redeemer in the midst of the unredeemed; the Physician among the lepers -- for God does not work through culture but through grace. He does not ask men to be refined; He asks them to be penitent.

Thus does God show that we become great not because of what we are, but because of what He gives.

God in His Infinite Wisdom had reached deep into the lower layers of humanity and picked out of its dregs two worthless derelicts; and He used one of them as the escort of His Eternal Son.

At the beginning of the Crucifixion they both cursed and blasphemed the Saviour. But suddenly the soul of one, lighted by fires from that Central Cross, turned to a King who was being mocked and asked to be one of His subjects: "Lord, remember me when thou shalt come into thy kingdom" *(Luke 23:42).*

Lord: He called Him Lord! A real King is so easy to approach!

Remember me: There was a touch of humor in asking God to remember. God had remembered him before he was born. That is why He is immortal. God had been following his soul down the corridors of time, and now the pursued asks the Pursuer to remember.

When thou shalt come into thy kingdom: How did the thief know He had a Kingdom? Maybe the crown of thorns spoke of a diadem, the crucifixion of a coronation, the nails of a sceptre, and the blood of royal purple. We can never judge people by the way they are dressed!

No prayer to God is ever unanswered. From the Central Cross there flashed back: "This day thou shalt be with me in Paradise" *(Luke 23:43).*

This day: Evil has its hour, but God has His day.

Thou: "And he calleth his own sheep by name *(John 10:3).* This was the foundation of Christian Democracy. The soul of an outcast is of such value that the Eternal Word addresses him in the second person singular: "Thou."

Shalt be with me in Paradise: I wonder why He said in Paradise? To be with Him is Paradise.

The mob on Calvary asked Him to come down from the Cross: the thief asked to be taken up! The masses would have believed if He preached a religion without a Cross; the thief found his faith by hanging on a cross. This is the supreme instance of one bringing good out of evil. It is doubtful if the thief would have found Goodness otherwise!

Why is it that this thief found salvation? Why, on the other hand, did Our Lord say to the chief priests and the ancients: "Amen I say to you, that the publicans and the harlots shall go into the kingdom of God before you" *(Matthew 21:3)*? Why did He lash out with whips at the merchants, and with His tongue scourge the so-called good people, calling them a "brood of vipers" and "whitened sepulchres"? And while speaking harshly to this group, why did he speak so kindly to the woman with five husbands, so gently to the publican Matthew, and so courteously to the good thief?

It can only be because the capacity for conversion is greater in the really wicked than in the self-satisfied and complacent. The very emptiness of soul of the sinners is in itself an occasion for receiving the compassion of God. Self-disgust is the beginning of conversion, for it marks the death of pride.

The prodigal began to be converted only when he was hungry: "There was a famine." He had left the Father's House saying: "Give me," but he came back saying: "Father, *make me* one of thy hired servants." As the Mother of Our Lord had said of her Son: "He hath filled the hungry with good things; and the rich he hath sent empty away" *(Luke 1:53)*.

May it not be that the conversion of the good thief is the key to the conversion of the modem world? Men will return to God, not because they are good, but because they recognize that they are evil. They will come to God through evil rather than through goodness. Or shall we say they will come to God through the Devil.

Countless are the instances mentioned in the Gospel of those who came to God after Satan was driven from their souls. The French Revolutionist Sorel predicted that the basic problem of the twentieth century would be the problem of evil.

The 19th century foreshadowed this in two of its most outstanding writers: Dostoevski, the Russian, and Nietzsche, the German. Nietzsche, representing one side of the problem of evil, believed that the world must pass from Christ to anti-Christ; Dostoevski, representing the other side, believed that the world would be saved by passing from anti-Christ to Christ.

Most typical of the latter approach is Professor C.E.M. Joad of the University of London, who explains the fanaticism for such creeds of Nazism, Fascism, and Communism as the yearning of irreligious minds to fill up the moral vacuum in their souls by an object of absolute adoration -- an evil god.

The universality of evil throughout the world frightened Joad, and "so pervasive and insistent have these evils become that it is at times difficult to avoid concluding that the Devil has been given a longer rope than usual for the tempting and corrupting of men."

None of the explanations given by his contemporaries concerning evil are satisfactory. The socialist explanation of evil in terms of economic inequality and injustice, Joad rejects; for if poverty is the root of all evil, then money must be the source of all virtue.

The psychological explanation of evil attributes evil to suppressed desires, thwarted sex libidos, and mother libidos, all of which could be abolished by popularizing aesthetics, by extending the blessings of the machine and the ballot.

These he rejected after asking himself: "Was no rich man ever cruel, was no unrepressed man ever tyrannical," "was no self-expressive child selfish"? With the posing of the question, there begins to file before the mind's eye that long line of absolute rulers, the sultans, the caliphs, the emperors and the kings, with the smaller fry, the school masters and the work house superintendents, and the slave overseers, the Squeerses and Brooklehursts, and Bumbles and Murdestones, bringing up the rear of the melancholy procession, who had money enough to be exempt from the cramping effects of poverty and power enough to be free from the repressive effects of authority.

Yet they used their power to increase, and often deliberately to increase, the misery of human beings with such consistency as to provoke Lord Acton's terrible verdict: "All Power corrupts and absolute power corrupts absolutely."

None of the modem explanations of evil, Joad argues, explains the fact of evil. "Evil is not merely a by-product of unfavorable circumstances; it is too wide-spread and too deep-seated to admit of any such explanations; so wide-spread, so deep-seated that one can only conclude that what the religions have taught is true, and that evil is *endemic in the heart of man.*"

"Endemic in the heart of man!" That is it. It is in our blood! It flows through our veins! It gives life to the brain when it thinks evil; it energizes the will when it kills; it fires the muscle when it drops bombs; and it persecutes the prayerful.

In the face of that evil which is endemic in the human heart, this truth emerges: It is one thing to be blind and another thing to know it.

There is hope for those who are deaf and who want to hear and for the lame who want to walk, and there is hope for the diseased who acknowledges the need of a physician and the sinner who feels the need of a redeemer.

The thief at the right conquered evil that way: By admitting his emptiness of soul he called upon God to save him! There is only one thing in the world worse than sin, and that is denying that we are sinners.

The tragedy of the modern world is that so many deny sin. Never before in the history of the world was there so much evil, and never before was there so little consciousness of it. Talk to a modern man about reconciling his soul with God and he will say: "What have I ever done to Him? I let Him alone, why should He not leave me alone?"

Why does he say this? For the same reason a healthy man would say to a surgeon who wanted to operate on him: "There is nothing wrong with me. Leave me alone." In like manner if you are your own law, if you set your own standards, and if you are your own god, then it is nonsense to ask to be reconciled to another god.

As a man gets more wicked he understands his wickedness less and less, just as when a man's fever climbs to a point of deliriousness, he understands his sickness less and less. He may even think himself so healthy that he wants to go to work. A moderately bad man always thinks he is good. We never know we were asleep until we wake up, and we never know what sin really is until we get out of it.

Only when you are sick, do you ask for a physician; and only when you recognize yourself as a sinner, do you ask for your Redeemer. Our Lord said: "They that are in health need not a physician, but they that are ill" *(Matthew 9:12).*

When, therefore, you reach a point where you cease calling yourself "idiotic" (and don't mean it) -- and begin to call yourself a "rotter" (and mean it) -- you are on the pathway of the good bandit that leads to conversion. The perception of guilt is the condition of conversion, as the perception of disease is the condition of remedy. So long as we think we are good we will never find God.

If therefore we think that we know it all, how can God teach us what we do not know?

We admit sometimes that we are ill tempered, or that we are intemperate, but will we ever admit that we are proud? We condemn pride so vociferously in others, but we deny that we have ever been guilty. The more conceited we are, the more we hate conceit in others. The more we say, "I am not conceited," the more we prove that we are conceited.

Our pride makes us look down on people, so that we can never look up to God. In fact because our pride admits no law and no authority other than ourselves, it is essentially anti-God.

All our other sins can be from ourselves; for example, avarice, lust, anger and gluttony. But pride comes direct from hell. By that sin fell the angels. It destroys the very possibility of conversion.

If therefore we can humble ourselves as did the thief at the right, and admit we have done wrong, then out of our creative despair we can cry to the Lord to remember us in our misery! The very moment we stop shutting and posing and begin to see ourselves as we really are, then in our humility we shall be exalted.

Let us examine our consciences. Let us ask ourselves not how *much* we know, but how much we do not know; not how good we are, but how bad we are. Let us judge ourselves not by the knowledge we possess, but by our consciences; not by our education, but by our habits; not by our politeness, but by our hearts.

As soon as we feel a great void in our souls, and realize that by our sinning we are no longer our own, and acknowledge that we are still thirsty at the border of a well, and admit that we have played the fool, and that our follies of the years mount up in their dark arrears, then out of a dark and swampy soul, we cry out with the thief -- as all

Catholics do when we go to Confession -- "Bless me Father, for I have sinned" -- "I am a sinner."

Such is the beginning of salvation. The thief died a thief, for he stole Paradise. And if we win Paradise we will be thieves too, for we will never deserve what we got -- the God of everlasting peace!

Seven Words to the Cross, 1944

Ninth Meditation

THE SECRET OF SANCTITY

There is only one thing in the world that is definitely and absolutely your own, and that is your will. Health, power, possessions, and honor can all be snatched from you, but your will is irrevocably your own, even in hell. Hence, nothing really matters in life, except what you do with your will. It is that which makes the story of the two thieves crucified on either side of Our Lord, for here is the drama of wills.

Both thieves at first blasphemed. There was no such thing as the good thief at the beginning of the Crucifixion. But when the thief on the right heard that Man on the Central Cross forgive His executioners, he had a change of soul.

He began to accept his sorrows. He took up his cross as a yoke rather than as a gibbet, abandoned himself to God's Will, and turning to the rebellious thief on the left said: "Neither dost thou fear God, seeing thou art under the same condemnation? And we indeed justly: for we receive the due reward of our deeds. But this man hath done no evil" *(Luke 23:40-41).*

Then from his heart already so full of surrender to His Saviour, there came this plea, "Remember me when thou shalt come into thy kingdom" *(Luke 23:42).* Immediately there came the answer: "Amen I say to thee: this day thou shalt be with me in paradise" *(Luke 23:43).*

"Thou." We are all individuals in the sight of God. He called His sheep by name. This word was the foundation of Christian democracy. Every soul is precious in God's sight, even those whom the state casts out and kills.

At the foot of the cross, Mary witnessed the conversion of the good thief, and her soul rejoiced that he had accepted the Will of God. Her Divine Son's second word promising Paradise as a reward for that surrender, reminded her of her own Second Word thirty years before, when the angel had appeared to her and told her that she was to be the Mother of Him Who was now dying on the Cross.

In her First Word, she asked how this would be accomplished since she knew not man. But when the angel said she would conceive of the Holy Spirit, Mary immediately answered: "Be it done to me according to thy word" *Fiat mihi* secundum verbum tuum. *(Luke 1:38)*

This was one of the great Fiats of the world. The first was at Creation when God said: *Fiat Lux*: "Let there be light"; another was in Gethsemani, when the Saviour, pressing the chalice of redemption to his lips, cried: *Fiat voluntas tua*: "Thy will be done" *(Matthew 26:42)*. The third was Mary's, pronounced in a Nazarene cottage, which proved to be a declaration of war against the empire of evil; *Fiat mihi* secundum verbum tuum: "Be it done to me according to thy word" *(Luke 1:38)*.

The Second Word of Jesus on Golgotha and the second Word of Mary in Nazareth teach the same lesson: *Everyone in the world has a cross, but the cross is not the same for any two of us*. The cross of the thief was not the cross of Mary. The difference was due to God's will toward each. The thief was to give life; Mary to accept life. The thief was to hang on his cross; Mary was to stand beneath hers. The thief was to go ahead; Mary to remain behind. The thief received a dismissal; Mary received a mission. The thief was to be received into Paradise, but Paradise was to be received into Mary.

Each of us, too, has a cross. Our Lord said: "If any man will follow me" *(Mark 8:34)*. He did not say: "Take up my cross." My cross is not the same as yours, and yours is not the same as mine. Every cross in the world is tailor made, custom built, patterned to fit one and no one else.

That is why we say: "My cross is hard." We assume that other persons' crosses are lighter, forgetful that the only reason our cross is hard is simply because it is our own. Our Lord did not make His Cross; it was made for Him. So yours is made by the circumstances of your life, and by your routine duties. That is why it fits so tightly. Crosses are not made by machines.

Our Lord deals separately with each soul. The crown of gold we want may have underneath it the crown of thorns, but the heroes who choose the crown of thorns often find that underneath it is the crown of gold. Even those that seem to be without a cross actually have one.

No one would have ever suspected that when Mary resigned herself to God's Will by accepting the honor of becoming the Mother of God, she would ever have to bear a cross. It would seem, too, that one who was preserved free from original sin should be dispensed from the penalties of that sin, such as pain. Yet this honor brought to her seven crosses and ended by making her the Queen of Martyrs.

There are, therefore, as many kinds of crosses as there are persons: crosses of grief and sorrow, crosses of want, crosses of abuse, crosses of wounded love and crosses of defeat.

There is the cross of widows. How often Our Lord spoke of them, for example, in the parable of the judge and the widow *(Luke 18:1-8)*; when He rebuked the Pharisees who "devour the houses of widows" *(Mark 12:40)*, when he spoke to the widow of Naim *(Luke 7:12)*, and when He praised the widow who threw two mites into the temple treasury *(Mark 12:42)*. Widowhood may have been particularly dear to Him, because His own mother was a widow, for Joseph His foster-father was presumably already dead.

When God takes someone from us, it is always for a good reason. When the sheep have grazed and thinned the grass in the lower regions, the shepherd will take a little lamb in his arms, carry it up the mountain where the grass is green, lay it down, and soon the other sheep will follow. Every now and then Our Lord takes a lamb from the parched field of a family up to those Heavenly Green pastures, so that the rest of the family may keep their eyes on their true home and follow through.

Then there is the cross of sickness, which always has a Divine purpose. Our Blessed Lord said: "This sickness is not unto death, but for the glory of God: that the Son of God may be glorified by it" *(John 11:4)*. Resignation to this particular kind of cross is one of the very highest forms of prayer. Unfortunately, the sick generally want to be doing something else other than the thing that God wants them to do.

The tragedy of this world is not so much the pain in it; the tragedy is that so much of it is wasted. It is only when a log is thrown into the fire that it begins to sing. It was only when the thief was thrown into the fire of a cross that he began to find God. It is only in pain that some begin to discover where Love is.

Because our crosses differ, soul will differ from soul in glory. We think too often that in Heaven there is going to be somewhat the same equality in social positions that we have here; that servants on earth will be servants in heaven; that the important people on earth will be the important people in heaven. This is not true.

God will take into account our crosses. He seemed to suggest that in the parable of Dives and Lazarus: "Son, remember that thou didst receive good things in thy lifetime, and likewise Lazarus evil things: but now he is comforted and thou art tormented" *(Luke 16:25)*.

There will be a bright jewel of merit for those who suffer in this world. Because we live in a world where position is determined economically, we forget that in God's world the royalty are those who do His Will. Heaven will be a complete reversal of values of earth. The first shall be last and the last first, for God is no respecter of persons.
A wealthy and socially important woman went to heaven. St. Peter pointed to a beautiful mansion and said: "This is your chauffeur's home." "Well," said she, "if that is his home, think what mine will be like." Pointing to a tiny cottage, Peter said: "There is yours." "I can't live in that," she answered. And Peter said: "I'm sorry, that is the best I could do with the material you sent me." Those who suffer as the thief did have sent ahead some fine material.

It makes no difference what you do here on earth; what matters is the love with which you do it. The street cleaner who accepts in God's name a cross arising from his state in life, such as the scorn of his fellowmen; the mother who pronounces her *Fiat* to the Divine Will as she raises a family for the Kingdom of God; the afflicted in hospitals who say *Fiat* to their cross of suffering are the uncanonized saints, for what is sanctity but fixation in goodness by abandonment to God's Holy Will?

It is typically American to feel that we are not doing anything unless we are doing something *big*. But from the Christian point of view, there is no one thing that is bigger than any other thing. The bigness comes from the way our wills utilize things. Hence mopping an office for the love of God is bigger than running the office for the love of money.

Most of our misery and unhappiness come from rebellion against our present state coupled with false ambition. We become critical of everyone above us, as if the cloak of honor, which another wears, was stolen from our shoulders. Rest assured that if it is God's Will that we do a certain task, it will be done, though the whole world would rise up and say "Nay." But if we get that honor by the abandonment of truth and humility, it will be bitter as wormwood and as biting as gall.

Each of us is to praise and love God in his own way. The bird praises God by singing, the flower by blooming, the clouds with their rain, the sun with its light, the moon with its reflection, and each of us by the patient resignation to the trials of his state in life.

In what does your life consist except two things? 1) Active duties. 2) Passive circumstances. The first is under your control; these do in God's name. The second is outside your control; these submit to in God's name. Consider only the present; leave the past to God's Justice the future to His Providence. Perfection of personality does not consist in knowing God's plan, but in submitting to it as it reveals itself in the circumstances of life.

There is really one shortcut to sanctity; the one Mary chose in the Visitation, the one Our Lord chose in Gethsemani, the one the thief chose on the Cross -- abandonment to the Divine Will.

If the gold in the bowels of the earth did not say *Fiat* to the miner and the goldsmith, it would never become the chalice of the altar. If the pencil did not say *Fiat* to the hand of the writer, we would never have the poem; if Our Lady did not say *Fiat* to the angel, she would never have become the House of Gold; if Our Lord did not say *Fiat* to the Father's Will in Gethsemani, we would never have been redeemed; if the thief did not say *Fiat* in his heart, he never would have been the escort for the Master into Paradise.

The reason most of us are what we are, mediocre Christians, "up" one day, "down" the next, is simply because we refuse to let God work on us. As crude marble, we rebel against the hand of the sculptor; as unvarnished canvas we shrink from the oils and tints of the Heavenly Artist. We are so "fearful lest having Him we may have nought else beside," forgetful that if we have the fire of Love, why worry about the sparks, and if we have the perfect round, why trouble ourselves with the arc.

We always make the fatal mistake of thinking that it is what we do that matters, when really what matters is what we let God do to us. God sent the angel to Mary, not to ask her to do something, but to let something be done.

Since God is a better artisan than you, the more you abandon yourself to Him, the happier He can make you. It is well to be a self-made man, but it is better to be a God-made man.

God will love you, of course, even though you do not love Him, but remember if you give Him only half your heart, He can make you only fifty percent happy. You have freedom only to give it away. To whom do you give yours? You give it either to the moods of the hour, to your egotism, to creatures or to God.

Do you know that if you give your freedom to God, in heaven you will have no freedom of choice, because once you possess the Perfect, there is nothing left to choose. And still you will be perfectly free, because you will be One with Him Whose Heart is Freedom and Love!

Seven Words of Jesus and Mary, 1945

WOMAN, BEHOLD THY SON;
BEHOLD THY MOTHER
Meditations on the Third Word from the Cross
Archbishop Fulton J. Sheen

First Meditation

WOMAN, BEHOLD THY SON

An angel of light went out from the great white Throne of Light and descended over the plains of Esdraelon, past the daughters of the great kingdoms and empires, and came to where a humble virgin of Nazareth knelt in prayer, and said, "Hail, full of grace!" These were not words; they were the Word. "And the Word became flesh." This was the first Annunciation.

Nine months passed and once more an angel from that great white Throne of Light came down to shepherds on Judean hills, teaching them the joy of a "Gloria in excelsis," and bidding them worship Him Whom the world could not contain, a "Babe wrapped in swaddling clothes and laid in a manger." Eternity became time, Divinity incarnate, God a man; Omnipotence was discovered in bonds. In the language of Saint Luke, Mary "brought forth her first-born Son . . .and laid Him in a manger." This was the first Nativity.

Then came Nazareth and the carpenter shop where one can imagine the Divine Boy, straitened until baptized with a baptism of blood, fashioning a little cross in anticipation of a great Cross that would one day be His on Calvary. One can also imagine Him in the evening of a day of labor at the bench, stretching out His arms in exhausted relaxation, whilst the setting sun traced on the opposite wall the shadow of a man on a cross. One can, too, imagine His Mother seeing in each nail the prophecy and the tell-tale of a day when men would carpenter to a Cross the One who carpentered the universe.

Nazareth passed into Calvary, and the nails of the shop into the nails of human malignity. From the Cross, He completed His last will and testament. He had already committed His blood to the Church, His garments to His enemies, a thief to Paradise, and would soon commend His body to the grave and His soul to His Heavenly Father. To whom, then, could He give the two treasures which He loved above all others, Mary and John? He would bequeath them to one another, giving at once a son to His Mother and a Mother to His friend. "Woman!" It was the second Annunciation! The midnight hour, the silent room, the ecstatic prayer had given way to the mount of Calvary, the darkened sky, and a Son hanging on a Cross. Yet, what consolation! It was only an angel who made the first Annunciation, but it is God's own sweet voice, which makes the second.

"Behold thy son!" It was the second Nativity! Mary had brought forth her First-born without labor, in the cave of Bethlehem; she now brings forth her second-born, John, in the labors of the Cross. At this moment Mary is undergoing the pains of childbirth, not only for her second-born, who is John, but also for the millions who will be born to her in Christian ages as "Children of Mary." Now we can understand why Christ was called "her First-born." It was not because she was to have other children by the blood of flesh, but because she was to have other children by the blood of her heart. Truly, indeed, the Divine condemnation against Eve is now renewed against the new Eve, Mary, for she is bringing forth her children in sorrow.

Mary, then, is not only the Mother of Our Lord and Saviour, Jesus Christ, but she is also our Mother, and this not by a title of courtesy, not by legal fiction, not by a mere figure of speech, but by the right of bringing us forth in sorrow at the foot of the Cross. It was by weakness and disobedience at the foot of the tree of Good and Evil that Eve lost the title, Mother of the Living; it is at the foot of the tree of the Cross that Mary, by sacrifice and obedience, regained for us the title, Mother of Men. What a destiny to have the Mother of God as my Mother and Jesus as my Brother!

PRAYER

O MARY! as Jesus was born to thee in thy first Nativity of the flesh, so we have been born of thee in thy second Nativity of the spirit. Thus thou didst beget us into a new world of spiritual relationship with God as our Father, Jesus as our Brother, and thou as our Mother! If a mother can never forget the child of her womb, then, Mary, thou shalt never forget us. As thou wert Co-Redemptrix in the acquisition of the graces of eternal life, be thou also our Co-Mediatrix in their dispensation. Nothing is impossible for thee, because thou art the Mother of Him who can do all things. If thy Son did not refuse thy request at the banquet of Cana, He will not refuse it at the celestial banquet where thou art crowned as Queen of the Angels and Saints. Intercede therefore to thy Divine Son, that He may change the waters of my weakness into the wine of thy strength. Mary, thou art the Refuge of Sinners! Pray for us, now prostrate at the foot of the Cross. Holy Mary, Mother of God, pray for us sinners, now and at the hour of our death. Amen.

The Seven Last Words, 1933

Second Meditation

THY KINGDOM COME

"Thy Kingdom Come"

"Woman, behold thy son."

When Our Lord taught us the "Our Father" He made the third petition a prayer that God's Kingdom, which is the kingdom of saints, might come. Now in His own last prayer, He addresses the saintliest of creatures: John the beloved disciple, and Mary, His Mother. He was dying on the cross for no other reason than to make us saints – and to be a saint means to be fixed in goodness. The saintliest creature God ever made was the Mother of His Divine Son, for she was not only "full of grace" but a co-Redeemer with her Son now suspended above her head. When Our Lord looked down to her and commended her to us in the person of John, saying: "Behold thy mother", He was equivalently telling us: "If you wish to be holy, behold thy mother; if you really wish that My Kingdom will come, then behold thy mother; if you will to be rooted in goodness and be perfect as your heavenly Father is perfect, then behold thy mother".

Our Lord made no exception; His Mother was given to all – to those who sin, to those who mourn, and to those who suffer.

Are you a sinner? Then go to Mary, for She knows something of the bitterness of your soul. Mary knows what it is for a soul to be without Jesus, for during the three days loss she merited to become the Refuge of Sinners. She was meriting the honor anew at this very moment. She would never have been given to sinners had there not been a crucifixion, there never would have been a crucifixion without sin, and there never would have been sin without sinner – and where sinners are, there are we. Mary, therefore, owes the dignity of her title to us, as sinners. Are you a sinner? Then hear her merciful Son lift me from despair with the words: "Behold thy mother."

Are you a mourner? Have you lost a sweet child, a kind father, a loving mother? Then you have lost only part of what you had. But Mary lost everything, for she lost God. To you, who mourn: "Behold thy mother."

In those moments of unbounded grief, when you are oppressed by your sins, and dripping tears from a wounded or broken heart; when you are sick of what you have and hunger after what you have not; when holiness seems such a distant goal and heaven so far off, then say to Mary: "Remember, Jesus, said to thee, concerning me as wicked as I am: 'Woman, behold thy son'."

The Seven Last Words and the Our Father, 1935

Third Meditation

THE SANCTUS

"Woman, behold thy son . . . behold thy mother."
– John 19:26-27.

Five days ago our Blessed Lord made a triumphal entry into the city of Jerusalem: Triumphant cries rang about His ears; palms dropped beneath His feet, as the air resounded with hosannas to the Son of David and praises to the Holy One of Israel. To those who would have silenced the demonstration in His honor, our Lord reminds them that if their voices were silent, even the very stones would have cried out. That was the birthday of Gothic Cathedrals.

They did not know the real reason why they were calling Him *holy*; they did not even understand why He accepted the tribute of their praise. They thought that they were proclaiming Him a kind of earthly king. But He accepted their demonstration because He was going to be the King of a spiritual empire. He accepted their tributes, their hosannas, their pæans of praise because He was going to His cross as a Victim. And every victim must be holy -- *Sanctus, Sanctus, Sanctus*. Five days later came the *Sanctus* of the Mass of Calvary. But at that *Sanctus* of His Mass, He does not say "holy" -- He speaks *to* the holy ones; He does not whisper "Sanctus" -- He addresses Himself *to* saints, to His sweet Mother Mary, and His beloved disciple, John.

Striking words they are: "Woman, behold thy son . . . behold thy mother." He was speaking now to saints. He had no need of saintly intercession, for He was the Holy One of God. But *we* have need of holiness, for every victim of the Mass must be holy, undefiled, and unpolluted. But how can we be holy participants in the Sacrifice of the Mass? He gave the answer: namely, by putting ourselves under the protection of His Blessed Mother. He addresses the Church and all its members in the person of John, and says to each of us: "Behold thy mother." That is why He addressed her not as "Mother" but as "Woman." She had a universal mission, to be not only His Mother, but to be the Mother of all Christians. She had been His Mother; now she was to be the Mother of His Mystical Body, the Church. And we were to be her children.

There is a tremendous mystery hidden in that one word "Woman." It was really the last lesson in detachment which Jesus had been teaching her these many years, and the first lesson of the new attachment. Our Lord had been gradually "alienating," as it were, His affections from His Mother, not in the sense that she was to love Him less, or that He was to love her less, but only in the sense that she was to love *us more*. She was to be detached from motherhood in the flesh, only to be more attached to that greater motherhood in the spirit. Hence the word: "Woman." She was to make us *other Christs*, for as Mary had raised the Holy One of God, so only she could raise us as holy ones for God, worthy to say *Sanctus, Sanctus, Sanctus*, in the Mass of that prolonged Calvary.

The story of the preparation for her role as Mother of the Mystical Body of Christ is unfolded in three scenes in the life of her divine Son, each one suggesting the lesson which Calvary itself was to reveal: namely, that she was called to be not only the Mother of God, but also the Mother of men: not only the Mother of holiness, but the Mother of those who ask to be holy.

The first scene took place in the Temple where Mary and Joseph found Jesus after a three-day search. The Blessed Mother reminds Him that their hearts were broken with sorrow during the long search, and He answers: "Did you not know that I must be about my Father's business?" Here He was equivalently saying: "I have another business, Mother, than the business of the carpenter shop. My Father has sent Me into this world on the supreme business of Redemption, to make all men adopted sons of My heavenly Father in the greater kingdom of the brotherhood of Christ,

Thy Son." How far the full vision of those words dawned upon Mary, we know not; whether she then understood that the Fatherhood of God meant that she was to be the Mother of men, we know not. But certainly, eighteen years later, in the second scene, the marriage feast of Cana, she came to a fuller understanding of that mission.

What a consoling thought it is to think that our Blessed Lord, who talked penance, who preached mortification, who insisted upon taking up the cross daily and following Him, should have begun His public life by assisting at a wedding festival! What a beautiful understanding of our hearts!

When in the course of the banquet the wine was exhausted, Mary, always interested in others, was the first to notice and the first to seek relief from the embarrassment. She simply said to our Blessed Lord, "They have no wine." And our Blessed Lord said to her, "Woman, what is that to me and to thee? my hour is not yet come." "Woman, what is that to me?" He did not call her "Mother," but "Woman" -- the same title she was to receive three years later.

He was equivalently saying to her: "You are asking Me to do something which belongs to Me as the Son of God. You are asking Me to work a miracle which only God can work; you are asking Me to exercise My divinity which has relationship to all mankind, namely as its Redeemer. But once that divinity operates for the salvation of the world, you become not only My Mother, but the Mother of redeemed humanity. Your physical motherhood passes into the wider world of spiritual motherhood, and for that reason I call you: 'Woman.'" And in order to prove that her intercession is powerful in that role of universal motherhood, He ordered the pots filled with water, and in the language of Crashaw the first miracle was worked: "the conscious waters saw their God and blushed."

The third scene happens within two years. One day as our Lord was preaching someone interrupted His discourse to say, "Thy mother . . . stands without, seeking thee." Our Blessed Lord said, "Who is my mother?" and stretching forth His hands toward His disciples He said: "Behold my mother and my brethren. For whosoever shall do the will of my Father, that is in heaven, he is my brother, and my sister, and mother." The meaning was unmistakable. There is such a thing as spiritual maternity; there are bonds other than those of the flesh; there are ties other than the ties of blood, namely spiritual ties which band together those of the Kingdom where reign the Fatherhood of God and the Brotherhood of Christ.

These three scenes have their climax at the Cross where Mary is called "Woman." It was the second Annunciation. The angel said to her in the first: "Hail, Mary." Her Son speaks to her in the second: "Woman." This did not mean she ceased to be His Mother; she is always the Mother of God; but her Motherhood enlarged and expanded; it became spiritual, it became universal, for at that moment she became *our mother.* Our Lord created the bond where it did not exist by nature as only He could do.

And how did she become the Mother of men? By becoming not only the mother, but also the spouse of Christ. He was the new Adam, she is the new Eve. And as Adam and Eve brought forth their natural progeny, which we are, so Christ and His Mother brought forth at the cross their spiritual progeny, which we are: children of Mary, or members of the Mystical Body of Christ. She brought forth her First-born at Bethlehem.

Note that St. Luke calls our Lord the *First-born* -- not that our Blessed Mother was to have other children *according to the flesh*, but only because she was to have other children *according to the spirit.* That moment when our Blessed Lord said to her, "Woman," she became in a certain sense the spouse of Christ and she brought forth in sorrow her first-born in the spirit, and his name was John. Who the second-born was we know not. It might have been Peter. It might have been Andrew. But we at any rate are the millionth-and-millionth-born of that woman at the foot of the Cross. It was a poor exchange indeed, receiving the son of Zebedee in place of the Son of God. But surely our gain was greater, for while she acquired but undutiful and often rebellious children, we obtained the most loving Mother in the world -- the Mother of Jesus.

We are children of Mary -- literally, *children.* She is our Mother, not by title of fiction, not by title of courtesy; she is our Mother because she endured at that particular moment the pains of childbirth for all of us. And why did our Lord give her to us as Mother? Because He knew *we could never be holy without her.* He came to us through her purity, and only through her purity can we go back to her. There is no *Sanctus* apart from Mary. Every victim that mounts that altar under the species of bread and wine, must have said the Confiteor, and become a holy victim -- but there is no holiness without Mary.

Note that when that word was spoken to our Blessed Mother, there was another woman there who was prostrate. Have you ever remarked that practically every traditional representation of the Crucifixion always pictures Magdalene on her knees at the foot of the crucifix? But you have never yet seen an image of the Blessed Mother prostrate. John was there and he tells in his Gospel that she stood. He saw her stand. But why did she stand? She stood to be of service to us. She stood to be our minister, our Mother.

If Mary could have prostrated herself at that moment as Magdalene did, if she could have only wept, her sorrow would have had an outlet. The sorrow that cries is never the sorrow that breaks the heart. It is the heart that can find no outlet in the fountain of tears which cracks; it is the heart that cannot have an emotional break-down that breaks. And all that sorrow was part of our purchase price paid by our Co-Redemptrix, Mary the Mother of God!

Because our Lord willed her to us as our Mother, He left her on this earth after He ascended into heaven, in order that she might mother the infant Church. The infant Church had need of a mother, just as the infant Christ. She had to remain on earth until her family had grown. That is why we find her on Pentecost abiding in prayer with the Apostles, awaiting the descent of the Holy Ghost. She was mothering the Mystical Body of Christ.

Now she is crowned in heaven as Queen of Angels and Saints, turning heaven into another marriage feast of Cana when she intercedes with her divine Saviour in behalf of us, her other children, brothers of Christ and sons of the heavenly Father.

Virgin Mother! What a beautiful conjunction of virginity and motherhood, one supplying the defect of the other. Virginity alone lacks something: there is an incompleteness about it; something unfulfilled; a faculty unused. Motherhood alone loses something: there is a surrender, an unflowering, a plucking of a blossom. Oh! For a *rapprochement* in which there would be a virginity that never lacked anything, and a motherhood that never lost anything! We have both in Mary, the Virgin Mother: Virgin by the overshadowing of the Holy Spirit in Bethlehem and Pentecost; Mother by the millions of her progeny from Jesus unto you and me.

There is no question here of confusing our Lady and our Lord; we venerate our Mother, we worship our Lord. We ask of Jesus those things which only God can give: mercy, grace, forgiveness. We ask that Mary should intercede for us with Him, and especially at the hour of our death. Because of her nearness to Jesus which her vocation involves, we know our Lord listens especially to her appeal. To no other saint can we speak as a child to its mother: no other virgin, or martyr, or mother, or confessor has ever suffered as much for us as she has; no one has ever established better claim to our love and patronage than she.

As the Mediatrix of all graces, all favors come to us from Jesus through her, as Jesus himself came to us through her. We wish to be holy, but we know there is no holiness without her, for she was the gift of Jesus to us at the *Sanctus* of His Cross. No woman can ever forget the child of her womb; then certainly Mary can never forget us. That is why we feel way down deep in our hearts that every time she sees another innocent child at the First Communion rail, or another penitent sinner making his way to the Cross, or another broken heart pleading that the water of a wasted life be changed into the wine of God's love, that she hears once again that word: "Woman, behold thy son."

Calvary and the Mass, 1936

Fourth Meditation

BLESSED ARE THE CLEAN OF HEART

"Blessed are the clean of heart: for they shall see God."
"(Son) behold thy mother, Woman, behold thy son."

On the hill of the Beatitudes, at the beginning of His public life, Our Lord preached: "Blessed are the clean of heart, for they shall see God." Now at the end of His life, on the Hill of Calvary, He speaks to the clean of heart: "(Son) behold your mother, Woman, behold your son."

This, of course, is not the beatitude of the world. The world is living today in what might be described as an era of carnality, which glorifies sex, hates restraint, identifies purity with coldness, innocence with ignorance, and turns men and women into Buddhas with their eyes closed, hands folded across their breasts, intently looking inward, thinking only of self.

It is just precisely against such a glorification of sex, and such egocentrism which is so characteristic of the flesh, that Our Lord reacted in His third Beatitude: "Blessed are the clean of heart."

The third Beatitude and the Third Word are related as theory to practice and as doctrine to example, for it was the purity of Our Lord that made the gift of his Mother possible. This is the one supreme lesson to be drawn from this word, namely, that Mary became Our Mother because her Divine Son was Purity itself. On no other condition could He have given her to us so completely and whole-heartedly.

In order to understand how Mary became Our Mother through purity, dwell for a moment on the nature of flesh. Flesh is essentially selfish even in its legitimate satisfaction. All its pleasures look to itself and not to another. Even the law of self-preservation implies, as the word itself states, a kind of selfishness. In its illegitimate pursuits, flesh is even more selfish still, for to satisfy itself it must tyrannize over others, and consume them to enkindle its own fires.

But God in his wisdom has instituted two escapes from the selfishness of the flesh: the Sacrament of Matrimony and the vow of chastity. Each not only breaks the circle of selfishness but makes possible a greater and wider field of service. Or to turn the truth around: the greater the purity of heart, the less the selfishness.

The first escape from the selfishness of the flesh, which God has instituted, is the Sacrament of Matrimony. Matrimony crushes selfishness, first of all, because it merges individuals into a corporate life in which neither lives for self but for the other; it crushes selfishness also because the very permanence of marriage is destructive of those fleeting infatuations, which are born with the moment and die with it; it destroys selfishness, furthermore, because the mutual love of husband and wife takes them out of themselves into the incarnation of their mutual love, their other selves, their children; and finally it narrows selfishness because the rearing of children demands sacrifice, without which, like unwatered flowers, they wilt and die.

But these are only negative aspects of Matrimony in relation to the flesh. What is more important to note is that matrimony cures selfishness by calling the flesh to the service of others. New horizons and vistas of devotion and sacrifice are opened to the eyes of flesh; others become more important than self; the ego becomes less circumscribed and more expansive. If reaches out to others, at times even forgetting self.

And so true is this that there is generally less selfishness in large families than in small. A husband and wife may live only for one another, but a father and mother must die to themselves in order to live for their offspring. All unregulated and egotistic attachments which destroy the integrity of a common life are left behind them. Where their heart is, there is their treasure also. They lay their flesh on the altar of sacrifice that others may live, and this is the beginning of love.

But God has provided still another escape from the selfishness of flesh, one more complete than the Sacrament of Matrimony, and that is the vow of chastity. The man or woman who takes this vow does so, not to escape the sacrifices which marriage demands, but to detach himself from all the ties of the flesh, in order that he may be free for greater service.

As St. Paul puts it: "He that is with a wife is solicitous for the things of the world, how he may please his wife; and he is divided. He that is without a wife is solicitous for the things that belong to the Lord, how he may please God."

The vow is a higher form of sacrifice than matrimony, simply because it purchases greater release from the claims of the flesh. The greater the purity the less the selfishness. He or she who takes it may be free to serve and love not just another man or woman and a few children, but all men and all women and all children in the bonds of charity in Christ Jesus Our Lord.

Marriage releases the flesh from its individual selfishness for the service of the family; the vow of chastity releases the flesh not only from the narrow and circumscribed family where there can still be selfishness, but also for the service of that family which embraces all humanity. That is why the Church asks those who consecrate themselves to the redemption of the world to take a vow and to surrender all selfishness, that they may belong to no one family and yet belong to all.

That is why in that larger family of the Kingdom of God, the priest is called "Father" -- because he has begotten children not in the flesh, but in the spirit. That is why the superior of a religious community of women is called

"Mother" -- she has her little flock in Christ. That too is why certain teaching orders of men are called "Brothers," and why women bound in religious life by the vow of chastity are called "Sisters."

They are all one family in which new relations have been established, not by their birth in the flesh but by their birth in Christ -- all selflessly seeking the glory of God and the salvation of sinners, under the one whom they love most on earth: their Holy Father, the successor of Peter, the Vicar of Jesus Christ.

Now if matrimony and the vow of chastity provide releases from the selfishness of the flesh, and if increasing purity prepares for a wider service of others, then what should we expect when we meet perfect purity?

If a person becomes less and less egocentric as he becomes more pure, then what should we look for in perfect sinlessness and perfect purity? If greater purity means greater selflessness, then what should we expect of innocence? The answer is: perfect sacrifice.

Given a character in whom there is no selfishness, either for his own comfort or even for his own life, and you have the sacrifice of the Cross. "For greater love than this no man hath, that a man lay down his life for his friends." Given a purity that rises above all family ties and bonds of blood, and then, as Our Lord told us: "He that doth the will of the Father in heaven is a father, a mother, a brother, and a sister."

Given a purity that is the Purity of Our Lord on the Cross, and you have someone so detached from the ego, so strange to selfishness, so thoughtless of the flesh that He looks upon His Mother, not *uniquely* as His own, but as the Mother of us all. Perfect Purity is perfect selflessness. That is why Christ gives His Mother to us, as represented in the person of John: "Behold thy mother."

He would not be selfish about her; he would not keep just for himself the loveliest and most beautiful of all mothers; He would share His own mother with us: and so at the foot of the Cross He gave her who is the Mother of God to us as the mother of men. No human person could do that because the ties of flesh and the selfishness of the flesh are too close. The flesh is too close to us to enable us to share our mother with others. But absolute purity can.

That is why the Beatitude of Purity is one with the Third Word, where selflessness, reaching its perfection in Purity, gave His life that we might be saved, and gave us His Mother that we might not be orphans.

Purity, then, is not something negative; it is not just an unopened bud; it is not something cold; it is not ignorance of life. Is justice merely the absence of dishonesty? Is mercy merely the absence of cruelty? Is faith merely the absence of doubt? Purity is not merely the absence of sensuality; it is selflessness born of love and the highest love of all.

Everyone with a vow is in love, but not in love with that which dies, but with that love which is eternal -- the love of God. There is a passion about chastity -- what Thompson calls a "passionless passion and wild tranquility."

Chastity is not an impossible virtue. Even those who have it not, may yet possess it. St. Augustine calls Mary Magdalen "the arch-virgin." Think of it! the "arch-virgin." He puts her next to the Blessed Mother in virginity; Magdalen, this common prostitute of the streets! She recovered purity, we might almost say, by receiving in anticipation of the Eucharist, the night she bathed the Feet of Our Lord with tears.

That day she came in contact with purity, and she so lived out its implications that within a short time we find her at the foot of the Cross on Good Friday. But who stands beside her? It is no other than the Blessed Mother.

What a remarkable companionship! a woman whose name a few months ago was synonymous with sin, and the Blessed Virgin! If Mary loved Magdalen, then why cannot she love us? If there was hope for Magdalen, then there can be hope for us. If she recovered purity, then it can be recovered by us. But how, except through Mary, for why is she called Mother Most Pure except to make us pure?

Everyone can go to Mary, not only converted sinners like Magdalen, but holy virgins and good mothers, for she is both Virgin and Mother. Virginity alone seems to lack something. There is a natural incompleteness about it -- a faculty unused. Motherhood alone seems to have lost something. There is something surrendered in motherhood. But in Mary there is "neither lack nor loss". ** There is Virginity and Motherhood -- "springtime of eternal May."

** (Sheila Kay Smith)

Purity, then, is not selfishness; it is surrender, it is thoughtfulness of others, it is sacrifice. It can even reach a peak where the Mother of Jesus can become our mother. Away then with that false maxim of the world which tells us that love is blind. It cannot be blind. Our Lord says it is not blind. "Blessed are the clean of heart, for they shall *see*" -- see even God. Mary, open our eyes!

The Cross and the Beatitudes, 1937

Fifth Meditation

THE SUFFERING OF THE INNOCENT

"Woman, behold thy son! (Son) Behold thy mother!"

Why do the innocent suffer? We do not mean the innocent who have suffering involuntarily thrust upon them, but rather those good souls who go out in search of suffering and are impatient until they find a cross. In other words, why should there be Carmelites, Poor Clares, Trappists, Little Sisters of the Poor, and dozens of penitential orders of the Church, who do nothing but sacrifice and suffer for the sins of men?

Certainly not because suffering is necessarily connected with personal sin. Our Lord told us that much, when to those who asked concerning a blind boy, "Who hath sinned, this man, or his parents . . .?", Our Lord answered "Neither."

If we are to find the answer we must go not merely to the suffering of innocent people, but to the suffering of Innocence itself. In this *Third Word* our attention is riveted upon the two most sinless creatures who ever trod our sinful earth: Jesus and Mary.

Jesus Himself was sinless by nature, for He is the all holy Son of God. Mary was sinless by grace, for she is "our tainted nature's solitary boast." And yet both suffer in the extreme. Why did He suffer Who had the power of God to escape the Cross? Why did she suffer who could have dispensed herself because of her virtue, or could have been excused by her Divine Son?

Love is the key to the mystery. Love by its very nature is not selfish, but generous. It seeks not its own, but the good of others. The measure of love is not the pleasure it gives -- that is the way the world judges it -- but the joy and peace it can purchase for others.

It counts not the wine it drinks, but the wine it serves. Love is not a circle circumscribed by self; it is a cross with arms embracing all humanity. It thinks not of having, but of being had, not of possessing but of being possessed, not of owning but of being owned.

Love then by its nature is social. Its greatest happiness is to gird its loins and serve at the banquet of life. Its greatest unhappiness is to be denied the joy of sacrifice for others. *That is why in the face of pain, love seeks to unburden the sufferer and take his pain, and that is why in the face of sin, love seeks to atone for the injustice of him who sinned.*

Because mothers love, do they not want to take the pain of their children's wounds? Because fathers love, do they not take over the debts of wayward sons to expiate their foolishness?

What does all this mean but the "otherness" of love? In fact love is so social it would reject emancipation from pain, if the emancipation were for itself alone. Love refuses to accept individual salvation; it never bends over man, as the healthy over the sick, but enters into him to take his very sickness.

It refuses to have its eyes clear, when other eyes are bedewed with tears; it cannot be happy unless everyone is happy, or unless justice is served; it shrinks from isolation and aloofness from the burdens and hungers of others. It spurns insulation from the shock of the world's sorrow, but insinuates itself into them, as if the sorrow were its very own.

This is not difficult to understand. Would you want to be the only person in all the world who had eyes to see? Would you want to be the only one who could walk in a universe of the lame? Would you, if you loved your family, stand on the dock and watch them all drown before your very eyes?

And if not, why not? Very simply, because you love them, because you feel so much one with them that their heartaches are your own heartbreaks.

Now apply this to Our Lord and His Blessed Mother. Here is love at its peak, and innocence at its best.

Can they be indifferent to that which is a greater evil than pain, namely sin? Can they watch humanity carry a cross to the Golgotha of death, while they themselves refuse to share its weight? Can they be indifferent to the outcome of love if they themselves *are* Love? If love means identification and sympathy with the one loved, then why should not God so love the world as to send His only begotten Son into it to redeem the world? And if that Divine Son loved the world enough to die for it, why should not the Mother of Love Incarnate share that redemption? If human love identifies itself with the pain of the one loved, why should not Divine Love suffer when it comes in contact with sin in man? If mothers suffer in their children, if a husband grieves in the sorrow of his wife, and if friends feel the agony of their beloved's cross, why should not Jesus and Mary suffer in the humanity they love?

If you would die for your family of which you are the head, why should not He die for humanity of which He is the Head? And if the deeper the love the more poignant the pain, why should not the Crucifixion be born of that Love?

If a sensitive nerve is touched it registers pain in the brain; and since Our Lord is the Head of suffering humanity, He felt every sin of every man as His own. That is why the Cross was inevitable.

He could not love us perfectly unless He died for us. And His Mother could not love Him perfectly, unless she shared that death. That is why His life was given for us, and her heart broken for us; and that, too, is why He is Redeemer and she is Redemptrix -- because they love.

In order more completely to reveal that a Cross was made up of the juncture of Love and sin, Our Lord spoke His *Third Word* to His Mother: "Woman, behold thy son"! He did not call her 'Mother' but 'Woman'; except when addressing John the next moment He added: "[Son] Behold thy Mother."

The term 'Woman' indicated a wider relationship to all humanity than 'Mother.' It meant that she was to be not only His Mother, but that she was also to be the Mother of all men, as He was the Saviour of all men. She was now to have many children -- not according to the flesh, but according to the spirit. Jesus was her first-born of the flesh in joy; John was her second-born of the spirit in sorrow; and we her millionth and millionth born.

If she loved Him Who died for all men, then she must love those for whom He died. That was His clear, unmistakable meaning. The love of neighbor is inseparable from the love of God. His love had no limits; He died for every man. Her love then must have no limits.

It must not be merely unselfish; it must even be social. She must be the Mother of every man. An earthly mother loves her own children most, but Jesus is now telling her that even John is her son, too, and John was the symbol of all of us.

The Father did not spare His Son, nor did the Son spare His Mother, for love knows no bounds. Jesus had a sense of responsibility for every soul in the world; Mary, too, inspired by His love, had a corresponding sense of responsibility. If He would be the Redeemer of the wayward children, she must be their Mother.

Now does that throw any light on the problem? Why do innocent, pure, good souls leave the world and its pleasures, feast on fasts, embrace the cross, and pray their hearts out? The answer is, *because they love.* "Greater love than this no man hath, that a man lay down his life for his friends."

They love the world so much that they want to save it, and they know there is no other way to save it, than to die for it. Many of us so love the world that we live *in* it and are *of* it, but in the end do nothing *for* it. Wrong indeed are they who say these innocent victims hate the world.

As soon as the world hears of a beautiful young woman or an upright young man entering the religious life, it asks: "Why did they leave the world?" They left the world, not because they hated the world, but because they loved it. They love the world with its human souls so much, that they want to do all they can for it; and they can do nothing better for it than to pray that souls may one day find their way back to God.

Our Lord did not hate the world; it hated Him. But He loved it. Neither do they hate the world; they are in love with it and everyone in it. They so much love the sinners in it, that they expiate for their sins; they so much love the Communists in it, that they bless them as they send them to their God; they so much love the atheists in it, that they are willing to surrender the joy of the divine presence that the atheist may feel less afraid in the dark.

They are so much lovers of the world that they may be said to be organic with it. They know that things and souls are so much interrelated that the good which one does has repercussion on the millions, just as ten just men could have saved Sodom and Gomorrah. If a stone is thrown into the sea, it causes a ripple which widens in ever greater circles until it affects even the most distant shore; a rattle dropped from a baby's crib affects even the most distant star; a finger is burnt and the whole body feels the pain.

The cosmos then is organic; but so also is humanity. We are all called to be members of a great family.

God is Our Father, Who sent His Son into the world to be Our Brother, and He on the Cross asked Mary to be Our Mother. Now if in the human body it is possible to graft skin from one member to another, why is it not possible also to graft prayer?

If it is possible to transfuse blood, why is it not possible also to transfuse sacrifice? Why cannot the innocent atone for the sinful?

Why cannot the real lovers of souls, who refuse to be emancipated from sorrow, do for the world what Jesus did on the cross and Mary did beneath it? The answer to this question has filled the cloisters.

No one on earth can measure the good these divine lovers are doing for the world. How often have they stayed the wrath of a righteous God! How many sinners have they brought to the confessional! How many deathbed conversions have they effected! How many persecutions have they averted!

We do not know, and they do not want to know, so long as love wins over hate. But let us not be foolish and ask: What good do they do for the world? We might as well ask: What good did the Cross do?

After all, only the innocent can understand what sin is. No one until the time of Our Lord ever thought of giving his life to save sinners, simply because no one was sinless enough to know its horrors.

We who have familiarized ourselves with it, become used to it, as a leprous patient after many years of suffering cannot wholly appreciate the evil of leprosy.

Sin has lost its horror; we never think of correlating it to the cross: we never advert to its repercussions on humanity.

> "Vice is a monster of so frightful mien,
> As to be hated, needs but to be seen;
> Yet seen too oft, familiar with her face,
> We first endure, then pity, then embrace."
>
> (Alexander Pope)

The best way to know sin is by not sinning. But Jesus and Mary were wholly innocent -- He by nature, she by grace; therefore, they could understand and know the evil of sin.

Having never compromised with it, there were now no compromises to be made. It was something so awful that to avoid it or to atone for it, they shrink not even from a death on the cross.

But by a peculiar paradox, though innocence hates sin, because it alone knows its gravity, it nevertheless loves the sinner. Jesus loved Peter who fell three times, and Mary chose as her companion at the foot of the cross, a converted prostitute.

What must the scandal mongers have said of that friendship as they watched Mary and Magdalen ascend and descend the hill of Calvary! But Mary braved it all, in order that in a future generation you and I might have hope in her as the "Refuge of sinners." Let there be no fear that she cannot understand our sinful misery because she is Immaculate, for if she had Magdalen as a companion then, why can she not have us now?

Dear Mother Immaculate, but seldom in history have the innocent suffered as they do today. Countless Marys and Johns stand beneath the cross guilty of no other crime than that they love the Man on the Cross. If there be no remission of sins without the shedding of blood, then let these innocent victims of hate in Russia, in Spain, and in Mexico, be the redemption of those who hate. We ask not that the hateful perish; we only ask that the sufferings of the just be the salvation of the wicked.

Thou didst suffer innocently because thou didst love us in union with thy Divine Son. Thus were we taught, that only those who cease to love ever flee from the Cross. The innocents who are slaughtered today are not the babes of Bethlehem; they are the grown-up children of Bethlehem's God -- men and women who save the Church today as Bethlehem's babes once saved Jesus.

Be thou their consolation, their joy, their Mother, O Innocent Woman who binds the sons of men to the Son of God in the unity of the Father and the Holy Ghost, world without end. Amen.

The Rainbow of Sorrow, 1938

Sixth Meditation

LUST

"Woman, behold thy son . . . behold thy mother."

Lust is an inordinate love of the pleasures of the flesh. The important word here is *inordinate* for it was Almighty God Himself who associated pleasure with the flesh. He attached pleasure to eating in order that we might not be remiss in nourishing and preserving our individual lives; He associated pleasure with the marital act in order that husband and wife might not be remiss in their social obligations to propagate mankind and raise children for the Kingdom of God.

The pleasure becomes sinful at that point where, instead of using it as means, we begin to use it as an end. To eat for the sake of eating is a sin, because eating is a means to an end, which is health. Lust, in like manner, is selfishness or perverted love.

It looks not so much to the good of the other, as to the pleasure of self. It breaks the glass that holds the wine; it breaks the lute to snare the music. It subordinates the other to self for the sake of pleasure. Denying the quality of "otherness," it seeks to make the other person care for us, but not to make us care for the other person.

We are living today in what might properly be called an era of carnality. As the appeal to the spiritual relaxes, the demands of the flesh increase. Living less for God, human nature begins to live only for self, for "no man can serve two masters: For either he will hate the one, and love the other: or he will sustain the one, and despise the other."

Peculiar to this era of carnality is the tendency to equate the perpetuity of marriage with the fleshly pleasure, so that when the pleasure ends the bond is presumed to be automatically dissolved. In America, for example, there is more than one divorce for every four marriages -- an indication of how much we have ceased to be a Christian nation and how much we have forgotten the words of Our Lord: "What therefore God hath joined together, let no man put asunder."

The regrettable aspect of it all is that with this increased sin there is a decreased sense of sin. Souls sin more, but think less about it. Like sick who are so moribund that they have no desire to be better, sinners become so calloused they have no yearning for redemption. Having lost their eyes, they no longer want to see; the only pleasure left them in the end is to mock and sneer at those who do.

It is never the pure who say that chastity is impossible, but only the impure. We judge others by ourselves, and attribute to others the vices from which we ourselves refuse to abstain.

Some reparation had to be made for the sin of lust which in Old Testament times became so hideous to God that He would have withheld the destruction of the cities of Sodom and Gomorrah could but ten just men have been found within their gates.

Our Lord began making reparation for it at the first moment of the Incarnation for He chose to be born of a virgin. Why did He choose to transcend the laws of nature? The answer is very simple. Original Sin has been propagated to every human being from Adam to this very hour, with the exception of Our Lady. The prolongation of this taint in human nature takes place through the carnal act, of which man is the active principle, for man was the head of the human race. Every time there is generation of one human being by another, through the union of man and woman, there is the propagation of original sin.

The problem confronting the Second Person of the Blessed Trinity in becoming man was: how become man without at the same time becoming sinful man, that is, man-infected by the sin to which all flesh is heir? How to become man without inheriting original sin? He had to be a true man in order to suffer for man, but He could not be a sinful man if He were to redeem man from sin. How could He be both man and yet sinless?

He could be man by being born of a woman; He could be sinless man, without original sin, by dispensing with man as the active principle of generation -- in other words, by being born of a virgin. Thus it was that when the Angel Gabriel appeared to Mary and told her that she was to conceive the Messias whose name would be called Jesus, she answered: "How can this be done, because I know not man?" She had made the vow of virginity and she intended to keep it.

The Angel answered that the conception of the Son of Man would take place without man, through the power of the Holy Ghost who would overshadow her. Being assured of her continued virginity, she accepted the motherhood of God Incarnate. "Be it done unto me, according to thy word."

So it was that reparation for sins of the flesh began the first moment of the Incarnation through the Virgin Birth. That same love He manifested for virginity in the beginning, He re-echoed in the first sermon of His public life: "Blessed are the clean of heart: for they shall see God."

Later on, to the Scribes and Pharisees who sought to malign His good name, He challenged them to find anything impure in His life: "Which of you shall convince me of sin?"

The final atonement and reparation is made on Calvary where, in reparation for all the impure desires and thoughts of men, Our Lord is crowned with thorns; where, in reparation for all the sins of shame, He is stripped of His garments; where, in reparation for all the lusts of the flesh,

He is almost dispossessed of His flesh, for according to Sacred Scripture, the very bones of His Body could be numbered.

We are so used to looking upon artistic crucifixes of ivory and the beautiful images in our prayer books, that we think of Our Blessed Lord as being whole on the Cross. The fact is that He made such reparation for sins of the flesh that His Body was torn, His Blood poured forth, and Scripture refers to Him on the Cross as a leper, as one struck by God and afflicted, so that "there is no beauty in Him, nor comeliness . . . that we should be desirous of Him."

Our Lord chose to go even further in reparation for the sins of lust by dispossessing Himself of the two most legitimate claims of the flesh. If there was ever a pure and legitimate claim in the realm of the flesh, it is the claim to the love of one's own Mother. If there is any honest title to affection in the universe of the flesh, it is the bonds of love that attach one to a fellow man. But the flesh was so misused by man and so perverted that Our Divine Saviour renounced even these legitimate bonds of the flesh in order to atone for the illegitimate.

He became totally un-fleshed, in order to atone for the abuse of the flesh, by giving away His Mother and His best friend. So, to His own Mother He looks and bids farewell: "Woman, behold thy son"; and to His best friend He looks and bids farewell again: "Behold thy mother."

How different from the world! A mother will deprive her son of an advanced education in a foreign land, saying: "I cannot give up my son"; or a wife will deprive her husband of good material advancement through a short absence, saying: "I cannot give up my husband." These are not the cries of noble love but of attachment. Our Lord did not say: "I cannot give up My Mother." He gave her up. He loved her enough to give her away for her life's plan and destiny, namely, to be *our* Mother.

Here was a love that was strong enough to forget itself, in order that others might never want for love. He made the sacrifice of His Mother that we might have her; He wounded Himself like the pelican, that we might be nourished by her motherhood. Mary accepted the poor exchange to carry out her Son's redemptive work. And at that moment when Jesus surrendered even the legitimate claims of the flesh and gave us His Mother, Mary, and His best friend, John -- selfishness died its death.

Two lessons are to be learned from this Third Word from the Cross:

1 -- The only real escape from the demands of the flesh is to find something more than the flesh to love; and 2 -- Mary is the refuge of sinners.

If we could ever find anything we loved more than the flesh, the demands of the flesh would be less imperative. This is the "escape" a mother offers her boy when she says: "Don't do anything of which your mother would ever be ashamed." If there is that higher love of his mother, the boy will always have a consecrated sense of affection, something for which he will be willing to make sacrifices.

When a mother makes such an appeal to her son she is merely re-echoing the lesson of the Saviour, who, in giving His Mother to us as our Mother, equivalently said: "My children, never do anything of which your Mother would be ashamed." Let a soul but love that Mother and He will love her Divine Son Jesus, Who, in order to make satisfaction for the unlawful pleasure of the flesh, surrendered to us His last and lawful attachment -- His Mother.

The psychology of this enthusiasm for a higher love of Jesus and Mary as an escape from the unlawful attachments of the flesh is this: by it we avoid undue concentration on lower loves and their explosions. Think about your mouth for five minutes, and you will have an undue concentration of saliva. Think about your heart for five minutes and you will believe you have heart trouble, though the chances are nine out of ten that you have not. Stand on a stage and think about your hands and they will begin to feel as big as hams.

The balance and equilibrium of the whole system is disturbed when an organ is isolated from its function in the whole organism, or divorced from its higher purpose. Those people who are always talking, reading, and thinking about sex are like singers who think more about their larynx than about singing. They make that which is subordinate to a higher purpose so all important that the harmony of life is upset.

But suppose that, instead of concentrating on an organ, one fitted that organ into a pattern of living -- then all the uneasiness would end. The skilled orator never feels his hands are awkward because, being enthused about his speech, he makes his hands subordinate to their higher purpose.

Our Lord practically said the same thing: "Be not solicitous . . . what you shall eat." So it is with the flesh. Cultivate a higher love, a purpose of living, a goal of existence, a desire to correspond to all that God wants us to be, and the lower passion will be absorbed by it.

The Church applies this psychology to the vow of chastity. The Church asks her priests and nuns to surrender even the lawful pleasures of the flesh, not because she does not want them to love, but because she wants them to love better. She knows that their love for souls will be greater as their love for the flesh is less, just as Our Lord died on the Cross for men because He loved His Own life less.

Nor must it be thought that the vow of chastity is a burden. Thompson has called it a "passionless passion, a wild tranquility." And so it is. A new passion is born with the vow of chastity, the passion for the love of God. It is the consolation of that higher love which makes the surrender of the lower love so easy. And only when that higher love is lost does the vow begin to be a burden, just as honesty becomes a burden only to those who have lost the sense of others' rights.

The reason there is a degeneration in the moral order and a decay of decency is because men and women have lost the higher love. Ignoring Christ their Saviour, who loved them unto the death on Calvary, and Mary who loved them unto becoming Queen of Martyrs beneath that Cross, they have nothing for which to make the sacrifice.

The only way love can be shown in this world is by sacrifice, namely, the surrender of one thing for another. Love is essentially bound up with choice, and choice is a negation, and negation is a sacrifice. When a young man sets his heart upon a maid and asks her to marry him, he is not only saying "I choose you"; he is also saying "I do not choose, I reject, all others. I give them all up for you." Apply this to the problem of lust.

Take away all love above the flesh, take away God, the crucifix, the Sorrowful Mother, salvation, eternal happiness -- and what possibility is there for choice, what is to be gained by denying the imperious and revolutionary demands of the flesh? But grant the Divine, and the flesh's greatest joy is to throw itself on the altar of the one loved where it counts its sorrow a cheap price for the blissful joy of giving.

Then its greatest despair is not to be needed; it could almost find it in its heart to inflict a wound that it might bind and heal. Such is the attitude of the pure: they have integrated their flesh with the Divine; they have sublimated its cravings with the Cross; having a higher love, they now make the surrender of the lower, that their Mother may never be put to shame.

Mary is the refuge of sinners. She who is the Virgin Most Pure is also the Refuge of Sinners. She knows what sin is, not by the experience of its falls, not by tasting its bitter regrets, but by seeing what it did to her Divine Son.

She looked upon His torn and bleeding flesh hanging from Him like rays of a purple sunset -- and she came to know how much flesh sinned by seeing what His flesh suffered. What better way in all the world was there to measure the heinousness of sin than by seeing when left alone with Him for three hours, what it could do to Innocence and Purity.

She is the Refuge of Sinners not only because she knows sin through Calvary, but also because she chose, during the most terrifying hours of her life, a converted sinner as her companion. The measure of our appreciation of friends is our desire to have them about us in the moment of our greatest need.

Mary heard Jesus say, "The harlots and publicans will enter the Kingdom of Heaven before the Scribes and Pharisees." So she chose the absolved harlot, Magdalen, as her companion at the Cross. What the scandalmongers of that day must have said when they saw Our Blessed Mother in the company of a woman who everyone knew was the kind who sold her body without giving away her soul.

Magdalen knew that day why Mary is the Refuge of Sinners, and certainly our day, too, can learn that if she had Magdalen as a companion then, she is willing to have us as companions now.

Mary's purity is not a holier-than-thou purity, a stand-offish holiness that gathers up its robes lest they be stained by the sinful; nor is it a despising purity which looks down upon the impure. Rather, it is a radiating purity that is no more spoiled by solicitude for the fallen than a ray of sunshine is sullied by a dirty window pane through which it pours.

There is no reason for the fallen to be discouraged. Hope is the message of Golgotha. Find a higher love than the flesh, a love pure, understanding, redeeming, and the struggle will be easy. That higher love is on the Cross and beneath it.

We almost seem to forget that there is a Cross at all. He begins to look more like a red rose and she begins to look like the stem. That stem reaches down from Calvary into all our wounded hearts of earth, sucking up our prayers and petitions and conveying them to Him. That is why roses have thorns in this life -- to keep away every disturbing influence that might destroy our union with Jesus and Mary.

ACKNOWLEDGEMENT

If Christ should come on earth some summer day
And walk unknown upon our busy street
I wonder how 'twould be if we should meet,
And being God – if He would act that way.

Perhaps the kindest thing that He would do
Would be just to forget I failed to pray
And clasp my hand, forgivingly, and say,
"My child, I've heard My Mother speak of you."

(Mrs. Frederick V. Murphy)

Victory Over Vice, 1939

Seventh Meditation

PRUDENCE

Behold thy son; behold thy mother.

The greatest crisis in the history of the world was the arrest and conviction of a Man found guilty of no other charge than an excess of love. What was tragic about that crisis reaching from a Garden to a Cross was: Man failed!

Peter, James, and John, who had been given the flashing light of the Transfiguration to prepare them for the dark night of Olives, slept as His enemies attacked. Judas, who had heard the Divine admonition to lay up treasures in Heaven, peddled his Master for thirty pieces of silver -- for Divinity is always sold out of all proportion to due worth.

Peter who had been made the Rock and Key-bearer, warmed himself by a fire and with an atavistic throwback to his fisherman days, cursed and swore to a maidservant that he knew not the man.

As Pilate submitted to the crowd the choice of Christ or a revolutionary upstart, the mob chose Barabbas. Finally, on Calvary where were the men? Where were those whom He cured? Peter was not there, nor his brother Andrew, nor James, nor any of the other Apostles except John, who might not have been there had it not been for the encouragement given him by Mary.

But though men failed in this crisis there is no instance of a single woman failing. In the four trials, the voice heard in His defense was that of a woman, Claudia Procul, the wife of Pontius Pilate, warning her husband not to do anything unjust to that just man. Events proved that the politician was wrong and the woman right.

On the way to Calvary it is the woman who offers consolation, first Veronica wiping away the blood and sweat from His Sacred Face to receive the reward of Its imprint on her towel; then the holy women to whom the Prisoner turned suggesting that only such multiplied mercies and charities as their own could avert catastrophe for their children.

Again on Calvary it is woman who is fearless, for there are several of them at the foot of the Cross. Magdalene, among them as usual, is prostrate. But there is one whose courage and devotion was so remarkable that the Evangelist who was there indicated the detail that she was "standing." That woman was the Mother of the Man on the Central Cross.

When we realize that He who is pinioned to that Cross is the Son of God and therefore possessed of Infinite Wisdom and Power, we are at first inclined to wonder why she should not have been spared the sorrow of Golgotha.

Since He had made her of incomparable beauty of body and soul, why should He not keep those eyes made for Paradise from gazing on a Cross? Why not shield ears attuned to the Divine Word from the blasphemies of ungrateful humans? Since preserved from original sin, why should its penalties be visited upon her? Must Mothers go to gallows with their sons? Must the innocent eat the bitter fruit planted by the sinful?

These are questions of false human wisdom; But God's ways are not our ways. Our Blessed Lord willed her presence there. Since He was the second Adam undoing the sin of the first, Mary would be the new Eve proclaiming the glory of womanhood in the new race of the redeemed.

The woman Eve would not be so cured that her most glorious daughter could not undo her evil. As a woman had shared in the fall of man, so woman should share in his redemption. In no better way could Our Lord reveal woman's role in the new order than by giving John, that disciple whom He loved above the others, to His Mother whom He loved above all: "Son! Behold thy Mother . . . Woman! Behold thy son! "

The Kingdom of God was born! Heavenly prudence had chosen the right means to reveal the new ties born of redemption. Mary was to be our Mother, and we her children.

The Saviour's death was at the same time a birth; the end of a chapter of crucifixion was the beginning of the chapter of a new creation.

As light is instantaneous in dispelling darkness so the Divine Saviour wills that not even a moment shall intervene between breaking down the attachments to Satan by sin and the incorporation of man into the Kingdom of God. She exchanges her Son for the advantages of the Passion and receives its first fruit -- John. He had kept His word: "l will not leave you orphans" *(John 14:18).*

On the Cross was Wisdom Incarnate, dying that we might live. If Our Saviour could have thought of any better means of leading us back to Him, He would have put us in other hands than hers.

There are many falsehoods told about the Catholic Church: One of them is that Catholics adore Mary. This is absolutely untrue. Mary is a creature, human, not Divine. Catholics do not adore Mary. That would be idolatry. But they do reverence her.

And to those Christians who have forgotten Mary, may we ask if it is proper for them to forget her whom He remembered on the Cross? Will they bear no love for that woman through the portals of whose flesh, as the Gate of Heaven, He came to earth?

One of the reasons why so many Christians have lost a belief in the Divinity of Christ is because they lost all affection for her upon whose white body, as a Tower of Ivory, that Infant climbed "to kiss upon her lips a mystic rose."

There is not a Christian in all the world who reverences Mary who does not acknowledge Jesus her Son to be in Truth the Son of the Living God. The prudent Christ on the Cross knew the prudent way to preserve belief in His Divinity, for who better than a Mother knows her son?

The gift of Mary did something to man, for it gave him an ideal love. To fully appreciate this fact dwell for a moment on the difference between two faculties: The intellect, which knows and the will, which loves.

The intellect always whittles down the object to suit itself. That is why the intellect insists on examples, explanations, and analogies. Every teacher must accommodate himself to the mentality of his class, and if the problem, which he is presenting, is abstract and complicated, he must break it up into the concrete, as Our Lord described the mysteries of the Kingdom of God in parables.

But the will never works that way. While the intellect pulls down the object of knowledge to its level, the will always goes out to meet the object.

If you love something, you lift yourself up to its level; if you love music you subject yourself to its demands, and if you love mathematics you meet its conditions. We tend to become like that which we love. Boys who love gangsters are already the making of gangsters. As our loves are, that we are. We scale mountains if the object loved is on a mountain; we jump down into the abyss if the object loved is there.

It follows that the higher our loves and ideals, the nobler will be our character. The problem of character training is fundamentally the inculcation of proper ideals.

That is why every nation holds up its national heroes, that citizens may become like to them in their patriotism and devotion to country.

If we have heroes and ideal prototypes for those who love sports, the stage, country, army and navy, why should there not be an ideal in the all-important business of leading a good life and saving our souls?

That is precisely one of the roles the Blessed Mother of our Divine Lord plays in Christian life: An object of love so pure, so holy, and so motherly that to be worthy of it we refrain from doing anything which might offend her.

There has hardly ever been a mother in the history of the world who did not at one time or another say to her son or daughter: "Never do anything of which your mother would be ashamed." But what these mothers say is only an echo from the Cross, when Our Divine Lord gave us His Mother as our mother. In giving her to us, He was equivalently saying: "Never do anything of which your Heavenly Mother would be ashamed."

The nobler the love, the nobler the character and what nobler love could be given to men than the woman whom the Saviour of the world chose as His own Mother?

Why is it that the world has confessed its inability to inculcate virtue in the young? Very simply because it has not co-related morality to any love nobler than self-love. Things keep their proportion and fulfill their proper role only when integrated into a larger whole.

Most lives are like doors without hinges, or sleeves without coats, or bows without violins; that is, unrelated to wholes or purposes which give them meaning.

If, for example, a speaker concentrates upon his hands, wonders whether he should put them in his pockets or behind his back, it will not be long until he feels he is all hands.

The modern emphasis on sex is a result of tearing a function away from a purpose, a part away from a whole. It can never be handled properly unless integrated to a larger pattern and made to serve it.

That is, to some extent, the role Our Blessed Mother plays in the moral life of our Catholic youth. She is that ideal love for which lesser and baser loves and impulses are sacrificed. Just as a skilled orator so integrates his hands into the pattern of speech that he is never conscious of their presence, so the Catholic youth maintains that healthy self-restraint out of respect for one whom he loves.

The level of any civilization is the level of its womanhood. What they are, men will be, for, to repeat, love always goes out to meet the demands of the object loved. Given a woman like the Mother of Our Lord as our supernatural Mother, you have one of the greatest inspirations for nobler living this world has ever known.

In this hour as never before the world needs to hear again this third word from the Cross. It needs the inspiration of the Good Woman. Unfortunately, the woman who is admired today is not the virtuous woman, but the beautiful woman -- and by beautiful is meant not that inner beauty of the king's daughter, but that beauty which is only skin deep and sometimes only powder deep.

Glance at the advertisements flashed across the pages and billboards of our country! They are for the most part pictures of women who ten years from now would not be accepted for the same advertisement, because they will have lost what they now possess -- a passing beauty.

Our modern world does not really love woman; it loves only her external beauty. If it loved woman, it would love woman as long as she is woman. But because it loves the mask of a woman, it ignores the woman when the mask disappears.

The alarming increase of divorces in our land and the consequent break-up of family life is due principally to the loss of love for the ideal in womanhood. Marriage has become identified with pleasure, not with love. Once the pleasure ceases, love ceases. The woman is loved not for what she is in herself but for what she is to others. The tragedy of such a state is not only what it does for woman, but also what it does for man.

How restore love for woman as *woman*? By giving as the object of life's love a woman who has given Life and Love to the world -- a Woman who is beautiful on the outside all the days of her life, because she is beautiful on the inside. That was the means Our Lord chose on the Cross to remake the world: Remake man by remaking the woman.

Conceived in the Divine Mind, sculptured by the creative fingers of the Heavenly Sculptor, touched by ever radiant color from the palette of heaven, the Artist on the Cross points to His masterpiece and says to man: "Behold the Woman!"

There is told a legend which illustrates the intercessory power of Our Blessed Lady: It seems that one day Our Blessed Lord was walking through the Kingdom of Heaven and saw some souls who had got in very easily. Approaching Peter at the Golden Gate He said: "Peter, I have given to you the keys to the Kingdom of Heaven. You must use your power wisely and discreetly. Tell Me, Peter, how did these souls gain entry into My Kingdom?" To which Peter answered: "Don't blame me, Lord. Every time I close the door, Your Mother opens a window."

When amidst the thousand and one allurements of this world you know not which way to turn, pray to the Woman -- the Virgin most prudent. She knows the true from the false, for in the language of Joyce Kilmer:

At the foot of the Cross on Calvary
Three soldiers sat and diced
And one of them was the devil
And he won the Robe of Christ.

I saw him through a thousand veils
And has not this sufficed?
Now, must I look on the devil robed
In the radiant robe of Christ?

He comes, his face is sad and mild
With thorns his head is crowned
There are great bleeding wounds in His feet
And in each hand a wound.

How can I tell, who am a fool
If this be Christ or no?
Those bleeding hands outstretched to me
Those eyes that love me so!

I see the robe – I look, I hope
I fear – but there is one
Who will direct my troubled mind.
Christ's Mother knows her Son.

O Mother of Good Counsel, lend
Intelligence to me
Encompass me with wisdom
Thou Tower of Ivory!

"This is the man of lies" she says
"Disguised with fearful art:
He has the wounded hands and feet
But not the wounded heart."

Beside the Cross on Calvary
She watched them as they diced
She saw the devil join the game
And win the Robe of Christ.

From "The Robe of Christ" from MAIN STREET AND OTHER POEMS, by Joyce Kilmer, copyright 1917 by Doubleday, Doran & Company, Inc.

The Seven Virtues, 1940

Eighth Meditation

A WORD TO THE SELFISH

The third group in the world who need to feel the impact of the Cross are the selfish.

By the selfish is here understood all those who feel that salvation is either an individual matter or else the concern of a particular class; that religion has no other right to exist than to remove the impediments of a selfish existence by slum clearance, social security, more playgrounds; and that all else, such as the regeneration of man from sin, or the culture of the soul, is a snare and a delusion.

When the selfish become learned they define religion, in the language of a contemporary philosopher, as "what a man does with his own solitariness"; when the selfish are in distress, they ask "why should God do this to me?" when the selfish sin, they say, "What harm does my sin do to anyone else?"

The selfish were on Calvary's hill in their representative who was the thief on the left! He had heard the blasphemy and pride of his companion thief broken, when out of a consciousness of sin he called to the Lord for mercy; but the experience left him untouched. One can be so close to God physically, and yet miss Him spiritually.

Turning to the Lord on the Central Cross, the thief on the left, in the supreme expression of selfishness, cried out with bitterness of soul: "If thou be Christ, save thyself and us" *(Luke 23:29).*

He was the first Marxist! Long before Marx, he was saying "Religion is the opium of the people."

A religion that thinks only of souls when men are dying, which bids them look to God at the moment when the courts are inflicting injustice, which talks about "pie in the sky" when stomachs are empty and bodies racked with pain, which talks about forgiveness when the social outcasts -- two thieves and a despised proletarian, a village carpenter -- are dying on a scaffold, is a religion that is the opium of the people.

"Save thyself and us" -- How modern! Salvation is for a class! Not everyone! Communism speaks only for the proletariat: "Save thyself and us." Fascism speaks only for the nation: "Save thyself and us." Nazism speaks only for the race: "Save thyself and us." The rich speak only for their class: "Save thyself and us."

Not a word about the salvation of the world, about His people whom He loved, about the Gentiles to whom He would send His Apostles; and above all else, not a word about His beloved Mother beneath His cross whose heart was already pierced by seven swords.

If there was to be salvation for the thief on the left it was not to be spiritual or moral, but physical: "Save thyself and us!" Save what? Our souls? No! Man has no soul! Save our bodies! What good is religion if it cannot stop pain, step down from a gibbet, rescue a class, or pamper selfish interests? Christianity is either a social gospel or it is a drug.

Our Lord did not answer that selfish thief directly, but He did answer Him indirectly when, looking down from the Cross, He addressed Himself to the two most beloved creatures on earth -- Mary, His Mother, and John, His Disciple. But He did not address them as "Mary" and as "John."

If He had called them by their names, they would have remained what they were; representatives of a certain class. If He had said "Mother," she would have been His Mother and no one else's. If he had said "John," he would

have been the son of Zebedee, and the son of no one else. So He called Mary "Woman" and John "Son." "Woman, behold thy son . . . son behold thy mother" *(John 19:26-27).*
He was saying that religion is not what a man does with his solitariness, but what he does with his relationships. And as if to prove for all time that religion is not selfishness, either of an individual or a "set" or a class, He called Mary and John into a relationship as wide as the world. In a certain sense He de-classified them.

She was no longer to be His Mother alone. As He was the new Adam, she would be the new Eve. He had told her about a year and a half before that there were other ties than those of flesh and blood, namely, the spiritual bond among those who do the will of God. "Behold my mother and my brethren. For whosoever shall do the will of God, he is my brother, and my sister and mother" *(Mark 3:34-35).*

Now He establishes that new relationship. As she was His Mother by the flesh, she would now be the mother of all "who are born, not of blood, nor of the will of the flesh, nor of the will of man, but of God" *(John 1:13).*

To herald her in this new relationship as the Mother of Christians, He calls her "Woman" -- it was a high summons to universal motherhood.

And John, who up to this point is the son of Zebedee, is not called John -- for that would have been to keep the ties of blood. He is addressed as "Son." "son, behold thy mother."

Jesus was the first born of Mary's flesh, but John was the first born of her Spirit at the foot of the Cross; and perhaps Peter was the second, Andrew the third, James the fourth, and we the millionth and millionth born.

He was setting up a new family, a new social relationship. In that context, economic and social questions would be settled, and not otherwise. "Seek ye first the kingdom of God and his justice, and all these things shall be added unto you" *(Luke 12:31).*

Religion is not an individual affair! A man can no more have an individual religion than he can have an individual government or an individual astronomy or mathematics. Religion is social, and so social is it that it is not limited to the criminal class, as the thief believed, not to any class, race, nation, or color. All these views are too aristocratic.

Snobbery can exist among proletarians as well as among dukes. The new totalitarian systems have produced "blue bloods" just as obnoxious as some of the blue bloods of monarchy.

This word of Our Lord furthermore reveals that all social duties flow out of these spiritual relationships. He did not say: "John, take care of My Mother," nor did He say: "Mary, look after John as you would me." No! Having established a new relationship between Mary and John, namely that of motherhood and sonship, the duties flowed quite naturally.

Religion is made the sharing of responsibilities. Mary had raised her Child, but now she was to adopt others and love them as sons, poor indeed though they were in comparison.

John had fulfilled his sonship to Zebedee, but now he was to take on new duties as her son and so live that he would never do anything of which his Mother would be ashamed.

Mary continued her duty of bearing the burden of others, for we find her on Pentecost in the midst of the Apostles, mothering the Infant Church as she mothered the Infant Jesus.

John too could never forget that word "son" which he heard from the Cross, as we find him some years after the Ascension writing to the Infant Church: "Behold what manner of charity the Father hath bestowed upon us, that we should be called, and should be the sons of God" *(1John 3:1).*

There is no Messianic race, no Messianic class, no Messianic color. Our Lord died for all men, and thus set up a new series of relationships with God. And from out of this new set of relationships, slum clearance and social justice and all the rest *follow* -- but not otherwise.

Hence Our Blessed Lord said nothing about slavery, because He knew that slavery would never be eradicated until men saw themselves related to one another on the basis of equality as children of God.

He did not discourse on the need of child clinics. He first proclaimed the value of a child to a pagan world by becoming a child among children.

He said nothing about the necessity of democracy. But He laid the foundation for it, when He told Pilate what we, over 1700 years later, wrote in the Declaration of Independence -- that all rights and liberties come from God.

He said nothing about the rights of labor. He first dignified it as a vocation by working as a carpenter.

He said nothing about treating servants decently, but He girded Himself with a towel and washed the feet of His own Apostles. "And whosoever will be first among you, shall be the servant of all" *(Mark 10:44).*

The classic example of the effect of the new relationship was the slave Onesimus, who ran away from his master Philemon. The slave came to Paul who made him a Christian. Paul then asked the slave to return to Philemon bearing a note in which Onesimus is called "my own son whom I have begotten in my bands. . . Do thou receive him as my own . . . Receive him . . . not now as a servant . . . but a most dear brother especially to me; but how much more to thee, both in the flesh and in the Lord" *(Philemon 1:10-16).* He was no longer a slave, because he was a Christian.

What barriers St. Paul would have broken down in his League of Nations: "There is neither Jew nor Greek" (that means, no race or political distinction); "there is neither bond nor free" (no economic distinction); "there is neither male nor female" (no sex distinction); "for you are all one in Christ Jesus" *(Galatians 3:28).*

When Chile and Argentina were about to go to war, it was the suggestion of a woman that the cannon of the two nations be melted, made into a statue of Christ and placed in the Andes at the border of each and be called "The Christ of the Andes." And it bears this inscription: "Sooner shall these mountains crumble than this pact of peace, entered into at the feet of Christ between these two nations, shall be broken." And that pact has never been broken!

Some day someone will read the Gospel: "Thou shalt love thy neighbor as thyself"; that is, love the other's interest as you do self interest. Not until all groups see themselves as bound in a new relationship to the common good, will they sacrifice their own special interests.

So long as every individual exists for himself, we shall have social discontent; so long as every class seeks only its own interest we shall have class warfare; and so long as each nation seeks its own interest exclusively, we shall have war.

After listening to that third word to the Cross we know that the equal distribution of economic goods does not make men brothers, but that, by making men brothers under the Fatherhood of God, economic goods are distributed. Equality of possessions does not make men brothers; but being brothers makes for economic equality.

The Prodigal Son thought he could have peace through distribution of economic wealth, but it was not until he had restored relations with his father that the distribution worked.

Communism of things will never work until we start with a communism of personal relationships. Individual selfishness cannot be corrected by class selfishness. Selfishness is insanity.

The author of Peer Gynt writes of the inmates of an insane asylum: "It is here that men are most themselves -- themselves and nothing but themselves -- sailing with outspread wings of self. Each shuts himself in a cask of self, the cask stopped with the bung of self and seasoned in a well of self. None has a tear for the other's woes or cares what any other thinks."

Centering on self, they hate themselves. Doing always what they like, they hate what they do. Having their own way, they block the way and lose their way. Unable to get along with themselves, they cannot get along with anyone else.

No wonder a young product of a progressive school once asked: "Must I always do what I want to do?" It is by no accident that this age which believed in self-expression has ended in self-disillusionment and disgust.

Our Lord spoke to the hating, raging, anti-Christian Saul on the Damascus road: "Saul, Saul, why persecutest thou me? It is hard for thee to kick against the goad" *(Acts 26:14)*. He used the figure of an ox hurting itself by kicking against the sharp nails of the cart. He was saying in effect: "When you rebel against Me, you are rebelling against yourself . . . You persecute Me, but you -- *you* are perishing."

Men, nations and systems always destroy themselves by seeking an order other than that based on the brotherhood of all men under the Fatherhood of God! Class consciousness must be transformed into "brother consciousness," or the world will perish. Freedom from God is really the freedom to destroy ourselves.

To the selfish comes the lesson from the Cross! Begin to live for others, and you will begin to live for self. Religion implies social relationships.

We did not wait until we were twenty-one and then, after studying the Constitution, decide to become Americans. We were born American -- born out of the womb of America. So likewise, in the spiritual order, we are born out of the womb of the Church. It is the Church founded by Christ which makes us Christian; it is not you or me, as a Christian, who adds our individuality to other individuals to form an institution!

Never therefore say: Religion is a purely personal matter. You can no more have your personal religion than you can have your personal sun. If your personal religion unites you to God, and my personal religion unites me to God, then is there not a common relationship between us to a common Father?

When we go to a concert, do we not give attention to the music, that is, do we not allow ourselves to be determined by something *outside* ourselves? Do we think that when people attend concerts, each one should do whatever he pleases, call out his own selections, take the baton from the conductor, or whistle his own tune?

Then why, when the subject is religion, where the Conductor is God, should we insist on our own individual ideas, or say religion is "what I think about God." Rather, religion is what God wants it to be, hence I must seek His will, not mine, discover His truth, not my opinion.

Nor is it true to say: "The way I conduct my own life is nobody's business but mine," or "it harms nobody else." Could you throw a stone in the sea without causing ripples which would affect even the most distant shore? How then do we think our moral actions can be devoid of social repercussions?

Morality is essentially a relationship of a threefold character: a relationship between my self and my conscience, between my self and my neighbor, and between my self and my God.

You cannot think of a single wrong deed in the world which does not disturb all three relationships -- even secret sins. Take, for example, a strong hatred which never expresses itself in violence.

First, it disturbs your relation to yourself; physically, by upsetting your stomach, spiritually by creating a tension between an ideal and a failure to attain it, and morally, later on, by remorse of conscience.

Secondly it disturbs your relation to your neighbor, by diminishing the content of love in the world. And if enough individuals did exactly what you did, it could cause a war.

Thirdly, it disturbs your relation to God, for if I am a motor made by God which runs best on the fuel of Divine Love which God supplies, it follows that I upset both myself and my happy relation to Him by trying to run the motor on the fuel of hate.

All quarrels, disagreements, wars, strifes, and dissensions begin with a false declaration of independence -- independence from God and independence from fellowman.

That incidentally is why the Jews on the one hand, and the Christians on the other, are on the wrong track when they try to break down intolerance by protests within their own group.

The Jews will never crush anti-Semitism so long as they protest against intolerance only within their ranks, or within their press, and completely ignore the intolerance shown to Christians. And the same is true of Christians. Not until they both protest out of a common relationship, until the Jew defends the Christian and the Christian the Jew, will there be peace.

One of the reasons why there has been such a great decline of belief in the Divinity of Christ outside the Church is because a proper understanding of the relationship existing between Christ and His Mother has been destroyed.

Would you, as a son, have much regard for anyone who said he liked you, but who refused to speak to your mother? Well, do you think Our Lord can feel any differently, particularly since He gave His Mother to us on the Cross?

Why not then, as a remedy for all selfishness, begin seeing ourselves bound to one another in every increasing relationship, first as common creatures of God, then as sons of the Heavenly Father, as brothers of Christ, as members of His Mystical Body vivified by one Spirit, governed by one Head, and as children of Mary, Our Mother, to whom -- as her children who never grow up -- we say in the language of Mary Dixon Thayer:

Lovely Lady dressed in Blue
Teach me how to pray!
God was just your little Boy,
Tell me what to say!

Did you lift Him up, sometimes,
Gently, on your knee?
Did you sing to Him the way
Mother does to me?

Did you hold His hand at night?
Did you ever try
Telling stories of the world?
O! And did He cry?

Do you really think He cares
If I tell Him things --
Little things that happen? And
Do the Angel's wings

Make a noise? And can He hear
Me if I speak low?
Does He understand me now?
Tell me for you know!

Lovely Lady dressed in Blue.
Teach me how to pray!
God was just your little Boy,
And you know the way.

(A Child on His Knees,
C/r Macmillan Co., New York)

Seven Words to the Cross, 1944

Ninth Meditation

THE FELLOWSHIP OF RELIGION

Have you ever said, in order to justify your selfishness, "After all, I have my own life to live?" The truth is you have not your own life to live, because you have to live it with everyone else. Religion is not what you do with your solitariness, but what you do with your relationships. You were born out of the womb of society, and hence the love of neighbor is inseparable from love of God. "If any man say: I love God, and hateth his brother; he is a liar. For he that loveth not his brother whom he seeth, how can he love God whom he seeth not? " *(1John 4:20).*

As danger multiplies, human solidarity becomes more evident. Human beings are closer to one another morally in a bomb shelter or shell-hole than they are in a brokerage office or at a bridge table. As sorrow increases, a sense of unity deepens. It is, therefore, only natural to suspect that the peak of tragedy in the lives of our Divine Lord and His Mother on Calvary should best reveal the communal character of religion.

It is particularly interesting to note that the Word Our Lord spoke to His Mother from the Cross is prefaced by St. John, in His Gospel, speaking of the seamless garment which had been worn by our Blessed Lord and for which the soldiers were now shaking dice. "The soldiers therefore, when they had crucified him, took his garments, (and they made four parts, to every soldier a part) and also his coat. Now the coat was without seam, woven from the top throughout" *(John 19:23).*

Why, out of all the details of the Passion, should he suddenly begin thinking about a robe? Because it was woven by Mary's hands. It was such a beautiful robe that these hardened criminals refused to tear it apart. Custom gave them the right to the perquisites of those whom they crucified. But here the criminals refused to divide the spoils. They shook dice for it, so that the winner had the whole robe.

After having yielded up His garments to those who shook dice for them, He on the Cross now yields up her who wove the seamless garment. Our Blessed Lord looks down to the two most beloved creatures He has on earth: Mary and John. He speaks first to His Blessed Mother. He does not call her "Mother," but "Woman."

As St. Bernard so lovingly put it, if He had called her "Mother," she would have been just His mother and no one else's. In order to indicate that she is now becoming the Mother of all men whom He redeems, He endows her with the title of universal motherhood: "Woman." Then indicating with a gesture of His head the presence of His beloved disciple, He added: "Behold thy son." He does not call him John, for if He did, John would have been only the son of Zebedee; he left him unnamed that he might stand for all humanity.

Our Lord was equivalently saying to His Mother: "You already have one Son and I am He. You cannot have another. All the other sons will be in Me as the branches are in the vine. John is one in Me and I in him. Hence I say not: 'Behold another son!' but 'Behold Me in John and John in Me.' "

It was a kind of testament. At the Last Supper He willed to mankind His Body and Blood. "This is my body! This is my blood!" Now He was willing His Mother: "Behold thy Mother." Our Blessed Lord was here establishing a new relationship; a relationship by which His own Mother became the mother of all mankind, and we in turn became her children.

This new bond was not carnal, but spiritual. There are other ties than those of blood. Blood may be thicker than water, but Spirit is thicker than blood. All men, whatever be their color, race, blood, are one in the Spirit: "For whosoever shall do the will of my Father, that is in heaven, he is my brother, and sister, and mother" *(Matthew 12:50).*

Mary had seen God in Christ; now her Son was telling her to see her Christ in all Christians. She was never to love anyone else but Him, but He would now be in those whom He redeemed. The night before He had prayed that all men might be one in Him, as there is but one life for the Vine and its branches. Now He was making her the custodian not only of the Vine but also of the branches through time and eternity. She had given birth to the King; now she was begetting the Kingdom.

The very thought of this Bride of the Spirit becoming the Mother of humanity is overwhelming, not because God thought of it, but because we so seldom ever think of it. We have become so used to seeing the Madonna with the Child in Bethlehem that we forget that same Madonna is holding you and me at Calvary.

At the manger, Christ was only a Babe; at Calvary, Christ was the head of redeemed humanity. At Bethlehem, she was the mother of Christ; on Calvary, she became the Mother of Christians. In the stable, she brought forth her Son without pain and became the Mother of Joy; at the Cross, she brought us forth in pain and became the Queen of Martyrs. In neither case shall a woman forget the child of her womb.

When Mary heard Our Blessed Lord establish this new relationship, she remembered so well when this spiritual fellowship began. Her third word, as His, was about the relationship. It was a long time ago.

After the angel announced to her that she was to be the Mother of God, which alone would have bound her to all humanity, the angel added that her elderly cousin, Elizabeth, was now with child: "And behold thy cousin Elizabeth, she also hath conceived a son in her old age: and this is the sixth month with her that is called barren. Because no word shall be impossible with God. And Mary said: Behold the handmaid of the Lord: be it done to me according to thy word. And the angel departed from her."

"And Mary rising up in those days, went into the hill country with haste into a city of Juda. And she entered into the house of Zachary and saluted Elizabeth. And it came to pass that when Elizabeth heard the salutation of Mary, the infant leaped in her womb. And Elizabeth was filled with the Holy Ghost. And she cried out with a loud voice and said: Blessed art thou among women and blessed is the fruit of thy womb. And whence is this to me that the mother of my Lord should come to me? For behold as soon as the voice of thy salutation sounded in my ears, the infant in my womb leaped for joy. And blessed art thou that hast believed, because those things shall be accomplished that were spoken to thee by the Lord" (*Luke 1:36-45*).

It is rightly assumed that no one may more justly claim immunity from service to others than a woman bearing a child. If one adds to this, *noblesse oblige*, the fact that this Woman bears within herself the very Lord of the Universe, then of all creatures she might rightfully claim dispensation from social bonds and duties to neighbor. Women in that condition come not to minister but to be ministered unto.

Here we have the spectacle of the greatest of all women becoming the servant of others. Not standing on her dignity saying, "I am the Mother of God," but recognizing the need of her aged cousin, this pregnant Queen, instead of awaiting her hour in isolation *as* other women, mounts a donkey, makes a five day journey over hill country, and with such a consciousness of spiritual fellowship that she does it, in the language of sacred Scripture, "with haste" *(Luke 1:39).*

Thirty-three years before Calvary, Mary recognizes that her mission is to bring her Lord to humanity; and with such a holy impatience is she filled that she begins it before her Son has seen the light of day. I love to think of her on this journey as the first Christian Nurse whose service to neighbor is inseparable from bringing Christ into the life of her patient.

There is no record of the exact words that Mary spoke. The Evangelist merely tells us that she saluted Elizabeth. But notice that just as soon as she saluted her cousin, new relationships were immediately established. Elizabeth no longer addresses her as cousin. She says, "Whence is this to me, that the mother of my Lord should come to me?" *(Luke 1:43).*

Mary is now not just a relative, or another mother of another child. She is called the "Mother of God!" But that was not the end of the relationship. Elizabeth's own child in her womb, who was to be called later by the Child in Mary's womb "the greatest man ever born of woman," now stirs in His mother's womb; we might almost say he danced to his birth in salutation to the King of Kings! Two unborn children establish a relationship before either had swung open the portals of flesh.

Notice how much Our Blessed Lady is made the link of bringing Christ to humanity. First of all, it was through her as a Gate of Heaven that He walked into this earth. It was in her as a Mirror of Justice that He first saw with human eyes the reflection of the world He had made. It is in her as a kind of living ciborium that He is carried to the First Communion rail of her cousin's home, where an unborn babe salutes Him as the Host who is to be the Guest of the world. It is through her intercession at Cana that He brings His Divine Power to supply a human need. And it is finally at the Cross that she who gave Christ to the world, now receives Him back again in us who have the high and undeserved honor to call ourselves Christian.

Because of this intimacy I wonder if it is not true that as the world loses veneration for Christ's mother, it loses also its adoration of Christ. Is it not true in earthly relationships that, as a so-called friend ignores your mother when he comes to your home, sooner or later he will ignore you? Conversely, as the world begins knocking at Mary's door, it will find that Our Lord Himself will answer.

If you have never before prayed to Mary, do so now. Can you not see that if Christ Himself willed to be physically formed in her for nine months and then be spiritually formed by her for thirty years, it is to her that we must go to learn how to have Christ formed in us? Only she who raised Christ can raise a Christian.

To develop that spiritual comradeship with Jesus and Mary, the Rosary is most effective. The word, Rosary, means a "garland of roses" culled from the Garden of Prayer. Each decade requires only between two and three minutes; thus the whole Rosary requires only a little over ten minutes.

If you do not say it all at once and on your knees, then say one decade when you arise in the morning, another decade on your way to work, another decade as you sweep the house or wait for your check at the noon lunch hour, another decade just before you go to bed; the last decade you can say in bed just before falling off to sleep.

When you are under twenty-five, you have time for only one decade before falling to sleep; when you get to be forty, you will have time for two; and when you are sixty, you will have time for a dozen.

Because the "Hail Mary" is said many times in the course of a Rosary, do not think of it as a sterile repetition, because each time it is said in a different setting or scene as you meditate, for example, on such mysteries as the Birth of Our Lord, the Crucifixion, the Resurrection, etc. You never thought as a child when you told your mother you loved her that it had the same meaning as it did the last time you told her. Because the background of the affection changed, its affirmation was new. It is the same sun that rises each morning, but it makes a new day.

What are some of the advantages of the Rosary?

1. If you say the Rosary devoutly, and all that it implies, every day of your life, you will never lose your soul.

2. If you wish for peace in your heart and in your family and an abundance of heavenly gifts on your household, then assemble your family each night and say the Rosary.

3. If you are anxious to convert a soul to the fullness of God's Love and Life, teach that person to say the Rosary. That person will either stop saying the Rosary or he will receive the gift of Faith.

4. If a sufficient army of us said the Rosary every day, the Blessed Mother would now, as in the past, obtain from Her Divine Son the stilling of the present tempests, the defeat of the enemies of human civilization, and a real peace in the hearts of tired and straying men.

5. If the cooling of your charity has made you unhappy on the inside and critical of others, then the Rosary, through meditation on Our Lord's great love for you on the Cross and your Mother's affection for you on Calvary, will rekindle your love of God and of neighbor and restore you to a peace which surpasses all understanding.

Do not think that in honoring Our Lady with the Rosary you are neglecting Our Lord. Did you ever know anyone who ignored you by being kind to your mother? If Our Lord said to you "Behold Thy Mother," it well behooves us to respect her whom Our Lord chose above all the creatures of earth. In any case remember, even though you wanted to, you could not stop with her. As Francis Thompson put it:

The celestial Temptress play,
And all mankind to bliss betray;
With sacrosanct cajoleries
And starry treachery of your eyes,
Tempt us back to Paradise!

Seven Words of Jesus and Mary, 1945

MY GOD! MY GOD! WHY HAST THOU FORSAKEN ME?
Meditations on the Fourth Word from the Cross
Archbishop Fulton J. Sheen

First Meditation

MY GOD! MY GOD! WHY HAST THOU FORSAKEN ME?

The first three words from the pulpit of the Cross were addressed to the three predilections of God: enemies, sinners, and saints. The next two words, the fourth and the fifth, betray the sufferings of the God-man on the Cross. The fourth word symbolizes the sufferings of man abandoned by God; the fifth word the sufferings of God abandoned by man.

When Our Blessed Lord spoke this fourth word from the Cross, darkness covered the earth. It is a common remark that nature is indifferent to our griefs. A nation may be dying of famine, yet the sun starts and plays upon the stricken fields. Brother may rise up against brother in a war which turns poppy fields into Haceldamas of blood; yet a bird, safe from the fire and shell, chants its little song of peace. Hearts may be broken by the loss of a friend; yet a rainbow leaps with joy across the heavens, making a terrible contrast between its smile and the agony it shines upon. But the sun refused to shine on the crucifixion! The light that rules the day, probably for the first and last time in history, was snuffed out like a candle when, according to every human calculation, it should have continued to shine. The reason was that the crowning crime of man, the killing of nature's Lord, could not pass without a protest from nature itself. If the soul of God were in darkness, so should be the sun which He had made.

Truly, all was darkness! He had given up His Mother and His beloved disciple, and now God seemingly had abandoned Him. "Eli, Eli, lamma sabacthani?" "My God! My God! Why hast Thou forsaken Me?" It is a cry in the mysterious language of Hebrew to express the tremendous mystery of a God "abandoned" by God. The Son calls His Father, God. What a contrast with a prayer He once taught: "Our Father, Who art in Heaven!" In some strange, mysterious way His human nature seems separated from His Heavenly Father, and yet not separated, for otherwise how could He cry, "My God, My God"? But just as the sun's light and heat can be withdrawn from us by the intervening clouds, though the sun remains in the sky, so there was a kind of withdrawal of His Father's Face in the terrible moment in which He took upon Himself the sins of the world. This pain and desolation He suffered for each of us, that we might know what a terrible thing it is for human nature to be without God, to be deprived of a Divine Remedy and Consolation. It was the supreme act of atonement for three classes of people: those who abandon God, those who doubt the presence of God, and those who are indifferent to God.

He atoned first of all for atheists, for those who on that dark midday half believed in God, as even now at night they half believe in Him. He atoned also for those who know God, but live as if they had never heard His name; for those whose hearts are like waysides on which God's love falls only to be trampled by the world; for those whose hearts are like rocks on which the seed of God's love falls only to be quickly forgotten; for those whose hearts are like thorns on which God's love descends only to be choked by the cares of the world. It was atonement for all who have had faith and lost it; for all who once were saints and now are sinners. It was the Divine Act of Redemption for all abandonment of God, for in that moment in which He was forgotten, He purchased for us the grace of never being forgotten by God.

It was also the atonement for that other class who deny the presence of God; for all those Christians who abandon all effort when they cannot feel God near them; for all who identify being good with feeling good; for all those skeptics beginning with the first who asked, "Why has God commanded you?" It was reparation for all the haunting questions of a doubting world:

"Why is there evil?" ... "Why does God not answer my prayers?" ... "Why did God take away my mother?" ... "why" .

. . "why" . . . "why"; and the reparation for all those queries was made when God asked a "why" of God.
Finally, it was atonement for all the indifference of the world which lives as if there had never been a crib at Bethlehem or a Cross at Calvary; it was atonement for all who shake dice while the drama of Redemption is being enacted; for all those who feel themselves as gods beyond all duties of worship and religion, yet bound by none. I suppose that after these twenty centuries the indifference of our modern world is more torturing and crucifying than the pains of Calvary. One can well believe that a crown of thorns, and that steel nails were less terrible to the flesh of our Saviour than our modem indifference which neither scorns nor prays to the Heart of Christ.

PRAYER

JESUS! Thou art now atoning for those moments when we are neither hot nor cold, members neither of heaven nor of earth, for now Thou are suffering between the two: rejected by the one, abandoned by the other. Because Thou wouldst not give up sinful humanity, Thy Heavenly Father hid His Face from Thee. Because Thou wouldst not give up Thy Heavenly Father, sinful humanity turned its back to Thee, and thus in holy fellowship Thou didst unite us both. No longer can men say that God does not know what a heart suffers in abandonment, for now Thou art abandoned. No longer can men complain that God does not know the wounds of an inquiring heart which feels not the Divine Presence, for now that sweet Presence is seemingly hid from Thee. Jesus, now I understand pain, abandonment, and suffering, for I see that even the sun has its eclipse. But Jesus, why do I not learn? Teach me that just as Thou didst not make Thy own Cross, neither shall I make my own, but accept the one Thou makest for me. Teach me that everything in the world is Thine, except one thing, and that is my own will; and since that is mine, it is the only real and true gift that I can ever bestow. Teach me to say, "Not my will, but Thine be done, O Lord." Even when I see Thee not, grant me the grace to believe and " although Thou slayest me, yet will I trust Thee. Tell me, how long, how long, O Lord, will I keep Thee writhing on the Cross?

The Seven Last Words, 1933

Second Meditation

THY WILL BE DONE ON EARTH AS IT IS IN HEAVEN

"Thy Will be done on earth as it is in heaven."

"My God, My God, why hast thou forsaken me?"

In the "Our Father" Our Lord asked us to resign ourselves to the will of the heavenly Father; on the Cross, he now resigned Himself to that same Divine Will. The real lesson hidden in these words is that now and then we face the unintelligible and mysterious things of life, and the only solution is to trust in the Will of God. "Thy will be done on earth as it is in heaven." We ask ourselves such questions as: "Why should I suffer? Why did God take away my mother? Why is there pain? Why do the innocent suffer? Why does God abandon me?" There is no answer on earth except: "Thy will be done."

Our Lord in this word is reemphasizing the lesson taught in the Book of Job. Job was sorely afflicted. He lost his children, his fortune; his wife turned against him, his friends abused him, and his whole body became afflicted with dread. And so he asked the question: "Why?"

"Why did I not die in the womb, why did I not perish when I came out of the belly, why was I received upon the knees, why was I suckled at the breasts; why is light given to him that is in misery and life to them that are in bitterness of soul?"

Job's friends tried to give him human explanations, to solve all of his riddles, to make everything reasonable, and to show how one part of the universe fits every other part. Now if the Book of Job were a purely human document, a trivial poet or a modern dramatist would have made God enter the scene and answer the questions of Job. And yet when God does come on the scene, what does God actually do? He does not answer the questions of Job. He asks Job more questions in a way that abolishes all foolish questions. He turns to Job and says: I will ask thee, and answer thou me. Where wast thou when I laid the foundations of the earth? . . Upon what are its bases grounded? Or who laid the cornerstone thereof . . . Who shut up the sea with doors, when it broke forth as issuing out of the womb: When I made a cloud the garment thereof and wrapped it in a mist as in swaddling bands?"

Then Job answered the Lord, and said I know that thou canst do all things, and no thought is hid from thee . . . Therefore I have spoken unwisely, and things that above measure exceeded my knowledge."

God insists on the inexplicableness of everything. The Maker of all things is astonished at the things He has made. Instead of proving to Job that it is a world explicable by science, He shows Job that it is a much stranger world than science ever suspected. The refusal of God to explain His design is itself a burning hint of His design: namely, the riddles of God are more satisfying than the solutions of men. And so, in the Book of Job, we see he was tormented not because he was the worst of men, but because he was the best. It was Good Friday that was prefigured in the wounds of Job.

The lesson for us is that many things are inexplicable here below, but they are only the details, e.g., "Why this pain?" "Why this loss?" "Why this sorrow?" The general principles remain true and unshakable: God is good, and He wills what is best for the soul. "My God, why hast thou forsaken me?" means forsaken only in appearance, not in reality. We may be lonely, but God is never out of our hearing. Our Lord has gone into the forests of suffering and loneliness, but He has left His footprints there, so we can find the way out. Take God's hand and follow Him in the dark, trusting, and believing. We cannot say He does not know what it is to be abandoned for He was abandoned on the cross. "Trust Him when dark doubts assail thee; trust Him when trust is small; trust Him when simply to trust Him is the hardest thing of all."

The Seven Last Words and the Our Father, 1935

Third Meditation

THE CONSECRATION

"My God, My God, why hast thou forsaken me?"
– Matthew 27:46.

The Fourth Word is the Consecration of the Mass of Calvary. The first three Words were spoken to men, but the last four Words were spoken to God. We are now in the final stage of the Passion. In the fourth Word, in all the universe, there is but God and Himself. This is the hour of darkness. Suddenly out of its blackness, the silence is broken by a cry -- so terrible, so unforgettable, that even those who did not understand the dialect remembered the strange tones: "*Eli, Eli, lamma sabacthani.*" They recorded it so, a rough rendering of the Hebrew, because they could never get the sound of those tones out of their ears all the days of their life.

The darkness which was covering the earth at that moment was only the external symbol of the dark night of the soul within. Well indeed might the sun hide its face, at the terrible crime of deicide. A real reason why the earth was made was to have a cross erected upon it. And now that the cross was erected, creation felt the pain and went into darkness.

But why the cry of darkness? Why the cry of abandonment: "My God, my God, why hast thou forsaken me?" It was the cry of atonement for sin. Sin is the abandonment of God by man; it is the creature forsaking the Creator, as a flower might abandon the sunlight which gave its strength and beauty. Sin is a separation, a divorce -- the original divorce from unity with God, whence all other divorces are derived.

Since He came on earth to redeem men from sin, it was therefore fitting that He *feel* that abandonment, that separation, that divorce. He felt it first internally, in His soul, as the base of a mountain, if conscious, might feel abandoned by the sun when a cloud drifted about it, even though its great heights were radiant with light. There was no sin in His soul, but since He willed to feel the effect of sin, an awful sense of isolation and loneliness crept over Him -- the loneliness of being without God.

Surrendering the divine consolation which might have been His, He sank into an awful human aloneness, to atone for the solitariness of a soul that has lost God by sin; for the loneliness of the atheist who says there is no God, for the isolation of the man who gives up his faith for things, and for the broken-heartedness of all sinners who are homesick without God. He even went so far as to redeem all those who will not trust, who in sorrow and misery curse and abandon God, crying out: "Why this death? Why should I lose my property? Why should I suffer?" He atoned for all these things by asking a "Why" of God.

But in order better to reveal the intensity of that feeling of abandonment, He revealed it by an external sign. Because man had separated himself from God, He, in atonement, permitted His Blood to be separated from His Body. Sin had entered into the blood of man; and as if the sins of the world were upon Him, He drained the chalice of His Body of His sacred Blood. We can almost hear Him say: "Father, this is My Body; this is My Blood. They are being separated from one another as humanity has been separated from Thee. This is the consecration of My Cross."

What happened there on the Cross that day is happening now in the Mass, with this difference: On the Cross the Saviour was alone; in the Mass He is with us. Our Lord is now in heaven at the right hand of the Father, making intercession for us. He therefore can never suffer again in His own human nature. How then can the Mass be the re-enactment of Calvary? How can Christ renew the

Cross? He cannot suffer again *in His own human nature* which is in heaven enjoying beatitude, but He can suffer again *in our human natures*. He cannot renew Calvary in His *physical body*, but He can renew it in His *Mystical Body* -- the Church. The Sacrifice of the Cross can be re-enacted provided we give Him our body and our blood, and give it to Him so completely that as His own, He can offer Himself anew to His heavenly Father for the redemption of His Mystical Body, the Church.

So the Christ goes out into the world gathering up other human natures who are willing to be Christs. In order that our sacrifices, our sorrows, our Golgothas, our crucifixions, may not be isolated, disjointed, and unconnected, the Church collects them, harvests them, unifies them, coalesces them, masses them, and this massing of all our sacrifices of our individual human natures is united with the Great Sacrifice of Christ on the Cross in the Mass.

When we assist at the Mass we are not just individuals of the earth or solitary units, but living parts of a great spiritual order in which the Infinite penetrates and enfolds the finite, the Eternal breaks into the temporal, and the Spiritual clothes itself in the garments of materiality. Nothing more solemn exists on the face of God's earth than the awe-inspiring moment of Consecration; for the Mass is not a prayer, nor a hymn, nor something said -- it is a Divine Act with which we come in contact at a given moment of time.

An imperfect illustration may be drawn from the radio. The air is filled with symphonies and speech. We do not put the words or music there; but, if we choose, we may establish contact with them by tuning in our radio. And so with the Mass. It is a singular, unique Divine Act with which we come in contact each time it is represented and re-enacted in the Mass.

When the die of a medal or coin is struck, the medal is the material, visible representation of a spiritual idea existing in the mind of the artist. Countless reproductions may be made from that original as each new piece of metal is brought in contact with it, and impressed by it. Despite the multiplicity of coins made, the pattern is always the same. In like manner in the Mass, the Pattern -- Christ's sacrifice on Calvary -- is renewed on our altars as each human being is brought in contact with it at the moment of consecration; but the sacrifice is one and the same despite the multiplicity of Masses. The Mass then is the communication of the Sacrifice of Calvary to us under the species of bread and wine.

We are on the altar under the appearance of bread and wine, for both are the sustenance of life; therefore in giving that which gives us life we are symbolically giving ourselves. Furthermore, wheat must suffer to become bread; grapes must pass through the wine-press to become wine. Hence both are representative of Christians who are called to suffer with Christ, that they may also reign with Him.

As the consecration of the Mass draws near our Lord is equivalently saying to us: "You, Mary; you, John; you, Peter; and you, Andrew -- you, all of you -- give Me your body; give Me your blood. Give Me your whole self! I can suffer no more. I have passed through My cross, I have filled up the sufferings of My physical body, but I have not filled up the sufferings wanting to My Mystical Body, in which you are. The Mass is the moment when each one of you may literally fulfill My injunction: 'Take up your cross and follow Me.'"

On the cross our Blessed Lord was looking forward to you, hoping that one day you would be giving yourself to Him at the moment of consecration. Today, in the Mass, that hope our Blessed Lord entertained for you is fulfilled. When you assist at the Mass He expects you now actually to give Him yourself.

Then as the moment of consecration arrives, the priest in obedience to the words of our Lord, "Do this for a commemoration of me," takes bread in his hands and says "This is my body"; and then over the chalice of wine says, "This is the chalice of my blood of the new and eternal testament." He does not consecrate the bread and wine together, but separately. The separate consecration of the bread and wine is a symbolic representation of the separation of body and blood, and since the Crucifixion entailed that very mystery, Calvary is thus renewed on our altar. But Christ, as has been said, is not alone on our altar; we are with Him. Hence the words of consecration have a double sense; the primary signification of the words is: "This is the Body of Christ; this is the Blood of Christ;" but the secondary signification is "This is my body; this is my blood."

Such is the purpose of life! To redeem ourselves in union with Christ; to apply His merits to our souls by being like Him in all things, even to His death on the Cross. He passed through His consecration on the Cross that we might now pass through ours in the Mass. There is nothing more tragic in all the world than wasted pain.

Think of how much suffering there is in hospitals, among the poor, and the bereaved. Think also of how much of that suffering goes to waste! How many of those lonesome, suffering, abandoned, crucified souls are saying with our Lord at the moment of consecration, "This is my body. Take it"? And yet that is what we all should be saying at that second:

I GIVE MYSELF TO GOD. HERE IS MY BODY. TAKE IT. HERE IS MY BLOOD. TAKE IT. HERE IS MY SOUL, MY WILL, MY ENERGY, MY STRENGTH, MY PROPERTY, MY WEALTH -- ALL THAT I HAVE. IT IS YOURS. TAKE IT! CONSECRATE IT! OFFER IT! OFFER IT WITH THYSELF TO THE HEAVENLY FATHER IN ORDER THAT HE, LOOKING DOWN ON THIS GREAT SACRIFICE, MAY SEE ONLY THEE, HIS BELOVED SON, IN WHOM HE IS WELL PLEASED. TRANSMUTE THE POOR BREAD OF MY LIFE INTO THY

DIVINE LIFE; THRILL THE WINE OF MY WASTED LIFE INTO THY DIVINE SPIRIT; UNITE MY BROKEN HEART WITH THY HEART; CHANGE MY CROSS INTO A CRUCIFIX. LET NOT MY ABANDONMENT AND MY SORROW AND MY BEREAVEMENT GO TO WASTE. GATHER UP THE FRAGMENTS, AND AS THE DROP OF WATER IS ABSORBED BY THE WINE AT THE OFFERTORY OF THE MASS, LET MY LIFE BE ABSORBED IN THINE; LET MY LITTLE CROSS BE ENTWINED WITH THY GREAT CROSS SO THAT I MAY PURCHASE THE JOYS OF EVERLASTING HAPPINESS IN UNION WITH THEE.

"CONSECRATE THESE TRIALS OF MY LIFE WHICH WOULD GO UNREWARDED UNLESS UNITED WITH THEE; TRANSUBSTANTIATE ME SO THAT LIKE BREAD WHICH IS NOW THY BODY, AND WINE WHICH IS NOW THY BLOOD, I TOO MAY BE WHOLLY THINE. I CARE NOT IF THE SPECIES REMAIN, OR THAT, LIKE THE BREAD AND THE WINE I SEEM TO ALL EARTHLY EYES THE SAME AS BEFORE. MY STATION IN LIFE, MY ROUTINE DUTIES, MY WORK, MY FAMILY -- ALL THESE ARE BUT THE SPECIES OF MY LIFE WHICH MAY REMAIN UNCHANGED; BUT THE *substance* OF MY LIFE, MY SOUL, MY MIND, MY WILL, MY HEART -- TRANSUBSTANTIATE THEM, TRANSFORM THEM WHOLLY INTO THY SERVICE, SO THAT THROUGH ME ALL MAY KNOW HOW SWEET IS THE LOVE OF CHRIST." AMEN.

Calvary and the Mass, 1936

Fourth Meditation

BLESSED ARE THE POOR IN SPIRIT

*"Blessed are the poor in spirit,
for theirs is the kingdom of heaven."*

"My God, My God, why hast thou forsaken me?"

At the beginning of His public life on the Hill of the Beatitudes our Lord preached: "Blessed are the poor in Spirit, for theirs is the Kingdom of Heaven." At the end of His life on the Hill of Calvary He now practices that poverty of Spirit by His Fourth Word from the cross: "My God, my God, why hast thou forsaken me?"

Both the Beatitude and the Word are foreign to the spirit of the world. Modern society is what might be characterized as acquisitive, for its primary concern is to acquire, to own, to possess; its aristocracy is not one of blood or virtue, but of money; it judges worth not by righteousness but in terms of possessions.

Our Blessed Lord came into the world to destroy this acquisitiveness and this subservience of moral to economic ends by preaching the blessedness of the poor in Spirit. It is worth noting immediately that "the poor in spirit" does not necessarily mean the indigent or those in straitened circumstances of life; "Poor in spirit" means interior detachment, and as such includes even some who are rich in the world's goods, for detachment can be practiced by the rich just as avarice can be practiced by the poor.

The poor in Spirit are those who are so detached from wealth, from social position, and from earthly knowledge that, at the moment the Kingdom of God demands a sacrifice, they are prepared to surrender all.

The Beatitude means then: Blessed are those who are not possessed by their possessions; blessed are they who whether or not they are poor in *fact* are poor in their inmost spirit.

Our Lord not only preached Poverty of Spirit; He also lived it, and He lived it in such a way as to conquer the three kinds of pride: -- the pride of what *one has*, which is economic pride; the pride of what one *is*, which is social pride; and the pride of what *one knows*, which is intellectual pride.

First of all, to counteract the wild exaltation of the economic, the pursuit of wealth as the noblest end of man, and the glorying in what one *has*, Christ became economically poor. He chose His Mother from the poorer classes who could afford to offer only doves in the Temple, and His foster father from the village tradesmen; and He Who owned the earth and the fullness thereof, chose for His birthplace a deserted shepherd's cave.

He was poor in His mission as He explained at Nazareth: "The Spirit of the Lord is upon me, wherefore he hath anointed me to preach the gospel to the poor." He was poor in His public life: "The foxes have holes, and the birds of the air nests; but the Son of man hath not where to lay his head."

He was poor in the eyes of government, for when asked to pay the tax, He had no money. He was poor in His death, for He was stripped of His garments -- the last remnant of earthly possessions --; He was executed on a cross erected at public expense, and buried in a stranger's grave.

Thus did He atone for those who are proud of what they have, by having nothing, and becoming the Universal Poor Man of the World. He who was rich became poor for our sakes that we might be rich, and He is therefore the only one in all history of whom both the rich and poor can say: "He came from our ranks. He is one of our own."

Reparation had to be made not only for the pride of wealth but also for the snobbery and pride of social position. The world is full of those who either through the accident of birth or circumstance count themselves better than their fellowmen and who glory in what they *are*.

These too He atoned for not only by veiling the glory of His Godhead under human form but also by the most poignant social abandonment. The very beginning of His life bears the record: "He came unto his own, and his own received him not." Cities abandoned Him; Bethlehem refused Him an inn; Nazareth drove Him from its gates; and Jerusalem stoned Him.

Truly indeed He could say: "A prophet is not without honor, but in his own country, and in his own house, and among his own kindred." Men abandoned Him. Some of His disciples hearing Him say He would give Himself humbly under the form of Bread said: "This saying is hard, and who can hear it?"... and they walked with Him no more.

Teachers of the Law abandoned Him, calling Him "a glutton, a wine-drinker, a friend of publicans and sinners." The needy abandoned Him and drew from Him the sweet complaint: "You will not come to me that you may have life."

One of His apostles abandoned Him for thirty pieces of silver, one for shame at the word of a maid-servant, and three for sleep. Even those whom He helped abandoned Him: "Were not ten made clean? and where are the other nine? There is no one found to return and give glory to God, but this stranger."

And now at the end of His life, the Roman governor could say: "Thy own nation ... has delivered Thee up to me." Thus did He Who is King of Kings become socially poor and an outcast from the snobs of the earth, in order that through that abandonment we might become -- let us pause at the very thought of it -- *children of God!*

Finally, He atoned for the intellectually proud, for all those who think they know, and who rely on the sufficiency of human knowledge without faith, by becoming spiritually poor.

During His Public Life, He rejoiced that the sublime truths of the Kingdom of Heaven were given only to the humble: "I confess to Thee, O Father, Lord of heaven and earth, because thou hast hid these things from the wise and prudent, and hast revealed them to little ones."

The night of His agony in the garden when that atonement for pride began in all horror, He described His soul as "sorrowful unto death"; and now on the Cross He lives the Beatitude of the Poor in Spirit by proclaiming the last and greatest poverty of all -- the spiritual poverty of seeming abandonment by God: "My God, Why hast thou forsaken me?"

Even the sun at mid-day hid its light as a symbol of the spiritual desolation of His soul. The Father had not really abandoned Him, but Our Lord restrained his Divinity from mitigating even with one drop of consolation the bitterness of His chalice.

The cry was one of abandonment, not one of despair. A soul that despairs never cries to God. Just as the keenest pangs of hunger are felt not by the dying man who is completely exhausted, but by the man battling for his life with the last ounce of strength, so abandonment is felt not by the ungodly and unholy, but by the most holy of men, Our Lord on the Cross.

This was the hardest reparation of all. It was not difficult to be economically poor; it was not so difficult to be socially poor and stripped of His friends; but it was hard to surrender Divine consolation in a moment of agony to atone for the self-wise, the intelligentsia, and the conceited, who refuse to bow their heads to the wisdom of God, for the atheists who live without God, and for the Communists who blot His name from the land of the living.

This word from the Cross was a revelation of how much mental agony there must be in the world in those minds and souls and hearts who are without God.

He knew at that one moment what it was to be without God! He knew something of the loneliness of godlessness and something of the misery of Communism, for it was the one moment in which He suffered the desolation of both, that we might have the consolation of never being without Him. By feeling without God, He redeemed those who live without Him.

Behold the Poor Man. Economically poor because stripped of garments; socially poor because deserted by friends; spiritually poor because abandoned by God. From that day to this, then: Blessed are the poor in Spirit. Blessed are the economically poor in spirit, for by desiring nothing, they possess all, even the mansions of the Father's House.

Some years ago when the Cloister of a Carmelite convent was broken by a Cardinal and opened to the public, a good Carmelite nun was showing a visiting priest through the convent. From the roof of it one could look over a valley, and on to an opposite hill where there stood a large and beautiful home that seemed to stand as a symbol for all that was sweet and beautiful and lovely in life.

Recalling the economic poverty of this poor nun, the visitor said to her, "Sister, just suppose that before you entered Carmel, you could have lived in that home. Suppose that you could have had all the wealth, refinement, and opportunities for worldly enjoyment that such a home would give you. Would you have left that house to have become a poor Carmelite?" And she answered, "Father, that *is* my house!"

Blessed also are the poor in spirit socially. Blessed are they who know of only one aristocracy -- the blue-bloods born at the Baptismal font and the royalty of the King of Kings.

There is going to be a tremendous transformation of social position at the last day, for God is no respecter of persons. Our social position in the Kingdom of God will depend not upon our human popularity of propaganda, but only upon those things we carry with us in the shipwreck of the world -- a clear conscience and the love of God.

The world has little use for either, that is why Our Lord warned us that a full-hearted love of Him would draw down the world's hatred: "Yea, the hour cometh, that whosoever killeth you, will think that he doth a service to God. And these things will they do to you, because they have not known the Father, nor me. But these things I have told you, that when the hour shall come, you may remember that I told you of them."

How completely His point of view reverses that of the world's estimate of position is evidenced in those equally striking words: "Blessed shall you be when men shall hate you, and when they shall separate you, and shall reproach you, and cast out your name as evil, for the Son of man's sake. Be glad in that day and rejoice; for behold, your reward is great in heaven."

Blessed finally are the poor in spirit intellectually. Blessed are the humble, and the teachable who like the Shepherds know they know nothing, or like the Wise Men who know they do not know everything. Faith in God, faith in prayer, hope in Christ, devotion to Our Blessed Mother, belief in the Eucharist and in infallibility -- all this may seem foolish to the self-wise, but "the foolishness of God is wiser than men."

Personally, we feel that if our eternal salvation were conditioned upon saving either one hundred corrupt men and women of the streets like Magdalen and Zacchaeus, or converting one proud university professor who felt his tiny mind had solved all the riddles of the universe, we should choose to go out and convert the hundred.

And there is a divine warrant for the choice, for Our Lord said to those who thought themselves wise: "Amen, I say to you, that the publicans and the harlots shall go into the Kingdom of God before you."

Why, then, are we proud? Why do we set all the energies of life on becoming rich: "What doth it profit a man, if he gain the whole world, and suffer the loss of his own soul?" Why do we seek social prestige and seek out the first places at tables -- the Divine injunction is just the contrary: "When thou art invited, go, sit down in the lowest place; that when he who invited thee cometh, he may say to thee: Friend, go up higher ... Because every one that exalteth himself shall be humbled; and he that humbleth himself shall be exalted."

Why are we proud? Whom in all the world could we find to love us in poverty, in friendless abandonment, and in ignorance, other than Our Lord. In the beautiful words of Francis Thompson:

"Strange, piteous, futile thing!
Wherefore should any set thee love apart?
Seeing none but I make much of naught." (He said),
"And human love needs human meriting:

How hast thou merited –
Of all man's clotted clay, the dingiest clot?

Alack, thou knowest not
How little worthy of any love thou art!
Whom wilt thou find to love ignoble thee,

Save Me, save only Me?
All which I took from thee I did but take,

Not for thy harms,
But just that thou might'st seek it in My arms.

All which thy child's mistake
Fancies as lost, I have stored for thee at home:

Rise, clasp My hand, and come."

If then we are called to be poor economically, poor socially, and poor intellectually, let us rejoice in the hope that for us is reserved the Kingdom of heaven, and for the present, see in our fleeting poverty "the shade of His hand, outstretched caressingly.

The Cross and the Beatitudes, 1937

Fifth Meditation

GOD AND THE SOUL

"My God! My God! Why hast thou abandoned me?"

The first three *Words* on the cross have reference to physical suffering: this *Fourth Word* has reference to moral suffering or sin. Physical suffering is pain; moral suffering is evil or sin.

Our world takes sin very lightly, regarding it too often as a relic of ages, which were ignorant of evolution and psychoanalysis. It is the contrary which is true: the more we know about death and its causes the more we know about sin, for in the language of Sacred Scripture, "the wages of sin is death."

Death and sin are identified and rightly so: death in the physical order corresponds to evil in the moral order. Death in the physical order is normally the domination of a lower order over a higher order.

For example, animals and men generally die through the slow oxidation and burning out of the organism. At that moment, when the oxidation of chemical order dominates the biological order, the phenomenon called death ensues.

Now man has not only a body, but also a soul. At that precise point, then, when the lower law of self dominates the higher law of charity, when the flesh dominates the spirit, when the love of earth gains supremacy over the love of God, there is the subversion of due order, and that domination of the lower over the higher order we call sin.

What death is to the body, that sin is to the soul, namely the surrender of life -- human in one case, divine in the other. That is why St. Paul calls sin a crucifixion or the killing of the Divine Life within us: "Crucifying again to themselves the Son of God, and making Him a mockery" *(Hebrews 6:6)*.

Since sin is the taking of Divine Life, it follows that nowhere else was sin better revealed than on Calvary, for there, sinful humanity crucified the Son of God in the flesh. Here sin comes to a burning focus. It manifests itself in its essence: the taking of Divine Life.

Moral evil reaches its greatest power in the taking of the life of the Man of Sorrows, for a world capable of killing the God-man is capable of doing anything.

Nothing else it can ever do will be worse, and all that it will ever do will be but the re-enactment of this tragedy. There, where character was perfect, and suffering most undeserved, the victory of evil was most complete.

If sin could have found a reason for being hateful towards God, the crime would have been less heinous. But His enemies could find no fault in Him except His all-compassing Goodness.

But goodness is the one thing sin cannot endure, for goodness is sin's constant reproach. The wicked always hate the good. The very unreasonableness of the judgment against Our Lord -- for even Pilate admitted he found the Man innocent -- was the mirror of the anarchy of sin.

Sin chose the battleground, set up the gallows of torture, influenced the judges, inflamed the crowds, and decided on the death of Divine Life.

It could have chosen no better way of revealing its nature. It refused to have God on earth, and so it lifted His Cross above the earth.

Sin wanted no shepherding calls to repentance, and so it fastened Him to a tree. "He came unto his own, and his own received him not." They abandoned Him at birth: they would now abandon Him in death. Thus would sin reach its most perfect expression: *for sin is the abandonment of God by man.*

But the Saviour is on the Cross not to go down to defeat, but to redeem from sin. How better can He atone for sin than by taking upon Himself one of its most bitter consequences?

Since sin is the abandonment of God by man, He now wills to feel its consequence: the abandonment of man by God. Such is the meaning of the *Fourth Word* uttered in the moment when darkness crept over Calvary like a leprosy: "My God, my God, why hast thou abandoned Me?"

Man rejected God. Our Lord willed to feel that rejection within Himself. Man turned away from God; He, Who is God united hypostatically with a human nature, now wills to feel that awful wrench, as if He Himself were guilty. It was all deliberate. He was laying His life down of Himself, even when they thought they were taking it away.

He willed to be identified with man, and now He resolves to travel the road to the end and to take upon Himself the terrible loneliness of sin. His pain of abandonment expressed in this *Fourth Word* was double: the abandonment by man and God.

Man abandons Him because He refuses to deny His Divinity; God seemingly abandons Him because He wills to forego divine consolation, to taste the bitter dregs of sin that the cup of sin may be emptied.

As a symbol of that double abandonment by heaven and earth, His cross is suspended between both, and yet uniting them for the first time since Adam abandoned God.

None of us knows the deeper meaning of the cry; no one can know. He alone Who is sinless can know the utter horror of sin which caused it.

But this we do know, that at this moment He permitted Himself to feel the solitariness and abandonment caused by sin. And yet His cry proves that though men do abandon Him, they never completely desert Him, for a man can no more shake off God than he can deny parentage.

That is why His cry of abandonment was prefaced with the cry of belief: "My God, my God!" Into it was concentrated the loneliness of every sinful heart that ever lived.

And yet with it all was the divine nostalgia -- the loneliness of the atheist who says there is no God and yet under starry skies believes in His Power.

So, too, the loneliness of fallen away Catholics, who have left the Church not for reasons but for things and who, like prodigal children, still dream of the happiness of the servants in the Father's house.

So, too, the loneliness of the enemies of religion who testify to its reality by the bitterness of their hate, for no man hates a mirage.

So, too, the loneliness of the pessimists who complain against the evil in the world, but only because they believe more deeply still in the reality of Justice.

So, too, the loneliness of sinners who hate themselves for hating virtue.

So, too, the loneliness of the worldly who live without religion, not because they deny it, but because they are "sore adread lest, having Him, [they] should have nought beside."

All in their own way are saying: "I abandon and yet I believe."

It is just that which makes one wonder if there is really any sinner who has ever gone so far down its dark, damp corridors as to forget that he left the light. The words on the Cross seem to say so much.

Not even those direct descendants of the executioners who pillage churches and crucify Christ's ambassadors have yet proved it, for how can one hate so intensely that which he believes to be only a dream?

If religion is the opium of the people, why, instead of putting men to sleep, does it awaken them to martyrdom? There is no explanation; only the Infinite can be infinitely hated and infinitely loved.

That is why sinners crucified Our Lord, and why the crucifixion made saints. Our Lord is the Infinite God.

It is hard for us to grasp the awfulness of sin, but if we cannot see it in its relation to the death of the all holy One of God, then we are beyond repentance.

The truth is that as long as sin endures, the Crucifixion endures. Clovis, the King of the Franks, on hearing for the first time the story of the Crucifixion said: "If I had been there with my army, this never would have happened." But the fact is, Clovis was there. So was his army. So were we.

The Crucifixion atoned not only for the sins of the past but also for the sins of the future.

"I saw the Son of God go by
Crowned with a crown of thorns.
'Was it not finished , Lord,' said I.
'And all the anguish borne?'

"He turned on me His awful eyes,
'Hast thou not understood?
Lo, every soul is a Calvary
And every sin a rood!' "

(Rachael A. Taylor)

Because our body seems closer to us than our soul, we are apt to think of pain as being a greater evil than sin. But such is not the case: "Fear ye not them that kill the body . . . but rather fear him that can destroy both soul and body in hell."

Thus the reality of sin in the Crucifixion and the idea of Hell became related. The Cross proves that life is fraught with tremendous issues; that sin is so terrible that full payment in justice could be made only by the death of God-made-man.

If sin cost the death of Divine Life, then the refusal to accept Redemption can mean nothing less than eternal death or Hell.

Life then is not a mere experience; it is a drama which involves issues of Eternal Life and Eternal Death. Those who would rob Justice of hell would rob Christ of His Cross.

Were we but animals, our choices would pass away with their fulfillment, but just as our thoughts are fastened to Truth, which is unchangeable, so, too, our resolves are registered on the scroll of Perfect Goodness, which is eternal.

If in our business we take from our cash registers the slip on which is recorded the debits and credits of the day, shall we be so unreasonable as to believe that we, who live by such an order, should ourselves be governed any differently?

Why then at the end of our day's work on earth, should not the Divine Bookkeeper find registered on our consciences our answer to the question of whether our life has been a failure or a success? Either we lose our soul or we find it; either we live or we die.

And if such a fate does not come at the end of our story, then the Cross is a mockery and life is vain. But seeing how high we can rise, and how low we can fall, we can see the importance of our choices -- the danger of being careless and the thrill of being brave.

As one writer has put it, "They are cowards who educate us to think that we are meant to stop at home in swaddling clothes, protected from fresh air and all possible dangers. They would make us soft and effeminate and unfit for the hurly-burly of life. This is no man's life but a tame travesty of it. All that is best in us revolts against coddling and the denial of all risk and adventure. What we need is some summons to the semi-divine courage which is latent in all of us, some challenge to risk all that we have for love. Imagine a man born of woman, ambling along on some old nag or wrapped up in some limousine to conquer the earth and to conquer himself and to make himself fit for the Divine Eros. I am tired of this cheapening of stupendous issues; I demand that Hell be given back to the world." (M. C. D'Arcy, S. J., The Pain of This World, p. 129.)

And if it be not given back to the world, then men will say, no matter how foul we become, all will be well with us in the end.

But as long as Hell remains we have a standard by which evil can be judged, by which those who trample the love of man and God under foot can be measured, by which those who attempt to drive God from the earth He made, can be weighed.

If a man wants to know his worth let him take one look at the Man on the Cross. There Love stands Crucified! If he crucified Love, then he is without Love; and to be without Love is Hell!

If he crucifies his lower self to be Christlike, then he is in love, and to be in love with Love is heaven.

Dear Saviour, open our eyes to see that our forgetfulness of the horror of sin is the beginning of our ruin. Too prone are we to blame finances, economics, and balances of trade for our ills, our woes; too unmindful are we that these are but the symptoms of our rebellion against Thy Divine Law.

Because we have rebelled against Thee, our Creator, creatures have turned against one another, and the world becomes one vast charnel house of hate and envy.

Give us light to see, O Lord, that it was sin which hardened itself into Thy nails, wove itself into Thy thorns, and congealed itself into Thy Cross.

But let us also see that if Thou didst take the Cross for us, then we must be worth saving; for if the Cross is the measure of our sin then the crucifix is the pledge of our redemption, through the same Christ Our Lord. Amen.

The Rainbow of Sorrow, 1938

Sixth Meditation

PRIDE

"My God, My God, why hast thou forsaken me?"

Pride is an inordinate love of one's own excellence, either of body or mind or the unlawful pleasure we derive from thinking we have no superiors. Pride being swollen egoism, it erects the human soul into a separate center of origin apart from God, exaggerates its own importance, and becomes a world in and for itself. All other sins are evil deeds, but pride insinuates itself even unto good works to destroy and slay them. For that reason, Sacred Scriptures says, "Pride goeth before destruction."

Pride manifests itself in many forms: *atheism*, which is a denial of our dependence on God, our Creator and our final end; *intellectual vanity*, which makes minds unteachable because they think they know all there is to know; *superficiality*, which judges others by their clothes, their accent, and their bank account; *snobbery*, which sneers at inferiors as the earmark of its own superiority, "they are not of our set"; *vain-glory*, which prompts some Catholic parents to refuse to send their boys and girls to Catholic colleges, because they would there associate only with the children of carpenters; *presumptuousness*, which inclines a man to seek honors and positions quite beyond his capacity; and *exaggerated sensitiveness*, which makes one incapable of moral improvements because of unwillingness to hear one's own faults.

Pride it was that made Satan fall from Heaven and man fall from grace. By its very nature such undue self-exaltation could be cured only by self-humiliation. That is why He who might have been born in a palace by the Tiber, as befitting His Majesty as the Son of God, chose to appear before men in a stable as a child wrapped in swaddling bands.

Added to this humility of His Birth was the humility of His profession -- a carpenter in an obscure village of Nazareth whose name was a reproach among the great. Just as today there are those who sneer at the humble walks of life, so too, there were then those who sneered: "ls not this the carpenter's son?" There was also the humility of His actions, for never once did He work a miracle in His own behalf not even to supply Himself with a place to lay His head.

Humility of example there was too, when on Holy Thursday night, He who is the Lord of heaven and earth, girds Himself with a towel, gets down on His knees, and with basin and water, washes the twenty-four calloused feet of His Apostles saying: "The servant is not greater than his lord . . . If then I being your Lord and Master have washed your feet; you also ought to wash one another's feet." Finally, there was humility of precept: "Unless you be converted, and become as little children, you shall not enter into the kingdom of heaven."

But the supreme humiliation of all was the manner of death He chose, for "He humbled Himself . . . even to the death of the cross." To atone for false pride of ancestry, He thrusts aside the consolation of Divinity; for pride of popularity, He is laughed to scorn as He hangs cursed upon a tree; for pride of snobbery, He is put in the company of thieves; for pride of wealth, He is denied even the ownership of His own deathbed; for pride of flesh, He was scourged until "there was no beauty in Him"; for pride in influential friends, He is forgotten even by those whom He cured; for pride of power, He is weak and abandoned; for pride of those who surrender God and their Faith, He wills to feel without God.

For all the egotism, false independence, and atheism, He now offers satisfaction by surrendering the joys and consolations of His Divine Nature. Because proud men forgot God, He permits Himself to feel God-lessness and it breaks His heart in the saddest of all cries: "My God, my God, why hast thou forsaken me?" There was union even in the separation; but they were words of desolation uttered that we might never be without consolation.

Two lessons emerge from this Word: 1 -- Glory not in ourselves for God resists the proud; and 2 -- Glory in humility for humility is truth and the path to true greatness. Why should we be proud? As St. Paul reminds us, "Or what hast thou that thou hast not received? And if thou hast received, why dost thou glory, as if thou hadst not received it?" Is it our voice, our wealth, our beauty, our talents of which we are proud? But what are these but gifts of God, anyone of which He might revoke this second?

From a material point of view, we are worth so little. The content of a human body is equivalent to as much iron as there is in a nail, as much sugar as there is in two lumps, as much oil as there is in seven bars of soap, as much phosphorus as there is in 2200 matches, and as much magnesium as it takes to develop one photograph. In all, the human body, chemically, is worth a little less than two dollars -- "O why should the spirit of mortal be proud?"

But *spiritually* we are worth more than the universe: "For what shall it profit a man, if he gains the whole world, and suffer the loss of his soul? Or what shall a man give in exchange for his soul?"

God resists the proud. The Pharisee who praised his own good deeds in the forefront of the Temple is condemned; the poor publican in the rear of the temple, who calls himself a sinner and strikes his breast in a plea for pardon, goes to his house justified. The harlots and the publicans who are conscious of their sin enter the kingdom of Heaven before the Scribes and the Pharisees, who are conscious of their righteousness.

The Heavenly Father is thanked for concealing His Wisdom from the self-wise and the conscious intellectuals and for revealing it to the simple: "I confess to thee, O

Father, Lord of heaven and earth, because thou hast hidden these things from the wise and prudent and hast revealed them to little ones."

Surely anyone who has had experience with the proud will bear witness to the truth of this statement: lf my own eternal salvation were conditioned upon saving the soul of one self-wise man who prided himself on his learning, or one hundred of the most morally corrupt men and women of the streets, I should choose the easier task of converting the hundred. Nothing is more difficult to conquer in all the world than intellectual pride. If battleships could be lined with it instead of with armor, no shell could ever pierce it.

This is easy to understand, for if a man thinks he knows it all, there is nothing left for him to know, not even what God might tell him. If the soul is filled to the brim with the ego, there is no place left for God. If a vessel is filled with water, it cannot also be filled with oil. So it is with the soul.

God can give His Truth and Life only to those who have emptied themselves. We must create a vacuum in our own souls to make room for grace. We live under the impression that we do more than we actually do. Take, for example, the simple fact of drinking liquid through a straw. We erroneously believe that we draw up the liquid through the straw. We do not, for strictly speaking there is no such thing as suction. All that we do is create a vacuum; the atmosphere presses down on the liquid with a weight equal to that of an ocean covering the earth to a depth of thirty-four feet. It is this pressure that pushes the liquid up through the straw when we create the vacuum.

So too in our spiritual lives. The good we accomplish is not through the action of ourselves, as much as it is through the spiritual pressure of God's grace. All we have to do is create a vacuum, to count ourselves as nothing -- and immediately God fills the soul with His Power and Truth.

The paradox of apostolate is, then: the less we think we are, the more good we do. It was only when Peter had labored all night and taken nothing, that Our Lord filled his boat with the miraculous draught of fishes. The higher the building the deeper the foundation; the greater the virtue the more the humility.

God's instruments for good in the world are for that reason only the humble; reducing themselves to zero they leave room for infinity, whereas those who think themselves infinite, God leaves with their little zero.

Even in the world we find a natural basis for humility. As long as we are small, everything else seems big. A boy mounts a broomstick that is no more than four feet long and yet to him it is a Pegasus traveling through space; he can hear the hoofs beating the clouds as he clings to the "whistling mane of every wind." His world is peopled with giants because he is so little; tin soldiers to him are real soldiers fighting real battles and the red of the carpet is the blood of the battlefield.

When he grows to be a big man, the giants shrink in size; the horses become broom-sticks, and the soldiers are painted tin no more than three inches high. In the spiritual order, it is the same; as long as there is a God who is wiser than we, greater than we, more powerful than we, then the world is a house of wonders.

Truth is then something so vast that not even an eternity can sound its depths. Love then is so abiding that not even heaven can dull its ecstasies. Goodness becomes so profound, that thanks must ever be on one's lips.

But just forget God, make yourself a god, and then your little learning is your title to omniscience. Then the saints become for you stupid fools; the martyrs, "fanatics"; the religious, "dumb"; confession, a "priestly invention"; the Eucharist, a "vestige of paganism"; heaven, a "childish fancy"; and truth, a "delusion." It must be wonderful to know so much, but it must be terrible to find out in the end that one really knows so little.

The second lesson to be derived from this Fourth Word from the Cross is that humility is truth. Humility is not an underestimation of our talents or gifts or powers, nor is it their exaggeration. A man who is six feet tall is not humble if he says he is only five feet four inches tall, just as he is not humble if he says he is seven feet tall. Humility is truth, or the recognition of gifts as gifts, faults as faults. Humility is dependence on God as pride is independence of Him.

It was that sense of independence or being without God which wrung out of the heart of Our Lord on the Cross this pitiable cry of abandonment: "My God, my God, why hast thou forsaken me?" The humble soul, conscious of his dependence on God, is always the thankful soul.

How many singers, orators, musicians, actors, doctors, professors ever think of thanking God for the special talents that made them outstanding in their profession? Out of the ten lepers who were made clean only one returned to give thanks. "Were not ten made clean? and where are the nine?" probably represents the proportion of the ungrateful who thank not because they are not humble.

The humble soul will always avoid praising his own good works and thus making void the virtue of his deeds. Self-praise devours merit; and those who have done good things to be seen by men, and who trumpet their philanthropies in the market places, will one day hear the saddest words of tongue or pen: "Thou hast already had thy reward."

The humble man, even though he be great in the eyes of the world, will esteem himself less than others, for he will always suspect that their internal greatness may far overreach his insignificant external greatness. He will therefore not flaunt his accidental superiority before his fellowman, for to do so is to prove one is not truly great. The really big men are the humble men; they are always approachable, kind, and understanding.

It is the little men who must put on airs. The really rich boy need not wear good clothes to impress his friends with his wealth, but the poor boy must do so to create the false impression of wealth. So it is with those who have nothing in their heads; they must be eternally creating the impression of how much they know, the books they have read, and the university from which they graduated.

The learned man never has to "seem" learned, as the saint never has to appear pious -- but the hypocrite does. The fact that so many men take honors seriously, change their voices, and cultivate poses, proves they never should have had the honors -- the honors were too big for them. They could not assimilate the honors; rather the honors assimilated them. Instead of wearing the purple, the purple wears them.

A sponge can absorb so much water and no more; a character can absorb so much praise and no more; the point of saturation is reached when the honor ceases to be a part of him and begins to stick out like a sore thumb. The truly great are like St. Philip Neri who one day, seeing a criminal being led off to prison, said: "There goes Philip Neri, except for the grace of God."

Suppose we began to be humble and esteemed others at least no less than ourselves. Suppose to those who wounded us with their slanderous darts, we answered: "Father, forgive!" Suppose to those who classified us with thieves, we made the best of it and converted them saying: "This day, Paradise." Suppose out of those who shamed us before relatives, as Jesus was shamed before His Mother, we made a new friend for our heavenly Mother: "Behold thy son!" Suppose to those beneath us in worldly dignity we humbled ourselves and asked them for a drink: "I thirst!"

Suppose we began to be truthful, and estimated ourselves at our real worth. If we did these things for but one hour, we would completely revolutionize the world. We are not wanting an example, for we have before our eyes Him who humbled Himself to the death on the Cross, who surrendered Divine consolation as Power put on the rags of weakness and Strength girded itself in abandonment, and, being God, appeared to be without God.

And why did He do this? Because we have been trying to lead our lives without God -- to be independent. By choosing the humiliation of the Cross in reparation for pride He takes us back again to the story of David and Goliath.

Goliath was a great giant clothed in an armor of steel and carrying in his hand a mighty sword. David was the shepherd boy without defensive steel and carrying no other weapon than a staff, and five little stones from a nearby brook. Goliath scorned him, saying: "Am I a dog, that thou comest to me with a staff?" David answered humbly, not trusting in his own power: "I come to thee in the name of the Lord . . ." The outcome we know. The boy with a stone killed the giant with the armor and sword.

The victory of David symbolized the reality of Good Friday. Pride is Goliath. Our Lord is the humble David who comes to slay pride with the staff of His Cross and five little stones -- five wounds, in hands, feet, and side. With no other weapon than these Five Wounds and the staff of the Cross do we gain victories over the Goliath of pride on the battlefield of our soul.

To the worldly they seem ill-fitted for battle, and impotent to conquer, but not if we understand God's plan from the beginning that: " . . . the foolish things of the world hath God chosen, that he may confound the wise; and the weak things of the world hath God chosen that he may confound the strong." It was with a cross and a crowned brow that God won the day. As Oscar Wilde puts it:

O smitten mouth! O forehead crowned with thorn!
O chalice of all common miseries!
Thou for our sakes that loved thee not has borne
An agony of endless centuries,
And we were vain and ignorant nor knew
That when we stabbed thy heart it was our own real hearts we slew.

Being ourselves the sowers and the seeds,
The night that covers and the lights that fade,
The spear that pierces and the side that bleeds,
The lips betraying and the life betrayed;
The deep hath calm: the moon hath rest: but we
Lords of the natural world are yet our own dread enemy.

Nay, nay, we are but crucified, and though
The bloody sweat falls from our brows like rain,
Loosen the nails – we shall come down I know,
Stanch the red wounds – we shall be whole again,
No need have we of hyssop-laden rod,
That which is purely human, that is Godlike, that is God.

(Oscar Wilde)

Victory Over Vice, 1939

Seventh Meditation

FAITH

My God! My God! Why hast thou forsaken me?

How many who profess no formal religion could tell what they disbelieve? The question is put that way because years ago many who did not have faith knew what they disbelieved and why; today those who do not have faith do not even know what they disbelieve. Having abandoned all certitudes, they have no standards by which to judge even their own agnosticism.

And now, with the depression, war and its consequent insecurity, they have begun to doubt their own doubts. The words 'progress' 'evolution' and 'science' which once thrilled them and gave them the illusion of faith, now leave them cold.

Many today feel that their life is discontinuous; that each act of their will is unrelated to any other; that their bad actions of the past, like a spent arrow, are gone and forgotten; that their life because ephemeral is unrelated to any responsibility, and that their last week's self is no longer their worry, nor what they will be next week their moral concern.

Their life is like a Japanese lantern, made up of thousands of designs, but without unity. They may know much, but they cannot put their fields of learning into a unity.

Their knowledge is like the shelves in a drug store, filled with bottles of wisdom one unrelated to another, but not like a living thing in which organs, cells and functions flow into a unity of purpose.

What they need to do is put a candle inside the Japanese lantern of their life: or a soul into their discontinuous chemical existence in order to recover the meaning of life; and that candle and that soul is faith.

Faith is not, as too many believe, an emotional trust; it is *not* a belief that something will happen to you; it is not even a will to believe despite difficulties. Rather faith is the acceptance of a truth on the authority of God revealing. It therefore presupposes reason. What *credit* is to business *that* faith is to religion.

Before extending you credit, the businessman must have a reason for extending that credit, namely, your ability to pay debts and your honesty. So it is with faith. You cannot start religion with faith, for to believe someone without a *reason* for belief is credulity and superstition.

The principal cause for the decline of religion in America is the irrational and groundless character of belief. Unless the foundation is solid the superstructure soon totters and falls. Try out the experiment and ask those who call themselves Christians why they believe and the majority of them will be found unable to give a reason.

When anyone asks us to join the Church he is not immediately accepted. He must first undergo instructions of between forty and one hundred hours extending over several months. Converts are not first told: "You must believe everything the Catholic Church teaches" but rather "You must have a *reason* for believing its teachings." Absolutely nothing is taken for granted. We do not say: "We will start with God." No! We start with the world. Using reason we, first prove the existence of God and His nature.

Enquiry precedes conviction. Enquiry is a matter for reason which weighs the evidence and says: "I ought to believe." But submission is an act of the will. It is at this point many fail, either because too absorbed by the pleasures of the world, or because fearful of the scorn of others.

But once it is admitted, thanks to the illumining grace of God, that Christ is the Son of God; there can be no picking and choosing among the parts of His Gospel.

Since Truth is life, it must like a living babe, be accepted in its entirety. Just as we are not falsely broadminded about life and accept a child on condition he has no arms, or only one eye, so neither can we say we will believe Christ when He talks about lilies of the field and not believe Him when He talks about the sanctity of the family. It is all or nothing. "He that gathereth not . . . scattereth" *(Matthew 12:30).*

That is why the condition of becoming a Catholic is the total, complete and absolute submission to the authority of Christ and its prolongation in the Church. A Catholic may be defined as one who made the startling discovery that God knows more than he does.

Faith is related to reason as a telescope to the eye, which does not destroy vision, but opens new worlds hitherto closed to it. We have the same eyes at night as we have in the day, but we cannot see at night because we lack normally the additional light of the sun.

Let two minds with exactly the same education, one without and the other with faith, look on a piece of unleavened bread in a monstrance. The one sees bread; the other adores the Eucharistic Lord. One sees more than the other because he has a light which the other lacks -- the light of faith.

For some illustrations of the virtue of faith we look in particular to the Fourth Word spoken from the pulpit of the Cross.

For almost three hours Our Lord hung upon the Cross, while the sun wore the crêpe of darkness in mourning for the Light of the World. Men might look on the sad spectacle of a Crucified Lord, but the sun could not endure it, and hid its face.

The Evangelists record the Fourth Word as being spoken when darkness covered the earth, which means that it was as night, not only in nature but in the heart and soul of Jesus. It was a moment of mysterious voluntary surrender of Divine consolation, a second of seeming God-forsakenness.

Man had already abandoned Him. They chose Barabbas to Him; they even begrudged Him enough of their earth to stretch out and die as they lifted Him above it on a tree.

Now God seems to abandon Him, as in the midst of the stygian blackness at high noon He spoke this time in Hebrew, the language of the Prophet and the Psalm. The tones were loud and clear: "Eli, Eli, lamma sabacthani" -- "My God, my God, why hast thou forsaken me?" *(Matthew 27:46).*

During His life some of His disciples left Him and walked with Him no more; only the night before at the Last Supper He said: "Behold, the hour cometh, and it is now come, that you shall be scattered every man to his own, and shall leave me alone . . ." *(John 16:32).*

That hour was upon Him now. He refused to be spared what His adopted brethren must share. He was "made sin" for us by taking upon Himself the condition which sin merited. What did sin merit? Abandonment by God.

Creatures turned against the Creator, the sheep rebelled against the Shepherd, the pilgrims left the fountains of living waters and dug for themselves broken cisterns that could hold no water. He willed to experience that isolation and abandonment. Hence the words: "Why hast thou forsaken me?"

And yet it was not total abandonment for it was prefaced by God: "My God, my God!" The sun does not abandon its task to light a world because temporarily overshadowed by a cloud. Because these misty shapes hide its light and heat, we still know a day of dawning is near.

Furthermore, the Fourth Word was a verse from a Psalm of faith which ends: "He hath not slighted nor despised the supplication of the poor man. Neither hath he turned away his face from me: and when I cried to him, he heard me" *(Psalm 21:25).*

In the perspective of this Word of Faith there are these three practical conclusions:

1) The object of faith is *God,* not the things of earth. Too many interpret faith as that which should release us from the ills of earth and assume that if we do suffer it is because we lack faith. This is quite untrue. Faith in God is no assurance that we will be spared the "arrows of outrageous fortune."

He was not. Why should we? It was His enemies who thought that if He were one with God, He should not suffer, for when He said: "Eli, Eli" they, imagining He called for Elias, sneered: "See whether Elias will come to deliver him" *(Matthew 27:49).* Because He was not delivered they concluded He must be wicked. No! Faith does not mean being taken *down* from a cross; it means be *lifted* up to heaven -- sometimes by a cross.

The only times some people think of God is when they are in trouble, or when their pocketbook is empty, or they have a chance to make it a little fatter. They flatter themselves that at such moments they have faith, when really they have only earthly hope for good luck.

It cannot be repeated too often: faith bears on the soul and its salvation in God, not on the baubles of earth.

2) Scripture states that when they crucified Christ, darkness covered the earth. That is exactly the description of our modern world. If the darkness of despair, the black-outs of peace make our world wander blindly, it is because we have crucified the Light of the World.

Witness within the last twenty years how religion has been nailed to the Cross in Russia, scourged in Germany, crowned with thorns in Spain, martyred in Poland and lashed in Mexico.

No wonder our statesmen know not which way to turn: they are either putting out or permitting to be put out the only Light which illumines the pathways of justice and peace.

It may be that our woes are the last stage of sin. For a century or more governments and people have abandoned God; now God is abandoning them. It is a terrible punishment when a just God strikes; but it is more terrible when He does not, but leaves us alone to our own devices to work out the full consequences of our sins.

We are at the end of a tradition and a civilization which believes we could preserve Christianity without Christ: religion without a creed, meditation without sacrifice, family life without moral responsibility, sex without purity, and economics without ethics.

We have completed our experiment of living without God and have proven the fallacy of a system of education which calls itself progressive because it finds new excuses for sins.

Our so-called progressiveness did we but realize it, is like unto the progressive putrefaction of a corpse. The soul is gone, and what we call change is only decay.

There is no stopping it except by reversing the process by which we drove God out of the world, namely by relighting the lamp of faith in the souls of men.

3) Here is a common burden of all believers in God. There is unfortunately a far greater unity among the enemies of God than among His friends. On the one hand, we have the spectacle of Hitler and Stalin burying their mutual hatreds because they found a greater hatred -- God and religion.

On the other hand, what are we believers in God doing to preserve religion, morality and culture? Too often we wage a civil war, attacking one another, while a common enemy storms our altars. This does not mean we must abandon creeds, and water down the milk of religion to a point where it would no longer nourish.

The Catholic Church for one would never do that, because since its truths are God-made they cannot be man-unmade. We are trustees not creators of faith.

But we do recognize that with Protestants and Jews we have God, morality and religion in common. In the name of God, let us, Jews, Protestants and Catholics, do two things: 1) Realize that an attack upon one is an attack upon all, since we are all one in God; it is not Tolerance we need, but Charity; not forbearance but love.

2) Begin doing something about religion, and the least we can do is to say our prayers: to implore God's blessings upon the world and our country; to thank Him for His blessings; and to become illumined in the fullness of His truth. There is entirely too much talk about religion and not enough action.

If we followed the same rules for health that we do about religion, we would all be bedridden. It is not enough to talk about the necessity of health; we must do something practical about it, for example, eat, exercise and rest.

So it is with religion. We must nourish ourselves with the truths of God, exercise our spiritual muscles in prayer, mortify ourselves of those things which are harmful to the soul, and be just as scrupulous in avoiding moral evil as we are in avoiding physical evil.

Faith being a virtue is a habit, -- not an acquired habit like swimming, but an infused habit given to us by God in Baptism. Being a habit it grows by practice.

The ideal is to reach a point in practice, where, like unto Our Lord on the Cross, we witness to God even amidst abandonment and the agony of a crucifixion.

The Seven Virtues, 1940

Eighth Meditation

A WORD TO THE INTELLIGENTSIA

Every age has its intelligentsia, and by the intelligentsia is here meant not the educated, but those who have been educated beyond their intelligence. A sponge can hold so much water; a person can hold so much education. When the point of saturation is reached in either, the sponge becomes a drip, and the person a bore.

All intelligentsia are proud because of the alleged superiority which their learning gives them. Their judgment of others is based on what they know rather than by conscience.

Religion, they judge by their own standards, and, whenever they write on the subject, their articles are entitled: "My idea of religion." Never do they seek to know God's idea of religion. Their own preconceived prejudices constitute the norm of judgment.

In the 17th century, the intelligentsia believed that any religion was acceptable which satisfied *individual* ideas of interpretation; in the 18th century, the intelligentsia believed that any religion was acceptable on condition it agreed with rational principles of their own making; in the 19th century, they believed any religion was good if it corresponded with their views on politics.

They claim that no educated person can believe in religion, for religion belongs in the same category as folklore, superstition, primitive taboos, and phobias. In the face of real learning, they talk comparative religion; in the face of simple faith, they mock and sneer. Voltaire always believed mockery was the best tool to destroy the infamy of Christianity.

The hall mark of culture is, to the intelligentsia, to be irreligious or anti-religious. They once doubted the existence of God, but nothing else; now they doubt not only themselves but the worthwhileness of humanity.

What impact does the Cross of Christ make upon them? One needs only to go to their intellectual progenitors to study their reaction.

The Fourth Word addressed to the Cross came from the intelligentsia of the time -- the Chief Priests, Scribes and Pharisees: "He saved others; himself he cannot save. If he be the king of Israel, let him now come down from the cross, and we will believe him. He trusted in God; let him now deliver him if he will have him; for he said: I am the Son of God" *(Matthew 27:42-43).*

The intelligentsia always know enough about religion to distort it, hence they took each of the three Titles which Christ had claimed for Himself, "Saviour," "King of Israel," and "Son of God," and turned them into ridicule.

"*Saviour*": So he was called by the Samaritans. Now they would admit He had saved others -- probably the daughter of Jairus, and the son of the widow of Naim, and Lazarus. They could afford to admit it now, for the Saviour Himself stood in need of salvation. "Others He saved, Himself He cannot save." The conclusive miracle to them was still lacking.

Poor fools! Of course He cannot save Himself. The rain cannot save itself if it is to bud the greenery. The sun cannot save itself, if it is to light a world; the soldier cannot save himself, if he is to save his country. And Christ cannot save Himself, if He is to save His creatures.

"*King of Israel*": That title the crowd gave Him after He fed the multitude, and fled into the mountains alone. They repeated it again on Palm Sunday when they strewed branches beneath His feet. Now that title was mocked as they sneer: "If He is King of Israel, let Him come down from the Cross."

Must all the Kings of earth be seated on golden thrones? Suppose Israel's King decided to rule from a cross, to be King not of their bodies through power, but of their hearts through love? Their own literature was full of the idea of a King Who would come to glory through humiliation.

How foolish then to mock a King because He refuses to come down from His throne. And if He did come down, they would be the first to say, as they did before that, He did it through the power of Beelzebub.

"Son of God," "He trusted in God," "Let God deliver Him if He wants Him, for He said: 'I am the Son of God' ": Irreligious forces have their holiday in moments of great catastrophe. In war time, they ask: "Where is Thy God now?" Why is it that in time of trouble, God is always put on trial and not man? Why in war, should the judge and the culprit change places as man asks: "Why does not God stop the war?"

Our Lord was robbed of the privilege of *acting* freely, when they fettered Him with ropes and riveted Him with steel. He was robbed of the privilege of *speaking* freely, when the soldier with a mailed fist in the court of Caiphas struck Him a blow on the cheek. He is now robbed of the privilege of *thinking* freely, as the intelligentsia laugh Him to scorn.

There is something of the mockery of hell in their sinister, diabolical language. Mockery is the greeting of hell, for having turned against God, souls in hell turn against one another, as man becomes a wolf to man.

A man literally consumes every other man; one lost soul preys fiendishly on the soul of his neighbor. The one who is nearest is always the one who is farthest away. It is the law of hell, that one hates his neighbor.

As criminals when caught in the net of justice turn against one another, so those who stumble into the realm of eternal darkness, gloat over the misery of every other soul in the region of death.

Thus did Christ hear Himself mocked! They do not know that they are already lost. They think He is. Therefore they, the really damned, mock one whom they believe is damned. Hell was triumphing in the human! Truly this was the hour of the power of the devils of hell.

To all the good on earth who have been mocked because of their faith in God -- you are not without an example. The sneer you receive in the office because out of love for this Good Friday Passion of your Saviour, you abstain from meat on Friday; the turned up lips and the barbed laughter you suffer because you pray, or because of your loyalty to the Church; the ridicule of your fellow soldiers as you kneel at your cot in the barracks and pray -- all these are but echoes of the taunts your Lord received on Calvary.

But do not come down from your cross! "Be glad and rejoice, for your reward is very great in heaven" *(Matthew 5:12).* "If we suffer we shall also reign with Him. If we deny Him, He will also deny us" *(2Timothy 2:12).*

Why does not He Who is the morning star, put out the darkness of this hour? Because this is a moment when He wills to make atonement for the sins of men. The essence of sin is twofold: it involves a turning *from* God, and a turning *to* creatures.

He Who is without sin, now wills to feel the two effects of sin. Because sin involves turning to creatures, He suffers *at the hand of men*: because sin involves a turning from God, He permits Himself to feel that Divine abandonment, as in the midst of rasping mockery He cries with a loud voice: "My God! My God! Why hast Thou Abandoned Me?"

This is His answer to the intelligentsia. Let them take their thought off learning for the moment and concentrate on conscience and its sin. Sin is separation from God! Sin is supreme loneliness! Sin separates man from God, man from man.

This disruptive power of sin which is permanent in hell, He now allows to devastate His inmost soul that He might suffer what we deserve for our sins.

That is why He left the mockery of hell unanswered, and the scorn of the intelligentsia unchallenged. The Scriptures say: "God will not be mocked." God will be mocked in the beginning! Not in the end!

That fellowship between God and man which was broken by sin, He now wills to feel as His own as His cry reveals that the essence of sin is not a mission, but a dismissal. This is what sin deserves: mockery from men, rejection by God. Such is the worm and fire of hell.

Think not that the cry of abandonment meant that He Who takes upon Himself the sins of the world, is not the Son of God. God could not be abandoned by God.

But God in the form of man could be abandoned, for in the strong language of St. Paul: "Christ hath redeemed us from the curse of the law, being made a curse for us: for it is written: Cursed is everyone that hangeth on a tree" *(Galatians 3:13).* The very words he quoted were taken from a Psalm written thousands of years before prophesying the very mockeries now hurled against the Cross!

The Son of David was quoting the songs of David. He Who is the Son of God was stirring the waters of the Son of Man with His own Spirit. The word made flesh was having recourse to His own words. The poet was reciting His own poetry.

It was the poetry of Redemption. The courts of justice, the mobs, the unrepentant, the intelligentsia had now done all they could to break Him down, by throwing back all His Love in His Face, but that Great Royal Love remains unbroken. For in the very dark moment when He felt the isolation and abandonment which sin merited, He in His human nature calls on God.

The way back to God for the intelligentsia is here indicated from Man's side and from God's.

From Man's Side

On man's side, that cry "My God" is the antithesis of the pride of the intelligentsia. It is a cry of humility and primordial obedience. Having arrived at the lowest depths of loneliness, man still asks for the right of being human. It is the confession of a duty-bound child; a prayer so subservient that man continues to seek God even in the darkness of abandonment.

Here Christ, taking on man's sin, asks God to deal justly with a creature predestined to be a child, and to open the door to the prodigal again. Sinful man is knocking! Adam hid after his sin. God asked: "Where art thou?" Now, the new Adam lays hold of Adam's loneliness of soul and asks God: "Where art Thou?"

This is the foundation of religion and the way of salvation to all the intelligentsia, viz.: by becoming obedient; by making a total surrender to God; by acknowledging creaturehood; by pleading for restored fellowship.

A man can thus feel the pains of hell, mockery and loneliness and still ask God why he is not acceptable in heaven. Nor in His word is there unbelief in misery or in the midst of the penalties of sin; never "is there a God" or even "God," but "My God, My God."

By laying oneself bare as the needy child, who cannot live in the loneliness of sin, man can still prove he takes no delight except in God: "For what have I in heaven? and besides Thee what do I desire upon earth?" *(Psalm 72:25).* That cry was the hope of man. It was the denial of the chaotic amidst chaos! We too can take our "Whys" to God!

Then follows the beautifully haunting realization that it really was not God who abandoned us; it was we who abandoned God. Adam hid from God after his sin -- so does man. God never really abandons man! Christ in His human nature was never separated from His Divine nature.

Because man is made for God, he feels sin as abandonment. It would be like a man who refused to eat saying: "O Food, why hast thou abandoned me?" Or parched lips of a man walking from a spring saying to the spring: "Water, why hast thou abandoned me?" As the stomach needs food, as parched lips need water, and the mind needs truth, so man needs God. We refuse to drink and then wonder why we are thirsty; we refuse to love God and wonder why we are unhappy.

From God's Side

If the way back to God on man's side is by the acknowledgment of creaturehood, from God's side the reconciliation is effected through love. Creatures run out of love when over-betrayed and mocked! They touch bottom and say: "I wash my hands of him."

But here Divine Love refuses to leave the sinner even in sin. We have no expression for the opposite of "washing our hands of a person" except "the Lord hath laid on Him the iniquity of us all" *(Isaiah 53:6).*

To bear sin meant to go on loving even in the midst of a crucifixion.

I can go on sinning despite His love, for I am free. But at the same time, when I see Christ still loving me even when I crucify Him; when I see Him still praying to God for me, even when I abandon Him, and never losing faith in me though I lose faith in Him, *by that very fact* I am made penitent, for how can I go on sinning in the face of love like that?

I may not be at the end of my journey, but I am at the end of my rebellion. I now see the nature of sin and cry: "Why am I abandoned?" I see the nature of God and cry: "My God, My God."

A child sins seriously. A mother suffers because of that sin, and the suffering varies in direct relationship to her love and the gravity of the sin. Because the mother loves the child, she cannot let the child suffer the effects of the sin alone. She enters into it and shares it. If the child sees the mother suffering, it will be drawn to penitence. Then the mother can forgive.

Christ so loved us that He took our sins upon Himself as if He were guilty, and draws us freely to repentance by the price He paid to save us. Hence forgiveness is no glib thing! The Cross was the supreme expression of the righteousness of God!

If the redemption of man were done without cost, it would insult us, for no man with a sense of justice wants to be "let off." It would insult God, for the whole moral order founded on justice would be impugned. The Cross is the eternal proof that no sin is forgiven through indifference.

God safeguards His justice even the very moment He forgives: "All we, like sheep, have gone astray, every one hath turned aside into his own way: and the Lord hath laid on him the iniquity of us all"*(Isaiah 53:6).* "Him, who knew no sin, he hath made sin for us, that we might be made the justice of God in him" *(2Corinthians 5:21).*

From the side of man and God therefore we come into relationship with God primarily as disobedient sons returning to a Holy and loving Father.

Intelligentsia! You are the most difficult class in the world to bring to God, not because you are wise, for no one is wise unless he has discovered truth.

To the self-wise who rejected Truth, Our Lord said: "the publicans and the harlots shall go into the kingdom of heaven before you" *(Matthew 21:31).*

Could it be possible that Paul was right in telling the intelligentsia of Corinth that the wisdom of the world is foolishness with God? Is character in the intellect alone, as you believe, or in the will which clings to God even in darkness as this world reveals?

Are all the intelligentsia happy? Are all the uneducated unhappy? Are you right in thinking that so long as a man is intellectually honest, his private morality is of no concern?

May it not be that the modern hatred of religion is to a great extent determined by the way men live? Do not men in the end delude themselves by making a creed fit the way they live, rather than making the way they live fit a creed? Is not mockery of religion but a vain attempt to ignore?

Why is it the intelligentsia are more interested in destroying faith in others than in giving others their own incertitude? You have told others that to believe in God is foolishness, but what wisdom did you give as a substitute? Why do you never think of making others better, but only "wiser" according to your own judgment?

A few years ago I instructed a young man in one of the large colleges of the East, which college incidentally was founded to teach religion. His classmates ridiculed him by buying rosaries and swinging them before his eyes as they passed him on the Campus. Why must the intelligentsia mock? Does learning really bring understanding?

Take an hour off tonight and meditate on the answer of Our Lord to the intelligentsia of His time. For all their mocking there was an answer -- the total, complete surrender to God -- the smiting of pride into nothingness. "And every height that exalteth itself against the knowledge of God, and bringing into captivity every understanding unto the obedience of Christ" *(2Corinthians 10:5)*. As you examine your conscience, ask yourselves:

Are you your own creator? Do you owe what is deepest in you to no other? Have you any more right than a rose to say there is no life beyond you? Is the freedom of your soul self-originating? Have you never done anything wrong in your life, and do you feel no need of atoning for it?

Did not Our Lord say: "Amen I say to you, unless you be converted and become as little children, you shall not enter into the kingdom of heaven" *(Matthew 18:3)*. By this He meant that you must put on a new mind: He does not ask you to be childish; He asks us to be childlike, i.e., to be docile, to be teachable.

When therefore, in the darkness, your soul feels disquieted and your conscience haunts you, think not that this is due to psychological explosions from an unconscious mind; it is rather the call of God.

As you lie awake at night and ponder over your sins, for the darkness brings out your own darkness; as you mourn the loss of relatives or friends and for the moment ponder on the problem of death; as you feel stirred by the purity, sacrifice and faith of others, even when you ridicule; as you try to throw off a thousand qualms of conscience a day -- ask yourself what these promptings really are!

They are actual graces: Divine solicitations, beckoning calls of the Shepherd to lost sheep.

Frustrate them not by introducing speculative questions, as did the woman at the well, when the root of your discontent is in your morals, not in your mind.

If you have been away from the Sacraments twenty years or more, cease justifying your rebellion against God by saying you no longer believe in the Sacrament of Penance. Your quasi-intellectual opposition is a camouflage for your moral cowardice. You are afraid to face your sins; so you attack the creed.

Get down on your knees! Humble yourselves before your God, for He heareth you before you call on Him. He knows your loneliness; He felt it on the Cross. He knows your needs; He bought them on Calvary.

Think not that Love has passed you by; it is only the bowl of human affection you drank dry -- not the chalice of salvation.

The Eternal still pleads, He refuses to destroy your freedom: "Come to Me all ye who labor and are heavily burdened." A humbled and contrite heart the Master will not despise, and from it may you pray in the language of the ancient prayer:

"Lord, make me an instrument of Thy peace; where there is hatred, let me sow love; where there is injury, pardon; where there is doubt, faith; where there is despair, hope; where there is darkness, light: and where there is sadness, joy."

"O Divine Master, grant that I may not so much seek to be consoled as to console; to be understood, as to understand; to be loved, as to love; for it is in giving that we receive, it is in pardoning that we are pardoned, and it is in dying that we are born to eternal life."

Seven Words to the Cross, 1944

Ninth Meditation

CONFIDENCE IN VICTORY

Perhaps at no time in modern history was there ever such a flight from life as at the present day. In much modern literature this is manifested either by a return to the primitive through sex, or through the subconscious.

In daily life, too, there is the flight from consciousness through alcoholism, or the flight from decision through indifference, or the flight from freedom by the denial of responsibility. All these are symptoms of despair. Many people as a result are cracking up, emotionally, mentally, and morally. Our problem is not to diagnose the malady, but to heal it.

Is there another way out, even in these dark days? For an answer one must go back to the darkest day the world ever saw, the day when the sun hid its face at noon, as if ashamed to shed its light on the crime men committed at Calvary. It recalled the dark moment of the Old Law when the High Priest, clothed not in gorgeous golden robes, but in simple white, entered into the darkness of the Holy of Holies, to sprinkle it with blood in atonement for the sins of the people. The people could not see him, nor could they hear him. They only knew that his being there was a matter of supreme importance, for not until he emerged might they feel that the weight of their sins had been lifted.

One day that symbol became a reality as darkness spread over the earth, blurring three crosses silhouetted against a black horizon. The True High Priest, clothed in Innocence entered into that place where God had hidden Himself because of man's sins, to sprinkle the Holy of Holies with His own Blood in reparation for the sins of men. We see nothing; there is only an awful silence, a thick gloom, relieved by one cry, sent up from a broken heart of self-abasement: "My God, My God, Why hast thou forsaken me?" *(Mark 15:34).*

These words were the first words of the prophetic Psalm 21, written 1000 years before this black day. Though the Psalm begins with sadness, it ends with joy, victory, and the assurance of spiritual sovereignty over the earth.

First, there is sorrow:

"O God, my God, look upon me: Why hast thou forsaken me?

"But I am a worm and no man: the reproach of men and the outcast of the people.

"All they that saw me have laughed me to scorn: they have spoken with the lips and wagged the head.

"He hoped in the Lord, let him deliver him: let him save him, seeing he delighted in him.

"They have dug my hands and feet. They have numbered all my bones.

"And they have looked and stared upon me. They parted my garments amongst them: and upon my vesture they cast lots.

Then comes the promise of victory:

"Ye that fear the Lord, praise him: all ye the seed of Jacob, glorify him.

"Let all the seed of Israel fear him: because he hath not slighted nor despised the supplication of the poor man.

"Neither hath he turned away his face from me: and when I cried to him he heard me.

"The poor shall eat and shall be filled: and they shall praise the Lord that seek him: their hearts shall live for ever and ever.

"All the ends of the earth shall remember, and shall be converted to the Lord: And all the kindreds of the Gentiles shall adore in his sight.

"For the kingdom is the Lord's; and he shall have dominion over the nations." *(Psalm 21:1-29)*

Mary standing at the foot of the Cross, knew her scriptures well. When she heard Our Lord begin Psalm 21, it reminded her of a song that she sang too. It was her fourth Word which she chanted in the home of Elizabeth, the greatest song ever written, "The Magnificat": "My soul doth magnify my Lord." It contains very much the same sentiments of Psalm 21, namely, the assurance of victory.

And Mary said: "My soul doth magnify the Lord. And my spirit hath rejoiced in God my Saviour. Because he hath regarded the humility of his handmaid: for behold from henceforth all generations shall call me blessed. Because he that is mighty hath done great things to me: and holy is his name. And his mercy is from generation unto generations, to them that fear him. He hath showed might in his arm: he hath scattered the proud in the conceit of their heart. He hath put down the mighty from their seat and hath exalted the humble. He hath filled the hungry with good things: and the rich he hath sent empty away. He hath received Israel his servant, being mindful of his mercy. As he spoke to our fathers: to Abraham and to his seed forever" *(Luke 1:46-55).*

There is something common to both these songs: both were spoken before there was any assurance of victory. In His fourth word from the Cross, the suffering figure looks forward through the darkness to the triumph of the Resurrection, and His spiritual dominion over the earth. In her fourth Word, the Woman, nine months before her child is born, looks down the long procession of the coming ages, and proclaims that when the world's great women like Livia, Julia, and Octavia shall have been forgotten, the ordinary law of human oblivion will be suspended in her favor, because she is the Mother of Him Whose Name is Holy, and Whose Cross is the Redemption of men.

How hopeless from a human point of view was the prospect of a Man of the Cross crying to God in darkness, ever exercising dominion over the earth that rejected Him! How hopeless from a human point of view was the prospect of an insignificant village maiden begetting a Son Who would be the Supreme Revolutionist of the centuries, exalting the poor to the family of the Godhead!

Both were really words of triumph, one of Victory before the battle was over, one of Overlordship before the Lord was born. To both Jesus and Mary, there were treasures in darkness, whether the darkness be on a black hill or in a dark womb.

Are you in the valley of despair? Then learn that the Gospel of Christ can be heard as Good News even by those whose life has been shattered by Bad News, for only those who walk in darkness ever see the stars.

All trusting implies something you cannot see. If you could see, there would be no occasion for trust. When you say you trust a man only insofar as you can see him, you do not trust him at all. Now to trust God means to hold fast to the truth that His purposes are good and holy, not because you see them, but in spite of appearances to the contrary.

The reason, therefore, why some souls emerge purified from catastrophe while other souls come out worse, is because the first had One in Whom they could trust and the second had none but themselves. The atheist therefore, is properly defined as the person who has no invisible means of support.

Have you ever noticed, as you talk to your fellowmen, the difference in the reaction to crisis on the part of those who have faith in God and His purposes and of those who have not? The man without faith was generally greatly surprised at the dark turn of events with two world wars in twenty-one years, the resurgence of barbarism and the abandonment of moral principles. But the man with faith in God was not so surprised. The sum came out just as he had expected; chaos was in the cards though they had not yet been dealt, for he knew that "unless the Lord build the house, they labor in vain that build it" *(Psalm 126:1)*.

Have you also observed that the person without faith finding his world of "progress" becoming so unprogressive, often reacted by blaming religion, by criticizing the Church, and even by blaspheming God for not stopping the war? Such egotists have some sense of justice, and since they refuse to blame themselves, then they must find a scapegoat.

But the man with faith, in the midst of taunts like that which came from the haughty monarch, "Who is the God that shall deliver you out of my hand" *(Daniel 3:15)*, answers as did the three youths in the fiery furnace: "For behold our God, whom we worship, is able to save us from the furnace of burning fire and to deliver us out of thy hands, O king. But if he will not, be it known to thee, O king, that we will not worship thy gods nor adore the golden statue which thou hast set up" *(Daniel 3:17-18)*. "Although he should kill me, I will trust in him" *(Job 13:15)*.

To bring out this difference between those who can call on God in darkness and those who do not, let us set in contrast a typical modern without faith, and a saint. As an example of the first take H. G. Wells who, for decades, hoped that "man with his feet on earth would one day have hands reaching among the stars."

When darkness fell over the earth in these last few years, he turned to pessimism. "There is no reason whatever to believe that the order of nature has any greater bias in favor of man than it had in favor of the ichthyosaur. In spite of all my disposition to a brave looking optimism, I perceive that now the universe is bored with him, is turning a hard face to him, and I see him being carried less and less intelligently, and more and more rapidly . . . along the stream of fate to degradation, suffering, and death."

Now hear St. Paul, who already had been persecuted, and who knew that the tyrant who held the sword would one day draw it across his neck:

"We are reviled: and we bless. We are persecuted: and we suffer it.

"We are blasphemed: and we entreat. We are made as the refuse of this world". *(1Corinthians 4:12-13).*

"Who then shall separate us from the love of Christ? Shall tribulation? Or distress? Or famine? Or nakedness? Or danger? Or persecution? Or the sword?

"For I am sure that neither death, nor life, nor Angels, nor principalities, nor powers, nor things present, nor things to come, nor might.

"Nor height, nor depth, nor any other creature, shall be able to separate us from the love of God which is in Christ Jesus our Lord *(Romans 8:35,38-39).*"

Take another comparison in time of trouble. Hear Bertrand Russell, a typical modern without faith in God. What is his hope for man?

"Man's origin, his growth, his hopes, fears, his loves, and beliefs, are but the outcome of accidental collocation of atoms. That no fire, no heroism, no intensity of thought and feeling, can preserve the individual beyond the grave; that all the labor of the ages, all devotion, all the inspiration, all the noonday brightness of human genius are destined to extinction, and that the whole temple of Man's achievement must be buried beneath the debris of a universe in ruins. Only on the firm foundation of unyielding despair can the soul's habitation be safely built."

Now turn to St. Augustine who lived in a world of despair when the Roman Empire that had survived for centuries fell, even as Satan fell from heaven, to the barbarians from the North.

"God, Who is not the Author of evil, but Who allowest it to exist in order to prevent greater evil.

"God Who art loved, knowingly or unknowingly, by everything that is capable of loving.

"God, in Whom all things are, yet Who receivest from the ignominy of creatures, no ignominy, from their malice, no malice, from their errors, no errors.

"God, from Whom to turn is to fall, towards Whom to turn, is to rise again, in Whom to dwell, is to find firm support; from Whom to depart is to die, to return to Whom, is to be restored to life, to dwell in Whom, is to live.

"God, Whom to forsake is the same as to perish, Whom to search for is the same as to love, Whom to see is the same as to possess.

"God, towards Whom faith urges, hope raises us, charity unites us. God, through Whom we triumph over our enemy.

"Thee I invoke.

"To Thee I address my prayers."

You see the difference! Now choose! Will you slip down into abysmal despair, or will you, like Christ in a blackness at high noon, and like Mary ere her Tree of Life had seen the earth, trust in God, His Mercy and His Victory?

If you are unhappy, or sad, or despondent, it is basically for only one reason: you have refused to respond to Love's plea: "Come to me, all you that labor and are burdened, and I will refresh you. Take up my yoke upon you and learn of me, because I am meek, and humble of heart: and you shall find rest to your souls" *(Matthew 11:28-29).* Everywhere else but in Him, the liberation promised is either armed or forced, and that can mean slavery. Only *nailed* love is free. Unnailed and uncrucified love can compel. Hands pinioned to a wooden beam cannot compel, nor can a lifted Host and an elevated Chalice constrain, but they can beckon and solicit.

That kind of love gives you these three suggestions for living in troubled times:

1) Never forget that there are only two philosophies to rule your life: the one of the Cross, which starts with the fast and ends with the feast. The other of Satan, which starts with the feast and ends with the headache. Unless there is the Cross, there will never be the empty tomb; unless there is faith in darkness, there will never be vision in light; unless there is a Good Friday, there will never be an Easter Sunday. In the beautiful assurance of our Lord: "Amen, amen, I say to you, that you shall lament and weep, but the world shall rejoice: and you shall be made sorrowful, but your sorrow shall be turned into joy " *(John 16:20).*

2) When bereavement comes, and when the "slings and arrows of outrageous fortune" strike, when like Simon of Cyrene a cross is laid on your reluctant shoulders, take that Cross to daily Mass and say to our Lord at the moment of consecration: "As Thou my Saviour in love for me dost say: 'This is My Body! This is My Blood!' so I say to Thee: 'This is my body! Take it. This is my blood! Take it. They are yours. I

care not if the accidents or species of my life remain, with my daily work, my routine duties. But all that I am substantially, take, consecrate, ennoble, spiritualize; turn my cross into a Crucifix, so that I am no longer mine, but Thine, O Love Divine!'"

3) Think not of Almighty God as a kind of absentee landlord with whom you hardly dare to be familiar, or to whom you go to fix your leaks, or to get yourself out of a mess. Think neither of God as an insurance agent, who can protect you against loss by fire. Approach Him not timidly as a stenographer might approach the boss for a raise, fearful, half believing that you will never receive what you seek. Do not fear Him with a servile fear, for God is more patient with you than you are with yourself. Would you, for example, be as patient with the wicked world today as He is? Would you even be as patient with anyone else who had the same faults as you? Rather, approach Him in full confidence and even with the boldness of a loving child who has a right to ask a Father for favors.

Though He may not grant all your wants, be sure that, in a certain sense, there is no unanswered prayer. A child asks his father for something that may not be good for him, e.g. a gun. The father, while refusing, will pick up the child in his arms to console him, giving the response of love, even in the denial of a request. As the child forgets in that embrace that he ever asked a favor, so in praying, you forget what you wanted by receiving what you needed -- a return of love. Do not forget either that there are not two kinds of answers to prayer, but three: One is "Yes." Another is "No." The third is "Wait."

You will find that, as you pray, the nature of your requests will change. You will ask less and less things for yourself and more and more for His love. Is it not true in human relationships that the more you love someone, the more you seek to give and the less you desire to receive? The deepest love never says: "Give me," but it does say: "Make me." You probably think that if Our Lord came into your room some night as you are praying, you would ask Him favors, or present your difficulties, or say: "When will the war end?" or "Should I buy General Motors stock? " or "Give me a million."

No! You would throw yourself on your knees and kiss the hem of His garment. And the moment He laid His hands on your head, you would feel such a peace and trust and confidence -- even in darkness -- that you would not even remember you had questions to ask, or favors to beg. You would consider them a kind of desecration. You would want only to look into His face, and you would be in a world which only lovers know. That would be the only Heaven you wanted!

Seven Words of Jesus and Mary, 1945

I THIRST
Meditations on the Fifth Word from the Cross
Archbishop Fulton J. Sheen

First Meditation

I THIRST

This is the shortest of the seven cries. Although it stands in our language as two words, in the original it is one. At the moment when Our Saviour resumes His sermon, it is not a curse upon those who crucify Him, not a word of reproach to the timid disciples at the border of the crowd, not a cry of scorn to the Roman soldiers, not a word of hope to Magdalen, not a word of love to John, not a word of farewell to His own mother. It is not even to God at this moment! Out from the depths of the Sacred Heart there wells through parched lips one awful word: "I thirst!"

He, the God-Man, who threw the stars in their orbits and spheres into space, who "swung the earth a trinket at his wrist," from Whose finger-tips tumbled planets and worlds, who might have said, "The sea is Mine and with it the streams in a thousand valleys and the cataracts in a thousand hills," now asks man -- man, a piece of His own handiwork -- to help Him. He asks man for a drink! Not a drink of earthly water, that is not what He meant, but a drink of love. "I thirst" -- for love!

The last word was a revelation of the sufferings of a man without God; this word was a revelation of the sufferings of God without man. The Creator cannot live without the creature, the Shepherd without the sheep, the thirst of Christ's love without the soul-water of Christians.

But what has He done to be entitled to my love? How much has God loved me? Oh, if I would know how much God has loved me, then let me sound the depths of meaning of that word "love," a word so often used and so little understood. Love, first of all, means to give and God has given His power to nothingness, His light to darkness, His order to chaos, and this is Creation. Love means to tell secrets to the one loved, and God has told in the Scriptures the secrets of His Nature and His high hopes for fallen humanity, and this is Revelation. Love means also to suffer for the one loved, that is why we speak of arrows and darts of love -- something that wounds -- and God is now suffering for us on the Tree of the Cross, for "greater love than this no man hath, than to lay down his life for his friend." Love means also to become one with the one loved, not only in the unity of flesh but in the unity of spirit, and God has so loved us as to institute the Eucharist, that we may abide in Him and He in us in the ineffable unity of the Bread of Life. Love wishes also to be eternally united with the one loved, and God has so loved us that He has promised us His Father's mansions, where a peace and a joy reign which the world cannot give and time cannot take away, and this is Heaven.

Certainly, love has exhausted itself. There is nothing more that Christ could do for His vineyard than He has done. Having poured forth all the waters of His everlasting Love on our poor parched hearts, it is no wonder that He thirsts for love. If love is reciprocal, then certainly He has a right to our love. Why do we not respond? Why do we let the Divine Heart die of thirst for human hearts? With what justice He might complain:

> Lo, all things fly thee, for thou fliest Me!
> Strange, piteous, futile thing!
> Wherefore should any set they love apart?
> Seeing none but I makes much of naught (He said),
> And human love needs human meriting:
> How hast thou merited –
> Of all man's clotted clay the dingiest clot?
> Alack, thou knowest not
> How little worthy of any love thou art!
> Whom wilt thou find to love ignoble thee,
> Save Me, save only Me?

(Francis Thompson, "The Hound of Heaven.")

PRAYER

DEAR JESUS! Thou hast given all for me, and yet I give nothing in return. How often Thou hast come to gather vintage in the vineyard of my soul, and hast found only a few clusters! How often Thou soughtest, and found nothing; knocked, and the door of my soul was closed to Thee! How often Thou didst ask for a drink, and I gave Thee only vinegar and gall!

How often, dear Jesus, I feared lest, having Thee, I must have naught besides. I forget that if I had the flame, I would forget the spark; if I had the sun of Thy love, I could forget the candle of a human heart; if I had the perfect round of Thy happiness, I could forget the broken arc of earth. O Jesus, my story is the sad story of a refusal to return heart for heart, love for love. Give me, above all human gifts, the sweet gift of sympathy for Thee.

Am I a stone and not a sheep
That I can stand, O Christ, beneath Thy Cross
To number drop by drop Thy Blood's slow loss,
And yet not weep?

Not so those women loved
Who with exceeding grief lamented Thee;
Not so fallen Peter weeping bitterly;
Not so the thief was moved;
Not so the sun and moon
Which hid their faces in a starless sky,
A horror of great darkness at broad noon
I, only I.

Yet give not o'er
But seek Thy sheep, true Shepherd of the flock,
Greater than Moses, turn and look once more
And smite a rock.

(Christina Rossetti)

The Seven Last Words, 1933

Second Meditation

GIVE US THIS DAY OUR DAILY BREAD

"Give us this day our daily bread."

"I thirst."

"Daily bread." At Capharnaum, He ministered to the needs of men by giving them food for their bodies. He told men to pray for bread: "Give us this day our daily bread"; but at Calvary, He asks for a drink. Then He gave His gift to the multitude; now the multitude must give their gift. He had been the Giver; now He would be the Receiver. From a torn body, He cried, "I thirst." Thirst is the most impatient of all sufferings; there is an imperious urgency about it – a fierce sting.

But it was not just a cry for water. We know that once before He asked the Samaritan woman for a drink, but when she drew the water from the well, there is no record that He took it. He was thirsting for her soul.

The lesson seems to be that God needs us. He is perfect, and yet He craves our love. He is all-powerful, and yet He is weak without our love. He is infinitely happy and yet unhappy without us. He is the fountain of Everlasting Waters, and yet He cries, "I thirst." He does seem to need us. How? Not, of course, in the sense that He is really imperfect, or that He is incomplete without us, but rather He needs us because we need Him.

The world is full of such examples. The charitable rich man thirsts for the poor. He does not need the poor man; from a worldly point of view, the poor man will take part of his substance. The poor man needs him only for food. But the rich man needs the poor man to exercise his charity. Truly can he say: "I thirst." I need you in order to be kind. In that sense, Our Lord thirsts for us because we need Him so.

He says to us: "I thirst" for you – you the unmortified because you need My spirit of sacrifice. You who would have a Calvary with hands unscarred and white have need of My hands that are pierced and red. I am the Redeemer. To you, who would never take up a cross, to you who need the spirit of penance, I cry: "I thirst." I thirst for you because your love of pleasure needs my love of sacrifice. I thirst for you because your love of the world needs my love of heaven. I do not thirst for you because I need you – for without you I never would have had the cross. I do not thirst for you because I need you for my happiness – for without you there would never have been sin. I thirst for you, not because I need you, but because you need me. Why then when I say "I thirst," do you, like the soldier, reach me bitter vinegar and gall?

The Seven Last Words and the Our Father, 1935

Third Meditation

THE COMMUNION

"I thirst." -- John 19:28.

Our Blessed Lord reaches the communion of His Mass when out from the depths of the Sacred Heart there wells the cry: "I thirst." This was certainly not a thirst for water, for the earth is His and the fullness thereof; it was not a thirst for any of the refreshing droughts of earth, for He calmed the seas with doors when they burst forth in their fury. When they offered Him a drink, He took it not. It was another kind of thirst which tortured Him. He was thirsty for the souls and hearts of men.

The cry was a cry for communion -- the last in a long series of shepherding calls in the quest of God for men. The very fact that it was expressed in the most poignant of all human sufferings, namely, thirst, was the measure of its depth and intensity. Men may *hunger* for God, but God *thirsts* for men. He thirsted for man in Creation as He called him to fellowship with divinity in the garden of Paradise; He thirsted for man in Revelation, as He tried to win back man's erring heart by telling the secrets of His love; He thirsted for man in the Incarnation when He became like the one He loved, and was found in the form and habit of man.

Now He was thirsting for man in Redemption, for greater love than this no man hath, that he lay down his life for his friends. It was the final appeal for communion before the curtain rang down on the Great Drama of His earthly life. All the myriad loves of parents for children, of spouse for spouse, if compacted into one great love, would have been the smallest fraction of God's love for man in that cry of thirst. It signified at once, not only how much He thirsted for the little ones, for hungry hearts and empty souls, but also how intense was His desire to satisfy our deepest longing.

Really, there should be nothing mysterious in our thirst for God, for does not the heart pant after the fountain, and the sunflower turn to the sun, and the rivers run into the sea? But that He should love us, considering our own unworthiness, and how little our love is worth -- *that is the mystery!* And yet such is the meaning of God's thirst for communion with us.

He had already expressed it in the parable of the Lost Sheep, when He said He was not satisfied with the ninety-nine; only the lost sheep could give Him perfect joy. Now the truth was expressed again from the Cross: Nothing could adequately satisfy His thirst but the heart of every man, woman, and child, who were made for Him, and therefore could never be happy until they found their rest in Him.

The basis of this plea for communion is Love, for Love by its very nature tends to unity. Love of citizens one for another begets the unity of the state. Love of man and woman begets the unity of two in one flesh. The love of God for man therefore calls for a unity based upon the Incarnation, namely, the unity of all men in the Body and Blood of Christ.

In order, therefore, that God might seal His love for us, He gave us to Himself in Holy Communion, so that as He and His human nature taken from the womb of the Blessed Mother were one in the unity of His Person, so He and we taken from the womb of humanity might be one in the unity of the Mystical Body of Christ. Hence, we use the word "receive" when speaking of communion with our Lord in the Eucharist, for literally we do "receive" Divine Life, just as really and truly as a babe receives the life of its mother.

All life is sustained by communion with a higher life. If the plants could speak they would say to the moisture and sunlight, "Unless you enter into communion with me, become possessed of my higher laws and powers, you shall not have life in you."

If the animals could speak, they would say to the plants: "Unless you enter into communion with me, you shall not have my higher life in you." We say to all lower creation: "Unless you enter into communion with me, you shall not share in my human life."

Why then should not our Lord say to us: "Unless you enter into communion with Me, you shall not have life in you"? The lower is transformed into the higher, plants into animals, animals into man, and man, in a more exalted way, becomes "divinized," if I may use that expression, through and through by the life of Christ.

Communion then is first of all the receiving of Divine Life, a life to which we are no more entitled than marble is entitled to blooming. It is a pure gift of an all-merciful God who so loved us that He willed to be united with us, not in the bonds of flesh, but in the ineffable bonds of the Spirit where love knows no satiety, but only rapture and joy.

And oh, how quickly we should have forgotten Him could we not, like Bethlehem and Nazareth, receive Him into our souls! Neither gifts nor portraits take the place of the beloved one. And our Lord knew it well. We needed Him, and so He gave us Himself.

But there is another aspect of Communion of which we but rarely think. Communion implies not only *receiving* Divine Life; it means also God *giving* human life. All love is reciprocal. There is no one-sided love, for love by its nature demands mutuality. God thirsts for us, but that means that man must also thirst for God. But do we ever think of Christ receiving Communion from us? Every time we go to the Communion rail we say we "receive" Communion, and that is all many of us do, just "receive Communion."

There is another aspect of Communion than receiving Divine Life, of which St. John speaks. St. Paul gives us the complementary truth in his Epistle to the Corinthians. Communion is not only an incorporation to the *life* of Christ;

it is also an incorporation to His *death.* "As often as you shall eat this bread, and drink the chalice, you shall show the death of the Lord, until He come."

Natural life has two sides: the anabolic and the katabolic. The supernatural also has two sides: the building up of the Christ-pattern and the tearing down of the old Adam. Communion therefore implies not only a "receiving" but also a "giving." There can be no ascent to a higher life without death to a lower one. Does not an Easter Sunday presuppose a Good Friday? Does not all love imply mutual self-giving which ends in self-recovery? This being so, should not the Communion rail be a place of exchange, instead of a place of exclusive receiving? Is all the *Life* to pass from Christ to us and nothing to go back in return? Are we to drain the chalice and contribute nothing to its filling? Are we to receive the bread without giving wheat to be ground, to receive the wine and give no grapes to be crushed? If all we did during our lives was to go to Communion to receive Divine Life, to take it away, and leave nothing behind, we would be parasites on the Mystical Body of Christ.

The Pauline injunction bids us fill up in our body the sufferings wanting to the Passion of Christ. We must therefore bring a spirit of sacrifice to the Eucharistic table; we must bring the mortification of our lower self, the crosses patiently borne, the crucifixion of our egotisms, the death of our concupiscence, and even the very difficulty of our coming to Communion. Then does Communion become what it was always intended to be, namely, a commerce between Christ and the soul, in which we give His Death shown forth in our lives, and He gives His Life shown forth in our adopted sonship? We give Him our time; He gives us His eternity. We give Him our humanity; He gives us His divinity. We give Him our nothingness; He gives us His all.

Do we really understand the nature of love? Have we not sometimes, in great moments of affection for a little child, said in language which might vary from this, but which expresses the idea, "I love that child so much, I should just like to possess it within myself?" Why? Because all love craves for unity. In the natural order, God has given great pleasures to the unity of the flesh. But those are nothing compared to the pleasure of the unity of the spirit, when divinity passes out to humanity, and humanity to divinity -- when our will goes to Him, and He comes to us, so that we cease to be men and begin to be children of God.

If there has ever been a moment in your life when a fine, noble affection made you feel as if you had been lifted into the third or the seventh heaven; if there has ever been a time in your life when a noble love of a fine human heart cast you into an ecstasy; if there has ever been a time when you have really loved a human heart -- then, I ask you, think of what it must be to be united with the great Heart of Love! If the human heart in all of its fine, noble, Christian riches can so thrill, can so exalt, can make us so ecstatic, then what must be the great heart of Christ? Oh, if the spark is so bright, what must be the flame!

Do we fully realize how much Communion is bound up with Sacrifice, both on the part of our Lord and on the part of us, His poor weak creatures? The Mass makes the two inseparable: there is no Communion without a Consecration. There is no receiving the bread and wine we offer, until they have been transubstantiated into the Body and Blood of Christ. Communion is the consequence of the Calvary: namely, we live by what we slay. All nature witnesses this truth; our bodies live by the slaying of the beasts of the fields and the plants of the gardens. We draw life from their crucifixion. We slay them not to destroy, but to fulfill; we immolate them for the sake of communion.

And now by a beautiful paradox of Divine Love, God makes His Cross the very means of our salvation. We have slain Him; we nailed Him there; we crucified Him; but Love in His eternal Heart willed not to be defeated. He willed to give us the very life we slew; to give us the very Food we destroyed; to nourish us with the very Bread we buried, and the very Blood we poured forth. He made our very crime a *happy fault*; He turned a Crucifixion into a Redemption; a Consecration into a Communion; a death into life everlasting.

And it is just that which makes man all the more mysterious! Why man should be loved is no mystery, but why he does not love in return is the great mystery. Why should our Lord be the Great Unloved; why should Love not be loved? Why then, whenever He says: "I thirst," do we give Him vinegar and gall?

Calvary and the Mass, 1936

Fourth Meditation

BLESSED ARE THY THAT HUNGER AND THIRST AFTER JUSTICE

"Blessed are they that hunger and thirst after justice: for they shall have their fill."

"I thirst."

At the beginning of His Public Life on the Hill of the Beatitudes, Our Lord preached the necessity of zeal: "Blessed are they that hunger and thirst after justice: for they shall have their fill." At the end of His Public Life on the Hill of Calvary He practiced that beatitude as there fell from His lips the cry of apostleship: "I thirst."

The world cannot understand either this Beatitude or this Word, for the world by its nature is seated in indifference. It is very fond of talking about religion, but dislikes doing anything about it. It dismisses zeal and intense love of God with the sneer of "mysticism," and regards religion as something incidental to human life, like poetry.

It is not uncommon, therefore, to find Catholics who say: "I knew I should not eat meat on Friday out of respect for the day on which Our Lord sacrificed His life for me, but I did not want to embarrass my host," or "I was staying with some unbelieving friends over the week-end and I did not want to embarrass them, so I did not go to Mass on Sunday," or "when they made fun of devotion to the Blessed Mother and ridiculed veneration of saints, and the crucifix, I said nothing, because I did not want to start an argument about religion."

Such is the indifference of the world -- a fear of being identified whole-heartedly with the God for whom we were made. If the world does hunger and thirst, it is always for something less than the justice of this Beatitude.

Communists, for example, hunger and thirst, but not for the Justice of God; they hunger and thirst for a system built, not upon love, but upon class-struggle and revolution. They seek to fill a want, but *only* the wants of the stomach.

It is just against such filling of the animal in us, and the starving of the spiritual, that Our Lord said: "Woe to you that are filled: for you shall hunger." "Your Father knoweth that you have need of all these things. Seek ye therefore first the kingdom of God, and his justice, and all these things shall be added unto you."

And against that compromising indifference which fears to assert God's justice, He warned: "Everyone therefore that shall confess me before men, I will also confess him before my Father who is in heaven. But he that shall deny me before men, I will also deny him before my Father who is in heaven"; and against justice that limits itself to economic rights and excludes the duties of man to his Maker, He said: "For I tell you, that unless your justice abound more than that of the Scribes and Pharisees, you shall not enter into the kingdom of heaven."

Not only negatively but positively did He preach the necessity of zeal for the Justice of the Kingdom of God. His circumcision was a kind of impatience to run His course of Justice which led to the Garden and the Cross; His teaching the Doctors in the Temple at twelve years of age was an impatience to teach men the sweetness of His Father's ways.

At the beginning of His Public Life we find Him driving merchants out of the Temple, in fulfillment of the prophecy of apostleship: "The zeal of thy house hath eaten me up." Later on, He made use of a dinner invitation to save the soul of Magdalen, and on a hot day made use of a common love of cold water to bring the Samaritan woman to a knowledge of everlasting fountains.

He came, He said, "not to destroy souls, but to save"; and, "seeing the multitude, he had compassion on them; because they were distressed, and lying as sheep having no shepherd." Then he said to His disciples: "The harvest indeed is great, but the laborers are few. Pray ye therefore the Lord of the harvest, that he send forth laborers into his harvest." His whole mission in life was one of zeal, a hunger and thirst for the Justice of God, which He perhaps best expressed in words of fire: "I am come to cast fire on the earth: and what will I, but that it be kindled? And I have a baptism wherewith I am to be baptized: and how am I straitened until it be accomplished!" "And other sheep I have, that are not of this fold: them also I must bring, and they shall hear my voice, and there shall be one fold and one shepherd."

And now at the end of His life, He yearns still more for justice as He who called himself the Fountain of Living Waters and He who was figuratively the Rock that gave forth water as Moses struck it in the desert, now lets well from out His Sacred Heart the shepherd's call to all the souls of the world: "I thirst."

It was not a thirst for earthly waters, for the earth and its oceans were His. And when they offered Him vinegar and gall as a sedative for His sufferings He refused it. It was therefore not a physical, but a spiritual thirst that troubled Him -- the thirst for the Beatitude of Justice -- an insatiable thirst for the souls of men.

The world that dislikes zeal for God's justice, first hated it in Him. It was His zeal that brought Him to the cross. The world loves the indifferent, the mediocre, the ordinary, but it hates two classes of people: those who are too good, and those who are too bad.

Hence, on Calvary we find Our Lord crucified with thieves. Both Innocence and Injustice fell foul of the law. Some go to the cross because they are too good for the majority or for the system; and others go to the cross because they are too bad for it.

The world hates the zealous, such as Our Lord, because they are a reproach to its mediocrity; it hates also the wicked, such as the thieves, because they are an annoyance to its self-complacency.

The race of quantity has always persecuted the race of quality. The good go down to death, because they are good; the wicked go to death because they are wicked -- the mediocre survive. As Our Lord put it: "The world cannot hate you; but me it hateth: because I give testimony of it, that the works thereof are evil." And if this was true of Our Lord, it must be true of us. The servant is not above the master.

If our passionate quest of God's cause makes us disliked by men, we cannot say we were not warned by Him who was hated first. "If the world hate you, know ye that it hath hated me before you. If you had been of the world, the world would love its own: but because you are not of the world, but I have chosen you out of the world, therefore the world hateth you . . . If they have persecuted me, they will also persecute you . . . That the word may be fulfilled which was written in their law: *They hated me without cause.*" Apostles of Christ, then, will never be popular. Their end is crucifixion.

And yet we must thirst for justice and be on fire for the Kingdom of God. And why? Because everything that is good diffuses itself. The sun is good, and it diffuses itself in light and heat; the flower is good, and it diffuses itself in perfume; the animal is good, and it diffuses itself in the generation of its kind; man is good, and he diffuses himself in the communication of thought; a Christian is good, and must therefore diffuse his Christianity, throw sparks from the flame of His love, enkindle fires in the inflammable hearts of men and speak of his Lover because He *is* Love, for "out of the abundance of the heart the mouth speaketh."

Strong love makes strong actions, and the measure of our zeal in bringing souls to the feet of Christ is the measure of our love of Him.

Converting souls to Christ then is not based on the pride of propaganda, but on a desire for perfection. An apostle desires to bring men and women to Our Lord not for the same reason a businessman wishes to increase his trade.

The businessman advertises to increase his profits; the Christian propagandizes to increase the happiness of others. He wants to bring souls to Our Lord for the same reason he wants to see the sun shine, the flowers bloom, and lambs grow into sheep -- because it is their perfection and therefore their happiness.

If a pencil is made for writing, we do not want to see it used for digging; if a bird is made for flying, we do not want to see it change places with the mole; if a soul is made for the fullness of Life, then we do not want to see it clip its wings and wallow in hatred, half-truths, and marred loveliness. We want to see it united with its perfection which is the Life and Truth and Love and Beauty of God.

That is why a Christian soul is apostolic -- it loves perfection, wholeness, completeness, happiness: God. And therefore it wants everyone to be God-like and God-ward.

And no cost is too great to achieve that end, for in the language of Paul: Who then shall separate us from the love of Christ? Shall tribulation? or distress? or famine? or nakedness? or danger? or persecution? or the sword? (As it is written: *For Thy sake we are put to death all the day long. We are accounted as sheep for the slaughter.*) But in all these things we overcome, because of Him that hath loved us. For I am sure that neither death, nor life, nor angels, nor principalities, nor powers, nor things present, nor things to come, nor might, nor height, nor depth, nor any other creature shall be able to separate us from the love of God, which is in Christ Jesus our Lord.

If there be hate, enmity, jealousy, and war on the face of the earth today is it not due in the last analysis to our want of zeal for the cause of God?

Just suppose that outside of the necessary structure of the Church, there was only one in all the world who believed in it, who received Communion, acknowledged the Primacy of Peter, and assisted at Holy Mass. Just suppose that that one zealous believer the first year converted one un-believer to Christ and His Church. Suppose that the next year these two each made a convert; then there would be four the second year.

And suppose the next year, these four made one apiece next year, then there would be eight converts at the end of the third year. Now how many would there be, from that one zealous believer, at the end of only thirty years? There would be in the communion rails of the church at the end of the 30th year, one billion, seventy-three million, seven hundred and forty-one thousand, eight hundred and twenty-four souls breaking their fast with the Bread of Life.

It is a tremendous thought, and a reminder of how much we have failed to do our duty and to spread the love and knowledge of Christ in the souls of men. Are we unmindful that thirst for justice will save our own souls? Have we forgotten the words of St. James: "He who causes a sinner to be converted from the error of his way, shall save his soul from death, and shall cover a multitude of sins."

Have we forgotten that the cold must burn, that the tepid must flame like torches of the night, that the Kingdom of heaven suffereth violence and only the violent shall bear it away? If we have, then we know why Our Lord cried: "I thirst." It is because we have reached Him the vinegar and gall of indifference.

Away with mediocrity! Lift up your hearts! The world is looking for light. Will you hide yours under bushels? The earth is looking for savor, will you let the salt lose its savor? Think of those Communists who are hungering for justice without knowing it! Think of the atheists who are starving for peace without knowing it! Think of the great mass of men and women in this country who set for themselves no higher life than that of animals, namely, to eat and drink, sleep and search for prey.

Think of those who hate the good, really because they hate their own wickedness! They have a passion for God hid beneath the ashes of their lives, but they presently live in fear "lest having Him they must have naught else besides."

We plead particularly for all Communists, who hate religion, who hate classes, and who hate God. But that does not mean we must hate them.

They are yearning for something which their own Communism cannot give them. They are hungering and thirsting for the justice of God, whether they know it or not. Therefore, we must not hate them just because they hate us. Rather, we must feel sorry for them because they miss so much, and because their zeal is bent on destruction rather than construction.

In fact, our sympathy for them should be so deep that we will strive to save them from the very ruins which, Samson-like, they pull down on their heads. This is our Christian duty, for we do not save our souls alone, but only in companionship with others.

On Judgment Day we shall be asked: Where are your children? If we can point to those whom we have saved, or can point to one Communist whom we have made a

Communionist, then we who hungered and thirsted shall be filled -- filled even from the fountains of God.

The Cross and the Beatitudes, 1937

Fifth Meditation

THE NEED OF ZEAL

"I thirst."

The *Fourth Word* is the *suffering of the soul* without God; the *Fifth Word* is the suffering of God without the soul. The cry, "I thirst," refers not to physical thirst.

It was His soul that was burning and His Heart that was on fire. He was thirsting for the souls of men. The Shepherd was lonely without His sheep; the Creator was yearning for His creatures; the First-born was looking for His brethren.

All during His life He had been searching for souls. He left heaven to find them among the thorns; it mattered little if they made a crown of them for Him, so long as He could find the one that was lost.

He said He came "not to call the just, but sinners," and His Heart thirsted for them now more than ever. He could not be happy until every sheep and every lamb was in His sheepfold. "Other sheep I have, that are not of this fold: them also I must bring . . . and there shall be one fold and one shepherd."

There was sorrow in His sad complaint during life; "You will not come to me"; but there is tragedy in the last cry: "I thirst."

There was probably no moment during the three hours of redemption in which Our Lord suffered more than in this. Pains of the body are nothing compared to the agonies of the soul.

Taking His life did not mean so much to Him, for He was really laying it down of Himself. But for man to spurn His Love -- that was enough to break His Heart.

It is difficult for us to grasp the intensity of this suffering, simply because none of us ever loves enough. We have not the capacity for love that He has, therefore we can never miss so much when it is denied.

But when our tiny little hearts are sometimes denied the love they crave, we do get some faint inkling of what must have gone on in His Own Great Heart.

The faithful loyal wife whose husband is snatched from her by death, the mother whose son refuses to visit her and bless her declining days with filial affection, the friend who has sacrificed all only to be betrayed by one for whom he gave all -- all these experience the keenest and bitterest of all human sufferings: the pangs of unrequited love. Such victims can and really do die of a broken heart.

But what is this love for another human being, compared to the love of God for man? The affection a human heart bears for another lessens as it multiplies the objects of its love, just as a river loses its fullness the more it divides itself into little streams.

But with God there is no decrease of love with the increase of objects loved, any more than a voice loses its strength because a thousand ears hear it.

Each human heart can break His Sacred Heart all over again; each soul has within itself the potentiality of another crucifixion. No one can love as much as Our Lord; no one therefore can suffer as much.

Added to this was the fact that His infinite Mind saw within that second, all the unfaithful hearts that would ever live until the end of time; all who would follow like Judas, and then betray; all who would fall and refuse His helping

Hand; in a word, all who would pass by His Cross and only stop, with the executioners to shake dice for His garments, while within a stone's throw of them would be the Prize so precious it was worth gambling their very lives away.

It was this picture of ungrateful men, which renewed the Agony of the Garden and caused His Death. He died of thirst in the desert of human hearts!

From this Word we discover this great lesson: the necessity of our loving our fellow men as Our Lord loves us.

If Jesus Christ thirsted for souls, must not a Christian also thirst? If He came to cast fire upon the earth, must not a Christian be enkindled? If He came to bring us the seed of Life, must not that seed fructify and bear fruit? If He lit a Light in our minds, must we not be illumined? Has He not called us to be His Apostles and His Ambassadors, in order that His Incarnation might be prolonged through the continued dispensation of the divine through the human?

A Christian then is a man to whom Our Lord has given other men. He breaks bread to the poor through our hands, He consoles the sick through our lips, He visits the sorrowful upon our feet, He sees the fields of harvest through our eyes, and He gathers the bundles into His everlasting barns through our toil.

To be worthy of the name Christian, then, means that we too, must thirst for the spread of the Divine Love; and if we do not thirst, then we shall never be invited to sit down at the banquet of Life.

Crowns shall be given only to the victors, and the chalice of everlasting wine only to those who thirst.

A Catholic who does not strive to spread his Faith is a parasite on the Life of the Church; he who is not girding his loins for apostolate is abdicating his seat on the dais of Christianity; he who is not bearing fruit is like a tree cut down on the road impeding the march of the army of God. He who is not a conquering spirit is a renegade.

The torch of Faith has been given to us not to delight our eyes but to enkindle the torches of our fellow men. Unless we burn and are on fire for the Divine Cause a glacial invasion will sweep the earth which will be the end, for "The Son of man, when he cometh, shall he find, think you, faith on earth?"

The measure of our apostolate is the intensity of our love. A human heart loves to talk about the object of his love, and loves to hear that object praised.

If we love Our Lord, then we will love to talk about His Holy Cause, for "out of the abundance of the heart the mouth speaketh." To those who have such love, there is never the excuse of a want of opportunity.

Our Lord has told us "the harvest indeed is great, but the laborers are few."

To the zealous Christian every country is a mission country; every banquet room a Simon's house where another Magdalen can be found; every ship another bark of Peter from which nets of salvation can be let down; every crowded city street another Tyre and Sidon where the whelps that eat the crumbs from the master's table can be rewarded for their faith; and every cross is a throne where thieves become courtiers.

There are those that would destroy every mark of the Saviour's feet from the face of the earth. There are those who would renew the Crucifixion by hating those who preach His love; the wicked today hide not the shame of their sins, but seek to find others and make others like unto themselves, in order to find consolation in their corporate decadence.

But these are not reason why Christians should go into the catacombs and leave the earth to the race of Cain. While these enemies of Divine Love live, they are still purchasable by Divine Grace and are potential children of the Kingdom of God. They are our opportunities.

Our Lord thirsted for them on the Cross, and we must thirst for them too, and love them enough to try to save them.

One thing is certain; we are not called to be Christians to damn them, but to save them, in order that all men may be one great redeemed humanity and Christ its Sacred Heart.

Some will always resist, but there are no hopeless cases. Sometime ago in Spain two hundred men were ordered shot when the Spanish people won over a city from the forces of anarchy.

These two hundred men had burned churches, murdered priests and nuns, ravaged virgins, and were now to expiate their crimes. The Carmelites who had suffered from their hands began a novena of prayer and fasting, that they might be converted to God before their death. Out of the two hundred, one hundred and ninety-eight at the end of the novena received the Sacraments and died in peace with their Saviour.

Something we must never forget is that every man wants to be happy, but he cannot be happy without God. Below the surface of every heart, down deep in its secret gardens, is a craving for that for which it was made, as even the caged bird still retains its love of flying.

As the Holy Father put it: "Beneath the ashes of these perverted lives there are to be found sparks which can be fanned into a flame." Even those who hate religion have never really lost it; if they had, they would not hate it so much.

The intensity of their hate is the proof of the reality of that which they hate. If they really lost religion, they would not spend all their energy attempting to make everyone else lose theirs; a man who has lost a watch does not go about persuading others to lose their watches.

Thus hate is but their vain attempt to despise. That is why we are not to consider them beyond evangelization.

They can still be brought back even at the last moment, as the thief, or as Arthur Rimbaud. Here was a man who blasphemed Christ intensely in this life by his writings; a man whose greatest thrill was to intoxicate anyone who spoke to him of God and Our Lady, in order to berate and even physically abuse him.

He even delighted in breaking his mother's heart to whom he wrote: "Happily this life is the only one; which is obvious, because one cannot imagine another life with more boredom in it than this one."

Then came his end, which is described for us in the language of François Mauriac: "Now imagine a human being who has great powers of resistance, who is much more masterful than I am, and who hates this servitude.

"Imagine a nature irritated and exasperated to distraction by this mysterious servitude and finally delivered over to an abandoned hatred of the cross.

"He spits on this sign which he drags after him and assures himself that the bonds which attach him to it could never stand out against a methodical and planned degradation of his soul and spirit.

"Thus he cultivates blasphemy and perfects it as an art and fortifies his hatred of sacred things with an armor of scornful contempt.

"Then suddenly, above this stupendous defilement, a voice rises, complainingly, appealingly; it is hardly so much as a cry, and no sooner has the sky received it than the echo is smothered by frightful jeers and by the laugh of the devil.

"As long as this man is strong enough, he will drag this cross as a prisoner his ball-chain, never accepting it. He will obstinately insist on wearing this wood along all the paths of the world. He will choose the lands of fire and ashes most suited to consume it.

"However heavy the cross becomes, it will not exhaust his hatred until the fateful day, the turning-point in his destiny, when he sinks down at last under the weight of the tree and under its agonizing embrace.

"He still writhes, pulls himself together and then sinks down again, hurling out a last blasphemy. From his hospital bed he brings abominable accusations against the nuns who are tending him; he treats the angelic sister as a fool and an idiot and then, at last, he breaks off. This is the moment marked from all eternity.

"The cross which has dragged him for thirty-seven years and which he has denied and covered with spittle, offers its arms to him: the dying man throws himself upon it, presses it to him, clings to it, embraces; he is serenely sad and heaven is in his eyes. His voice is heard: 'Everything must be prepared in my room, everything must be arranged. The chaplain will come back with the Sacraments. You will see. They're going to bring the candles and the lace. There must be white linen everywhere. . . .' "

No! Religion is not the opium of the people. Opium is the drug of deserters who are afraid to face the Cross -- the opiate that gives momentary escape from the Hound of Heaven in pursuit of the human soul.

Religion, on the contrary, is the elixir which spurs a soul on to the infinite goal for which it was made. Religion supplies the profoundest desires.

The greatest thirst of all is the thirst of unrequited love -- the hand reached out which never grasps; the arms outstretched which never embrace the hand knocking on a door which is never opened. It is these things religion satisfies by making man think less about his passing desires and more about his ultimate desire.

His passing desires are multiple and fleeting -- gold one minute, food another, pleasure another. But his ultimate desire is unique and abiding -- the perfect happiness of everlasting joy and peace. It is our duty to lead men to the realization of this desire.

Those who hate religion are seeking religion; those who wrongly condemn are still seeking justice; those who overthrow order are seeking a new order; even those who blaspheme are adoring their own gods -- but still adoring.

From certain points of view, they are all prisoners of Divine Love; they are confusing desires with *the* desire, passions with love.

They are all living in the shadow of the Cross, they are all thirsting for the Fountain of Divine Life. Their lips were made to drink - and we must not refuse to reach them the cup.

The Rainbow of Sorrow, 1938

Sixth Meditation

GLUTTONY

"I thirst."

Gluttony is an inordinate indulgence in food or drink, and may manifest itself either in taking more than is necessary, or in taking it at the wrong time, or in taking it too luxuriously. It is sinful because reason demands that food and drink be taken for the necessities and conveniences of nature not for pleasure alone.

The Gospel describes Dives as being guilty of this sin. There is no mention in the story given to us by Our Blessed Lord that Dives was a wicked man. We have no record of him underpaying his servants or of being guilty of any moral turpitude. Our Lord tells us only that he was "clothed in purple and fine linen; and feasted sumptuously every day."

And there was a certain beggar named Lazarus, who lay at his gate full of sores, desiring to be filled with the crumbs that fell from the rich man's table, and no one did give him; moreover the dogs came, and licked his sores. And it came to pass that the beggar died and was carried by the angels into Abraham's bosom. And the rich man also died; and he was buried in hell. And lifting up his eyes when he was in torments, he saw Abraham afar off, and Lazarus in his bosom. And he cried and said: "Father Abraham, have mercy on me, and send Lazarus, that he may dip the tip of his finger in water, to cool my tongue; for I am tormented in this flame."

And Abraham said to him: "Son, remember that thou didst receive good things in thy lifetime, and likewise Lazarus evil things, but now he is comforted; and thou art tormented. And besides all this, between us and you, there is fixed a great chaos: so that they who would pass from hence to you, cannot, nor from thence come hither."

And he said: "Then, father, I beseech thee, that thou wouldst send him to my father's house, for I have five brethren, that he may testify unto them, lest they also come into this place of torments." And Abraham said to him, "They have Moses and the prophets; let them hear them." But he said, "No, father Abraham; but if one went to them from the dead, they will do penance." And he said to him, "If they hear not Moses and the prophets, neither will they believe, if one rise again from the dead."

If there is any indication of the present degeneration of society better than another, it is the excess of luxury in the modern world. When men begin to forget their souls, they begin to take great care of their bodies. There are more athletic clubs in the modern world than there are spiritual retreat houses; and who shall count the millions spent in beauty shops to glorify faces that will one day be the prey of worms.

It is not particularly difficult to find thousands who will spend two or three hours a day in exercising, but if you ask them to bend their knees to God in five minutes of prayer, they protest that it is too long. Added to this is the shocking amount that is yearly spent, not in the normal pleasure of drinking, but in its excess.

The scandal increases when one considers the necessary wants of the poor which could have been supplied by the amount spent for such dehumanization. The Divine judgment upon Dives is bound to be repeated upon many of our generation, who will find that the beggars for whose service they refused to interrupt their luxuries, will be seated at the Banquet of the King of Kings, while they, like Dives, will be the beggars for but a drop of water.

Some reparation had to be made for gluttony, drunkenness, and excessive luxury. That reparation began at the birth of Our Lord, when He who might have pulled down the heavens for His house-top and the stars for His chandeliers, chose to be rejected by men and driven as an outcast to a cave in the hillsides of the least of the cities of Israel.

The very first sermon He preached was a plea for detachment: "Blessed are the poor in spirit, for theirs is the kingdom of heaven." He began His public life by fasting forty days and bade men, "Be not solicitous for your life, what you shall eat, nor for your body, what you shall put on."

Traveling about as an itinerant prophet, He admitted He was as homeless as at His birth and that the beasts and birds had a better habitation than He: "The foxes have holes, and the birds of the air, nests; but the Son of Man hath not where to lay His head." There was no luxury in the way He dined, for we know of but one meal that He himself prepared, and it consisted only of bread and fish.

Finally, at the Cross, He is stripped of His garments and denied a death-bed, in order to go out of His own world as He came into it -- Lord of it and yet possessing nothing. The waters of the sea were His and all the fountains of the earth had sprung up at His word; He it was who drew the bolt of Nature's waterfalls and shut up the seas with doors; He it was who said: "Whosoever drinketh of this water shall thirst again; but he that shall drink of the water that I will give him, shall not thirst for ever. If any man thirst, let him come to me, and drink."

But now He lets fall from His lips the shortest of the seven cries from the Cross and the one that expresses the keenest of all human sufferings in reparation for those who have had their fill: "I thirst."

A soldier immediately put a sponge full of vinegar on a stick and pressed it to His mouth. Thus was fulfilled the prophecy uttered by the Psalmist a thousand years before: "In my thirst they gave me vinegar to drink."

He who fed the birds of the air is left unfed; He who changed water into wine now thirsts; the everlasting fountains are dry; the God-man is poverty-stricken. The Divine "Lazarus" stands at the door of the world and begs for a crumb and a drop, but the door of generosity is closed in His face.

Thus was reparation made for the luxury of eating and drinking. When Mirabeau was dying, he called for opium, saying, "You promised to spare me needless suffering . . . Support this head, the greatest head in France." When Christ is dying, He refuses the drug to alleviate His suffering. He deliberately wills to feel the most poignant of human wants, that He might balance in the scales of justice those who had more than they needed.

He even made Himself the least of all men by asking them for a drink -- not a drink of earthly water. That is not what He wanted, but a drink for His thirsty heart -- a drink of love: *I thirst for love.*

This word from the Cross reveals that there is a double hunger and a double thirst: one of the body, the other of the soul. On many previous occasions Our Lord had distinguished between them: "Woe to you that are filled: for you shall hunger. Woe to you that now laugh: for you shall mourn and weep." "Blessed are ye that hunger now, for you shall be filled. Blessed are ye that weep now, for you shall laugh."

Then to the multitude who followed Him across the sea in search of bread, He said: "Labour not for the meat which perisheth, but for that which endureth unto life everlasting, which the Son of man will give you."

To the Samaritan woman who came to draw water at Jacob's well He foretold: "Whosoever drinketh of this water shall thirst again; but he that shall drink of the water that I will give him, shall not thirst forever: But the water that I will give him, shall become in him a fountain of water, springing up into life everlasting." But above all other references to the food and drink of the inner man as contrasted with that of the outer man, He promised the supreme nourishment of Himself: "For my flesh is meat indeed, and my blood is drink indeed."

It is in the light of this double hunger and thirst of body and soul that the distinction between dieting and fasting becomes clear. The Church fasts; the world diets. Materially there is no difference, for a person can lose twenty pounds one way as well as the other. But the difference is in the intention.

The Christian fasts not for the sake of the body, but for the sake of the soul; the pagan fasts not for the sake of the soul, but for the sake of the body. The Christian does not fast because he believes the body is wicked, but in order to make it pliable in the hands of the soul, like a tool in the hands of a skilled workman.

That brings us down to the basic problem of life. Is the soul the tool of the body, or the body the tool of the soul? Should the soul do what the body wants, or should the body do what the soul wants? Each has its appetites and each is imperious in the satisfaction of its wants. If we please one, we displease the other, and vice versa. Both of them cannot sit down together at the banquet of life.

The development of character depends on which hunger and thirst we cultivate. To diet or to fast -- that is the problem. To lose a double chin in order to be more beautiful in the eyes of creatures or to lose it in order to keep the body tamed and ever obedient to the spiritual demands of the soul -- that is the question. Human worth can be judged by human desires.

Tell me your hungers and your thirsts and I will tell you what you are. Do you hunger for money more than for mercy, for riches more than for virtue, and for power more than for service? Then you are selfish, pampered, and proud.

Do you thirst for the Wine of Everlasting Life more than for pleasure, and for the poor more than for the favor of the rich, and for souls more than for the first places at table? Then you are a humble Christian.

The great pity is that so many have been so concerned with the body that they neglect the soul, and in neglecting the soul, they lose the appetite for the spiritual. Just as it is possible in the physiological order for a man to lose all appetite for food, so it is possible in the spiritual order to lose all desire for the supernatural. Gluttonous about the perishable, they become indifferent to the everlasting.

Like deaf ears, which are dead to the environment of harmony and blind eyes which are dead to the environment of beauty, so warped souls become dead to the environment of the Divine.

Darwin tells us in his autobiography that in his love for the biological he lost all the taste he once had for poetry and music, and he regretted the loss all the days of his life. Nothing so much dulls the capacity for the spiritual as excessive dedication to the material.

Excessive love of money destroys a sense of value; excessive love of the flesh kills the values of the spirit. Then comes a moment when everything seems to rebel against the higher law of our being. As the poet has put it, "All things betrayest thee, who betrayest me." Nature is so loyal to its Maker that it is always in the end disloyal to those who abuse it. "Traitorous trueness and loyal deceit" is its best poetic description, for in faithfulness to Him it will always be fickle with us.

The Fifth Word from the Cross is God's plea to the human heart to satisfy itself at the only satisfying fountains. God cannot compel men to thirst for the holy in place of the base, or for the divine rather than the secular. That is why

His plea is merely an affirmation: "I thirst," meaning, "I thirst to be thirsted for." And His thirst is our salvation.

A twofold recommendation is hidden in this short sermon from the Cross: first, to mortify bodily hunger and thirst, and second, to cultivate a spiritual hunger and thirst.

We are to *mortify bodily hunger and thirst,* not because the flesh is wicked, but because the soul must ever exercise mastery over it, lest it become a tyrant. Quite apart from avoiding all excesses, the Cross commits us even to the minimizing of expenditures for luxuries, for the sake of the poor. How many ever think of foregoing an elaborate dinner and theater party, or a debut, out of genuine sympathy and affection for Christ's poor? Dives did not, and he lost his soul because of that forgetfulness. How many in less ample circumstances even mortify themselves one movie a month in order to drop its equivalent in the poor box, that He who sees in secret may reward in secret?

The Divine counsel concerning such restraint of bodily appetites is unmistakable. On one occasion, when Our Lord was invited to the home of the Prince of the Pharisees, He addressed the host himself saying: "When thou makest a dinner or a supper, call not thy friends, nor thy brethren, nor thy kinsmen, nor thy neighbors who are rich; lest perhaps they also invite thee again, and a recompense be made to thee. But when thou makest a feast, call the poor, the maimed, the lame, and the blind; And thou shalt be blessed, because they have not wherewith to make thee recompense; for recompense shall be made thee at the resurrection of the just."

The money we spend in the excesses of bodily hunger and thirst will do us no good on the last day; but the poor whom we have assisted by our restraint and mortification will stand up as so many advocates before the bar of Divine Justice, and will plead for mercy on our souls, even though they once were heavily laden with sin.

The Heavenly Judge cannot be bought with money, but He can be swayed by the poor. On that last day, the only one that really counts, will be fulfilled the beautifully prophetic words of the Mother of Our Lord: "He hath filled the hungry with good things; and the rich he hath sent empty away."

When such surrenders of the superfluous food and drink are made for the soul's sake, let it all be done in a spirit of joy. "And when you fast, be not as the hypocrites, sad. For they disfigure their faces, that they may appear unto men to fast. Amen, I say to you, they have received their reward. But thou, when thou fastest, anoint thy head, and wash thy face; that thou appear not to men to fast, but to thy Father who is in secret; and thy Father who seeth in secret, will repay thee."

We are, in addition, to *cultivate a spiritual hunger and thirst.* Mortification of the bodily appetites is only a means, not an end. The end is union with God, the soul's desire. "Taste and see that the Lord is sweet." The great tragedy of life is not so much what men have suffered, but what they have missed. It comes within the compass of a few to satisfy their earthly desires with wealth, but there is no man living, who, if he willed it, could not enjoy the spiritual food and drink that God serves to all who ask.

And yet how few there are who ever think of nourishing their souls. How few there must have been in Jerusalem to have drawn from Our Lord the sweet complaint: "How often would I have gathered together thy children, as the hen doth gather her chickens under her wings, and thou wouldst not?"

Well indeed might the Saviour say to us, as we listen to the cry: "I thirst," the words he addressed to the woman at the well: "If thou didst know the gift of God, and who He is that saith to thee, Give me to drink; thou perhaps wouldst have asked of him, and he would have given thee living water."

But how many ask? Consider the greatest gift of God to men: the Bread of Life and the Wine that germinates virgins. How few avail themselves of the Divine presence to break their fast each morning on the Heavenly food of the soul!

How many are sufficiently conscious that Our Lord is present in the tabernacle, to pay a daily visit to Him in His Prison of Love? And if we do not, what does it witness to but the deadening of our spiritual sense. Our body would miss a dessert more than our soul would miss a Communion.

No wonder Our Crucified Redeemer thirsted for us on the Cross -- thirsted for our unresponsive hearts and dulled souls. And let us not think that His thirst is a proof of His need, but of our own. He does not need us for His perfection any more than we need the flower that blooms outside our window for our perfection. In dry seasons we desire rain for the flower, not because we need the rain, but because the flower needs it.

In like manner, God thirsts for us, not because He needs us for His happiness, but because we need Him for our happiness. Without Him it is impossible for us to develop. Just as certain diseases, such as rickets and anemia, arise in the body from a deficiency of necessary vitamins, so too our characters fail because of a deficiency of the Spirit.

The vast majority of men and women in the world today are so under-developed spiritually, that if a like deficiency showed in their bodies, they would be physical monstrosities.

How many millions of minds there are today that are devoid of one single satisfying truth that they can carry through life to sustain them in their sorrows and console them at their death? How many millions of wills there are that have not yet found the goal of life and which, because they are presently without it, flit like butterflies from one colored emotion to another, unable to find repose?

Let them cultivate a taste for something more than bread and circuses; let them sound the depths of their beings to discover there the arid wastes crying for the refreshment of everlasting fountains. Of course these emaciated hungry souls are not altogether to blame. They have heard preachers without end preaching, "*Go to Christ!*" But what does that mean? Go back 1900 years? If so, then have they not a right to doubt the Divinity of Him who could not project Himself through time?

Look up to heaven? If so, then what has become of His blessing, His forgiveness of sinners, His Truth that He said would endure unto the end of time? Where is His authority? His Power? His Life now? If it is not someplace on earth, then why did He come to earth? To leave only the echo of His words, the record of His deeds, and then to slip away leaving us only a history and its teachers?

Somewhere on earth today is His truth: "He that heareth you, heareth me." Somewhere on earth is His Power: "Behold, I have given you power . . ." Somewhere on earth is His Life: "The bread that I will give, is my flesh, for the life of the world." Where find it?

There is an institution on the face of the earth that claims to be that, and to those who have knocked at its portals and have asked for a drink has come the elixir of Divine Life and with it the peace that comes to those who drink and never thirst again, and eat and never hunger again.

To each and every one of us, inside and outside the Church, our Lord asks: "Will you accept the cup of My Love?" He took our cup of hate and bitterness in Gethsemane, and its dregs were so bitter that they made Him cry out: "My Father, if it be possible, let this chalice pass from me."

But He drank every drop of it. If He drank our cup of hates why do we not drink His chalice of pardon? Why then, when He cries, "I thirst," do we reach Him vinegar and gall?

I cannot tell the half of it, yet hear
What rush of feeling still comes back to me,
From that proud torture hanging on His Cross,
From that gold rapture of His Heart in Mine.
I knew in blissful anguish what it means
To be a part of Christ, and feel as mine
The dark distresses of my brother limbs,
To feel it bodily and simply true,
To feel as mine the starving of His poor,
To feel as mine the shadow of curse on all,
Hard words, hard looks, and savage misery,
And struggling deaths, unpitied and unwept.
To feel rich brothers' sad satieties,
The weary manner of their lives and deaths,
That want in love, and lacking love lack all.
To feel the heavy sorrow of the world
Thicken and thicken on to future hell,
To mighty cities with their miles of streets,
Where men seek work for days, and walk and starve,
Freezing on river-banks on winter nights,
And come at last to cord or stream or steel.
The horror of the things our brothers bear!
It was but naught to that which after came,
The woe of things we make our brothers bear,
Our brothers and our sisters! In my heart
Christ's Heart seemed beating, and the world's whole sin, --
Its crimson malice and grey negligence, --
Rose up and blackening hid the Face of God.

(Arthur Shearly Cripps)

Victory Over Vice, 1939

Seventh Meditation

TEMPERANCE

"I Thirst."

There is a world of difference between what we *need* and what we *want.* We *need* those things which are essential for a normal, comfortable human existence; but we *want* more than that. Our needs are quickly satisfied, but our wants rarely.

The day our Blessed Lord multiplied the loaves and fishes the Evangelist records that each person had his fill and was satisfied. But just suppose that Our Lord instead of giving food which they needed, miraculously multiplied money and gave each of them the equivalent of a ten dollar bill. How many, do you think, would have been satisfied with one bill? Money is a want; food is a need.

Because our needs are limited, but our wants are unlimited, a virtue is necessary to restrain our inordinate appetites and desires -- and that virtue is called temperance. It has for its object the regulation of the sensible appetites by reason.

The two strongest appetites in man are eating and drinking which sustain his individual life and the sexual act which propagates his social nature. Excesses in these appetites are the sources of the two sins of gluttony and lust. Temperance is the virtue which moderates them for the sake of the soul.

Temperance must not be confused either with Puritanism, which because of the abuse of a thing would take away its use; nor with license, which would interpret all restraint as an infringement of liberty. Rather, there is a golden mean, as revealed in Our Lord's first miracle at Cana, where He changed water into wine to satisfy the individual appetite and blessed the married couple for the satisfaction of the creative instinct.

There is no consolation here for those gloomy souls who would kill the joy of living, nor for those frivolous souls who would isolate pleasure from the end of living, namely, the salvation of the soul.

Temperance reaches its peak in Him who came to preach the hard way of the cross, and yet began it by serving wine and assisting at a marriage feast. For that reason, the extremists who want all fast or all feast were never pleased with His Temperance.

As He said to them on one occasion: "For John came neither eating nor drinking; and they say: He hath a devil. The Son of man came eating and drinking, and they say: Behold a man that is a glutton and a wine drinker a friend of publicans and sinners" *(Matthew 11:18-19)*. It is so hard to please those who are looking for faults.

Finally, on the Cross He gave us His Fifth Word -- the revelation of the philosophy of temperance. Racked by the burning fever of crucifixion, like a dying soldier on a battlefield His lips craved for water. There was a physical foundation of the cry: "I thirst" *(John 19:28)*.

But it looked to something else. St. John who was at the foot of the Cross records that He said it *“that the scriptures might be fulfilled" (John 19:28)*.

A thousand years before the Psalmist had prophesied that hour: "And they gave me gall for my food, and in my thirst they gave me vinegar to drink" *(Psalm 68:22)*.

The cry was not a cry of weakness, nor selfishness, but a proclamation that the material exists for the spiritual; the appetites and thirsts of earth must be the stepping stones to the hunger and thirst for the kingdom of God and His Justice.

From this Word we learn two lessons of Temperance: First *the material exists for the spiritual.* Christ expressed a physical thirst for a spiritual reason, namely, the fulfillment of prophesy as a proof of His divinity. In like manner, every material thing on the face of this earth, from salt to flesh, must be for us, a means, not an end -- a bridge, not a goal of life.

A glutton does not respect this order; he does not eat to live, but lives to eat. He subordinates life to one of its conditions. The glutton or the drunkard is really a person without a sense of humor. He takes food and drink too seriously; he always misses the reference.

He takes drink so seriously that he forgets it was meant to assist locomotion, not to impede it; he takes flesh so seriously that he forgets it was meant to solder life, not to scorch it.

Why are there so many unhappy marriages today? Because instead of marrying for the reason that human love is the vestibule to the Divine, they marry wondering how long they will be married. On the way back from the Justice of the Peace they are already preparing for divorce as one says to the other: "I will love you for two years and six months."

There was once a time when a man who married a woman would no more have thought of divorcing her than of murdering her. But those were the days when men loved because they believed in God; now they lust because they believe in Freud -- for if this world is all there is, then why not get all you can and by whatever means you can.

It is only in the Church today that "life without lust is born," because she teaches that the use of flesh conditions salvation. But in our modern divorce-mad world "lust without life shall die."

Because temperance teaches us that the earthly exists for the heavenly, the motive of a Christian is far different from the motive of a pagan.

Take two persons who by cutting down on their food lose twenty pounds each. Materially, twenty pounds off a pagan is the same as twenty pounds off a Christian. But the motive in each case is quite different. The pagan diets; the Christian fasts. The pagan diets for the sake of his bodily appearance; the Christian fasts for the sake of his soul. Each received his corresponding reward, either the praise of men who love leanness or the praise of God who loves virtue.

The tragedy of so much dieting, from a Catholic point of view, is how much restraint, or shall we say fat, that goes to waste. That is why one of the first questions in our Catechism is: "Of which should we take more care, our soul or our body?" And the answer is: "We should take more care of our soul, for 'what doth it profit a man, if he gain the whole world, and suffer the loss of his immortal soul?'"

It is the rigid adherence to this principle that the material exists for the spiritual, which makes the Catholic school one of the greatest training grounds for character in the world. Little children are taught as soon as they enter school to 'give up' certain things during Lent -- not because candy is bad, but in order that they might be self-controlled and self-possessed. It is the contrary to the pagan philosophy of 'self-expression' or doing whatever you please.

A boiler that refuses to keep within the limits and blows up is self-expressive. A drunkard is self-expressive or liquor-possessed because he is not self-possessed. Liquor is not his servant; he is its slave. We Catholics do not eat meat on Friday because we love our Lord. That is the day on which He died, and out of loving memory for this redemption we give up the pleasure of meat -- and most of us Catholics hate fish -- because He gave up His life for us. Is that anything to be scorned?

The basis of the Catholic secret of temperance and discipline is exchange. All life is founded on exchange: "What exchange shall a man give?" We get light in exchange for heat; bread in exchange for a dime. If you want to be an expert in mathematics you have to give up being an expert in tennis; if you want to give your body all its satisfactions, you have to give up the joys of the soul. We have to pay for everything.

Every joy demands that another be left untouched. Every step forward requires an austerity, but that is not because there are no rewards on the other side of the hill, but only because we cannot see what is on the other side of the hill.

We must choose then between God and Mammon; flesh and spirit. "No man can serve two masters." If we want to save our soul for eternity, we must discipline our body in time. And we do this not with sadness but with gladness, after the example of Him "who having joy set before him endured the Cross."

A saint is always joyful, but our modern pleasure-hunter is always melancholy. He is not really happy, because he laughs too much. His laughter is artificially stimulated from the outside by a stooge with a wise-crack; it is not a joy that proceeds from the inside because of a duty fulfilled out of love of God. Happiness comes from self-possession through temperance, not from self-expression through license.

The second lesson of temperance in this Fifth Word is given us by the soldier who shared his wine with Our Lord. The cry of Our Lord was not addressed to anyone in particular, but as others wondered what to do, he did it. Scripture says "*he ran.*"

There was no irresoluteness about his service; only one thought dominated his mind: "His need is greater than mine." The Gospel notes that he *filled* the sponge. It was unusual for an executioner to share rations with the one to be executed, but there was something very un-criminal about that man on the central cross.

The wine he gave was not much, but God considers not the gift of the giver, but the love of the giver. The soldier could not reach the lips of Our Lord so he placed the sponge on a reed and touched it to the lips of the Saviour. He had shared his wine with his Creator, and if he knew it, also with his Saviour. And until the crack of doom his act like that of Magdalene shall be recorded among men.

As he restrained himself in the use of his lawful possessions out of love of the suffering, so must we share our treasures out of love for the poor. Here again the motive of sharing is more important than the deed. The reward we will get for our giving depends on the intention of our giving.

We love those who love us -- but there is no great reward in this, for "do not the heathens this." But we must love even our enemies that we may be children of Our Father who is in heaven. Loving enemies out of a divine intention is worth more than loving friends out of a personal satisfaction.

The philanthropists who give millions to erect art museums, libraries, and playgrounds out of purely humanitarian reasons, will not further their eternal salvation as much as the poor widow who gives a nickel to a poor man on the street because in his need she sees the poverty of Christ. It is simply a matter of bookkeeping.

Suppose you wanted to establish a credit for purchases. Naturally, if you deposited your money on credit in a furniture store, you could not expect it to be honored at an automobile factory. In like manner, if you give lavishly to be credited by mankind, you cannot expect to be credited by Christ for eternal salvation. Millions given to perpetuate a family name will avail the soul nothing at the moment of judgment.

This does not mean that money given for art institutes and playgrounds do not avail for eternal salvation, but that they avail only on condition they were given for that motive, that is, in His name: "For whosoever shall give you to drink a cup of water in my name, because you belong to Christ: Amen I say to you, he shall not love his reward" *(Mark 9:40)*.

St. Paul, emphasizing that charity or the love of God alone makes deeds profitable unto salvation, is even more emphatic: "If I should distribute all my goods to feed the poor, and if I should deliver my body to be burned, and have not charity, it profiteth me nothing" *(1Corinthians 13:3)*.

There is a story told of a woman who gave a fortune motivated by human glory, and very occasionally a meager gift for a spiritual intention. When she went to heaven St. Peter showed her a tiny insignificant little house, which was dwarfed by all the mansions surrounding it. "I cannot live in that," said the woman. St. Peter answered: "Sorry, lady. That was the best I could do with the materials you sent me."

It is one of the paradoxes of Christianity that the only things that are really our own when we die is what we gave away in His name. What we leave in our wills is snatched from us by death; but what we give away is recorded by God to our eternal credit, for only our works follow us. It is not *what* is given that profits unto salvation; it is *why* it is given.

That is why a friendly meal given to an enemy in the name of Him Who loved us when we were His enemies, is worth more on the day of our judgment than a ten-million-dollar hospital given to perpetuate a family name.

There is no injustice in this. Each gets the reward he wanted: In one instance, the love of Christ; in the other the memory of men. Of the latter Our Lord said the saddest words ever spoken: "They already have their reward."

For those who wish to cultivate the virtue of temperance and to be self-possessed, these two specific recommendations are made: First, each day practice at least three trivial mortifications, for example, giving up the ninth cigarette, holding back the sarcastic word, returning a kindly answer to a sneer, or sealing the lips on the scandal you just heard, which probably, like all scandals, is 99 44/100 percent untrue.

Second, the magnitude of the mortification is not as important as the love of God for which it is done. Great sacrifices without love are worthless for the soul; nor because they are great does it follow they were done with love; it is the motive that matters -- do them out of love of God.

Then amid the crosses and trials of life, you may catch their relation to the Cross, which alone gives a pattern to the contradiction of life. May we all, like unto the soldier, Joyce Kilmer, as he trudged across the fields of France, see in every aching shoulder, feverish brow, and burning hand, the vision of Christ with His Cross:

My shoulders ache beneath my pack
(Lie easier, Cross, upon His back).

I march with feet that burn and smart
(Tread, Holy Feet, upon my heart).

Men shout at me who may not speak
(They scourged Thy back and smote Thy cheek).

I may not lift a hand to clear
My eyes of salty drops that sear.

(Then shall my fickle soul forget
Thy Agony of Bloody Sweat?)

My rifle hand is stiff and numb
(From Thy pierced palm red rivers come).

I Thirst

Lord, Thou didst suffer more for me
Than all the hosts of land and sea.
So let me render back again
This millionth of Thy gifts. Amen.

The Seven Virtues, 1940

Eighth Meditation

A WORD TO THE MODERNS

The fifth group with a distinct reaction to religion are the Moderns. The Moderns are those who believe in moderation. They hate excesses either good or evil; compromise is the very essence of life; they have an "open mind" -- in fact so open that they never close it on anything absolutely right and true; they are what the Scriptures call "luke-warm," but they prefer to call themselves "broad."

The Moderns are good persons by the standards of the world; they have their daughter married in a Church, where she was never baptized; they like Easter Sunday services and particularly the Fashion Parade which follows; in discussions, they feel that a pretty good case can be made out for the existence of some Power behind the Universe.

They read seven books a year -- all novels, chosen because they were either widely advertised or because their neighbor read them; they serve on hospital boards, parent-teachers associations, contribute to birth-control clinics and Russian relief; but always within the limit allowed by income tax.

They send their children to the best schools they can afford; never send them to church, but let them go to the movies at least twice a week; they take their politics from a radio commentator; their economics from their son who has had one year of it under a Marxist Professor in college. They think there are too many divorces, but after all we are not living in the Middle Ages; they believe that the majority is always right; that religion does add some sentiment and symbolism to life -- in a word, they are what their neighbors would call "good" people.

Their words are correct; their manners courteous; they shrink from giving pain to others; they discountenance profligacy; cursing and swearing are vulgar: they are the Good Moderns.

Being sceptical and doubting the very existence of truth they regard any enthusiasm for religion as a folly. Religion for them is more often an occasion for derision than conversion; they boast of their objectivity but it consists merely in surveying all planets but inhabiting none.

They love to seek truth, but scrupulously avoid the responsibility of finding it; they want to be auditors at all classes, but to be pupils of none; they find it easier to doubt, than to examine.

They never want to know whether a thing is right or wrong, but whether it is "progressive" or "reactionary," "liberal" or "contemporary"; they love to make distinctions between the "historical Jesus" and the "Christ of Paul" and say they would be Christian tomorrow if "all the accretions and perversions" were eliminated. They follow that one avocation in life in which there is no apprenticeship -- criticism.

Transactions of business speculations in stocks, the ephemeral happenings of the day, the superficial wisdom of commentators -- all these find a way directly to their hearts. But religion to them is weariness, when it is not humorous. Religion they say, makes them melancholy and they want to relax.

What is the reaction of the "moderns" to the Cross? We need only go back to their ancestors who addressed the Fifth Word to the Cross.

The Gospels call them "by-standers at the Cross." These original Moderns loved their puns and their humor at the expense of religion. The occasion for it was the Fourth Word of Our Lord from the Cross: "My God, My God, why hast Thou forsaken Me?" It was spoken in Hebrew: "Eli, Eli, Lemma Savacthani."

The bystanders knew very well what that meant. But to those who willed to mock, it was a fine opportunity for a pun. Pretending that they understood him to say "Eloi" rather than "Eli" or the "Elias" rather than "God," they said: "this man calleth Elias" -- "Let us see whether Elias will come to deliver him" *(Matthew 27:47-49) (Mark 15:34-36).* The lance thrust of this word consists in the fact that they make the self-vaunted Messias summon a man who must come before the Messias.

It was a typical attitude of many who think *religion means something else than it actually does*: mistaking Eloi for Eli, Elias for God, religion for social service; contemplation for dreaming; mortification for morbidity; confession for psychoanalysis, and the Papacy for politics. The dilettantes and moderns always think we are calling on Elias when we are actually calling on God.

Their very words indicated passivity, indifference and false caution: "Let us see if Elias will come to deliver him" *(Matthew 27:49).* Wait! Take your time! Do not do anything rash! Wait and see what the Church does about Marxism! Wait and see if it will change its marriage laws! Do not be in a hurry to give your soul to God!

The difficulties of the moderns are always verbal, never real. Those who remain away from God suffer from confusion of their own making. They think the Church is something else than it is, as the bystanders mistook God for Elias.

It is not what they know that is true, which keeps them from salvation; it is what they know that is wrong! They realize this when they come into the Church. Church windows from the outside look like meaningless lead tracings, but from the inside looking out, they reveal patterns of exquisite beauty and loveliness.

As Our Lord did not answer those who mocked Him in the Fourth Word, neither does He answer those who mock Him now. The perfect soul never permits itself to be drawn down to the level of those who mock, for "mockery is the fume of little hearts."

But He did answer them indirectly. To the bystanders, the dilettantes, the over cautious moderns, He did give the key to salvation: the need of fire for a cause as burning as thirst.

There is no pain of the human body comparable to thirst. Who has not heard of "the panting thirst that scorches in the breath of those that die the soldier's fiery death"?

For almost Three Hours now He had remained bareheaded, except for a crown of thorns, under that burning blinding sun, while from four fountains there poured out life in the form of blood. It was therefore natural for Him to ask for a drink!

He, the God-man! He, Who shut up the sea with doors as it did burst forth as issuing out of a womb; He, Who threw stars in their orbits and spheres into space; He, Who said: "He that believeth in me shall never thirst" (*John 6:35*); He, Who once stood up in the Temple on the last day of a solemn feast, and cried out in a loud voice: "If any man thirst, let him come to me, and drink" *(John 7:37)*, now speaks not to God, nor to the executioners, nor to His Mother, but to man. He asks man for a drink: "I thirst!"

There was genuine thirst there, for no one could be crucified without it. But under that physical symbol of thirst was hidden a spiritual thirst, and St. John who was at the foot of the cross made it known: He spoke that the Scriptures might be fulfilled! What Scriptures? His own words: "I was thirsty, and you gave me to drink" *(Matthew 25:35)*. It was therefore a thirst to be thirsted for -- a thirst for the salvation of souls.

While the bystanders were like ice, He was on fire; while they coursed in shallow streams, He launched out into the deep; while they only stand and wait, He plunges in that one cry through both fire and water; while the Moderns were saying: "Let us see" Our Lord was answering: "No, be athirst! Be afire! I am come to cast fire on the earth: and what will I, but that it be kindled?" *(Luke 12:49).*

Religion is not for calculating love. One must love life like wine and drink death like water. Religion is love and:

Love is not love
Which alters, when it alteration finds,
Or bends with the remover to remove.
O! No! it is an ever-fixed mark
That looks on tempests, and is never shaken; . . .
Love's not Time's fool, though rosy lips and cheeks
Within his bending sickle's compass come
Love alters not with his brief hours and weeks
But bears it out even to the edge of doom.

(Shakespeare)

Our Lord chose persons of that kind for His Disciples: Sons of thunder like James and John, who would have called down lightning from heaven on the Samaritans, but whose zeal once rightly directed, truly thundered through the world.

He chose hot blooded, fiery, impetuous Peter, swinging a sword recklessly at night, and yet out of love for God, breathing his last on a Cross upside down, thinking it unbecoming to die like the Lord.

He chose Magdalen, passionate and sensuous, the kind of woman who gave her body without giving her soul, and yet the one who under the touch of Christ's fiery hand gave her body in penance to save souls in grace.

There is no place for spineless characters in religion. "I know thy works, that thou art neither cold nor hot. I would thou wert cold, or hot. But because thou art lukewarm and neither cold, nor hot, I will begin to vomit thee out of my mouth" *(Revelation 3:15-16).* Such is God's disdain for the indifferent.

There is more possibility for conversion in a passion wrongly directed, than in indifference. Where there is fire, its direction can be changed by God's grace, so that it will burn upward rather than downward, and thus enkindle goodness rather than vice.

But where there is indifference and false tolerance and spineless broadmindedness that looks at all causes and espouses none -- there is no chance.

There are many potential saints in prison, and many potential devils in the service of God. In both cases there is thirst: thirst for Satan or thirst for God. And either thirst could be reversed.

Lenin, for example, was a St. Francis in reverse, as St. Francis was a Lenin in reverse. Both started with the idea of violence: Lenin believed in social reform by violence to a class; St. Francis believed in social reform by violence to himself.

They were both right in their starting point: violence: "The kingdom of heaven suffereth violence, and the violent bear it away" *(Matthew 11:12).* It was the direction of that violence that made the difference between the two!

Hate and love spring from the same passion, as laughter and sorrow drink from the same fountain of tears. The difference is in the motive and the end for which they live. Religion is something that must be either hated or loved. It cannot be watched!

Too many people get credit for being good, when they are only passive. They are too often praised for being broadminded when they are so broadminded they can never make up their minds about anything. They are like the icebergs in the cold streams of the North; they cannot help being icebergs! But let those icebergs get down into the warm gulfstream of the south and yet remain icebergs: then *they* will have character!

Moderns! Wait not for a proof of your own making as did the bystanders at the Cross. They dictated the terms upon which they would accept the Divinity of Christ: you dictate terms upon which you will accept the Divinity of the Church. You are looking for bargains in religion, and there are none.

The Church has never yet had a sale on beliefs; it has never compromised on a single Divine Truth to win a soul. There are plenty of religious shops that have, and that is why today so many of them are ending in bankruptcy.

What is particularly interesting is that those religious shops who compromised on God's Truth to win you Moderns, are the very ones whom you Moderns today reject.

Moderns! The proofs for the Divinity of Christ are never so overwhelming as to destroy your freedom; they are sufficient to convince you, but not to compel you. Christ will never batter down the door of your reason: "Behold, I stand at the door and knock." The latch is on our side of the door, not on God's side.

The proper aim of speculation is not merely to destroy falsehood – but to preserve and consolidate the structure of truth. There is a grave danger in too much analysis:

> "Little by little we subtract
> Faith and fallacy from fact,
> The illusory from the true,
> And starve upon the residue."

You may have greater *knowledge* of uncorrelated facts than most people -- Moderns often do, but you have done nothing with your *wills*. Did you ever stop to think that there is such a thing as knowledge increasing through love?

You must, of course, first know to love, but then you must love to know, for the knowledge from the outside that comes from investigation is nothing compared to the knowledge that comes from the *inside* by love.
When you know a thing you draw it to yourself; when you love a thing you draw yourself to it.

Have you ever tried to love God even on the basis of the little knowledge that you did have? If you had, your knowledge would have grown by leaps and bounds. "If any man will do the will of him; he shall know of the doctrine, whether it be of God, or whether I speak of myself" *(John 7:17)*.

You Moderns will never be convinced of religion by argument, for the chances are you have sufficient knowledge. You need *good* will. The best cure for "sceptic poisoning" is love. Develop fire and enthusiasm -- God has no use for tepid souls.

Love your neighbor with an unselfish, dedicated, passionate love, and you will find God. Visit the sick in the hospitals, the poor in the slums. Give them some of your possessions, but also listen to them.

Notice the different attitudes of those who have faith and those who lack it; how peaceful some are in suffering, and how rebellious others are. Slowly you will come to see that if God can make so much difference in their lives, what a difference He would make in your own.

Suffer deeply in sympathy with others; love them in an unselfish way and you will learn more than you ever learned from books. Elias will never come to you, but Christ will come in suffering and in need.

"For I was hungry, and you gave me to eat; I was thirsty and you gave me to drink; I was a stranger and you took me in: naked, and you covered me: sick, and you visited me; I was in prison and you came to me" *(Matthew 25: 35-36).*

Our Lord said: "I thirst." This was the crucified way of saying "Come to me, all you that labour, and are burdened, and I will refresh you" *(Matthew 11:28).* God always puts Himself on the attitude of wanting something as an excuse to give us something.

"Give me to drink," He said to the Woman at the well. But He Who asked also said: "If thou didst know the gift of God, and who he is that saith to thee, Give me to drink, thou perhaps wouldst have asked of him, and he would have given thee living water" *(John 4:10).* He thirsts for us, only because we need Him so! It is not His loss if we love Him not; it is ours.

Without Him our hearts are panting, our lips are parched. Tomorrow we think the rocks of the world will give us fountains, but the next day we find them dry. Each new day brings on its new deception and vain glimmer of the same mirage.

Finally, the Word of Our Lord from the Cross reveals the secret of your unhappiness: it is your moderation. You have no great loves: you are not on fire; you never thirst. Even we who know the Saviour and His Cross have been infected by your passivity. We have become like you -- lukewarm.

The cohorts of Satan today have more passion for the spreading of evil, than many of the children of God have for the spreading of Truth. As Prometheus stole the fire from heaven, so the Pentecostal fires have been stolen from our altars and are now blazing in the temples of anti-God.

All of us are Moderns in a certain sense; we do not love Love as we ought. God is a consuming fire and we are puny embers. Christ came to cast fire upon the earth, and we throw up a smoke screen.

We are all waiting for Elias to take Him down! Why do we not do it and do it *now*! We go up to Calvary but we come down uncrucified! Woe! Woe unto us that come down from Golgotha's Hills with hands unscarred and white.

From the Cross, the Saviour cries, I thirst, and we reach Him vinegar and gall. If the Cross means anything, it means that our human goodness is not enough. Well may He say to us:

You call Me Master, and obey Me not.
You call Me Light, and see Me not.
You call Me Way, and walk not.
You call Me Life, and desire Me not,
You call Me Wise, and follow Me not,
You call Me fair, and love Me not,
You call Me rich, and ask Me not,
You call Me eternal, and seek Me not,
You call Me gracious, and trust Me not,
You call Me noble, and serve Me not.
You call Me mighty, and honor Me not,
You call Me just, and feed Me not.
If I condemn thee, blame Me not.

(Engraved on an old slab in the
Cathedral of Lubeck, Germany)

Seven Words to the Cross, 1944

Ninth Meditation

RELIGION IS A QUEST

Every human heart in the world without exception is on the quest of God. Not everyone may be conscious of it; but they are conscious of their desire for happiness which some in ignorance, perversity, or weakness identify with the tinsel and baubles of earth. It is as natural for the soul to want God as for the body to want food or drink. It was natural for the prodigal son to be hungry; it was unnatural to live on husks. It is natural to want God; it is unnatural to satisfy that want with false gods.

On the other hand, not only is the soul on the quest of God, but God is on the quest of the soul, inviting everyone to His Banquet of Love. But since love is free, His invitation is rejected in the Gospel language either because they have just married, or because they have bought a farm, or because they must try a yoke of oxen.

This double quest of the Creator for the creature and the creature for the Creator is revealed in the Fifth Word of our Lord from the Cross, and the Fifth Word of our Lady, pronounced when her Son was only twelve years of age.

One day Our Blessed Lord said to the multitude: "If any man thirst, let him come to me and drink" *(John 7:37)*. But on the Cross, He, from whose fingertips toppled planets and worlds, He Who filled the valleys with the song of a thousand fountains now cries, not to God, but to man: "I thirst" *(John 19:28)*. The physical pain of being nailed to a cross, lingering for hours without food or drink beneath an Oriental sun, the parched dryness that came from loss of blood, now expresses itself not in peevish impatience but in a simple declaration of thirst.

There is nothing in the whole story of the Crucifixion which makes Our Lord seem so human as this one Word. And yet that thirst could not have been only physical, for the Gospel tells us that He said it in order that the Scriptures might be fulfilled. It, therefore, was spiritual as well as physical. God was on the quest of souls, trusting that one of the trivial ministrations of life, the offering of a cup in His name, might bring the offering within the sweet radiance of His Grace. The Shepherd was still out after the sheep, at the moment when He was giving His Life for the flock!

Mary standing in the shadow of her Son's hard death-bed heard His Word and knew that it was more than a plea for relief. She remembered so well the Psalm from which it was taken. Hearing it, she was reminded of the time she thirsted, too. It was just when her little Son reached the legal age of twelve. During the Feast of the unleavened bread, instituted in remembrance of the Exodus from Egypt, Mary and Joseph joined the pilgrimage to the Holy City. After seven days, according to custom, the multitude departed in the afternoon, the men leaving by one gate, the women by another, to reunite at the halting place of the first night. Joseph and Mary left, each thinking the Child was with the other, only to discover at nightfall that He was not with either.

If the trumpets of doom had sounded, their hearts would have been less heavy. For three days they flushed the hills and the caravans, and on the third day they found Him. We know not where He was during those three days. We can only guess. Perhaps He was visiting Gethsemani where His Blood, twenty-one years later would crimson the olive roots; perhaps He stood on Calvary's hill and saw this sad hour. In any case, on the third day they found Him in the temple, teaching the doctors of the law. Mary said: "Son, why hast thou done so to us? Behold thy father and I have sought thee sorrowing" (*Luke 2:48*). In a land where women were reticent, where men were always masters, it was not Joseph who spoke. It was Mary. Mary was the mother, Joseph was the foster-father.

When Abraham drew near to God, a "great and darksome horror seized upon him" *(Genesis 15:12)*, and when the Lord appeared, "Abraham fell flat on his face" *(Genesis 17:3)*. When Jacob saw the Lord, he trembled saying: "How terrible is this place" *(Genesis 28:17)*. When Moses came in the presence of God, "Moses hid his face" *(Exodus 3:6)*. And yet here, a woman addresses Him Who is the Author of Life, through whom all things were made and without Whom nothing is made, as "*Son*." She called Him that by right and not by privilege. That one word shows the intimate relationship between the two, and it was probably her usual way of addressing Him in Nazareth.

Here was a creature on the quest of God. As our Blessed Lord's thirst on the Cross revealed the Creator in search of man, Mary's words revealed its complementary truth that the creature is in search of God.

If each is seeking for the other, why do they not find? God does not always find man because man is free, and like Adam man can hide from God. Like a child who hides from his mother when he does something wrong, so does man turn from God when he sins. God then always seems "so far away;" but the truth is, it is man who is "far away." Sin creates a distance. Respecting human freedom, God calls, but He does not force. "I thirst" is the language of liberty.

God is closer to us than we suspect, as Paul told the Athenians. He may be somewhat disguised and appear like a gardener as He did to Mary Magdalen, or like a chance acquaintance on a roadway, as He did to the disciples of Emmaus. What must have been the chagrin, therefore, of the inn-keepers of Bethlehem when they discovered that they had refused hospitality to the Mother of Our Lord! If they ever met Our Blessed Mother later on, they probably chided her saying: "Why did you not tell us that you were the Mother of Jesus?" If any of the bystanders at the Crucifixion within the next forty days saw the Risen and Glorified Saviour, how they must have mourned in their hearts, saying: "If I had only known, it was You Who asked for a drink."

Why is it that in religion we want a proof and a manifestation so strong that it will overwhelm our reason and destroy our freedom? That God will never grant! On man's side, the regret will continue even until Judgment! When Christ shall say: "I was thirsty and you gave me not to drink" *(Matthew 25:42)*.

"The angels keep their ancient places;
Turn but a stone, and start a wing!
'Tis ye, 'tis your estranged faces,
That miss the many-splendoured thing."

From the Fifth Word of Jesus and Mary there emerges the lesson that the apostolate of religion should start with the assumption that everyone wants God. Bigots? Do they want Our Lord and His Church? Certainly they think more about the Church than some who belong to it. Be not too hard on them.

They do not really hate the Church. They hate only what they mistakenly believe to be the Church. If I had heard the same lies about the Church that they have heard, and if I had been taught the same historical perversions as they, with my own peculiar character and temperament, I would hate the Church ten times more than they do. At least they have some zeal and some fire. It may be misdirected, but with God's grace it can be channeled into love as well as hate.

These souls who peddle anti-religion tracts or anti-Catholic publications are to be regarded in exactly the same light as St. Paul before his conversion. And as he preached and lectured against the Church, after assisting at the killing of the most brilliant of the early Churchmen, St. Stephen, there were many believers who despaired. Prayers were multiplied to God: "Send someone to refute Paul." And God heard their prayers. God sent Paul to answer Paul. A bigot made the best Apostle.

In my radio audience a few years ago was a young woman who used to sit before the radio and ridicule and scoff and wisecrack at every word. She is now enjoying the fullness of Faith and the Sacraments. In another town was a man who used to make records of these broadcasts, then take them to a nearby convent, and play them for the sisters, who had no radio. But he mitigated this act of kindness by making a running commentary of ridicule while the record played. He recently built the new Sisters' school in that city. Everyone is on the quest of God, and if the soul gives God a chance, God will win.

God is thirsting too, for those who have lost the Faith. The position of the fallen-away Catholic is rather unique. The seriousness of his fall is to be measured by the heights from which he fell. His reaction to the Church is either hate or argument. In both cases he bears witness to the Divinity of the Church. The hate is his vain attempt to despise. Since his conscience which was informed by the Spirit in the Church will not let him alone, he will not let the Church alone.

But the general truth still holds true: assume that he is on the quest of the Divine, otherwise he would not think so much about it. Hence never, never, never argue with a fallen away Catholic. He may tell you, for example, that he left because he could not believe in Confession. Do not believe it. He left because he refused in his pride to confess his sins. He wants to argue to salve his conscience; but he needs absolution to heal it. Like the woman at the well, who had five husbands, he wants to keep religion in the realm of the speculative. What he needs is to have it brought down in the realm of the moral, as our Blessed Lord did for that woman. His difficulty is not with the Creed: it is with the commandments. Having tasted the best, he is miserable without it.

We do not help him by telling him why the road he took was wrong. He knows it. He even knows the right road. We can help him best, like the father of the prodigal, by going out on the road to meet him and make the return journey easy, for every prodigal wants to get back home.

Sinners too, want God. That is to say, conscious sinners. One need hardly ever tell such a sinner how wicked he is. He knows it a thousand times better than you. His conscience has pointed an accusing finger at him in his sleep; his fears have emblazoned his sins on his mind; his neurosis, anxieties, and unhappiness have been like trumpets of his inner death.

This consciousness of sin is not yet conversion, for up to this point a soul may be repenting like Judas, only to itself. One can be mad at oneself for playing the fool, or be ashamed at one's misdeeds, or be sad at being discovered, but there is no true repentance without a turning to God. The consciousness of sin creates the vacuum; grace alone can fill it.

You say: "I am a sinner. I will not be heard." If God will not hear a sinner, why did he praise the publican in the rear of the Temple, who struck his breast saying: "O God, be merciful to me a sinner" *(Luke 18:13)* There were two sinners on Calvary on either side of our Lord. One was saved because he asked to be saved. Did not our Divine Saviour say: "Come to me, all you that labor and are burdened" *(Matthew 11:28)* -- and who is more heavily burdened than a sinner? Unlike all other religions, Christianity starts with the sinner. In a certain sense, it begins with human hopelessness. You have to be good to enter most other religions; you become a Christian on the assumption that you are not good.

God will find you, if your will does not refuse to be found. Hence, avoid those selfish and petty acts which may deaden and stunt you in the one great moment, when surrender to the Divine Will can bring peace. In that case we become like the cobbler of Charles Dickens. For years he had been a prisoner in the Bastille, where he cobbled shoes. He became so enamored of the walls, the darkness, and the task's monotony that when he was liberated, he built a cell at the center of his English home. On days when skies were clear and birds were singing, the taps of the cobbler in the dark could still be heard. So men, by habitual residence in imprisoning moods, render themselves incapable of living in wider horizons, the great hopes and faith of religion.

Stunt not your spiritual life by looking for faults. You do not say Shakespeare cannot write because you heard a poor actor butcher the soliloquy of Hamlet; you do not reject the beauty of music because you hear an occasional moaner or groaner on the radio; you do not disbelieve in medicine because your doctor has a cold.

Give God a chance. The prolongation of his Incarnate Life in the Church is an offer, not a demand. It is a gift, not a bargain. You can never deserve it, but you can receive it. God is on the quest of your soul. Whether you will know peace depends on your own will. "If any man will do the will of him, he shall know of the doctrine, whether it be of God, or whether I speak of myself" *(John 7:17).*

Seven Words of Jesus and Mary, 1945

IT IS FINISHED
Meditations on the Sixth Word from the Cross
Archbishop Fulton J. Sheen

First Meditation

IT IS CONSUMMATED

From all eternity God willed to make man to the image of His eternal Son. After having painted the heavens with blue and the earth with green, God then made a garden, beautiful as only God knows how to make a garden beautiful, and in it placed man made to conform to the image of God's Son. In some mysterious way the revolt of Lucifer echoed to earth, and the image of God in man was blurred and ruined.

The Heavenly Father in His divine mercy willed to restore man to his pristine glory. In order that the portrait might once more be true to the Original, God willed to send to earth His Divine Son according to whose image man was made, that the earth might see once more the manner of man God wanted us to be. In the accomplishment of this task, only Divine Omnipotence could use the elements of defeat as the elements of victory. In the Divine economy of Redemption, the same three things which cooperated in our fall shared in our redemption. For the disobedient man Adam, there was the obedient man Christ; for the proud woman Eve, there was the humble virgin Mary; for the tree of the garden, there was the tree of the Cross. The Redemption was now completed. The work which His Father had given Him to do was accomplished. We were bought and paid for. We were won in a battle fought not with five stones like those with which David slew Goliath, but with five wounds, hideous scars on hands and feet and side; in a battle fought not with armor glistening under a noonday sun, but with flesh hanging like purple rags under a darkened sky; in a battle where the cry was not "Crush and kill," but "Father, forgive"; in a battle fought not with spitting steel, but with dripping blood; in a battle in which he who slew the foe lost the day. Now the battle was over. For the last three hours He had been about His Father's business. The artist had put the last touch on His masterpiece and with the joy of the strong He uttered the song of triumph: "It is finished."

His work is finished, but is ours? It belongs to God to use that word, but not to us. The work of acquiring Divine life for man is finished, but not the distribution. He has finished the task of filling the reservoir of Calvary's sacramental life, but the work of letting it flood our souls is not yet finished. He has finished the foundation; we must build upon it. He has finished the ark, opening His side with a spear and clothing Himself in the garment of His precious blood, but we must enter the ark. He stands at the door and knocks, but the latch is on the inside, and only we can open it. He has enacted the consecration, but the communion depends on us; and whether our work will ever be finished depends entirely on how we relive His life and become other Christs, for His Good Friday and His passion avail us nothing unless we take up His Cross and follow Him. Sin is the great obstacle to the accomplishment of that task, for as long as there is sin in the world, Christ is crucified anew in our hearts.

I saw the Son of God go by
Crowned with the crown of thorn.
"Was it not finished, Lord?" I said,
"And all the anguish borne?"

He turned on me His awful eyes:
"Hast Thou not understood?
Lo! Every soul is Calvary,
And ever sin a rood."

(Rachel Annand Taylor)

PRAYER

Dear Jesus! redemption is Thy work; atonement is mine, for atonement means at-one-ment with Thy life, Thy truth, and Thy love. Thy work on the Cross is finished, but my work is to take you down, for –

> Whenever there is silence around me
> By day or by night --
> I am startled by a cry,
> It came down from the cross --
> The first time I heard it,
> I went out and searched --
> And found a Man in the throes of crucifixion,
> And I said, "I will take you down,"
> And I tried to take the nails out of His feet,
> But He said, "Let them be
> For I cannot be taken down
> Until ever man, every woman, and every child
> Come together to take Me down."
> And I said, "But I cannot bear Your cry.
> What can I do?
> And He said, "Go about the world --
> Tell everyone that you meet --
> There is a Man on the cross."
>
> (Elizabeth Cheney)

Thou art on the Cross, but we must take Thee down. Thou hast been hanging there long enough! Through Thy Apostle, Paul, Thou hast told us that those who are Thine crucify their flesh and its concupiscences. My work, then, is not finished until I take Thy place upon the Cross, for unless there is a Good Friday in my life, there will never be an Easter Sunday; unless there is a garment of a fool, there will never be the white robes of wisdom; unless there is the crown of thorns, there will never be the glorified body; unless there is the battle, there will never be the victory; unless there is the thirst, there will never be the Heavenly

Refreshment; unless there is the Cross, there will never be the empty tomb. Teach me, Jesus, to finish this task, for it is fitting that the sons of men should suffer and thus enter into their glory.

The Seven Last Words, 1933

Second Meditation

FORGIVE US OUR TRESPASSES AS WE FORGIVE THOSE WHO TRESPASS AGAINST US

"Forgive us our trespasses as we forgive those who trespass against us."

"It is consummated."

Everyone who ever came into the world came into it to live. Our Lord, on the contrary, came not into it to live, but to die. His one supreme task was to lay down His life for the redemption of many. The forgiving of the trespasses of man by blotting out sin was the unique business His Father had assigned to Him. Now that duty was done. He had made it possible for us to pray: "Forgive us our trespasses as we forgive those who trespass against us," and so now He cries out with joy of victory won: "It is consummated."

God labored for six days in the creation of the world, at the end of which came the divine applause of a work completed: "And God saw that it was good." For thirty-three years God made man, burned with desire to be baptized with the blood of Redemption; and now at the end of the three hours on the cross, God saw once more "that it was good." It took only a word to create, but it took a life to redeem.

What a lesson for us! How few of us ever finish the tasks assigned to us. The world is full of souls that are like unfinished symphonies, and half-completed Gothic Cathedrals – souls who have begun the poem of their life but have never written the last line; souls that paint pictures and leave out the borders; souls that never have the joy of looking on a perfect work, seeing that it is good, and then, catching an echo from the Cross, crying out the song of victory: "It is finished".

Calvary is a place of great impatience. Many souls follow Our Lord to the Mount of Beatitudes, but refuse to follow Him to Calvary; some carry their cross to Calvary, but when they get there, they lay it down; some are stripped of the garments of doubt, but refuse to be nailed in the fullness of sacrifice; others are nailed but unfasten themselves before the elevation of the cross; others are crucified but answer the challenge of the world and come down after one hour, after two hours, within a minute of the sound of three. The world is full of half-crucified souls. Few there are who stay until the very end; few there are who know what it is to give all, to see the work well done, and experience the thrill of a victory won. Would that there were a single day in our life, in which we could honestly say – I have given God all! "It is finished."

The Seven Last Words and the Our Father, 1935

Third Meditation

THE ITE, MISSA EST

"It is finished." – John 19:30.

Our Blessed Saviour now comes to the *Ite, missa est* of His Mass, as He utters the cry of triumph: "It is finished."

The work of salvation is finished, but when did it begin? It began back in the agelessness of eternity, when God willed to make man. Ever since the beginning of the world there was a Divine "Impatience" to restore man to the arms of God.

The Word was impatient in heaven to be the "Lamb slain from the beginning of the world." He was impatient in prophetic types and symbols, as His dying face was reflected in a hundred mirrors stretching through all Old Testament history. He was impatient to be the real Isaac carrying the wood of His sacrifice in obedience to the commands of His heavenly Abraham. He was impatient to fulfill the mystic symbol of the Lamb of the Jewish Pasch, who was slain without a single bone of its body being broken. He was impatient to be the new Abel, slain by his jealous brethren of the race of Cain, that His Blood might cry to Heaven for forgiveness. He was impatient in His mother's womb, as He saluted His precursor John. He was impatient in the Circumcision, as He anticipated His blood-shedding and received the name of "Saviour." He was impatient at the age of twelve, as He reminded His Mother that He had to be about His Father's business. He was impatient in His public life, as He said He had a baptism wherewith He was to be baptized and He was "straightened until it be accomplished." He was impatient in the Garden, as He turned His back to the consoling twelve legions of angels, to crimson olive roots with His redemptive Blood. He was impatient at His Last Supper, as He anticipated the separation of His Body and Blood under the appearance of bread and wine. And then, impatience closed as the hour of darkness drew near at the end of that Last Supper -- He sang. It was the only time He ever sang, the moment He went to His death.

It was a trivial matter for the world if the stars burned brightly, or the mountains stood as symbols of perplexity, or the hills made their tribute to valleys which gave them birth. What was important was that every single word predicted of Him should be true. Heaven and earth would not pass away until every jot and tittle had been fulfilled. There was only a little iota remaining, one tiny little jot; it was a word of David's about every prediction being fulfilled. Now that all else was fulfilled, He fulfilled that iota; He, the true David, quoted the prophetic David: "It is finished."

What is finished? The Redemption of man is finished. Love had completed its mission, for Love had done all that it could. There are two things Love can do. Love by its very nature tends to an Incarnation, and every Incarnation tends to a Crucifixion. Does not all true love tend toward an Incarnation? In the order of human love, does not the affection of husband for wife create from their mutual loves the incarnation of their confluent love in the form of a child? Once they have begotten their child, do not they make sacrifices for it, even to the point of death? And thus their love tends to a crucifixion.

But this is just a reflection of the divine order, where the love of God for man was so deep and intense that it ended in an Incarnation, which found God in the form and habit of man, whom He loved. But our Lord's love for man did not stop with the Incarnation. Unlike everyone else who was ever born, our Lord came into this world to redeem it. Death was the supreme goal He was seeking. Death interrupted the careers of great men, but it was no interruption to our Lord; it was His crowning glory; it was the unique goal He was seeking.

His Incarnation thus tended to the Crucifixion, for "greater love than this no man hast, that he lay down his life for his friends." Now that Love had run its course in the Redemption of man, Divine Love could say: "I have done all for my vineyard that I can do." Love can do no more than die. It is finished: "Ite, missa est."

His work is finished. But is *ours*? When He said, "it is finished," He did not mean that the opportunities of His life had ended; He meant that His work was done so perfectly that nothing could be added to it to make it more perfect -- but with us, how seldom that is true. Too many of us *end* our lives, but few of us see them *finished*. A sinful life may end, but a sinful life is never a finished life.

If our lives just "end," our friends will ask: "How much did he leave?" But if our life is "finished" our friends will ask: "How much did he take with him?" A finished life is not measured by years but by deeds; not by the time spent in the vineyard, but by the work done. In a short time a man may fulfill many years; even those who come at the eleventh hour may finish their lives; even those who come to God like the thief at the last breath, may finish their lives in the Kingdom of God. Not for them the sad word of regret: "Too late, O ancient Beauty, have I loved Thee."

Our Lord finished His work, but we have not finished ours. He pointed the way we must follow. He laid down the Cross at the finish, but we must take it up. He finished Redemption in His physical Body, but we have not finished it in His Mystical Body. He has finished salvation, we have not yet applied it to our souls. He has finished the Temple, but we must live in it. He has finished the model Cross, we must fashion ours to its pattern. He has finished sowing the seed, we must reap the harvest. He has finished filling the chalice, but we have not finished drinking its refreshing draughts. He has planted the wheat field; we must gather it into our barns. He has finished the Sacrifice of Calvary; we must finish the Mass.

The Crucifixion was not meant to be an inspirational drama, but a pattern act on which to model our lives. We are not meant to sit and watch the Cross as something done and ended like the life of Socrates. *What was done on Calvary avails for us only in the degree that we repeat it in our own lives.*

The Mass makes this possible, for at the renewal of Calvary on our altars we are not on-lookers but sharers in Redemption, and there it is that we "finish" our work. He has told us: "And I, if I be lifted up from the earth, will draw all things to myself." He finished His work when He was lifted up on the Cross; we finish ours when we permit Him to draw us unto Himself in the Mass.

The Mass is that which makes the cross visible to every eye; it placards the Cross at all the crossroads of civilization; it brings Calvary so close that even tired feet can make the journey to its sweet embrace; every hand may now reach out to touch its Sacred Burden, and every ear may hear its sweet appeal, for the Mass and the Cross are the same. In both there is the same offering of a perfectly surrendered will of the beloved Son, the same Body broken, the same Blood flowed forth, the same Divine Forgiveness. All that has been said and done and acted during Holy Mass is to be taken away with us, lived, practiced, and woven into all the circumstances and conditions of our daily lives. His sacrifice is made our sacrifice by making it the oblation of ourselves in union with Him; His life given for us becomes our life given for Him. Thus do we return from Mass as those who have made their choice, turned their backs upon the world, and become other Christs for the generation in which we live -- living potent witnesses to the Love that died that we might live with Love.

This world of ours is full of half-completed Gothic cathedrals, of half-finished lives and half-crucified souls. Some carry the Cross to Calvary and then abandon it; others are nailed to it and detach themselves before the elevation; others are crucified, but in answer to the challenge of the world "Come down," they come down after one hour . . . two hours . . . after two hours and fifty-nine minutes. Real Christians are they who persevere unto the end. Our Lord stayed until He had finished.

The priest must likewise stay at the altar until the Mass is finished. He may not come down. So we must stay with the Cross until our lives are finished. Christ on the Cross is the pattern and model of a finished life. Our human nature is the raw material; our will is the chisel; God's grace is the energy and the inspiration.

Touching the chisel to our unfinished nature, we first cut off huge chunks of selfishness. Then by more delicate chiselings we dig away smaller bits of egotism until finally only a brush of the hand is needed to bring out the completed masterpiece -- a finished man made to the image and likeness of the pattern on the Cross. We are at the altar under the symbol of bread and wine; we have offered ourselves to our Lord; He has consecrated us.

We must therefore not take ourselves back, but remain there unto the end, praying unceasingly, that when the lease of our life has ended and we look back upon a life lived in intimacy with the Cross, the echo of the Sixth Word may ring out on our lips: "It is finished."

And as the sweet accents of that *Ite, missa est* reach beyond the corridors of Time and pierce the "hid battlements of eternity," the angel choirs and the white-robed army of the Church Triumphant will answer back: *"Deo gratias."*

Calvary and the Mass, 1936

Fourth Meditation

BLESSED ARE THE PEACE-MAKERS

"Blessed are the peace-makers: for they shall be called the children of God."

"It is consummated."

At the beginning of His public life on the Hill of the Beatitudes, Our Lord preached: "Blessed are the peace-makers: for they shall be called the children of God." At the end of His life on the hill of Calvary, He practiced that Beatitude as, concluding peace between man and God, He uttered the triumphant cry: "It is consummated."

Like all the other Beatitudes, this was at utter variance with the spirit of the world, where right is might, and where pugnacity and aggressiveness are virtues. This is putting it mildly, for in our generation there has arisen a philosophy of life whose first principle is class struggle.

Never before in the history of the world did any political system profess, and much less act, on the motive of hate. We have it now in Communism, which has almost drowned out the voice of the Prince of Peace.

But what is the peace spoken of in this Beatitude? The most perfect definition of peace ever given was that of St. Augustine: *"Peace is the tranquility of order."* It is not tranquility alone, for some nations such as Russia are tranquil through fear.

Rather, it is the tranquility of order in which there is no oppression from without, but rather a subordination of all things to the sovereign good which is God. Therefore, the subjection of senses to reason, reason to faith, and the whole man to God as his eternal end and final perfection -- that is the basis of peace.

It was just such a tranquility of order which Our Lord brought to earth as the angels sang at His birth: "Glory to God in the highest, and on earth peace to men of good will." He bade His disciples to have peace with one another. Into whatsoever house they entered, they were first to say: "Peace be to this house."

The very Beatitude we are considering is a blessing on such peacemakers, and His words over Jerusalem a reminder of His sorrow at those who loved not peace: "If thou also hadst known, and that in this thy day, the things that are to thy peace; but now they are hidden from thy eyes."

The night of His arrest in the garden, when Peter drew his sword and cut off the right ear of the servant of the high priest, Our Lord rebuked him saying: "Put up again the sword into its place: for all that take the sword shall perish with the sword." Touching the ear of the wounded servant He made it whole.

The next afternoon, He who came to preach peace was put to death in the first world war of man against his Redeemer; but before He died He pronounced the last and final words of peace: "It is finished."

What is finished? War is finished! The war against sin! The war against evil! The war against God! The work of atonement, which is *at-one-ment* with God, was completed. He has finished his Father's decade of the sorrowful mysteries, and the glorious ones were now about to begin.

The last farthing was paid. The Treaty of Peace was signed: "Blessed are the peacemakers." And now that He has made peace, He could cry in triumph: "It is finished." It was not just an armistice; it was victory; it was a consummation -- something done that could not be undone -- Peace with God.

Thus far we have spoken of peace which Our Lord brought to earth. Now we must consider a difficulty against it. If Christ is the Prince of Peace, and if they who take the sword perish with it, and if a kingdom divided against itself will be brought to desolation, and if the Resurrection greeting is *Pax,* then how reconcile these other seemingly contradictory words of Our Lord: "Do not think that I came to send peace upon earth: I came not to send peace, but the sword". "Think ye, that I am come to give peace on earth? I tell you, no; but separation. For there shall be from henceforth five in one house divided three against two, and two against three. The father *shall be divided* against the son, and the son against the father, the mother against the daughter, and the daughter against the mother, the mother-in-law against her daughter-in-law and the daughter-in-law against her mother-in-law." "He that hath not, let him sell his coat and buy a sword."

The explanation of these apparent contradictions is to be found in the words He addressed to His apostles the night of the last supper in which He made an important distinction between two kinds of peace: "My peace I give unto you; *not as the world giveth,* do I give unto you." "These things I have spoken to you, that *in me* you may have peace. *In the world* you shall have distress: but have confidence: I have overcome the world." There is a difference then between His Peace and the peace of the world.

It is evident from these words that Our Lord offers a peace and a consolation that He alone can confer, a peace that comes from the right ordering of conscience, from justice, charity, love of God and love of neighbor. And blessed are those peace-makers who continue to spread that message of peace, for they shall be called the children of God; that is, they shall be recognized as possessing a divine characteristic which shall stamp them as God-like.

But these very lovers of peace, who follow in His footsteps, who take up their crosses daily, who love Him more than all the world, who surrender all to be completely His, who trust in the Providence that feeds the birds, who have the faith of little children, and who love Christ and therefore seek that *interior peace* of conscience that only Christ can give -- they will by that very fact be hated by the world.

The poor in spirit will be hated by those who pursue self-interest; the meek will be opposed by the self-assertive; those who hunger and thirst after justice will be scorned by the indifferent; the merciful will be ridiculed by the unforgiving; the pure of heart will be the laughingstock of the Freudians. The world whose false peace is based on self-love will make war against those whose peace is based on conscience.

In that sense, Our Lord brought the sword -- we might say, He even made war, war against war, war against selfishness, war against sin, war against godlessness. And if His war against evil brought him to the cross, then His followers who preach His peace must also expect to be crucified.

The son who enters the priesthood rather than business may be hated by his father; the daughter who enters the convent rather than the social whirl may be hated by her mother; and the mother-in-law who pleads for the sanctity of the marriage bond may be hated by the daughter-in-law; and the daughter-in-law who is received into the Church to enjoy the security of its truth and the life of its Eucharist, may be hated by her mother-in-law. This is the meaning of Our Lord's words about a house being divided against itself.

A young man goes to college. He could there join an Oriental sun cult, or become a Buddhist, or a Confucianist, or start a new religion of his own, and his parents would probably only remonstrate; but let him join the Church and there would be war!

Truly indeed: "I came not to bring peace but the sword" -- but Our Lord encouragingly reminds that young man that the war against him is only temporary. "In the world you shall have distress; but have confidence: I have overcome the world."

The Prince of peace then brings war -- war against a false peace, war against tranquility without order. If there is anything in life of which we must beware it is the danger of a false peace. Our Lord could have made a false peace with the world.

Did not the very ones who put Him to death ask Him to make terms with them? Did they not shout up to the throne: "Come down from the cross and we will believe"; in other words, "Come down and make a false peace. You are too insistent in the rights of your heavenly Father. You are too uncompromising about sin. You are too intolerant about your divinity. Can you not see that your claim to be the Son of God and Redeemer of the world is upsetting the world? Did you not hear one of the judges say to you last night 'One man must die for the nation to keep peace'? Come down and we will have peace."

Yes, if He had come down, there would have been peace; but a false peace! Our Lord stayed on the Cross until it was finished. He would not compromise His divinity. He would not compromise obedience to His Father's will. He would not minimize the horror of sin.

And so He stayed on the cross making war against evil until the battle was over, like a dying soldier who feebly fights with ebbing strength until his cause is victorious. That is why He could cry at the end: "It is consummated."

So, too, we must beware of a false peace. The Communists for example ask us to join them in a League for Peace, but we cannot, simply because it is a false Peace. Communists want peace among non-Communist nations only because it offers them a better opportunity for their propaganda, which ends in the destruction of peace.

Furthermore, to a Communist there is no real peace until all nations are subject to the Communist regime and the leadership of Stalin. Communism thus becomes identified with the overthrow of the family, of religion, of justice, and of God. Such is peace as the world gives it.

Because we refuse to accept that false peace, because we refuse to come down from our cross and join in their false peace based on injustice, we bring down upon our heads their violence and their hate. But we cannot expect the world to treat us differently than it treated Our Lord.

Peace for us means a right conscience, not a dictatorship over the proletariat; it means the tranquility of order, not the overthrow of society; it means loving our enemies, not despising them; it means something in the inside of a man's soul, not something outside like a sickle and a hammer.

We must beware, then, of concluding a false peace; of selling the Saviour for thirty pieces of silver because He does not make us rich; of denying Him before men because of the ridicule of maid servants; of sleeping in hours of great need; and above all else, of stepping down from the cross, even after two hours and fifty-nine minutes of the world's crucifixion.

We must be prepared to suffer scorn, if for no other reason than because we are peace-makers; we must ever be ready to be hated by the world, for Our Lord told us we would be hated because of Him. We must stay until "it is finished," even though that staying makes our fellow-men hate us.

This life is not a victory; this life is a war, and *God hates peace in those who are destined for war!*

The Cross and the Beatitudes, 1937

Fifth Meditation

A PLANNED UNIVERSE

"It is finished."

In the face of the undeserved suffering of the just, the unmerited prosperity of the wicked, the misery of the merciful, the pleasures of the sinful, many will ask this question: Is this a planned universe, or is it the plaything of chance?

This question would have been unanswerable in this life had not Goodness itself descended into the level of the world's woe, deliberately and willfully. But once the Best freely goes down to the worst, and fits it into His plan and purpose, then no man can ever be without hope.

If a man who knows nothing about electricity is told that a bolt of electricity more powerful than lightning is to be released by a scientist in a small laboratory, that man will not fear the result, so long as he is certain that the scientist knows what he is doing.

He reasons that the scientist understands the nature of electricity, even though he does not. If the scientist hurls that otherwise destructive fire in a tiny room, it must be because he knows how to control its force. In other words, he has a plan or purpose.

In like manner, if God, Who could have foregone the trials and sorrows of man, and yet by a free act descends to man, assumes his nature, and unites it with His Own Divine Nature, and then with eyes open and with full knowledge of the world's iniquity, walks into it and even embraces it, it must be because it fits into His Divine pattern.

Our Blessed Lord did not walk blindly into a world capable of crucifying virtue, as you and I might walk into an unknown forest. He came into it as a doctor into his hospital, with full knowledge of how to deal with pain.

His whole course was charted beforehand; nothing took Him by surprise. At any given moment He had the Power to overcome. But He would not use the Power regardless of how much He was challenged, until He *willed* it.

It is this Divine Knowledge which explains His rejoinder to Mary and Joseph in the temple, when He was only twelve years of age: "Did you not know that I must be about my Father's business?" Already He talks of a plan, and in particular of a plan that is made in Heaven.

It also explains His many prophecies concerning His death, its time, its place, and its circumstances, and the almost impatient urge He had to realize it. "I have a baptism wherewith I am to be baptized: and how I am straitened until it be accomplished!"

Death then would not be a stumbling block to Him as it was to Socrates, for whom it was but an unwanted interruption of his teaching. For Our Lord, death was the goal He was seeking, the supreme objective of His mission on earth.

Everyone else who ever came into the world, came into it to live. Our Lord came into it to *die*. But that death with its scourgings and tears would not come to Him in an unguarded moment.

Many times during His life when His enemies sought to kill Him, He said His "hour was not yet come." When "the hour" He set did come, He refused the help of heaven and earth to postpone it or escape it.

He refused heaven's help, for had He not said: "Thinkest thou that I cannot ask my Father, and he will give me presently more than twelve legions of angels?" He refused earth's help, for He told Peter: "Put up thy sword into the scabbard." His enemies did not come to Him: He went to them. And He went saying: "This is your hour, your hour of darkness. Your hour when I allow you to do with Me whatever you please; the hour when I might turn my back upon the ills of humanity, but in which I drink its chalice of bitterness even to its very dregs." He "Having joy set before him, endured the cross."

Bodily suffering, mental anguish, bitter disappointment, the false judgment of justice, the betrayal of true friendship, the court's perversion of honesty, and the violent separation from a mother's love -- all these He took upon Himself knowingly, freely, deliberately, and purposely.

Then after three hours of crucifixion, surveying all the prophecies made about Him in Old Testament days, and the prophecies He had made of Himself, and seeing them all fulfilled and the last stitch drawn on the tapestry of His Life and the pattern completed, He uttered His sixth word -- a word of triumph: "It is finished."

That cry meant: This is a planned universe. Suffering fits into it, otherwise He would have refused it. The cross fits into it, otherwise He would not have embraced it. The crown of thorns fits into it, otherwise He would not have worn it.

Nothing was accidental; everything was ordered. His Father's business was completed. The plan was finished.

The full significance of the plan was not revealed until three days later, when the Seed which fell to the ground arose into the newness of Life. It was this plan Our Lord gave to the disciple at Emmaus: "Ought not Christ to have suffered these things and so to enter into his glory?"

In other words, unless there is a Good Friday in our lives, there will never be an Easter Sunday; unless we die to this world, we shall not live in the next unless there is the crown of thorns, there will never be the halo of light; unless there is the cross, there will never be an empty tomb; unless we lose our life, we shall not find it; unless we are crucified with Christ, we shall never rise with Christ.

Such is the plan, and on our choice depends eternal issues. Our attitude toward the inescapable cross immortalizes us, either for gain or loss.

And though the plan seems hard, it is not blind, for Our Lord has not merely told us to follow Him -- He has led the way. We can follow His footsteps out of the dark forest of our sufferings, but we can never say: He does not know what it means to suffer.

He suffered first to teach us how to bear it. He did not say: "Go to the Cross," but He did say: "Come, follow Me." Because He was God, He knew that men would not go just because they were told, but that they would follow if an example were given.

Our Lord made use of the contradictions of life to redeem us; we must make use of the same contradictions to apply the fruits of that redemption. His plan is finished for He is now enjoying glory. Our plan is not yet finished, for we have not yet saved our souls.

But everything we do must be directed to that one supreme goal, for "what doth it profit a man, if he gain the whole world, and suffer the loss of his own soul." Is not that the reason why, in God's plan of the universe, suffering generally comes at the end instead of at the beginning? This is a fact.

Youth is full of hopes; age is burdened with cares. Paradise came at the beginning of human history, and seven vials of wrath will come at its end. The angels sang at His birth, but His executioners blasphemed at His death.

Even in religion, the greatest spiritual joys seem to come at ordination, or at reception of the veil, or at conversion, or at the marriage ceremony.

Later on, God seems to withdraw His consoling sweetness, as a mother no longer coaxes a grown child with candy, in order to teach us that we must walk on our own feet, and work for the joys beyond.

As reasonable beings, we must ask why suffering, sadness, disillusionment, and cares, all seem to come in the evening of life?

The first reason seems to be to remind us that earth is not a paradise, and that the life, truth, and love we crave, is not to be found here below.

As Abraham was told to go out of his country, so we seem to be told by life's bitterness to go out of ourselves, to look beyond and upwards to the completion of our task.

It is the burn of the fire that makes the child snatch his hand away, and it is the burden and bitterness of life that makes us draw ourselves away from earth. God is, as it were, urging us on to finish our lives and not merely to have them end, as the animals that rise to eat and then lie down to die.

Then, too, God permits these crosses in the twilight of our lives in order to supply the defects of our love. If we gave our young bones to the world, our sufferings remind us that we can still give our dry bones to God.

The crucifixion gave the good thief his one good opportunity for making amends for his failure to love, and enabled him by an act of love to purchase Paradise that very day.

Too many of us are like St. Augustine, who during the delirious viciousness of early life, said: "I want to be good, a little later on, dear Lord, but not now."

It takes a cross to jolt us back again into the plan, just as many mechanical devices are restored to order by a jolt. Life's wrenches and throbs do more than anything else to convince us that we can never find happiness on earth; and if happiness could be found here, man would never so universally have sought God.

> "If there had anywhere appeared in space
> Another place of refuge, where to flee
> Our hearts had taken refuge in that place,
> And not with Thee.
>
> "For we against creation's bars had beat
> Like prisoner eagles, through great worlds had sought
> Though but a foot of ground to plant our feet
> Where Thou wert not.
>
> "And only when we found in earth and air
> In Heaven or hell, that such might nowhere be
> That we could not flee from Thee anywhere
> We fled to Thee."
>
> (Richard Trench)

This Sixth Word explains that really astounding fact that we have in this life greater capacities for pain than for pleasure.

We can enjoy pleasures, but if we continue in them abnormally they reach a point where they turn into pain. They do not lead us on and on to richer Elysian fields; rather do they turn back on us and wound us. Even the very repetition of a pleasure dulls the pleasure itself. Tickling begins with laughter and ends with pain.

But with pain it is different. In moments of intense suffering, we feel we could not bear it if it continued a minute longer. It goes on beyond that minute, and yet we tap new layers of endurability. But never does pain pass into pleasure. No toothache ever becomes fun just because it lasts a week.

Now why is it that we have greater resources for pain than for pleasure? The real reason is this: if we live our lives as God intended that we should, then we should leave pain behind in this world and enjoy everlasting bliss in the next. Pleasure is reserved for the next world; that is why it plays traitor to us here. Pain is not intended for the next world; that is why we can exhaust it here. Pain exists in the next world only for those who refuse to exhaust it here as an exchange for everlasting life.

That brings up the supreme problem of a happy death. A happy death is a masterpiece. Our Lord labored on His masterpiece from eternity, for He is the "Lamb slain from the beginning of the world." We must labor on ours from the beginning too, for as the tree falls, there it lies.

At the moment of death nothing will be useful to us -- except God. If we have Him, then we shall recover everything in Him.

For that reason, a Christian is never in full possession of his life until the day of his death. That is why the Church calls it a *Natalitia* -- birthday, the birthday into Eternal life. Eternal exile is only for those who made the earth their fatherland.

No masterpiece was ever completed in a day. It takes years for the artist to discipline his mind and hand, and then years again to chisel away the stubbornness of the marble to make the form appear. The greatest masterpiece of all -- a Happy Death -- must be prepared for by practice.

We learn how to die by dying, dying to our selfishness, our pride, our envy, our sloth, a thousand times a day. This is what Our Lord meant when He said: "If any man will come after me, let him . . . take up his cross daily, and follow me." We cannot die well unless we practice dying.

Then when the time comes for the last stroke we shall be skilled in it, and we shall not be taken by surprise.

Our tower will have been completed; whether it be high or low will matter not. It only matters that we finish the plan Our Lord has given us to do. And may we all, as an old Irish saying has it: "Be in heaven half an hour before the devil knows we're dead."

The Rainbow of Sorrow, 1938

Sixth Meditation

SLOTH

"It is finished."

Sloth is a malady of the will that causes us to neglect our duties. Sloth may be physical or spiritual. It is physical when it shows itself in laziness, procrastination, idleness, softness, indifference, and nonchalance. It is spiritual when it shows itself in an indifference to character betterment, a distaste for the spiritual, a hurried crowding of devotions, lukewarmness, and failure to cultivate new virtue.

The classic description of the effects of sloth is to be found in the book of Proverbs: "I passed by the field of the slothful man, and by the vineyard of the foolish man: And behold, it was all filled with nettles, and thorns had covered the face thereof, and the stone wall was broken down. Which when I had seen, I laid it up in my heart, and by the example I received instruction. Thou wilt sleep a little, said I, thou wilt slumber a little, thou wilt fold thy hands a little to rest: And poverty shall come to thee as a runner, and beggary as an armed man."

Of such indifference to duty Our Lord spoke in the Apocalypse: "But because thou art lukewarm, and neither cold, nor hot, I will begin to vomit thee out of my mouth."

The Life and teaching of Our Lord lend no support to the slothful man. When yet only twelve years of age He speaks of being about His "Father's business" which was nothing less than redeeming the world. Then for eighteen years He worked as a manual laborer transforming dead and useless things into the child's crib, the friend's table, Nazarene roofs, and the farmers' wagons, as symbols of His later work by which He would transform hard money changers and prostitutes into useful citizens of the Kingdom of Heaven.

Beginning a public life with calloused hands He preached the Gospel of work: "I must work the works of Him that sent me, whilst it is day; the night cometh, when no man can work." His whole life, in His own words, was spent not in receiving, but in giving: "the Son of man is not come to be ministered unto, but to minister, and to give his life as a redemption for many."

He earned the right to teach the necessity of work, and lest we live under any illusions that any other work is more important than the saving of souls, even the burial of our fathers, He said to the disciple who asked for such permission: "Follow me, and let the dead bury their dead."

To the young man who wished to be His disciple but first wanted to bid farewell to friends at home, Our Lord said: "No man putting his hand to the plough, and looking back, is fit for the kingdom of God." Laboring for bread alone is no fulfillment of His commandment, for to those who wanted more bread He pleaded, "Labor not for the meat which perisheth, but for that which endureth unto life everlasting, which the Son of man will give you."

The business of salvation is no easy task. There are two roads through this world and two gates into the future life. "Enter ye in at the narrow gate; for wide is the gate, and broad is the way, that leadeth to destruction, and many there are who go in thereat. How narrow is the gate, and strait is the way that leadeth to life: and few there are that find it!"

Curiously enough, His invitation goes out only to those who labor for the eternal prize: "Come to me, all you who labor, and are burdened, and I will refresh you. Take up my yoke upon you, and learn of me, for I am meek, and humble of heart: And you shall find rest to your souls. For my yoke is sweet, and my burden light."

So completely had He fulfilled the smallest detail of His Father's business that on the very night of His Agony, in the Upper Room in the presence of His Apostles, He could raise His eyes to heaven and pray: "Father . . . I have glorified thee on earth; I have finished the work which thou gavest me to do." Then the following afternoon, as the Carpenter is put to death by His own profession, He cries out from the Cross in a loud voice the final reparation for sloth and the song of triumph: "It is consummated."

He did not say, "I die," because death did not come to take Him. He walked to it to conquer it. The last drop in the chalice of redemption was drained; the last nail had been driven in the mansion of the Father's House; the last brush touched to the canvas of salvation! His work was done!

But ours is not. It is important to realize this for there are the slothful who justify themselves by saying they need only faith in Christ to save their souls. Surely He who worked so hard for the world's redemption, came not to dispense His followers from work. The servant is not above the master. Faith in Him alone does not save, for "faith without good works is dead." It is not enough for the student to have faith in his teacher's knowledge; he must also study. It is not enough for the sick to have faith in their doctor; their organism must cooperate with him and his medicine. It is not enough to believe that Washington was the "father of our country"; we must also assume and fulfill our duties as American citizens.

In like manner, it is not enough to believe in Christ; we must live Christ and, to some extent, die Christ-like. His words permit of no equivocation: "And he that taketh not up his cross, and followeth me, is not worthy of me. He that findeth his life, shall lose it and he that shall lose his life for me, shall find it."

St. Paul understood the labor involved in being a Christian and wrote the same message to the Romans: "For if we have been planted together in the likeness of His death, we shall be also in the likeness of his resurrection." What He hath done with His human nature, we must do with ours

-- plant it in the soil of the Cross and await the Resurrection of the Eternal Easter.

Later on, to the Corinthians, Paul repeated it: "As you are partakers of the sufferings, so shall you be also of the consolation." And St. Peter, who knew well the scandal of the Cross pleaded for joy in reliving the Cross: "But if you partake of the sufferings of Christ, rejoice that when his glory shall be revealed, you may also be glad with exceeding joy."

There is no hope for the spiritually slothful in these injunctions. Our Lord is the die; we must be stamped by it. He is the pattern; we must be remodelled to it. The Cross is the condition; we must be nailed to it. Our Lord loved His Cross so much that He keeps its scars even in His glory. He who had won victory over death, kept the record of its wounds.

If so precious to Him, they cannot be meaningless for us. In their preservation is the reminder that we too must be signed with those signs and sealed with those seals.

On Judgment Day, He will say to each of us: "Show Me your hands and feet. Where are your scars of victory? Have you fought no battles for truth? Have you won no wars for goodness? Have you made no enemy of evil?"

If we can prove we have been His warriors and show the scars on our apostolic hands, we shall enjoy the peace of victory. But woe unto us who come down from the Calvary of this earthly pilgrimage with hands unscarred and white!

Two lessons emerge from this Sixth Word from the Cross witnessing to His finished work and our own unfinished tasks: First, we must beware of spiritual sloth, for its penalties are tremendous; and second, we must work for a complete life.

The Gospel records three instances of sloth. There were the foolish virgins, chaste but lazy. The wise virgins fill their lamps with oil and wait to hear the step of the approaching bridegroom. The foolish virgins do not think of oil, and tired of waiting, they fall asleep. When the bridegroom comes, the wise virgins light their lamps and welcome the bridegroom. The foolish virgins go out to buy oil, but everybody is asleep, the shops are closed. They go back to the wedding feast, but the door is closed. They cry: "Lord, Lord, open to us." But His answer is: "Amen, I say to you, 1 know you not ..." Our Lord concludes the parable with these words: "Watch, ye, therefore, because you know not the day nor the hour."

The second instance of sloth was the parable of the barren fig tree: "And the next day, when they came out from Bethania, he was hungry. And when he had seen afar off a fig-tree having leaves, he came if perhaps he might find anything on it. And when he was come to it, he found nothing but leaves. For it was not the time for figs. And answering, he said to it: 'May no man hereafter eat fruit of thee any more forever."

The third was the parable of the buried talent. He who received five talents earned another five; he who had received two earned another two; but he who received one hid it in the ground. Of him the lord of the servants said, "Wicked and slothful servant! . . . Take ye away therefore the talent from him, and give it him that hath ten talents. For to every one that hath shall be given, and he shall abound: but from him that hath not, that also which he seemeth to have shall be taken away. And the unprofitable servant cast ye out into the exterior darkness. There shall be weeping and gnashing of teeth."

Common to these three parables is the danger of sloth and the necessity of work. Purity without good works will not save us any more than it saved the foolish virgins. Those who do nothing run the risk of losing the little they have. In other words, it is possible to lose our souls by doing nothing.

"How shall we escape if we neglect . . .?" We lose our souls not only by the evil we do, but also by the good we leave undone.

Neglect the body, and the muscles stiffen; neglect the mind, and imbecility comes; neglect the soul, and ruin follows. Just as physical life is the sum of the forces which resist death, so the spiritual life is to some extent the sum of the forces which resist evil. Neglect to take an antidote for a poison in the body, and we die by our neglect. Neglect to take precaution against sin, and we die the death merely because of neglect.

Heaven is a city on a hill, hence, we cannot coast into it; we have to climb. Those who are too lazy to mount can miss its capture as well as the evil who refuse to seek it. Let no one think he can be totally indifferent to God in this life and suddenly develop a capacity for Him at the moment of death.

Where will the capacity for Heaven come from if we have neglected it on earth? A man cannot suddenly walk into a lecture room on higher mathematics and be thrilled by its equations if all during life he neglected to develop a taste for mathematics. A heaven of poets would be a hell to those who never learned to love poetry. And a heaven of Divine Truth, Righteousness, and Justice would be a hell to those who never studiously cultivated those virtues here below. Heaven is only for those who work for heaven.

If we crush every inspiration of the Divine; if we drown every Godward inspiration of the soul; if we choke every inlet to Christ -- where will be our relish for God on the last day? The very things we neglected will then be the very cause of our ruin. The very things that should have ministered to our growth will then turn against us and minister to our decay.

The sun which warms the plant can under other conditions also wither it. The rain which nourishes the flower can under other conditions rot it. The same sun shines upon mud that shines upon wax. It hardens the mud but softens the wax. The difference is not in the sun, but in that upon which it shines.

So it is with God. The Divine Life that shines upon a soul who loves Him, softens it into everlasting life; that same Divine Life which shines upon the slothful soul, neglectful of God, hardens it into everlasting death.

Heaven and Hell are in like manner both effects of Divine Goodness. Their difference comes from our reaction to that goodness, and to that extent are also our creations. Both God and man are in different senses creators of heaven and hell.

A little heed then to this word from the Cross: "It is consummated." We finish our vocation as He finished His -- on a cross and nowhere else. Only to the doers of the truth, and not to its preachers or its hearers, comes the reward of the crown. Doing implies the spending not of what we *have*, but of what we are.

We need have no undue fear for our health if we work hard for the Kingdom of God; God will take care of our health if we take care of His cause. In any case, it is better to burn out than to rust out.

Burning the candle at both ends for God's sake may be foolishness to the world, but it is a profitable Christian exercise -- for so much better the light. Only one thing in life matters: Being found worthy of the Light of the World in the hour of His visitation.

"Take ye heed," He said. "Take ye heed, watch and pray. For ye know not when the time is. Even as a man who going into a far country, left his house, and gave authority to his servants over every work, and commanded the porter to watch. Watch ye therefore (for you know not when the lord of the house cometh: at even, or at midnight, or at the cock crowing, or in the morning), lest coming on a sudden, he find you sleeping. And what I say to you, I say to all: Watch."

Not only must we beware of spiritual sloth, but we must also work for a completed life. The important word in the struggle against sloth is "finished". The world judges us by results; Our Lord judges us by the way we fulfill and finish our appointed tasks. A good life is not necessarily a successful life.

The sowers are not always the reapers. Those whom God destines only to sow receive their reward for just that, even though they never garnered a single sheaf into everlasting barns. In the parable of the talents, the reward is according to the development of potentialities and the completion of appointed duties.

One day Our Lord "sitting over against the treasury, beheld how the people cast money into the treasury, and many that were rich cast in much. And there came a certain poor widow, and she cast in two mites, which make about half a cent. And calling his disciples together, he saith to them: Amen, I say to you, this poor widow hath cast in more than all they who have cast into the treasury. For all they did cast in of their abundance; but she of her want cast in all she had, *even* her whole living."

The result was trivial for the treasury, but it was infinite for her soul. She had not half done her duty, she had finished it. This is what is meant by completed living.

In the Christian order, it is not the important who are essential, nor those who do great things who are really great. A king is no nobler in the sight of God than a peasant. The head of government with millions of troops at his command is no more precious in the sight of God than a paralyzed child. The former has greater opportunities for evil, but like the widow in the Temple, if the child fulfills his task of resignation to the will of God more than the dictator fulfills his task of procuring social justice for the glory of God, then the child is greater. "God is no respecter of persons."

Men and women are only actors on the stage of life. Why should he who plays the part of the rich man glory in his gold and rich table and consider himself better than one who plays the role of the beggar begging a crumb from his table. When the curtain goes down they are both men. So when God pulls down the curtain on the drama of the world's redemption, He will not ask what part we played, but only how well we played the role assigned to us. The Little Flower has said: that one could save one's soul by picking up pins out of love of God.

If we could create worlds and drop them into space from our fingertips, we would please God no more than by dropping a coin into a tin cup. It is not *what* is done, but *why* it is done that matters. A bootblack shining a pair of shoes inspired by a Divine motive is doing more good for this world than all the Godless conventions Moscow could ever convene.

It is the intention which makes the work. Duties in life are like marble, canvas, and stone. Marble becomes valuable because of the image given to it by the sculptor; canvas is ennobled by the picture of the artist; and stone is glorified by the pattern of the architect.

So it is with our works. The intention gives them value as the image gives the marble value. God is not interested in what we do with our hands, or our money, or our minds, or our mouths, but with our *wills*. It is not the work but the worker that counts.

Let those souls who think their work has no value recognize that by fulfilling their insignificant tasks out of a love of God, those tasks assume a supernatural worth. The aged who bear the taunts of the young, the sick crucified to their beds, the ignorant immigrant in the steel mill, the street cleaner and the garbage collector, the wardrobe mistress in the theater and the chorus girl who never had a line, the unemployed carpenter and the ash collector -- all these will be enthroned above dictators, presidents, kings, and cardinals if a greater love of God inspires their humbler tasks than inspires those who play nobler roles with less love.

No work is finished until we do it for the honor and glory of God. "Whether you eat or drink, or whatever else you do, do all to the glory of God." When our lease on life runs out there are two questions will be asked. The world will ask: "How much did he leave?" The angels will ask: "How much did he bring with him?"

The soul can carry much, but in its journey to the judgment seat of God it will be freighted down only with that kind of goods which a man can carry away from a shipwreck -- his good works done for the glory of God. All that we leave behind is "unfinished." All that we take with us is "finished."

May we never die too soon! This does not mean not dying young; it means not dying with our appointed tasks undone. It is indeed a curious fact that no one ever thinks of Our Lord as dying too young! That is because He finished His Father's business. But no matter how old we are when we die, we always feel there is something more to be done.

Why do we feel that way, if it is not because we did not do well the tasks assigned to us. Our task may not be great; it may be only to add one stone to the Temple of God. But whatever it is, do each tiny little act in union with your Saviour, who died on the Cross, and you will *finish* your life. Then you will never die too young!

But if, impatient, thou let slip thy cross,
Thou wilt not find it in this world again,
Nor in another; here, and here alone
Is given thee to suffer for God's sake.
In other words we shall more perfectly

Serve Him and love Him, praise Him, work for Him,
Grow near and nearer Him with all delight;
But then we shall not any more be called
To suffer, which is our appointment here,
Canst thou not suffer then one hour, -- or two?
If He should call thee from thy cross to-day,
Saying, It is finished! – that hard cross of thine
From which thou prayest for deliverance,
Thinkest thou not some passion of regret
Would overcome thee? Thou wouldst say, "So soon?
Let me go back and suffer yet awhile
More patiently; -- I have not yet praised God."
And He might answer to thee, -- "Never more.
All pain is done with." Whensoe'er it comes,
That summons that we look for, it will seem
Soon, yea too soon. Let us take heed in time
That God may now be glorified in us;
And while we suffer, let us set our souls
To suffer perfectly: since this alone,
The suffering, which is this world's special grace
May here be perfected and left behind. . . .
Endure, Endure, -- be faithful to the end!

(Harriet Eleanor Hamilton-King)

Victory Over Vice, 1939

Seventh Meditation

JUSTICE

"It is consummated."

Calvary is not a history everyone likes to hear recalled, and generally those who most shrink from the sight of the Saviour on the Cross are the very ones who delight in the grotesque murder stories in our tabloids, and follow with bold interest the harrowing details of a sex crime.

Why is it that the lover of horror cannot stand the sight of the crucifix? Why is it that the fanatics of murder stories are so cold to the story of the world's greatest sacrifice? The answer is that unlike all other crimes the crucifix is self-accusing.

We can look on other scenes of injustice without feeling we are involved in them; but we cannot look on a crucifix without feeling that we had something to do with it, either for better or worse; either as a robber brought before his victim for judgment, or as a drowning man brought before his rescuer for thanks.

In the face of all things else we can remain somewhat indifferent, for in human injustice the issues of right and wrong are not always clear-cut. But on Calvary there is an absoluteness; there are no streaks of grey, no blurred edges, only a straight collision of black and white, of good and evil -- and there is no 'No Man's Land' between them.

It is the epitome of the struggle of the world; we are involved in it to the extent that we are involved in the conflict of good and evil. It would be convenient at times if we could wash our hands of the whole affair as Pilate tried to do; but deeper than the blood on Lady Macbeth's hands, not all the waters of the seven seas could wash away those spots incarnadined.

In the Crucifix is symbolized the perennial crisis in the soul of every man, the choice between the illusory end of time and the imponderable ends of eternity. First are focused all the microscopic conflicts of good and evil that go on in every conscience; or, to put it another way, every man's soul is Calvary written small. That is why the Crucifix is inescapable; we either shrink from it or we embrace it; but we cannot be indifferent to it. Slinking away from it like a frightened animal is only the dishonest way of saying it is 'self-accusing.'

It is part of that perverse psychology which makes us suit our thinking to the way we live, rather than suiting the way we live to our thinking. There are really only two classes of souls in all the world: those who have the courage to contemplate the Crucifix and the cowards who run from it.

For those who are brave enough to look at the Crucifix there is a revelation of the moral order -- not a moral order based on abstractions, theories, and hypotheses, but a moral order revealed in a Person of absolute goodness who has met the impact of human evil.

It is more like a mirror than a scene, for it reveals not something unrelated to us, but ourselves, our moral beggary, our perversities and our defeats.

Like nothing else in all the world, it seems to ask the questions: "Where do you stand?" "Which side do you propose to take from this moment on -- My side, or the side of moneyed Judas, cowardly Pilate, crafty Annas, or lustful Herod?" We cannot escape an answer.

If on that Cross were someone who himself had been wrong and failed and had compromised with goodness, we could plead an excuse. But here neutrality is impossible, because there is no question of something more good or less good -- there is only right and wrong.

No answer is the wrong answer. By the answer we give, we judge ourselves. We cannot be on both sides, any more than we can be in Light and Darkness at the same time.

No wonder so many dislike the sight of a Crucifix; no wonder they hate their consciences; no wonder they try to drown its warnings in noise and excitement; no wonder they change the subject of conversation when anyone mentions death, or sneer when they are reminded of sin.

The Cross they can look at, for that might be only a symbol of the contradictions of life; but the Crucifix -- they call it 'horrible' when they mean it is accusing.

They may run away from it during life, but they will meet it at the Eternal Judgment, when the Son of Man shall come bearing the Cross in triumph in the clouds of heaven, to render to every man according to his works.

The modern mood of mutilating the Gospel, choosing some texts and ignoring others, makes men miss the purpose of the life of Christ. He came on earth not primarily to preach, but to *redeem*. He came less to live than to die.

His mission was not one of mere benevolence, nor to create a revolution in politics or economics, nor to heal, nor to leave a humanitarian ethics -- all these were secondary to the one absorbing purpose of His life, the redemption of man.

The sublime declaration of His coming is set down by St. John: "God so loved the world, as to give his only begotten Son; that whosoever believeth in him, may not perish, but may have life everlasting" *(John 3:16)*. Those who regard Christ as no more than a teacher cannot explain either His death or the desire for it.

If a fisherman sitting calmly on a dock throws himself into the sea to prove that he loves his neighbor who is calmly seated beside him, the act is meaningless. But if his neighbor actually fell in and the fisherman jumped into the sea to give up his life to save him, then we should say: "Greater love than this no man hath" *(John 15:13).*

In like manner, the plunging of Christ into the sea of human suffering is explicable only on the assumption that we were in danger of being drowned by sin. He came to pay a debt and by His obedience in the flesh to expiate our disobedience, and form to Himself a new race of men: He by whom the world was made *(Philippians 2: 8-11).*

What often happens in the economic order, happened in the moral order; man contracted a bigger debt than he could pay. A sin against Divine Love is greater than man alone can repair.

But if God undertook to forgive the debt through mercy, justice would have been unrequited. God of course could pay the debt of man's sin, but He could not in justice; do it apart from man.

A judge will not permit a stranger to walk off the street into a courtroom and take the death sentence of a murderer. In like manner, God could not pay *our* debt unless He became in some way involved in it.

This the Son of God, Jesus Christ, did by becoming man, assuming a human nature like unto us in all things save sin. He did not merely substitute for us, nor take our place; there is an identification of Him with us. He is the Head of our sin-laden race. In a certain sense He and we are one Person -- the new Adam.

Strictly speaking, Our Lord is man in an absolute sense, not just *a* man; His humiliation was not so much in assuming a human nature, but in making Himself one with us in the sinful conditions which we created.

He came not into an ideal world, but into this world of sin and suffering -- not as a stranger to this life and lot, but as one bearing the burden of the world's sin in Himself, though Himself sinless. He submitted to put on the form and habit of man, and to prove His obedience to the Divine Will in the face of temptation, as you and I must do it.

He willed to become the target of the hatred and scorn and mockery of God, and the effect of it was awful, for He faced sin in both its accumulated and massed power and in its experiential delights.

He humbled Himself in taking upon Himself the temporal penal consequences, which are the result of the moral disorder which sin wrought. By His submission to them for our sake He made in Himself the expiation for our sinful nature, becoming, as it were, the living crucible in which the dross of our sinful lives is burned away, that we might be once again pure gold consecrated to God's holy purposes.

It was not that our sins were transferred to Him that we might be guiltless, but that by accepting allegiance with our human nature, He willed to be visited upon Him the conditions which our sins deserved.

Not as a mere man bearing a limited share of the world's burden for sin did He suffer, but as the God-Man whose human suffering embraced within itself the uttermost suffering which sin can bring -- physical and mental pain consequent on human mortality; utter self-abnegation for the pride and avarice of men; and defenseless crucifixion for the world's arrogance and brute force.

Thus did He will that in Him our suffering might be transmuted from penalty into expiation, and be the beginning of a new life in Him.

That is why when the hour comes for Him freely to lay down His life, He offers no defense. As a guilty person, He stands before the Judges; silently He listens to the charges and the condemnation; all forces of evil are allowed their free play.

Finally, the Cross was not merely the outbreak of human passion -- it was the violent expression of anti-God. It was sin in its essence -- the attempted destruction of Divinity.

Sin is self-mutilation, the destruction of personality -- when it takes the form of pride, it crowns Goodness with thorns; when it takes the form of dishonesty, it nails hands to a Cross; when it takes the form of hate, it blasphemes the dying; when it takes the form of lust, it crucifies.

Nothing less than bloodshed could have been sin's worst crime and registered sin's deepest hurt.

Evil must work its power to the bitter end, use all its hatred, exhaust all its deceits, unsheathe all of its bloody swords, that being exhausted, Goodness may be revealed as triumphant.

And now that evil was spent in the final act of crucifixion, seeing that in Justice the last farthing was paid in the red coin of His blood and the mortgage against man paid back, He uttered His Cry of Triumph: "It is consummated."

All history, pagan and Jewish, looked forward to this moment; Heaven and earth were separated -- now they could be united.

The Pontiff or Bridge-builder has spanned the shores of eternity and time, and the Bridge is the Cross. The last rivet has been put in place; the last nail driven . . . It is consummated.

This is the meaning of a Crucifix: His death is not necessitated by the perverse will of sinful men, and, therefore, is not a martyrdom; but rather a willing submission to their perverse will in order to awaken men to the malignity of their sin and thereby win them over to repentance.

In this one and the same act there stands revealed the awful malignity of sin and the Goodness of God, for it is the Victim who forgives. It was the beauty and loveliness of the God-Man Christ which on the one hand made the crime so great, and on the other hand made the Divine forgiveness so final and so certain.

That Figure on the Cross bore to the full not only the physical effects of sin which any man might suffer, and not only the mental effects of sin which all of us ought to feel, but the spiritual effects of sin which only He could feel because being sinless, He was not part of it. Only the sinless know the horror of sin.

If you can stand the gaze of a Crucifix long enough, you will discover these truths. First, if sin cost Him, Who is Innocence, so much, then I who am guilty cannot take it lightly; second, there is only one thing worse in all the world than sin -- and that is to forget I am a sinner; third, more bitter than the Crucifixion must be my rejection of that Love by which I was redeemed.

Every law, physical or moral, has its penalties. If I disobey the law of health, nature penalizes me with sickness. If I disobey the moral law, I cannot eternally hope to escape its consequences as though I had not violated it.

Some time may intervene between the sowing and the harvest, the wheat and the cockle may be permitted to grow together; but there one day comes the day of judgment, when the wheat is gathered into barns and the cockle is burned.

Suppose now you admitted that you were a sinner, and you wished to be justified by that Redemption. How would you put the two together? How would you tie up a sinful heart with that Cross? How span 1900 years to make Redemption effective in you -- now at this hour? This is a very practical question and merits an answer.

It would be easy to answer, if that Cross could be lifted out of the rocks of Calvary by some giant hand and set down in the very midst of our cities and in the center of our plains.

Suppose such a miracle actually happened, so that instead of looking back in memory and imagination to Calvary as something that happened we could see Calvary re-enacted before our very eyes, so truly and really that we could gain the same merit as if we stood on Good Friday beneath the shadow of the Cross.

Suppose in some visible way we could "show the death of the Lord until he come" *(1Corinthians 11:26)*, that we might incorporate ourselves to it as Mary and John did on Calvary.

We have a right to expect that the Memorial of His Passion be prolonged to this hour, for did He not give that Memorial the night before He died by consecrating bread and wine into His own body and blood, and tell His Apostles to do it in memory of Him?

If that Redemptive Death could be so visibly re-enacted in our days of war and woe and misery, then the Cross would not be a memory, but an action; not a prayer but a renewed sacrifice; not a thing unrelated to us, but something made available for our participation.

It almost sounds too good to be true. But that is precisely what has happened! For Catholics, the Mass is Calvary renewed! On the Cross He was alone; in the Mass we are with Him. In that sense, Christ is still on the Cross.

The Seven Virtues, 1940

Eighth Meditation

A WORD TO THE SENSATIONALISTS

The sixth irreligious group are the Sensationalists: those for whom religion must always be dramatic, *i.e.*, they judge it by their feelings rather than by their minds and wills; their religion is a titillation rather than a sanctification; a "feeling good" rather than being good; a startling overtone rather than a quiet, subdued minor.

They accuse the Church of doing nothing because it is not doing anything sensational; as they might say, "There is nothing in the papers" because there was no riot, no murder mystery, no scandal in high life and no train wreck.

If, for example, I announced that next Sunday I would broadcast standing on my head to symbolize that the world was topsy turvy, and if in that ecstasy of modernity, I called the posture "iambic-dithyrambic", I would have most of the newspaper photographers of New York in the studio. Headlines would appear: "Remarkable new symbolism: Father Sheen stands on his head." My radio audience would pick up about 1000 per cent. But if I announced that next Good Friday night I would preach on the Cross, few would listen.

There is nothing so calculated to win many modern minds to religion as playing the fool, catering to the gallery, and making salvation dramatic.

The Sensationalists were represented at the Cross by the Roman soldiers of whom Luke writes: "And the soldiers also mocked him, coming to him, and offering him vinegar and saying: If thou be the King of the Jews save thyself" *(Luke 23:36-37).*

These men were not Jews, nor citizens of conquered Israel; they were proud legionnaires of Rome's screaming eagles. Why then did they refer to Him mockingly as the King of the Jews? Because in keeping with the spirit of paganism, they thought all gods were national gods.

Babylon had its god; the Medes and Persians had theirs; the Greeks had theirs, and so did the Romans have their own. The implication was that of all the national gods, none seemed poorer and weaker than the God of Israel, Who could not save Himself from a tree.

Their mockery is something like we hear today. "Germany prays to God; America prays to God; England prays to God; On Whose side is God?" The implication being that God must necessarily be a geographical Deity restricted to one people, one race and one nation.

The answer of course to that taunt is, that if we prayed as we should, we would all be on the same side, because the perfect prayer is: "Thy Will be done." The very fact that we ask a question of that kind proves we do not understand that God is the Father of all. Too many are worried about whether God is on our side, and heedless as to whether we are on God's side.

But there was something more significant still in their mockery; these men were sensationalists: hence they expected religion to be dramatic -- just as dramatic as unloosening fetters and turning a cross into a throne.

In their eyes, God could justify himself only by doing a stunt, by being eccentric, pandering to their love of excitement. They wanted a Life of Christ like Hollywood might do it, with love scenes between Judas and Magdalen.

That is why they asked Him to step down from the Cross. They wanted an incident that would make them say "Ah" when their eyes saw it, rather than that one which would make them say "I believe" when their minds, under the grace of God, knew it.

All through the ages there have been groups who despise the unobtrusive in religion. In the Old Testament, Naaman came to Elias the prophet to be cured of leprosy. He expected a dramatic cure. But the man of God told him to "Go and wash in the Jordan." In disgust at such a simple, common-place suggestion, Naaman turned and went away in a rage.

Satan too believes in the dramatic. One of the temptations on the Mount, was to suggest to Christ that He throw Himself down from the pinnacle unhurt, summoning to Himself legions of angels bearing Him up lest He dash His Foot against a stone.

And now the sensationalists at the Cross with their jaded appetites, and their sadistic impulses make the same appeal. Come down from the Cross with rose buds in place of scars, garlands in place of a crown of thorns, and with power instead of sacrifice.

Just suppose He did come down unscarred from that cross. Would these sensationalists have believed? They probably would have summoned a professor from Athens to prove it was all an illusion.

While these soldiers were asking for something as dramatic as the King of the Jews unloosening His manacles of steel, Our Blessed Lord said in His language a very simple word, a word which meant: "The drama is already over." And the word He spoke was a word of quiet triumph: “It is finished.”

To those soldiers, it must have been as preposterous as if you came into a theater about 8:30 one evening and while you asked: "When is the curtain going up" -- someone on the stage announced: "I am very sorry, the play is over.

The curtain is already rung down. You have missed the plot. It is finished."

Sensationalists miss Divinity for just that reason: the true religion is always unspectacular. The foolish virgins go to buy oil for their lamps and when they come back they find the Bridegroom already returned. And the door closed. It was so undramatic.

A beautiful maiden knocks at the door of an inn, and an innkeeper tells her there is no room. Into a stable she enters and there a child is born. It was God's entrance into the world. But it was so undramatic.

A collector of taxes is seated at his table counting money and a passer-by calls to him: "Come, follow Me." Matthew becomes an Apostle. It was so undramatic.

Three common criminals in the eyes of Roman law carry their crosses up a hill. One of them Our Saviour forgives and rescues him into Paradise. It was so undramatic.

In fact, it was boring. So the soldiers took dice and sat down and shook them to see who would have His garments. There within a stone's throw of them -- was being enacted the tremendous drama of redemption, and they only sat and gambled.

All life is a gamble as we only know it! Some throw dice and play for such small stakes, like garments and wealth; others throw a life and play for the stake of eternal salvation.

But it was so undramatic! They missed their play and lost! But the man on the Cross was saying His cause had won. "It is finished."

What did He mean: "It is finished"? Three times this phrase is used in Sacred Scripture: at the beginning of human history, at the end and in the middle of history. At the beginning, for in Genesis we read: "So the heavens and the earth were *finished*, and all the furniture of them" *(Genesis 2:1)*.

At the end of time, we hear that Word sounding throughout the world: " . . . And there came a great voice out of the temple from the throne saying: It is done" *(Revelation 16:17)*. Between these two extremes, we hear Our Lord on the Cross dividing all history into a period before and after His coming, binding both unto Himself in this sixth utterance from the Cross: "It is finished."

The Word in humiliation, by Whom the world was made, now takes the world once again into His Hands and surrenders it to the Father saying: The curtain may now go up on the reign of the Spirit. The world is ready for the last act.

This Word so undramatically spoken revealed that Christ was not only true God, but also true man.
First, it revealed Him as the Son of God, for as the Eternal Word He was, as it were, making His report to the Father, that the redemption of man was now finished and the time was ripe for the sending of the Holy Spirit into the souls of men to make them children of God. What was so wonderfully created, could now be more marvelously regenerated.

In the beginning of the world God saw that it was good and rejoiced; now the Son sees that it is better and breaks out into a poem of joy: "It is perfected." For "where sin abounded, grace did more abound" *(Romans 5:20)*. "For as by the disobedience of one man, many were made sinners; so also by the obedience of one, many shall be made just" *(Romans 5:19)*. Through all eternity the Father says to His Son: "Thou art my Son, this day have I begotten Thee." Now the Son says to the Father: "Thou art my Father; this day have I finished it."

This cry of victory also revealed His human nature, for by it the sinner is now acquitted of his sin, the last farthing is paid, the handwriting of debt blotted out and man restored to union with God. All the debts outstanding against man were paid, for being man, He suffered as man.

But being God, His suffering had infinite value. "For God indeed was in Christ, reconciling the world to himself, not imputing to them their sins; and he hath placed in us the word of reconciliation" *(2Corinthians 5:19)*. From now on He can await the Father's rending of the grave on Easter morn, in the final proclamation that it was not He that died; it was sin.

This word was not the sigh of a sufferer finding relief; it was the word of a Divine Artist finishing the work His Father had given Him to do -- finished at about the age of 33.

Thus, the perfecting of creation by redemption, and the restoration to fallen man of the dignity of Divine adoption, was rendered all the more undramatic because He did not finish His Work with an autobiography. Rather, His autobiography was a biography. He did not say: "I finished it"; but "It is finished."

He is not the subject of the Greatest work which was wrought on this poor and sinful earth of ours. The servant Jahoe does not name Himself, but rather speaks of the whole Program which God wrought through Him. Nor is He saying: "Thank God I have not been unsuccessful" or "I will be remembered." The "it" rather than the "I" closes an autobiography of the Son, as if it were a biography written by the Father and the Holy Spirit. He could not endure the thought of a book entitled: "My Three Years in Israel."

He is not one of the world's "great men." "Great men" are always dramatic. As if their works needed justification, they ring down the curtain of life with a great "I am." Great men always reveal themselves: This Man on the Cross concealed Himself. Therefore, He was God as well as man.

Sensationalists! Salvation is not sensational. Faith is not emotional; the redemption is not dramatic. You can sit in the very shadow of the Cross as did the soldiers, and still miss its meaning.

You can justify your refusal to come to God because of scandals. So did the soldiers. It was an awful scandal that Christ the Son of God should swing impotent from a peg.

From that quiet, undramatic word that His work was perfected, learn that no one is as unsensational as God. He comes in the zephyrs, not in thunder. Therefore, look for God in the commonplace. That they should seek God, if happily they may feel after him or find him, although he be not far from every one of us: For in him we live, and move, and are.

Do you ever remember an evening when the deadening sounds of the world faded away and you found yourself gazing down a new avenue of spiritual yearning? That was the voice of God. That was an actual grace. Did you ever feel a remorse, a sense of emptiness, a disgust with excesses, or wish for inner peace? That was the voice of God.

Make this experiment whether you believe in God or not. At your first opportunity stop in a Catholic Church for a visit. You need not believe as we Catholics do, that Our Lord is really and truly present in the tabernacle. But just sit there for an hour, and within that Hour you will experience a surpassing peace the like of which you never before enjoyed in your life.

You will ask yourself as a sensationalist once asked me when we made an all-night vigil of adoration in the Basilica of Sacre Coeur in Paris: "What is it that is in that Church?" Without voice or argument or thundering demands, you will have an awareness of something before which your spirit trembles -- a sense of the Divine.

God walks into your soul with silent step. God comes to you, more than you go to Him. Every time a channel is made for Him, He pours into it His fresh gift of grace. And it is all done so undramatically -- in prayer, in the sacraments, before the altar, in loving service of fellowman.

Never will His coming be what you expect, and yet never will it disappoint. The more you respond to His gentle pressure, the greater will be your freedom.

Too long have you wanted to be "just yourself." Can't you think of anything better than that? How about living as a Child of God?

Seven Words to the Cross, 1944

Ninth Meditation

THE HOUR

The most current philosophy of life today is self-expressionism: "Let yourself go;" "Do whatever you please." Any suggestion of restraining errant impulses is called a masochistic survival of the dark ages. The truth is that the only really self-expressive people in the world are in the insane asylum. They have absolutely no inhibitions, no conventions, and no codes. They are as self-expressive as hell, i.e., in complete disorder.

Self-expressive lives in this sense are self-destructive. Yet there is a way to be truly self-expressive in the sense of self-perfection. But this is impossible without sacrifice. Incompleteness is always the lot of the undisciplined. To understand this lesson, we turn to Calvary.

When Our Blessed Lord uttered His Fifth Word to the Cross, "I thirst" *(John 19:28)*, a soldier nearby -- soldiers are always mentioned kindly in the Scripture -- put some wine on a hyssop, and placing it at the end of a long reed reached it to the mouth of Our Blessed Lord, who tasted the wine. The Evangelist adds, "Jesus therefore, when he had taken the vinegar, said: 'It is consummated'" *(John 19:30)*.

Three times this word is used in Sacred Scripture: at the beginning of the world, at the end, and in between. In creation, the Heavens and earth are described as "finished." At the end of the world, a Great Voice is heard coming out of the Temple saying: "It is finished." And now, from the Cross, it is heard again. The word does not mean, "Thank God, it is over." It means it is perfected, the debt had been paid, the work that He had come to do had been completed.

When Mary at the foot of the Cross saw that soldier offer Him wine and heard Him say, "It is consummated," she thought of the moment when it all began. There was wine there too, but not enough. It was the marriage feast of Cana. When in the course of the banquet the wine gave out, the first to observe the lack of wine was not the steward. It was Our Blessed Mother. She notes human needs even before those commissioned to supply them.

Our Blessed Mother said to Our Lord a simple prayer: "They have no wine" *(John 2:3)*. That was all. And her Son answered: "Woman". He did not call her Mother. "Woman, what is that to me and to thee? My hour is not yet come" *(John 2:4)*. Why "Woman"? He was equivalently saying to her: "Mary, you are My Mother. You are asking Me to begin My public life, to declare Myself the Messiah, the Son of God, by working My first miracle. The moment I do that first miracle you cease to be just My Mother. As I reveal myself as Redeemer, you become in a certain sense a co-redemptrix, the Mother of all men. That is why I address you by the title of universal Motherhood: 'Woman'. It will be the beginning of your womanhood."

But what did He mean by saying: "My hour is not yet come?" Our Blessed Lord used that word "hour" often in relation to His Passion and Death. When, for example, His enemies took up stones to throw at Him in the temple, the Evangelist says, "His hour was not yet come" *(John 7:30)*. The night of the Last Supper, He prayed: "Father, the hour is come. Glorify thy Son, that thy Son may glorify thee" *(John 17:1)*. Then when Judas came out into the Garden, Our Blessed Lord said: "This is your hour" *(Luke 22:53)*. The Hour meant the Cross.

The working of His first miracle was the beginning of the hour. His sixth word from the Cross was the end of that hour. The Passion was finished. The water had been changed into wine; the wine into blood. It is perfected. The work is done.

From these words the lesson emerges that, between the beginning of our assigned duties and their completion and perfection, there intervenes an "hour," or a moment of mortification, sacrifice, and death. No life is ever finished without it. Between the Cana when we launch the vocation of our lives, and that moment of triumph when we can say we succeeded, there must come the interval of the Cross. Our Lord could have had no other motive in asking us to take up our cross daily than to perfect ourselves. It was almost like saying, between the day you begin to be a concert pianist and the day you triumph in concert work, there must come the "hour" of hard study, dull exercises, and painful addiction to work.

It is very likely that the reason for the answer Our Lord gave the Greeks when they visited Him: "Unless the grain of wheat falling into the ground die, itself remaineth alone. But if it die, it bringeth forth much fruit" -- was to remind them that death is a condition of life. Athens conceivably might have made Him a teacher, but Jerusalem with its Hour would make Him a Redeemer.

The Christ Who is our Head is not a Christ unscarred, but a Christ slain and risen and bearing in His glorified Body the marks of "the Hour" on hands and feet and side. As St. Paul says: "And they that are Christ's have crucified their flesh, with the vices and concupiscences" *(Galatians 5:24).*

Short of this self-discipline by which we humble our pride and restrain our selfishness, our lives are unfinished and incomplete. Most lives are frustrated because they have left out the Cross. They think the endless Day of Eternity can be won without the Crucial Hour of Calvary. Nature abhors incompleteness. Cut off the leg of a salamander and it will grow another. The impulses we deny in our waking life are often completed in our dreams. Our mutilated souls in one way or another, are trying to complete their incompleteness and to perfect their imperfection.

In the spiritual life this is a conscious, deliberate process: the application of the "Hour" of Christ's Passion to ourselves, that we may share in His Resurrection. "That I may know him and the power of his resurrection and the fellowship of his sufferings: being made conformable to His death" *(Philippians 3:10).*

Our Lord, after rising from the tomb, told the disciples on the way to Emmaus that "the Hour" was the condition of His glory. "O foolish and slow of heart to believe in all things which the prophets have spoken. Ought not Christ to have suffered these things and so to enter his glory?" *(Luke 24:25-26).* Without some systematic detachment on our part, therefore, it is impossible to advance in charity.

The finished man or the perfected man is the non-attached man, non-attached to a craving for power, publicity, and possessions; non-attached to anger, ambition, and avarice; non-attached to selfish desires, lusts, and bodily sensations. The practice of non-attachment to the things which stunt our soul, is one of the things meant by "the Hour." It is a going "against the grain"; a being on God's side even against oneself, a renouncement for the sake of recovery.

By what signs will you know whether your life is unfinished? Among others we mention these: First, the habit of criticism is the best indication of an incomplete life. Our sense of justice is so keen and deep that we do not have it ourselves; we compensate for the lack by trying to make everyone else just. Criticism of others is thus an oblique form of self-commendation. We think we make the picture hang straight on our wall by telling our neighbors that all his pictures are crooked. Like the lark who flutters with great agitation over her nest, we exhibit most flagrantly the very things we seek to hide.

When you say of another's failing, "That is one thing I can not stand", you reveal the very thing to which you are most unconsciously inclined. We personalize and objectify our unrecognized failings by talking of the failings of others. We hate in others the sins to which we are most likely to be addicted. When Our Lord said, "Judge not, that you may not be judged" *(Matthew 7:1)*, He also meant that you are judged by your judgment of others! You have given yourself away! You are trying to make up for not having the "Hour" by giving others a miserable day.

Another proof of incompleteness is revealed in criticism of religion, either explicit or implicit. If you are a rationalist and regard faith as a superstition, you probably are very fond of ghost stories. You complete your incompleteness by a flight into the incredulous. If you regard all the mysteries of religion as so much worthless superstition, why do you read so many detective stories? You are filling up your need of heavenly mystery with murder mystery.

Why is it that the impure like to read books attacking the purity of others? Why are those who are notoriously undisciplined and unmoral also most contemptuous of religion and morality? They are trying to solace their own unhappy lives by pulling the happy down to their own abysmal depths. They erroneously believe that Bibles and religions, Churches and priests have in some way foisted the distinction between right and wrong in the world, and that if they would be done away with, they could go on sinning with impunity. They measure progress by the height of the pile of discarded moral truths.

A third mark of incompleteness is in a state of continual self-reference. The egocentric is always frustrated, simply because the condition of self-perfection is self-surrender. There must be a willingness to die to the lower part of self, before there can be a birth to the nobler. That is what Our Lord meant when He said: "For he that will save his life shall lose it; and he that shall lose his life for My sake shall find it" *(Matthew 16:25)*.

Many married women who have deliberately spurned the "hour" of childbearing, are unhappy and frustrated. They never discovered the joys of marriage because they refused to surrender to the obligation of their state. In saving themselves, they lost themselves! It takes three to make love, not two: you and you and God. Without God people only succeed in bringing out the worst in each other. Lovers who have nothing else to do but love one another, soon find there is nothing else. Without a central loyalty, life is unfinished.

The youth of America remain juvenile longer than in any other country of the world! The reason is, that so-called "progressive" education, by neglecting self-discipline in favor of unbounded self-expression, has denied them the one thing that would make them really progressive. To leave out the "hour" of self-renunciation is to make impossible the day of self-development.

It is only by dying to our lower self, that we live to the higher: it is only by surrendering that we control: it is only by crushing our egotism that we can develop our personality. How does the plant get its power to develop? By being unresponsive and unrelated to others, or by surrendering and adjusting itself to its environment that it may survive. How can we enjoy the swim except by surviving the shock of the first cold plunge; how can we enjoy the classics except after the dull routine of grammar? How can we live to the higher life of God unless we make ourselves receptive by self-denial?

Once you have surrendered yourself, you make yourself receptive. In receiving from God, you are perfected and completed. It is a law of nature and grace that only those who give, will ever receive. The Sea of Galilee is fresh and blue and gives life to all the living things within its sunlit waters -- not because it receives waters, but because it gives them. The Dead Sea, on the contrary, is dead, simply because it has no outlet. It does not give and, therefore, it never receives. No fish can live in its waters, no beast can thrive upon its shores. Not having had its Calvary of surrender, it never has its Pentecost of Life and Power.

If nothing pleases you, it is because you do not please yourself. If you rarely find a person or thing you like, it is because you do not like yourself. Life does not allow egocentricity to establish its own order, for to life, selfishness is disorder. But how shall this disordered self be oriented to others except by discipline? That is why in the center of the Kingdom of God there is a Cross.

Seven Words of Jesus and Mary, 1945

FATHER, INTO THY HANDS
I COMMEND MY SPIRIT
Meditations on the Seventh Word from the Cross
Archbishop Fulton J. Sheen

First Meditation

FATHER, INTO THY HANDS I COMMEND MY SPIRIT

When Adam had been driven from the Garden of Paradise, and the penalty of labor imposed upon him, he went out in quest of the bread he was to earn by the sweat of his brow. In the course of that search, he stumbled upon the limp form of his son Abel, picked him up, carried him upon his shoulders, and laid him on the lap of Eve. They spoke to him, but Abel did not answer. He had never been so silent before. They lifted his hand, but it fell back limp; it had never acted that way before. They looked into his eyes, cold, glassy, mysteriously elusive; they had never been so unresponsive before. They wondered, and as they wondered, their wonder grew. Then they remembered: "For in what day soever thou shalt eat of the tree, thou shalt die the death." *It was the first death in the world.*

Centuries whirled around into space, and the new Abel, Christ, is now put to death by His jealous brethren of the race of Cain. The life that came out from the boundless deep now prepares to return home. His sixth word was a cry of retrospect: "I have finished the work." His seventh and last word is one of prospect: "I commend My Spirit." The sixth word was man-ward; the seventh word was God-ward. The sixth word was a farewell to earth; the seventh His entrance into Heaven. Just as those great planets only after a long time complete their orbit and return again to their starting-point, as if to salute Him who sent them on their way, so He who had come from Heaven had finished His work and completed His orbit, now goes back to the Father to salute Him, who sent Him out on the great work of the world's redemption: "Father, into Thy hands I commend My Spirit."

The Prodigal Son is returning to His Father's house, for is not Christ the Prodigal? Thirty-three years ago He left His Father's eternal mansion and went off into the foreign country of this world. Then He began spending Himself and being spent; dispensing with an infinite prodigality the divine riches of power and wisdom, and bestowing with a heavenly liberality the divine gifts of pardon and mercy. In this last hour His whole substance is wasted among sinners, for He is giving the last drop of His precious blood for the redemption of the world. There is nothing to feed upon except the husks of human sneers, and the vinegar and gall of bitter human ingratitude. He now prepares to take the road back to His Father's house, and when yet some distance away, He sees the face of His Heavenly Father He breaks out into the last and perfect prayer from the pulpit of the Cross: "Father, into Thy hands I commend My Spirit."

All the while Mary is standing at the foot of the Cross. In a short time, the new Abel slain by His brethren, will be taken down from the gibbet of salvation and laid in the lap of the new Eve. It will be the death of Death! But when the tragic moment comes it may seem to the tear-dimmed eyes of Mary that Bethlehem has come back. The thorn-crowned head which had nowhere to lay itself in death, except on the pillow of the Cross, may, through Mary's clouded vision, seem the head which she drew to her breast at Bethlehem. Those eyes at whose fading even the sun and moon were darkened were to her the eyes that glanced up from a crib of straw. The helpless feet riveted with nails once more seem to her the baby feet at which were cast gold, frankincense, and myrrh. The lips now parched and crimsoned with blood, seem the ruddy lips that once at Bethlehem nourished themselves on the Eucharist of her body. The hands that can hold nothing but a wound, seem once more the baby hands that were not quite long enough to touch the huge heads of the cattle. The embrace at the foot of the Cross seems the embrace at the side of the crib. In that sad hour of death which always makes one think of birth, Mary may feel that Bethlehem is returning again.

PRAYER

NO, MARY! Bethlehem is not come back. This is not the crib, but the Cross; not birth, but death; not the day of companionship with Shepherds and Kings, but the hour of a common death with thieves; not Bethlehem, but Calvary.

Bethlehem is Jesus, as thou, His sinless mother, gave Him to man; Calvary is Jesus, as sinful man gave Him back to you. Something intervened between Thy giving at the manger and Thy receiving at the Cross, and that which intervened is my sins. Mary, this is not thy hour; it is my hour -- my hour of wickedness and sin. If I had not sinned, death would not now hover on its black wings about His crimsoned body: if I had not been proud, the atoning crown of thorns would never have been woven; if I had been less rebellious in treading the broad way which leads to destruction, the feet would never have been pierced with nails; if I had been more responsive to His shepherding calls from the thorns and thistles, His lips would have never been on fire; if I had been more faithful, His cheeks would never have been blistered with the kiss of Judas.

Mary, it is I who stand between His birth and His approaching redemptive death. I warn thee, Mary, think not when thy arms come to clasp Him, that He is white as He came from the Father; He is red as He came from me. In a few short seconds, thy Son shall have surrendered His soul to His Heavenly Father, and His body to thy caressing hands. The last few drops of blood are falling from that great chalice of Redemption, staining the wood of the Cross and crimsoning the rocks soon to be rent in horror; and a single drop of it would be sufficient to redeem ten thousand worlds. Mary, my Mother, intercede with thy Divine Son for forgiveness of the sin of changing thy Bethlehem into Calvary. Beg Him, Mary, in these last remaining seconds, to grant us the grace of never crucifying Him again nor piercing thy own heart with seven swords. Mary, plead to thy dying Son that as long as I live . . . Mary! Jesus is dead. ... Mary!

The Seven Last Words, 1933

Second Meditation

DELIVER US FROM ALL EVIL. AMEN.

"Deliver us from all evil. Amen"

"Father, into thy hands I commend my spirit."

There is no deliverance from evil except in heaven. That too is why the final petition of the 'Our Father' which asks that we be delivered from evil is balanced by the last words of Our Lord from the cross commending His Soul into the hands of His Heavenly Father.

There is evil in the world, and as long as we remain here below, we must struggle against it. God might have made a different world, a world in which we would have sprouted virtue by the same necessity that the sun rises, and fire burns, and iron is hard. But then where would merit and character have been? All life is a trial. I can be one of God's heroes only because I might have been one of God's cowards; I can be one of the patriots of the Kingdom of God, only because I might have been one of its traitors; I can be a saint of the Cross only because I might also be a devil. There is no epic of the certainties of life; no crowns of merit rest suspended over those who do not fight; there are no aureoles except for those who might have turned back and yet pushed on.

Christ's eyes now look downward as the last few drops of blood reluctantly wed themselves to the rocks, splitting them open like hungry mouths. There is always a strange power in the eyes of the dying, which enables them to follow the ones they love, even when other senses are mute and dead. His eyes are now resting on the same object He rested on when He was born – His sweet and beloved Mother. She felt His eyes fixed on her. She looked up, the eyes closed, the head dropped, there was the rupture of a heart through the rapture of love, and there Mary stood beneath the cross – a childless Mother, bereaved of God.

Sleep on tired world! Your God is dead. Sleep on creatures! You now have creation to yourself. Sleep on Jerusalem! You have slain the Prophet Who would have made you a Heavenly City. Sleep on sinners! The Heart that filled you with remorse is pierced with a lance. Sleep on, all ye who hate, for the wings of love are broken. Sleep on atheists; you have killed your God. Sleep in your false sleep – you can do more than nature can, for it awakes and shudders at your crime. Sleep on for your few brief moments, but remember some day you will awaken and one vision will meet your eyes: The Vision of Love Crucified on a Cross.

May you throw yourself beneath it, and in the ecstasy of knowing God as your Father may you pray the prayer of Salvation: "Our Father, Who art in heaven – like Thy Son – into Thy hands I commend my spirit."

The Seven Last Words and the Our Father, 1935

Third Meditation

THE LAST GOSPEL

"Father, into thy hands, I commend my spirit." – Luke 23:46.

It is a beautiful paradox that the Last Gospel of the Mass takes us back to the beginning, for it opens with the words "In the beginning." And such is life: the last of this life is the beginning of the next. Fittingly indeed, then, that the Last Word of our Lord was His Last Gospel: "Father, into thy hands I commend my spirit." Like the Last Gospel of the Mass, it too takes Him back to the beginning, for He now goes back to the Father whence He came. He has completed His work. He began His Mass with the word: "Father." And He ends it with the same word.

"Everything perfect," the Greeks would say, "travels in circles." Just as the great planets only after a long period of time complete their orbits, and then go back again to their starting point, as if to salute Him who sent them on their way, so the Word Incarnate, who came down to say His Mass, now completes His earthly career and goes back again to His heavenly Father who sent Him on the journey of the world's redemption. The Prodigal Son is about to return to His Father's House, for is He not the Prodigal Son? Thirty-three years ago He left the Father's House and the blessedness of heaven, and came down to this earth of ours, which is a foreign country -- for every country is foreign which is away from the Father's House.

For thirty-three years He had been spending His substance. He spent the substance of His Truth in the infallibility of His Church; He spent the substance of His Power in the authority He gave to His apostles and their successors. He spent the substance of His Life in the Redemption and the Sacraments. Now every drop of it is gone, He looks longingly back again to the Father's House, and with a loud cry throws His Spirit into His Father's arms, not in the attitude of one who is taking a plunge into the darkness, but as one who knows where He is going -- to a homecoming with His Father.

In that Last Word and Last Gospel which took Him back to the Beginning of all beginnings, namely, His Father, is revealed the history and rhythm of life. The end of all things must in some way get back to their beginning. As the Son goes back to the Father; as Nicodemus must be born again; as the body returns to the dust -- so the soul of man which came from God must one day go back to God.

Death is not the end of all. The cold clod falling upon the grave does not mark *finis* to the history of a man. The way he has lived in this life determines how he shall live in the next. If he has sought God during life, death will be like the opening of a cage, enabling him to use his wings to fly to the arms of the divine Beloved. If he has fled from God during life, death will be the beginning of an eternal flight away from Life and Truth and Love -- and that is hell.

Before the throne of God, whence we came on our earthly novitiate, we must one day go back to render an account of our stewardship. There will not be a human creature who, when the last sheaf is garnered, will not be found either to have accepted or rejected the divine gift of Redemption, and in accepting or rejecting it to have signed the warrant of his eternal destiny.

As the sales on a cash register are recorded for the end of our business day, so our thoughts, words, and deeds are recorded for the final Judgment. If we but live in the shadow of the Cross, death will not be an ending but a beginning of eternal life. Instead of a parting, it will be a meeting; instead of a going away, it will be an arriving; instead of being an end, it will be a Last Gospel -- a return to the beginning. As a voice whispers, "You must leave the earth," the Father's voice will say, "My child, come unto Me."

We have been sent into this world as children of God, to assist at the Holy Sacrifice of the Mass. We are to take our stand at the foot of the Cross and, like those who stood under it the first day, we will be asked to declare our loyalties. God has given us the wheat and the grapes of life, and as the men who, in the Gospel, were given talents, we will have to show return on that divine gift.

God has given us our lives as wheat and grapes. It is our duty to consecrate them and bring them back to God as bread and wine -- transubstantiated, divinized, and spiritualized. There must be harvest in our hands after the springtime of the earthly pilgrimage.

That is why Calvary is erected in the midst of us, and we are on its sacred hill. We were not made to be mere on-lookers, shaking our dice like the executioners of old, but rather to be participants in the mystery of the Cross.

If there is any way to picture Judgment in terms of the Mass, it is to picture it in the way the Father greeted His Son, namely, by looking at His hands. They bore the marks of labor, the callouses of redemption, and the scars of salvation. So too when our earthly pilgrimage is over, and we go back to the beginning, God will look at both of our hands. If our hands in life touched the hands of His divine Son they will bear the same livid marks of nails; if our feet in life have trod over the same road that leads to eternal glory through the detour of a rocky and thorny Calvary, they too shall bear the same bruises; if our hearts beat in unison with His, then they too shall show the riven side which the wicked lance of jealous earth did pierce.

Blessed indeed are they who carry in their Cross-marked hands the bread and wine of consecrated lives signed with the sign and sealed with the seal of redemptive Love. But woe unto them who come from Calvary with hands unscarred and white.

God grant that when life is over, and the earth is vanishing like a dream of one awakening, when eternity is flooding our souls with its splendors, we may with humble and triumphant faith re-echo the Last Word of Christ: "Father, into thy hands I commend my spirit."

And so the Mass of Christ ends. The *Confiteor* was His prayer to the Father for the forgiveness of our sins; the *Offertory* was the presentation on the paten of the Cross of small hosts of the thief and ourselves; the *Sanctus* was His commending ourselves to Mary, the Queen of Saints; the *Consecration* was the separation of His Blood from His Body, and the seeming separation of divinity and humanity; the *Communion* was His thirst for the souls of men; the *Ite, missa est* was the finishing of the work of salvation; the *Last Gospel* was the return to the Father whence He came.

And now that the Mass is over, and He has commended His Spirit to the Father, He prepares to give back His Body to His Blessed Mother at the foot of the Cross. Thus once again will the end be the beginning, for at the beginning of His earthly life He was nestled on her lap in Bethlehem, and now, on Calvary, He will take His place there once again.

Earth had been cruel to Him; His feet wandered after lost sheep and we dug them with steel; His hands stretched out the Bread of everlasting life and we fastened them with nails; His lips spoke the Truth and we sealed them with dust. He came to give us Life and we took away His. But that was our fatal mistake. We really did not take it away. We only tried to take it away. He laid it down of Himself. Nowhere do the Evangelists say that He died. They say, "He gave up the ghost." It was a willing, self-determined relinquishment of life.

It was not death which approached Him, it was He who approached death. That is why, as the end draws near, the Saviour commands the portal of death to open unto Him in the presence of the Father. The chalice is gradually being drained of its rich red wine of salvation. The rocks of earth open their hungry mouths to drink, as if more thirsty for the draughts of salvation than the parched hearts of man; the earth itself shook in horror because men had erected God's Cross upon its breast. Magdalene, the penitent, as usual clings to His feet, and there she will be again Easter morn; John, the priest, with a face like a cast moulded out of love, listens to the beating of the Heart whose secrets He learned and loved and mastered; Mary thinks how different Calvary is from Bethlehem.

Thirty-three years ago Mary looked down at His sacred face; now He looks down at her. In Bethlehem heaven looked up into the face of earth; now the roles are reversed. Earth looks up into the face of heaven -- but a heaven marred by the scars of earth. He loved her above all the creatures of earth, for she was His Mother and the Mother of us all. He saw her first on coming to earth; He shall see her last on leaving it. Their eyes meet, all aglow with life, speaking a language all their own. There is a rupture of a heart through a rapture of love, then a bowed head, a broken heart. Back to the hands of God He gives, pure and sinless, His spirit, in loud and ringing voice that trumpets eternal victory. And Mary stands alone a Childless Mother. Jesus is dead!

Mary looks up into His eyes which are so clear even in the face of death: "High Priest of Heaven and earth, Thy Mass is finished! Leave the altar of the Cross and repair into Thy Sacristy. As High Priest Thou didst come forth from the sacristy of Heaven, panoplied in the vestments of humanity and bearing Thy Body as Bread and Thy Blood as Wine.

Now the Sacrifice has been consummated. The Consecration bell has rung. Thou didst offer Thy Spirit to Thy Father; Thy Body and Thy Blood to man. There remains now nothing but the drained chalice. Enter into Thy Sacristy. Take off the garments of mortality and put on the white robes of immortality. Show Thy hands, and feet, and side to Thy heavenly Father and say: "With these was I wounded in the house of those that love me."

"Enter, High Priest, into Thy heavenly Sacristy, and as Thy earthly ambassadors hold aloft the Bread and Wine, do Thou show Thyself to the Father in loving intercession for us even unto the consummation of the world. Earth has been cruel to Thee; but Thou wilt be kind to earth. Earth lifted Thee on the Cross, but now Thou shalt lift earth unto the Cross. Open the door of the heavenly Sacristy, O High Priest! Behold, it is now we who stand at the door and knock!

"And Mary, what shall we say to Thee? Mary, Thou art the Sacristan of the High Priest! Thou wert a Sacristan in Bethlehem when He did come to Thee as wheat and grapes in the crib of Bethlehem. Thou wert His Sacristan at the Cross, where He became the Living Bread and Wine through the Crucifixion. Thou art His Sacristan now, as He comes from the altar of the Cross wearing only the drained chalice of His sacred Body.

"As that chalice is laid in your lap it may seem that Bethlehem has come back again, for He is once more yours. But it only seems -- for in Bethlehem He was the chalice whose gold was to be tried by fire; but now at Calvary He is the chalice whose gold has passed through the fires of Golgotha and Calvary. In Bethlehem He was white as He came from the Father: now He is red as He came from us. But thou art still His Sacristan! And as the Immaculate Mother of all hosts who go to the altar, do thou, O Virgin Mary, send us there pure, and keep us pure, even unto the day when we enter into the heavenly Sacristy of the Kingdom of Heaven, where thou wilt be our eternal Sacristan and He our eternal Priest."

And you, friends of the Crucified, your High Priest has left the Cross, but He has left us the Altar. On the Cross He was alone; in the Mass He is with us. On the Cross He suffered in His physical Body; on the altar He suffers in the

Mystical Body which we are. On the Cross He was the unique Host; in the Mass we are the small hosts, and He the large host receiving His Calvary through us. On the Cross He was the wine; in the Mass, we are the drop of water united with the wine and consecrated with Him. In that sense He is still on the Cross, still saying the Confiteor with us, still forgiving us, still commending us to Mary, still thirsting for us, still drawing us unto the Father, for as long as sin remains on earth, still will the Cross remain.

> "Whenever there is silence around me
> By day or by night
> I am startled by a cry.
> It came down from the Cross.
> The first time I heard it
> I went out and searched --
> And found a man in the throes of Crucifixion. And I said: 'I will take you down,'
> And I tried to take the nails out of His Feet, But He said: 'Let them be
> For I cannot be taken down
> Until every man, every woman, and every child Come together to take me down.'
> And I said: 'But I cannot bear your cry. What can I do?'
> And He said: 'Go about the world --
> Tell every one that you meet
> There is a Man on the Cross.'"

(Elizabeth Cheney)

Calvary and the Mass, 1936

Fourth Meditation

BLESSED ARE THEY THAT MOURN

"Blessed are they that mourn; for they shall be comforted."

"Father into thy hands I commend my spirit."

At the beginning of His Public Life on the Hill of the Beatitudes, Our Lord preached: "Blessed are they that mourn; for they shall be comforted." At the end of His Public Life on the Hill of Calvary, He found that blessed comfort: "Father, into your hands I commend my spirit."

Like all the other beatitudes, this beatitude of mourning is quite different from the beatitude of the world: "Eat, drink, and be merry, for tomorrow we die." The world never regards mourning as a blessing, but always as a curse. Laughter is the gold it is seeking, and sorrow is the enemy it flees.

It can no more understand the beatitude of mourning, than it can understand the cross. In fact, the modern man steels himself even against the suffering of another by wearing the mask of indifference, quite unmindful that such a thickening of his spiritual skin, though it may sometimes protect him from sorrow, nevertheless shuts in his own morbidity until it festers and corrupts.

But it must not be thought that the beatitude of Our Lord is either a condemnation of laughter and joy or a glorification of sorrow and tears. Our Lord did not believe in a philosophy of tragedy any more than we do. As a matter of fact, He upbraided the Pharisees because they wore long faces and looked sad when they fasted, and His Apostles summed up His Life and Resurrection in the one word "Rejoice."

The difference between the beatitude of the world, "Laugh and the world laughs with you," and the beatitude of Our Lord, "Blessed are they that mourn," is not that the world brings laughter and Our Lord brings tears. It is not even a choice of having or not having sadness; it is rather a choice of where we shall put it: at the beginning or at the end. In other words, which comes first: laughter or tears?

Shall we place our joys in time or in eternity, for we cannot have them in both. Shall we laugh on earth, or laugh in heaven, for we cannot laugh in both. Shall we mourn before we die or after we die, for we cannot mourn in both. We cannot have our reward both in heaven and on earth.

That is why we believe one of the most tragic words in the life of Our Lord is the word He will say to the worldly at the end of time: "You have already had your reward."

Which of the two roads then shall we take: the royal road of the Cross, which leads to the Resurrection and Eternal Life, or the road of selfishness which leads to Eternal Death? The first road is filled with thorns, but if we traverse it far enough, we find it ends in a bed of roses; the other road is filled with roses, but if we traverse it far enough, it ends in a bed of thorns.

But we cannot take both roads or make the best of both worlds, because we cannot love both God and Mammon, any more than we can be both alive and dead at the same time. No man can serve two masters: "either he will hate the one, and love the other; or he will sustain the one, and despise the other."

If we save our life in this world, we lose it in the next; if we lose our life in this world, we save it in the next. If we sow in sin, we reap corruption; if we sow in truth, we reap life everlasting. But we cannot do both.

With which, then, shall we begin -- the fast or the feast? This is the problem of the beatitudes. Our Lord begins with the fast and ends with the feast; the world begins with the feast and ends with want.

The contrast between these two philosophies is recorded on every page of the Gospel. Dives was rich on this earth, but he had not even a drop of cold water after his death; Lazarus was a beggar on earth, but he became a rich man in the bosom of Abraham. Therefore, in the words of Our Lord: "Woe to you that now laugh: for you shall mourn and weep"; "Blessed are ye that weep now, for you shall laugh."

It is not surprising then to find that Our Lord, who came into such utter conflict with the evil of the world, should be described as the "Man of Sorrows," and one "Who in the days of His flesh with a strong cry and tears, offering up prayers and supplications to Him that was able to save Him from death, was heard for his reverence."

There is no record in the Gospels that He ever laughed, though there are many records of His tears. He openly wept at the grave of His friend Lazarus. He wept over the city that was to kill Him, and amidst tears glistening on that heavenly face bemoaned: "Jerusalem, Jerusalem, thou that killest the prophets, and stonest them that are sent unto thee, how often would I have gathered together thy children, as the hen doth gather her chickens under her wings, and thou wouldest not!"

And not a long time afterwards He wept tears of crimson in the garden, as the "desperate tides of the great world's anguish forced through the channels of a single heart." And finally on the Cross after three hours of blood-weeping, He comes to the end of His mourning.

Tears and crucifixions are not final; they are only the momentary death that even the seed endures before it bursts into the bloom and blossom of life.

Had He not said: "Blessed are ye that weep now, for you shall laugh." He had had his fast, now He would have the feast; He had worn the thorns, now He would have the diadem of gold; He had mourned; now He would rejoice.

And in fulfillment of the beatitude of mourning, He lets ring out over Golgotha's hills in a commanding voice the last word He ever uttered on this earth as a suffering man, and it was a word of joy and triumph: "Father, into Thy hands I commend My spirit." It was the word of one who is strong and vigorous. No one was taking His life away. He was laying it down of Himself, and nowhere does Sacred Scripture say that He died.

Death was not coming to Him; it was He who was going to it. Death did not open its portals to Him; He unlocked them of Himself, for He knew whither He was going.

His last hour was not like the pushing out of a boat into a trackless sea bound for unknown lands and under starless skies. His goal was fixed. He knew where He was going. The exiled King was going back home; the Prodigal Son was returning to the Father's house; the Heavenly Planet that thirty-three years before started out on its orbit to illumine a world, now returns to salute Him who sent Him on His way; the Great Captain now goes back to His native land, bearing the glorious scars of victory.

The sorrowful mysteries are over; now begin the glorious ones. Truly indeed, "Blessed are they that mourn, for they shall be comforted."

The sorrow of Our Lord is over. He who mourned is comforted. But how about us? Which beatitude are we going to follow? Are we going to take all our laughter here below, or save some of it for eternity? Are we going to flee the cross now, or are we going to embrace it? Are we going to plan our life so that at the end we can say: "Father, into your hands I commend my spirit." If we are, then we must mourn. But why must we mourn?

We must mourn, first of all, because the world will make us mourn if we follow the Redeemer's beatitudes. If we practice meekness, the world will try to provoke us to anger; if we are merciful, the world will accuse us of not being just; if we are clean of heart, the world will shout "Prudes"; if we hunger and thirst after justice, we shall not succeed; if we are peace-makers, the world will say we are cowards; if we are poor in spirit, the world will look down upon us.

In a word, suffering naturally follows the Christian's conflict with the evil of the world. Because we have been taken out of the world, the world will hate us. The servant is not above the master; if it made Him weep crimson tears, it will make us weep too.

That is the first reason, then, why we must mourn: Because we have chosen the Man of Sorrows. But "blessed are ye when they shall revile you and persecute you, and speak all that is evil against you, untruly for my sake: Be glad and rejoice, for your reward is very great in heaven."

There is another reason why we should mourn, and that is because of the sorrow we caused Our Lord's Blessed Mother. We can never grieve enough for grieving her who is Our Mother too. And we did make her suffer, for there is never a wicked deed done in the world, but that there is an innocent victim.

The repercussion of sin is enormous. We throw a stone into the sea, and it causes a ripple that disturbs even the most distant shore. Calvary had its innocent victim too -- one who had no share in bringing Our Lord to the cross, in fact the only one who could ever say: "I am innocent of the blood of this man" -- that innocent victim was Mary.

What had she done to deserve the Seven Swords? What crimes had she committed to rob her of her Son? She had done nothing; but we have. We have sinned against Her Divine Son; we have sentenced Him to the Cross; and in sinning against Him we wounded her.

In fact, we thrust into her hands the greatest of all griefs, for she was not losing a brother, or a sister, or a father, or a mother, or even just a son -- she was losing God. And what greater sorrow is there than this!

And finally, we should mourn for the greatest of all reasons, namely, because of what our sins have done to Him. If we had been less proud, His crown of thorns would have been less piercing; if we had been less avaricious, the nails in the Hands would have been less burning; if we had traveled less in the devious ways of sin, His feet would not have been so deeply dug with steel; if our speech had been less biting, His lips would have been less parched; if we had been less sinful, His agony would have been shorter; if we had loved more, He would have been hated less.

There is a personal equation between that Cross and us. Life with its rebellions, its injustices, its sins, all played a role in the Crucifixion. We can no more wash our hands of our guilt than Pilate could wash his as he held them up under a noon-day sun and declared himself innocent.

It was not so much the Crucifixion that hurt and wounded, it was not Annas, it was not Caiphas, it was not the executioners, for "they knew not what they did"; it was not His enemies who caused His greatest sorrow: "If my enemies had done this, I could have borne it."

It was we who grieved Him most, for we know what we do; we have tasted His sweetmeats; we have broken Bread with Him; we are His familiars. That is our sorrow -- that He who came to heal the broken hearts, had His own Heart broken by us.

But mourning is not despair. If we have crucified Christ, there is pardon: "Father, forgive them"; if we have pierced Mary's heart, there is pardon still: "Son, behold thy mother"; if there are tears in our eyes, they shall be wiped away: "Blessed are they that mourn, for they shall be comforted."

Think not, then, that the beatitude of mourning means the enthronement of sorrow, for it ends in the triumphant flight into the Father's embrace. All of you, therefore, who for months and years have lain crucified on beds of pain, remember that an hour will come when you will be taken down from your cross, and the Saviour shall look upon your hands and feet and sides to find there the imprint of His wounds, which will be your passport to eternal joy; for being made like Him in His death, you shall be made like Him in His glory.

All you husbands, wives, brothers, and sisters who have been bereaved of loved ones, remember that the Good Shepherd has taken His sheep to the green pastures that you, like other sheep, might follow your beloved even to the arms of Love.

To you whose life is as a fountain of tears for sins, remember that just as baptismal water washed away your original sin, so your tears will wash away your actual sins, and a day will come when God himself will wipe them all away.

To you who have lost faith, who have fear of confession, who dread casting yourself at the feet of Our Lord for absolution; remember that even your fear and your sin is a mourning, for you are most miserable on the inside.

You have broken your own heart, but be not disturbed. Take it to the anvil of Calvary, and under the fires of Love it shall be mended into that wholeness where it will never sorrow again, because when God mends a heart, it loses its capacity to sorrow and can only rejoice.

To all you who mourn, He has said: "Blessed are you, for you shall be comforted." You have had your fast with Christ, now you shall have His feast. He has saved much for you; He kept something back when He was on earth. He has reserved it for those who have wept.

And that thing which he has kept for eternity, which will make your life's crucifixion seem as naught, which will make your eternity a blissful ecstatic passionless passion of love, which will be the ending of all beatitudes and the crown of all living, that thing which He has guardedly treasured for eternity, and which will make heaven heaven, will be -- His Smile!

The Cross and the Beatitudes, 1937

Fifth Meditation

ETERNAL FREEDOM

"Father, into thy hands I commend my spirit."

"Fear ye not them that kill the body . . . but rather fear him that can destroy both soul and body in hell." Calvary is wrapped up in these words of Our Blessed Lord, for therein is revealed the supreme struggle of every life, -- the struggle to preserve our spiritual freedom. We cannot serve both God and Mammon; we cannot save our life both for time and eternity; we cannot feast both here and hereafter; we cannot make the best of two worlds; either we will have the fast on earth and the feast in heaven, or we will have the feast here and the fast in eternity.

In order then to purchase our freedom with the glorious Christ, we may have to suffer the slavery of earth. Real freedom consists in keeping our soul our own, even though we have to lose our body to preserve it.

Sometimes it can be preserved easily, but there may arise occasions when it demands even the sacrifice of our life.

A moment may come in the life of a politician, for example, when, in order to keep his independence, he must sacrifice the ease and influence which comes with the bribe.

To every Christian in like manner, there comes the supreme moment when he must choose between temporal pleasure and eternal freedom. In order to save our souls, we must often run the risk of losing our bodies.

Our Divine Saviour had the choice put before Him on Calvary, where He kept His soul free at the cost of His life. He went down into the bodily slavery of the Cross in order to keep His soul His own.

His majesty He surrendered to the supremacy of His enemies; His hands and feet He enslaved to their nails; His body He submitted to their grave; His good name He subjugated to their scorn; His blood He poured forth captive to their lance; His comfort he subjected to their planned pain; and His life He laid down as a serf at their feet. But His spirit He kept free and for Himself.

He would not surrender it, for if He kept His freedom, He could recover everything else He had already given into their hands.

They knew that, and so they tried to enslave His Spirit by challenging His Power: "Come down from the cross, and we will believe."

If He had Power to step down from that Cross, and yet refused, He was not a crucified prisoner, but their Judge on His Judgment Seat and their King on His Throne. If He had the Power to come down, and did come down, then He would have been submitted to their will and thus become their slave.

He refused to do the human thing -- to come down from the Cross. He did the divine thing, and stayed there! By so doing, He kept His soul His own.

Therefore, He could do with it whatever He pleased. All during His life He did the things that were pleasing to His Heavenly Father; now He would do them at His death.

Laying hold of His spirit, for He was master of Himself, He sent it back again to His Father, not with a hoarse cry of rebellion, not with a weak murmur of stoical endurance, not with the quivering uncertain tones of a Hamlet debating "to be or not to be," but with the loud, strong, triumphant voice of One Who was free to go to whom He pleased, and willed to go only back home: "Father, into Thy Hands I commend My Spirit."

That was the one, inescapable, untouchable thing in His life and every life: the spirit.

We can hammer iron, because it is material; we can melt ice, because we can warm it with our fires; we can break twigs, because we can get them into our hands; but we cannot crucify Faith, we cannot melt Hope, we cannot break Charity, and we cannot murder Justice, because all these things are spiritual and therefore, beyond the power of enslavement.

In a higher sense, the soul of every man is the last and impregnable fortress of character. As long as he wills to keep his spirit his own, no one can take it away, even though they take his life.

That spirit man can freely give away or sell, for example, into the slavery of drink, but it is his own as long as he chooses to keep it.

Our Lord kept His Spirit free at the most terrible of all costs, to remind us that not even the fear of a crucifixion is a reason for stepping down from the most glorious of all liberties -- the power to give our soul to God.

Unfortunately, freedom has lost its value for the modern world. It understands freedom too often as the right to do whatever you please, or the absence of constraint. This is not freedom but license, and very often anarchy.

Freedom means not the right to do what you *please*, but the right to do what we *should* in order to attain the highest and noblest ends of our nature.

An aviator is free not when he disregards the law of gravitation because it suits his fancy, but when he obeys it in order to conquer it and fly. Liberty then is a means, not an end; not a city, but a bridge.

When we say, "We want to be free," the obvious question is, "Free from what?" "Free from interruption." "Very well, but why?" "Because I want to travel to a certain place where I have business." Then freedom becomes meaningful. It implies a knowledge of a goal or a purpose.

Now human nature has a goal, namely, the using of this world as a stepping stone to the perfection of our personality, which is the enjoyment of perfect happiness.

But if we never stop to ask ourselves why we are here, or where we are going, or what is the purpose of life, then we are changing our direction, but we are not making progress; neither are we free.

If we forgot our real destiny, we cut up our lives into tiny, successive, and incomplete destinies, like a man who is lost in a forest, going first one way and then another.

If he had a single distant point, say a church steeple, beyond and outside the forest, he would be free either to go out of the forest or remain in it, and he would be making progress as he approached the church steeple.

So it is with life: if we have a fixed goal then we can make progress toward it; but it is sheer nonsense to say we are making progress if we constantly change our goal. As long as the model remains fixed, we are free to paint it, but if the model one moment is a rose and the next moment a nose, then art has lost not only its freedom but its joy.

This last and final Word on the Cross reminds us that Our Lord never lost sight of His goal! and because He did not, He sacrificed everything else to keep Himself free to attain it. Surplus baggage must often be dropped in order to run freely to refuge.

That is why Our Lord told the rich man to leave his bags of gold behind, for thus he could more perfectly run the course to eternal life. Our Lord Himself dropped everything, even His life.

But He dropped it as a seed into the ground and picked it up again in the freshness of the risen life of Easter Sunday.

From this sacrifice of His life in order to keep His Spirit free from the Father, we must learn not to be overcome by the sorrows and trials and disappointments of life. The danger is that forgetting the ideal, we may concentrate more on saving our body than on saving our soul.

Too often we blame persons and things for being indifferent to our pains and aches, as if they were primary. We want nature to suspend its sublime tasks, or we want persons to leave their round of duties, not just to minister to us in our necessities, but to soften us with their sympathy.

Forgetting that sometimes the work is more than the comfort, we become like those sick at sea who feel the ship should stop, hundreds should be delayed, and the port be forgotten, just to minister to their sickness.

Our Blessed Lord on the Cross might have made all nature minister to His wounds, He might have turned the Crown of thorns into a garland of roses: His nails into a sceptre, His blood into royal purple, His Cross into a golden throne, His wounds into glittering jewels. But that would have meant the ideal of sitting at the right hand of the Father in His Glory, was secondary to an immediate and temporary earthly comfort.

Then the purpose of life would have been less important than a moment in it; then the freedom of His Spirit would have been secondary to the healing of His Hands; then the higher self would have been the slave of the lower self -- and that is the one thing we are bidden to avoid.

"God strengthen me to bear myself
That heaviest weight of all to bear
Inalienable weight of care.

"All others are outside myself
I lock my door and bar them out,
The turmoil, tedium, gad-about.

"I lock my door upon myself,
And bar them out; but who shall bar
Self from myself, most loathed of all?

"If I could set aside myself
And start with lightened heart upon
The road by all men overgone!

"God harden me against myself
This coward with pathetic voice
Who craves for ease, and rest, and joys.
"Myself arch-traitor to myself
My hollowest friend, my deadliest fore
My clog whatever road I go.

"Yet One there is can curb myself
Can roll the strangling load from me
Break off the yoke and set me free."

(Christina Rossetti)

There is no escaping the one thing necessary in the Christian life, namely saving our souls and purchasing the glorious liberty of the children of God. The crucifixion ends, but Christ endures. Sorrows pass, but we remain. Therefore we must never come down from the supreme end and purpose of life; the salvation of our souls.

Often the temptation will be strong and the temporal advantages will seem great; but at those moments, we must recall the great difference between the solicitation of a sinful pleasure and the appeal of our heavenly destiny.

Before we have a sinful pleasure, it is attractive and appealing. After we have it, it is disgusting. It was not worth the price; we feel we were cheated and that we sold ourselves out of all proportion to our due worth, as Judas felt when he sold the Saviour for thirty pieces of silver.

But with the spiritual life it is different. Before we have intimate union with Christ and His Cross, it seems so distasteful, so contrary to our nature, so hard and so uninviting. But after we have given ourselves over to Him, it gives a peace and a joy which surpasses all understanding. That is why so many miss Him and His joy. They stand so far away they never learn to know Him. Like the poet they ask:

> "Must Thou, Designer Infinite
> Char the wood ere Thou canst limn with it?"

Must the wood be subject to fire before we can paint with it as charcoal? Is death the condition of life? Is the discipline of study the path to knowledge? Are long hours of tedious practice, the road to the thrill of music? Must we lose our lives in time in order to save them for eternity? Yes. That is the answer.

But it is not so hard as it seems, for, as St. Paul tells us: "The sorrows of this life are not worthy to be compared to the joys that are to come." How often as little children, when our little toys were broken, we thought life was no longer worth living, for the universe was in ruins; and then, surveying the wreck which seemed so hopeless, we cried ourselves to sleep.

May not those once great sorrows which faded into insignificance with maturity be but the symbol of the trivialities of our present burdens, compared to the joys which await us in the mansions of the Father's House?

Only let us not be fooled by those who say human life has no purpose, and who, in the language of a scientist, say that life is like a lit candle and that when the candle is done the flame goes out, and that is the end of us all.

But what this scientist forgot to tell us is that light is not something in the candle, but something which emanates from it; something associated with matter but separable and distinct from it. For even when the candle has burned out, the light continues to emit itself at the rate of 186,000 miles a second, beyond the moon and stars, beyond the Pleiades, the nebulas of Andromeda, and continues to do so as long as the universe endures.

And so when the candle of our life burns low, may we have kept our soul so free, that like a flame it will leap upwards to the Great Fire at which it was enkindled, and never stop until its light meets that Heavenly Light which ages ago came to this world as its Light, to teach us all to say at the end of our earthly pilgrimage here, as He said at the close of His: "Father, into Thy Hands I commend My Spirit."

The Rainbow of Sorrow, 1938

Sixth Meditation

COVETOUSNESS

"Father, into thy hands, I commend my spirit."

Covetousness is an inordinate love of the things of this world. It becomes inordinate if one is not guided by a reasonable end, such as a suitable provision for one's family, or the future, or if one is too solicitous in amassing wealth, or too parsimonious in dispensing it.

The sin of covetousness includes therefore both the intention one has in acquiring the goods of this world and the manner of acquiring them. It is not the love of an excessive sum that makes it wrong, but an inordinate love of any sum.

Simply because a man has a great fortune, it does not follow that he is a covetous man. A child with a few pennies might possibly be more covetous. Material things are lawful and necessary to enable us to live according to our station in life, to mitigate suffering, to advance the Kingdom of God, and to save our souls.

It is the pursuit of wealth as an end instead of a means to the above ends, that makes a man covetous.

In this class of the covetous are to be placed the young woman who marries a divorced man for his money; the public official who accepts a bribe; the lawyer; the educator or clergyman who sponsors radical movements for Red gold; the capitalist who puts profits above human rights and needs, and the laborer who puts party power above the laborer's rights.

Covetousness is much more general in the world today than we suspect. It once was monopolized by the avaricious rich; now it is shared by the envious poor.

Because a man has no money in his pockets is no proof that he is not covetous; he may be involuntarily poor with a passion for wealth far in excess of those who possess.

History bears witness to the fact, that almost every radical economic revolutionist in history has been interested in only one thing: -- booty. The only poor people who ever attacked the rich and sought nothing for themselves were Our Lord and His followers, like St. Francis of Assisi.

There are very few disinterested lovers of the poor today; most of their so-called champions do not love the poor as much as they hate the rich. They hate all the rich, but they love only those poor who will help them attain their wicked ends.

Such covetousness is ruinous for man, principally because it hardens the heart. Man becomes like unto that which he loves, and if he loves gold, he becomes like it -- cold, hard and yellow. The more he acquires, the more he suffers at surrendering even the least of it, just as it hurts to have a single hair pulled out even though your head is full of them.

The more the sinfully rich man gets, the more he believes he is needy. He is always poor in his own eyes. The sense of the spiritual thus becomes so deadened, that its most precious treasures are bartered away for the trivial increases, as Judas sold his Master for thirty pieces of silver.

As St. Paul tells us, "The desire for money is the root of all evils, which some coveting have erred from the faith." *(1Timothy 6:10)* The Providence of God becomes less and less a reality, and if it still retains value, it is reduced to a secondary role; God is trusted as long as we have a good bank account.

When things go well we are quite willing to dispense with God, like the young man in the Gospel who came to our Lord only because he was being deprived of some of his father's estate. "Master, speak to my brother that he divide the inheritance with me." It was only when economic confusion arose that the young man had recourse to the Divine.

There are many in the world today who think that the only reason for the existence of the Church is to improve the economic order and if they do not have their fill, they assail the Church for failing. Well indeed might the Church answer in the words of Our Lord: "O man, who hath appointed me judge and divider over you?"

To turn man's heart away from perishable things to the eternal values of the soul, was one of the reasons for the Lord's visit to the earth. His teaching from the beginning, was not only a warning against covetousness, but a plea for a greater trust in Providence.

"Do not lay up for yourselves treasures upon the earth, where moth and rust consume, and where thieves break through and steal; but lay up for yourselves treasures in heaven, where neither moth nor rust consumes, and where thieves do not break through nor steal. For where thy treasure is, there will thy heart be also." *(Matthew 6:19-21)*

I say to you therefore, do not be anxious about your life, what you shall eat or what you shall drink; nor about your body, what you shall wear. Is not the life of more consequence than the food, and the body than the clothing? Look at the birds of the sky, how they neither sow nor reap nor gather into barns yet your heavenly Father feeds them! Are you not of much more value than they? Yet who among you by anxious thought is able to add a single span to his life?

And why should you worry about clothing? Observe the field-lilies, how they grow; they neither toil nor spin; yet I tell you that even Solomon in all his magnificence was not arrayed like one of them. But if God so clothes the grass of the field, which exists today and is thrown in the oven tomorrow, will He not much rather clothe you, O you of little faith?

"Do not therefore worry saying, "What shall we eat?" "What shall we drink?" or "What shall we wear?" for the heathen seek after all these things; and your heavenly Father knows that you need them all. But seek first the kingdom of God and His holiness, and all these things shall be given you besides. Do not then be anxious about tomorrow, for tomorrow will take care of itself. Quite enough for the day is its own trouble." *(Matthew 6:25-34)*

The man who unduly loves riches is a fallen man, because of a bad exchange; he might have had heaven through his generosity, and he has only the earth. He could have kept his soul, but he sold it for material things. Camels will pass through eyes of needles more easily than the covetous will pass through the gates of heaven. It was easy of course to condemn the rich; our world is too full of those who are doing it now. But our economic revolutionists do it because they envy wealth, not because they love poverty.

It was not so with Our Divine Saviour. He Who condemned Dives and the man who ordered bigger barns the very day he died, and who thundered that no man could serve God and Mammon, lived His gospel. Not in a hospital, or a home, or a city, but in a stable in the fields did He bow entrance into the world He made. Not with money did He make money in the markets of exchange, but as a poor carpenter.

He earned His living with the two most primitive instruments used: wood and hammer. During His three years of preaching, not even a roof could He claim as His own: "The foxes have burrows, and the birds of the sky have nests; but the Son of Man has not a place where He may lay His head." *(Matthew 8:9,20)*

Then, at His death, He had no wealth to leave; His Mother He gave to John; His body to the tomb; His blood to the earth; His garments to His executioners. Absolutely dispossessed, He is still hated, to give the lie to those who say religion is hated because of its possessions.

Religion is hated because it is religion, and possessions are only the excuse and pretext for driving God from the earth. There was no quarreling about His will; there was no dispute about how His property would be divided; there was no lawsuit over the Lord of the Universe.

He had given up everything in reparation for covetousness, keeping only one thing for Himself that was not a thing -- His Spirit. With a loud cry, so powerful that it freed His soul from His flesh and bore witness to the fact that He was giving up His life and not having it taken away, He said in farewell: "Father, into Thy Hands I commend My Spirit."

It rang out over the darkness and lost itself in the furthermost ends of the earth. The world has made all kinds of noise since to drown it out.

Men have busied themselves with nothing to shut out hearing it; but through the fog and darkness of cities, and the silence of the night, that awful cry rings within the hearing of everyone who does not force himself to forget, and as we listen to it we learn two lessons:

1. *The more ties we have to earth, the harder will it be for us to die.*
2. *We were never meant to be perfectly satisfied here below.*

In every friendship hearts grow and entwine themselves together, so that the two hearts seem to make only one heart with only a common thought. That is why separation is so painful; -- it is not so much two hearts separating, but one heart being torn asunder.

When a man loves wealth inordinately, he and it grow together like a tree pushing itself in growth through the crevices of a rock. Death to such a man is a painful wrench, because of his close identification with the material. He has everything to live for, nothing to die for. He becomes at death the most destitute and despoiled beggar in the universe, for he has nothing he can take with him. He discovers too late that he did not belong to himself, but to things, for wealth is a pitiless master.

It would not allow him during life to think of anything else except increasing itself. Now he discovers too late that by consecrating himself to filling his barns, he was never free to save the only thing he could carry with him to eternity: -- his soul. In order to acquire a part, he lost the whole; he won a fraction of the earth, now he will need only six feet of it.

Like a giant tied down by ten thousand ropes to ten thousand stakes, he is no longer free to think about anything else than what he must leave. That is why death is so hard for the covetous rich.

On the contrary, as the ties to earth become lessened, the easier is the separation. Where our treasure is, there is our heart also. If we have lived for God, then death is a liberation. Earth and its possessions are the cage that confines us and death is the opening of its door, enabling our soul to wing its way to its Beloved for which it had only lived and for which it only waited to die.

Our powers of dispossession are greater than our powers of possession; our hands could never contain all the gold in the world, but we can wash our hands of its desire. We cannot own the world, but we can disown it. That is why the soul with the vow of poverty is more satisfied than the richest covetous man in the world, for the latter has not yet all he wants, while the religious wants nothing; in a certain sense the religious has all and is perfectly happy.

It was such poverty of spirit raised to its sublimest peaks, which made the death of Our Lord so easy. He had no ties to earth. His treasure was with the Father, and His Soul followed the spiritual law of gravitation.

Gold, like dirt, falls; charity, like fire, rises: "Father, into Thy Hands I commend My Spirit."

The death of Our Lord on the Cross reveals that we are meant to be perpetually dissatisfied here below. If earth were meant to be a Paradise, then He who made it would never have taken leave of it on Good Friday. The commending of the Spirit to the Father was at the same time the refusal to commend it to earth. The completion or fulfillment of life is in heaven, not on earth.

Our Lord in His last Word is saying that nowhere else can we be satisfied except in God. It is absolutely impossible for us to be perfectly happy here below. Nothing proves this more than disappointment. One might almost say the essence of life is disappointment. We look forward to a position, to marriage, to ownership, to power, to popularity, to wealth, and when we attain them, we have to admit, if we are honest, that they never come up to our expectations.

As children we looked forward to Christmas; when it came and we had our fill of sweets and tested every toy or rocked every doll, and then crept into our beds, we said in our own little heart of hearts: "Somehow or other, it did not quite come up to expectations." That experience is repeated a thousand times in life.

But why is there disappointment? Because when we look forward to a future ideal, we endow it with something of the infinity of the soul. I can imagine a house with ten thousand rooms studded with diamonds and emeralds, but I shall never see one. I can imagine a mountain of gold, but I shall never see one.

So with our earthly ideals. We color them with the qualities of our spiritual soul. But when they become realized, they are concrete, cabined, cribbed, confined. A tremendous disproportion thus arises between the ideal we conceived and the reality before us.

That disproportion between the infinite and the finite is the cause of disappointment. There is no escaping this fact. We have eternity in our heart, but time on our hands. The soul demands a heaven, and we get only an earth. Our eyes look up to the mountains, but they rest only on the plains. It is easier to strangle our ideals than it is to satisfy them. He who attains his earthly ideal, smashes it.

To touch an ideal in this world is to destroy the ideal. "No man is a hero to his valet." We are no longer thirsty at the border of a well. The satisfaction of earthly ideals turns against us, like a cruel retort from one we paid an underhand compliment.

But there is no reason for being pessimists or cynics. Disappointment is no proof that there is no ideal, but only that it is not here. Just as we would have no eyes were there no beauties to see, and as we would have no ears were there no harmonies to hear, so we would have no appetite for the infinite were there no God to love.

In Him alone is the reconciliation of the chase and the capture. Here on this earth we are buffeted between the two. The chase has its thrill for it is the pursuit of an ideal, the quest for satisfaction, and the march to victory. The capture too has its thrill for it is possession, enjoyment and peace.

But while we live in time we can never enjoy both together. The capture ends the excitement of the chase; and the chase without a capture is maddening, like having a refreshing spring withdrawn from our parched lips as we draw near to it.

How to combine the chase without the ennui of capture, and the capture without losing the joy of the chase? It is impossible here below, but not in heaven, for when we attain unto God, we capture the Infinite and because He is Infinite it will take an eternity of chase to discover the undiscoverable joys of Life, Truth, Love and Beauty.

Such is the meaning behind the last and farewell word from the Cross. Centuries ago the sun shone upon plants and trees and imprisoned within them its light and heat. Today we dig up that light and heat in coal, and as its flames mount upward we pay back our debt to the sun.

So now the Divine Light, that for thirty-three years has been imprisoning itself in human hearts, goes back again to the Father, to ever remind us that only by completing a similar circuit and commending our souls to the Father, do we find the answer to the riddle of life, and the end of disappointment and the beginning of eternal peace for our eternal hearts.

Everything is disappointing except the Redemptive Love of Our Lord. You can go on acquiring things but you will be poor until your soul is filled with the love of Him Who died on the Cross for you. As the eye was made for seeing and the ear for hearing, so your spirit was made to be re-commended back again to God.

If it had any other destiny the dying words of the Saviour would have betrayed that destiny. The spirit has a capacity for the infinite; the knowledge of one flower, the life of a single hour, the love of a minute do not exhaust its potencies. It wants the fullness of these things; in a word -- it wants God.

The tragedy of our modern life is that so many put their pleasures in *desires* rather than in *discovery*. Having lost the one purpose of human living, namely God, they seek substitutes in the petty things of earth.

After repeated disappointments, they begin to put their happiness not in a pleasure, but in the *hunt* for it, in butterfly existences that never rest long enough at any one moment to know their inner desires; running races hoping they will never end; turning pages but never discovering the plot; knocking at doors of truth and then dashing away lest its portals be opened and they be invited in. Existence becomes a flight from peace, rather than an advance; a momentary escape from frustration instead of its sublimation in victory.

Every now and then there comes to some a light through the clouds of Calvary and the echo of the word commending a spirit to God, but instead of making a supreme effort to satisfy the goal of life, they crucify it.

"But the husbandmen said one to another, this is the heir; come, let us kill him and the inheritance shall be ours. And laying hold of him, they killed him and cast him out of the vineyard."

Thus do some men believe that if they could drive God from the earth, the inheritance of sin would be there without remorse; and if they could but silence conscience, they could inherit peace without justice. It was just this mentality that sent Our Lord to the Cross. If the voice of God could be stifled, they believed they could enjoy the voice of Satan in peace.

Now take a different outlook on the world. How many, even of those who have killed conscience, can say: "I am happy; there is nothing I want"? But if you are not brave enough to say that, then why not seek? And why not seek in the one direction in which you know happiness lies?

At death, you will leave *everything*, but there is one thing you will not leave -- your desire to life. You want the one thing the Cross brings you: -- Life through death.

In its effulgence, the mystery of existence becomes clear. The Cross refers to *me*, personally and individually, as if no one else in the world ever existed. On the cross He has traced for me in sacrifice, which is the sublimest of gestures, a program of life; submission to the Divine Will. He went down the dark road of Gethsemane to Calvary's death out of devotedness to God's glory and my salvation.

For my culpable self-indulgence, He atones by surrender of Himself. "He was wounded for our iniquities; He was bruised for our sins. The chastisement of our peace was upon Him." *(Isaiah 5:3-5).*

If this Master of the world's symphony would miss my single note of virtue in the harmony of the universe; if this Captain of Wars would miss my spear in His battle for Goodness; if this Artist would miss my little daub of color in the masterpiece of redemption; if this Cosmic Architect would note the absence of my little stone in the building of His temple; if this Tree of Life would feel the fall of but my little leaf to the sinfulness of earth; if this Heavenly Father would miss me in the empty chair at the banquet spread for the millions of the children of God; if this Orator from the Pulpit of the Cross would note my inattention as I turned to glance at an executioner; if God cares that much for me, then I must be worth something since He loves me so!

But if Himself He come to thee, and stand
Beside thee, gazing down on thee with eyes
That smile, and suffer; that will smite thy heart,
With their own pity, to a passionate peace;
And reach to thee Himself and the Holy Cup
(With all its wreathen stems of passion-flowers
And quivering sparkles of the ruby stars),
Pallid and royal, saying 'Drink with Me;'
Wilt thou refuse? Nay, not for Paradise!
The pale brow will compel thee, the pure hands
Will minister unto thee; thou shalt take
Of that communion through the solemn depths.
Of the dark waters of thine agony,

With heart that praise Him, that yearns to Him
The closer through that hour. Hold fast His hand,
Though the nails pierce thine too! take only care
Lest one drop of the sacramental wine
Be spilled, of that which ever shall unite
Thee, soul and body to thy living Lord!

(Harriet Eleanor Hamilton-King)

Victory Over Vice, 1939

Seventh Meditation

CHARITY

"Father, into thy hands I commend my spirit."

Charity is the perfection of Justice. As Aristotle put it so wisely: "Where Justice is, there is a further need of friendship; but where friendship is, there is no need of justice. "Complementing that last thought, St. Augustine said: "Love God and do whatever you please," for if you love God you will never do anything to offend Him.

It was therefore fitting that the Sixth Word, reflecting the Justice of God which fulfilled the will of the Father in its smallest detail, should be followed by the Seventh Word of Charity: "Father, into Thy Hands I commend My Spirit." It was like the seventh day of Creation. During the six words the Son of God labored forgiving enemies, pardoning thieves, solacing a mother, atoning for faithlessness, pleading for love, atoning for injustice, and now He takes His rest and goes back home.

Love is to a great extent a stranger on earth; it finds momentary satisfactions in human hearts, but it soon becomes restless. It was born of the Infinite and can never be satisfied with anything less. In a certain sense, God spoiled us for any other love except Himself, because He made us out of His Divine Love.

Born of His Everlasting Fire, the earthly sparks of affection can but kindle our hearts. We are all kings in exile; prodigals from the Father's House. As flames must mount upward to the sun, so He Who came from the Father must go back again to the Father: Love must return to Love. "Father, into Thy Hands I commend My Spirit."

It is noteworthy that He said these words with a loud voice. No one was taking His life away. It was not like the love expressed by a dying parent to his child; such love is begotten of a heart meeting the impact of the inevitable. But in the case of Our Lord, it was completely and absolutely unforced -- the deliverance of freedom.

Thus did He teach us that all love on this earth involves choice. When, for example, a young man expresses his love to a young woman and asks her to become his wife, he is not just making an affirmation of love; he is also negating his love for anyone else. In that one act by which he chooses her, he rejects all that is not her.

There is no other real way in which to prove we love a thing than by choosing it in preference to something else. Words and sighs of love may be, and often are, expressions of egotism or passion; but deeds are proofs of love.

When God put Adam and Eve in the garden, the preservation of their gifts was conditioned upon fidelity to Him. But how prove fidelity except by choice, namely by obeying God's Will in preference to any other will.

In the freedom of choosing a fruit to a garden, was hidden the test of their love. By their decision, they proved they loved something else more than God.

After the Resurrection, Our Lord prefaced the conferring of the powers of jurisdiction on Peter as the Rock of the Church, by asking the question: "Simon, Son of John, lovest thou Me more than these?" Three times the question is asked, because three times Peter had denied Our Lord -- Once again, love is tested by preference.

The beginning and the end of the public life of Our Lord reveals this same basic quality of love. On the Mount of Temptation and on the Mount of Calvary, Satan and wicked men throw bribes into the balance to influence His choice. Surveying all the grandeur of earth, Satan in a frightening boast said: "All these kingdoms are mine." He offered them all to Our Lord if falling down He would adore him. Jesus could have the world if He would give up heaven.

Now on the other mount, it is satanic men who tempt as they shout: "Come Down and we will believe." "Come Down from your belief in the Heavenly Father." "Come Down from your belief in Divinity." "Come Down from the cross and we will believe." Jesus could have believers if He would give up the Cross, but without the Cross Jesus could not be the Saviour.

But as He did not fall down before Satan, neither did He come down from the cross, for perfect love is the choice of Divine Love. He would choose the Father's Will either to this wealth or His bodily comfort. And that is why: "Greater love than this no man hath, that he lay down His life for his friend."

Now His love was not just declared by word, but proven by deed. He could enjoy the fruit of perfect love: "Father, into Thy Hands I commend My Spirit."

For us, there can be but one conclusion: it is not enough to bear a Christian name, we must also merit the name. "Not everyone that saith 'Lord, Lord' shall enter into the Kingdom of heaven." We can prove we love Our Lord only by choosing Him in preference to anything else. The condition of returning to the Father's hands on the last day is the choice of His Cross and all that it implies.

At any moment of our existence we can test whether we are truly Christian, and that test will be the obedience to His commandments: "He that hath my commandments and keepeth them, he it is that loveth me. And he that loveth me shall be loved of my Father, and I will love him and manifest myself to him. And my Father will love him and we will come to him and make our abode with him" *(John 14: 21-23).*

This brings us to the second lesson of Charity. In this Seventh Word, Our Lord did not express Love of the Father in terms of keeping commandments: it was a personal relationship; that of Father and Son. Even in the text: "He that loveth my commandments and keepeth them, he it is that loveth me," the possessive adjective is to be noted. The commandments are not abstract laws separable from His Person; they are one with Him.

"If you love *Me* keep My *commandments.*" Perfect love is therefore quite distinct from obedience to commandments as laws. Laws are for the imperfect; love is for the perfect. Law is for those who want to know the minimum; love is for those who are interested in the maximum. Laws therefore are generally negative: "Thou shalt not . . ."; love is affirmative: "Love the Lord, thy God, with thy whole heart."

Imperfect Christians are concerned only with keeping the laws of the Church; they want to know how far they can go without committing a mortal sin; how near they can get to hell without falling in; how much wrong they can do short of punishment; how they can please God without displeasing themselves.

The perfect Christian is never interested in borders, or the minimum, because love is never measured. Mary Magdalene did not count out the drops of the precious ointment as she poured them on the feet of Our Divine Saviour. Judas did; he counted the cost.

But Magdalene, because she loved, broke the vessel and gave everything, for love has no limits. St. Paul, in like manner, could think of no better way of describing the love of Christ for sinners than to say: "He emptied himself."

There is no law that those who love should give gifts to their beloved; there are no laws that mothers should love children. Where there is love, there is no law, because love has no limits.

There was no boundary to the cross; the arms outstretched even into infinity portrayed the universal efficacy of Redemption. There was no counting the cost: "Not my will but Thine be done." He even refused to touch a drink which might have dulled His senses, and thus deprive His will of complete self-devotion for men.

Like Magdalene, He broke the chalice of His Life, and poured out "plentiful Redemption." Such perfect love could be compensated only by a return to perfect love: "Father, into Thy Hands I commend My Spirit."

The essence of Christianity is love, yes! But not love as our world understands it; not loving those who love us, but loving even those who hate us. Love is not in the organism, but in the will; not in affection, but in intention; not in satisfaction, but in preference to the choosing of God above everything.

Every soul then, even those who irritate, annoy and hate us must be looked upon as a potential lover of Christ, and every Christian must be regarded as a kind of consecrated host.

The most degraded man on the face of the earth is precious, and Christ died for Him. That poor soul may have made the wrong choice, but that is not for us to decide. While he has life, he has hope. He might not seem lovable to us, but he is loved by God.

The perfection of all virtue is charity; love of God and love of our neighbor. Whether or not we, like Christ, shall deliver our soul into the Father's hands on the last day, depends entirely upon the use we make of our freedom.

When we abuse it, our conscience tells us that we are our own worst enemy. "Now I know that when I nailed thee to a Cross it was my own heart I slew." All sin is self-mutilation.

Most of us are kept back from a perfect love of God, "... fearful lest having Him, we should have naught else beside." There is a fear of losing something by obedience to Him; a hesitation of venturing all on God. Could we but see that when we have the sun we need not the candle, then all would be easy.

God grant us the light to see that in loving Him we have everything, and with that light, the grace to die with His words on our lips: "Father, into Thy Hands I commend My Spirit."

The Seven Virtues, 1940

Eighth Meditation

A WORD TO THE THINKERS

The greatest problem of life is life itself. Remember how it puzzled Hamlet. What was the end of life? Would he want to continue to exist or not? When he died, would that be the end of him? Or would he go on living as in a dream? If there were nothing beyond this life, then well we might take it with a dagger, said Hamlet. If there is a life beyond, then we must worry about our conscience. Hamlet was very uncertain:

> "To be, or not to be: that is the question.
> Whether 'tis nobler in the mind to suffer
> The slings and arrows of outrageous fortune
> Or to take arms against a sea of troubles,
> And, by opposing, end them? To die, to sleep
> No more . . . 'Tis a consummation
> Devoutly to be wished. To die, to sleep.
> To sleep, perchance to dream; ay, there's the rub!
> For in that sleep of death what dreams may come
> When we have shuffled off this mortal coil,
> Must give us pause. There's the respect
> That makes calamity of so long life.
> For who would bear the whips and scorns of time,
> Th' oppressor's wrong, the proud man's contumely,
> The pangs of despised love, the law's delay,
> The insolence of office, and the spurns
> That patient merit of th' unworthy takes,
> When he himself might his quietus make
> With a bare bodkin? Who would these fardels bear,
> To grunt and sweat under a weary life,
> But that the dread of something after death,
> The undiscovered country from whose bourn
> No traveller returns, puzzles the will,
> And makes us rather bear those ills we have
> Than fly to others that we know not of?
> Thus conscience does make cowards of us all."

Now, turn from Hamlet's uncertainty of life to the Seventh Word that came from the Cross in loud, clear tones when there was a rupture of the heart through a rapture of love, as Christ bowed His Head and died: "Father, into Thy hands I commend my Spirit."

No doubt here; no problem here as to whether it's a sleep or a dream, or whether one should make his exit from the world with a dagger. Here was absolute certainty about the issue of life. Life is a return to the God Who made us. We came from God. To God again we go.

The Greeks had a theory that the perfect movement was the circular movement, because the beginning was the end; and in a certain sense that was right.
The beginning of our life which was God, is also the end. We came from His creative Hands, and then, like a planet, when we have completed life's orbit, we go back to Him Who sent us on our way.

Life is like the coals, which in the prehistoric past as trees and foliage sucked in the fire and light of the sun, kept them hidden for years in the bowels of the earth, but finally when placed in the hearth give back to the sun that which they took from it.

And now the Son of God, like the Prodigal Son, goes back to the Father's House. For thirty-three years He has been in the foreign country of this earth, 'wasting His substance' among us, spending now even His last drop of blood. "And now glorify thou Me, O father, with thyself, with the glory which I had, before the world was, with thee" *(John 17:5)*. "I have glorified thee on earth; I have finished the work which thou gavest me to do" *(John 17:4)*. Now He could return home. "Father, into thy hands I commend my spirit."

Among those who gathered around the Cross was a centurion, so called because he commanded about 100 men, and who had duties similar to the sergeant of our army. The

Gospel generally speaks well of centurions. As a soldier, he was often brought into contact with death.

On this particular occasion He had nailed Our Lord to the Cross, then sat down, shook dice for His garments and watched Him die. But there was something peculiar about that Figure on the Central Cross.

Often the tongues of those crucified had to be cut out to prevent their blasphemies. But here was one Who forgave those who sent Him to His Death. Then too he noted that as the end grew near, He seemed to be getting stronger, as if Death were not coming to meet Him, but He was going out to meet it. He was not dying on this Cross as other men died in bed.

The very second of death, He spoke in a loud, clear voice, as if men were not taking away His life, but He was laying it down of Himself: "Father, into thy hands I commend my Spirit." These were not words of death, but of life. While He was accommodating Himself to death, it was only a milestone on the roadway in the onward march of life.

It made the sergeant think! Are we just animals who eat and sleep and then lie down to die and rot, or is there something after death, a God into Whose Hands we go to render an account of our stewardship. He shook off the thought for a moment, but was rekindled to it when the earth shook and the dead rose from their graves and walked.

He went on thinking about life and death as he broke the legs of the two thieves, for they were not yet dead. Coming to the Central Cross and finding Christ dead, He ran a spear into His Side. Blood and water came out; the Divine Miser had hoarded up a few drops, to prove that Death is not the end of life.

These drops trickled down the spear, touched the centurion's hand, and tradition has it that he was immediately cured of a life-long affliction. In any case, he glorified God by saying: "Indeed this was the Son of God" *(Matthew 27: 54) (Luke 23:47) (Mark 15:39).*

A soldier had found faith on a battlefield; a thinker discovered the answer to life's riddle in the midst of death. This life is not the end of all. That soldier became the representative of that seventh and last type who come in contact with the Cross, namely, the thinkers.

The term here is used in contradistinction to the intelligentsia, who *think* they are educated. By the thinkers is here understood all who concern themselves with the ultimate of life: why was I born, why am I here and whither am I going?

The thinkers do not necessarily mean the educated, nor even those who spend their life in meditation. But rather those who, once they are brought in contact with the spectacle of death, think the whole problem through.

One wonders what John thought when he saw that lance go into the side of his Lord. I wonder if he remembered that incident of the night before when Peter used a sword too, to cut off the ear of the servant of the High Priest.

I wonder too, if John recalled what the Saviour answered to Peter: "Put up again thy sword into its place: for all that take the sword shall perish with the sword" *(Matthew 26:52).*

Why then did not this sergeant perish with his sword? Because Our Lord seemed to suggest that it is all right if you use the sword against Me, but do not use it against your neighbor. That is why our Lord said to the soldiers: "I have told you that I am He. If therefore you seek Me, let these go their way" *(John 18:8).*

There was a woman there along with John -- the Mother of James and John whom Our Lord called 'sons of thunder.' Now there is thunder. The whole earth is trembling! And only one 'son of thunder' is there. Where is James? Why is he not there?

I wonder if she remembers, that good mother, the day that she went to Our Lord and said to Him: "Say that these my two sons, may sit, the one on thy right hand, and the other on thy left, in thy kingdom" (Matthew 20:21).

Mothers are always doing that. They are always manoeuvring for their boys to get them into the right place. And the mother of these boys was no exception. She wanted to be sure that they would be in the upper classes.

And what did He say: "You know not what you ask. Can you drink the chalice that I shall drink?" *(Matthew 20:22)*. Only one of them could! Ah! The Kingdom of God is so different from the kingdom of men.

Mary Magdalen was there too. Poor Mary! Wherever there is ointment being poured forth, Mary will be there, and this time it is He Who pours out the crimson ointment of salvation. She saw it on the ground, and she suspected some of it was on her beautiful hair. As she once broke a vessel and gave everything in Simon's house, she now sees that Our Blessed Lord has done the same thing. He broke a vessel too when He gave all; and the odor filled the house: 'The House of the World!'

Then there was Mary, His Mother. It is peculiar about mothers that their children never grow up; even when they die they still seem like children. Her mind goes back to a night long ago, when War began -- the war against evil. She can recall so well looking out through the cracks in a stable roof and seeing a great star in the background of angels' wings, blazing in the night. To her it looked as if the Heavenly Father had hung out His Service Flag: His Son had gone to war!

Ye Mothers of the world, think ye not that she knows what it means to have a boy go to war! She remembers so well the night that He went out to battle, armed only in the flesh of man. And then the Battle came! This is not Bethlehem, Mary! This is Calvary! This is war! And unlike all the mothers of the world, you are in it. A queer war in which even mothers march upon the field! And you were wounded: pierced by seven swords! Everywhere the smell of death: nails, hammers, wounds, ghastly sights!

Mary -- look up from the battlefield as thou didst look up from the crib. It is still dark! Dark in mid-afternoon. The sun has dimmed its light! It seems so far away! It looks exactly like a star! Remember the White Star of Christmas? Well -- this is different! Mary! You are the first Gold Star Mother of the World!

Seven Words to the Cross, 1944

Ninth Meditation

THE PURPOSE OF LIFE

Probably the word most often used in the contemporary scene is the word *Freedom*. If the sick talk most about health, because health is endangered, may it be that the modern talk about freedom means that we are in danger of losing it? It is indeed possible that while we fight to keep our enemies from binding chains to our feet, we become our own enemy by binding chains to our souls.

What I am trying to say is there are two kinds of freedom; a freedom *from* something, and a freedom *for* something; an external freedom from restraints, and an internal freedom of perfection; a freedom to choose evil and a freedom to possess the good.

This inner freedom the typical modern man does not want, because it implies responsibility and, therefore, is a burden -- the awful burden of answering, what is the purpose of your life? That is why theories which deny man's inner freedom are so popular today, e.g., Marxism, which destroys freedom in terms of historical determination; Freudianism, which dissolves freedom in the determination of the subconscious and the erotic; totalitarianism, which drowns individual freedom in the totality.

The root of all our trouble is that freedom for God and in God has been interpreted as freedom from God. Freedom is ours to give away. Each of us reveals what we believe to be the purpose of life by the way we use that freedom. For those who would know the supreme purpose of freedom, turn to the life of Our Lord and Our Lady.

The first word Our Lord is recorded as speaking in the Scripture is at the age of twelve: "I must be about my father's business" *(Luke 2:49)*. During His public life, He re-affirmed His obedience to His Father: "I do always the things that please him" *(John 8:29)*. Now on the Cross, when He goes out to meet death, and freely surrenders His life, His last words are: "Father, into thy hands I commend my spirit" *(Luke 23:46)*. The last words of other men are spoken in whispers, but He spoke these words in a loud voice.

Death, therefore, did not come to Him; He went to death. No one took His Life away; He laid it down of Himself. He was strong enough to live, but He died by an act of will. This was not an emphasis on dying, but an affirmation of uninterrupted Divine Life. It was the beginning of His return to the glory which He had with the Father, before the foundations of the world were laid.

“Father” -- note the word of Eternal Parenthood. He did not say "Our Father" as we do, for the Father was not His and ours in the same way. He is the natural Son of the Father; we are only the adopted sons.

“Into Thy Hands" -- These were the hands the prophet called "good"; the hands that guided Israel to its historical fulfillment; the hands that provided good things even for the birds of the air and the grass of the field.

"I commend my Spirit" -- Surrender! Consecration. Life is a cycle. We come from God and we go back again to God. Hence the purpose of living is to do God's will.

When Our Blessed Mother saw Him bow His head and deliver His spirit, she remembered that last Word that she ever is recorded to have spoken in Scripture. It was to the wine steward at the marriage feast of Cana: "Whatsoever He shall say to you, do ye" *(John 2:5)*. What a beautiful valedictory! They are the most magnificent words that ever came from the lips of a woman: "Whatsoever He shall say to you, do ye." At the Transfiguration, the Heavenly Father spoke from the Heavens and said: "This is my beloved Son . . . Hear ye him" *(Matthew 17:5)*. Now our Blessed Mother speaks and says, "Do His will."

The sweet relationship of three decades in Nazareth now draws to a close and Mary is about to give Emanuel to us all, and she does it by pointing out to us the one and only way of salvation: complete consecration to her Divine Son. Nowhere in the Scripture is it ever said that Mary loved her son. Words do not prove love. But that love is hidden under the submission of her mind to Him and her final injunction to us: "Whatsoever He shall say to you, do ye."

Both the last recorded word of Jesus and the last recorded word of Mary were words of surrender: Jesus surrendered Himself to the Father; Mary asked us to surrender ourselves to the Son. This is the law of the universe. "For all are yours: And you are Christ's. And Christ is God's" *(1Corinthians 3:22-23).*

Now face the problem squarely: What do you do with your freedom? You can do three things with it:

1) Keep it for your selfish desires.
2) Break it up into tiny little areas of trivial allegiance or passing fancies.
3) Surrender it to God.

1) If you keep freedom only for yourself, then because it is arbitrary and without standards, you will find it deteriorating into a defiant self-affirmation. Once all things become allowable, simply because you desire them, you become the slave of your choices. If your self-will decides to drink as much as you please, you soon find not only that you are no longer free not to drink, but that you belong to drink and not drink to you. Boundless liberty is boundless tyranny. This is what Our Lord meant when he said: "Whosoever committeth sin is the servant of sin." *(John 8:34)*

(2) The second way out is to become a dilettante, by using your freedom like a hummingbird, hovering first over this flower, then over that, but living for none and dying without any. You desire nothing with all your heart, because your heart is broken into a thousand pieces. You thus

become divided against yourself; a civil war wages within you, because you swim in contradictory currents.

You change your likes and desires when dissatisfied, but you never change yourself. You are then very much like the man who complained to the cook at breakfast that the egg was not fresh and asked her to bring another. She brought in an egg a minute later, but when he got to the bottom of it, he found it was the same old egg turned upside down. So it is always the same self; what has changed is the desire, not the soul. In that case, even your interest in others is not real.

In your more honest moments, you discover that you have dealt with them on the basis of self-interest; you let them speak when they agree with you, but you silence them when they disagree; even your moments of love are nothing but a barren exchange of egotisms; you talk about yourself five minutes, and he talks about himself five minutes, but if he takes longer he is a bore.

No wonder such people often say: "I must pull myself together." Thus do they confess that they are like broken mirrors, each reflecting a different image. In essence this is debauchery, or the inability to choose one among many attractions; the soul is diffused, multiple, or "legion" as Satan called himself.

(3) Finally, you can use your freedom as Christ did on the Cross, by surrendering His Spirit to the Father, and as Mary bade us at Cana, by doing His Will in all things. This is perfect freedom: the displacement of self as the center of motivation, and the fixation of our choices, decisions, and actions on Divine Love. "Thy Will be done on earth as it is in Heaven."

We are all like limpets that can live only when they cling to a rock. Our freedom forces us to cling to something. Freedom is ours to give away; we are free to choose our servitudes. To surrender to Perfect Love is to surrender to happiness and thereby be perfectly free.

Thus to "serve Him is to reign." But we are frightened. Like St. Augustine in his early life we say: I want to love you, dear Lord, a little later on, but not now." Fearful of One Who comes to us purple-robed and cypress-crowned, we ask: "Must Thy harvest fields be dunged with rotten death?" Must gold be purified by fire? Must hands that beckon bear the red livid marks of nails? Must I give up my candle, if l have the sun? Must I give up knocking if the door of love is opened? Do we not act toward God and Mary as a child who resents the affectionate embrace of its parents, because it is not our mood to love?

Francis Thompson so reflected when he heard these words from the mouth of a child:

> "Why do you so clasp me,
> And draw me to your knee?
> Forsooth, you do but chafe me,
> I pray you let me be:
> I will be loved but now and then
> When it liketh me!'
>
> So I heard a young child,
> A thwart child, a young child
> Rebellious against love's arms,
> Make its peevish cry.
> To the tender God I turn: --
> 'Pardon, Love most High!
> For I think those arms were even Thine,
> And that child even I."

As Pascal said: "There are only two kinds of people we can call reasonable: either those who serve God with their whole heart because they know Him, or those who search after Him with all their heart because they do not know Him."

There is, therefore, some hope for those who are dissatisfied with their choices, and who want. If you do just that, you create a void. Far better it is for you to say: "I am a sinner," than to say: "I have no need of religion." The empty can be filled, but the self-intoxicated have no room for God. Could we but make the surrender, we would cry out with Augustine "Too late, O ancient Beauty, have I loved Thee," as we have discovered in the language of the great poet:

"O gain that lurk'st ungained in all gain!
O love we just fall short of in all love!
O height that in all heights art still above!
O beauty that dost leave all beauty pain!
Thou unpossessed that mak'st possession vain."

Seven Words of Jesus and Mary, 1945

Acknowledgments

To the Archbishop Fulton John Sheen Foundation in Peoria, Illinois for there help and encouragement in the creation of this book series on the Seven Last Words.

We would also like to acknowledge the Most Rev. Daniel R. Jenky, C.S.C., Bishop of Peoria, in appreciation for his many years of leadership and fidelity to Archbishop Sheen's cause for canonization.

www.archbishopsheencause.org

To the staff at Sophia Institute Press for their invaluable assistance.

Their mission to nurture the spiritual, moral and cultural life of souls and to spread the gospel of Christ in conformity with the authentic teachings of the Roman Catholic Church is very much appreciated.

www.sophiainstitute.com

To the good folks at Bishop Sheen Today. We value your guidance, support, and prayers in helping us to share the wisdom of Archbishop Fulton J. Sheen with a whole new generation of readers. Your apostolic work of sharing his audio and video presentations along with his many writings to a worldwide audience is very much appreciated.

www.bishopsheentoday.com

And lastly, to Archbishop Fulton J. Sheen, whose teachings on the Holy Hour and prayer continue to inspire many to love God more and to appreciate the gift of the Church. May we be so blessed as to imitate Archbishop Sheen's love for the saints, the sacraments, the Eucharist, and the Blessed Virgin Mary. May the Good Lord grant him a very high place in heaven!

About the Author

Fulton J. Sheen (1895–1979)

Archbishop Sheen, best known for his popularly televised and syndicated television program, Life is Worth Living, is held today as one of Catholicism's most widely recognized figures of the twentieth century.

Fulton John Sheen, born May 8, 1895 in El Paso, Illinois was raised and educated in the Roman Catholic faith. Originally named Peter John Sheen, he came to be known as a young boy by his mother's maiden name, Fulton. Over the course of many dedicated, steadfast years, he was ordained a priest of the Diocese of Peoria at St. Mary's Cathedral in Peoria, IL on September 20, 1919.

Following his ordination, Sheen moved overseas to further his education, and earned a doctorate in Philosophy from The Catholic University of Louvain in Belgium in 1923. That same year, he received the Cardinal Mercier Prize for International Philosophy, becoming the first ever American to earn this distinction.

Upon returning to America after varied and extensive work throughout Europe, Sheen continued to preach, as well as teach theology and philosophy at the Catholic University of America in Washington DC from 1927 until 1950.

Starting in 1930, Sheen became a host on a weekly Sunday night radio broadcast called The Catholic Hour. This broadcast captured many devoted listeners, reportedly drawing an audience of four million people every week for two decades.

In 1950, he became the National Director of the Society for the Propagation of the Faith, raising money to support the missions. During the 16 years that he held this position, he raised millions of dollars to support the missionary activity of the Church. These efforts influenced tens of millions of people all over the world, bringing them to know Christ and his Church. In addition, his own preaching and personal example brought about many converts to Catholicism.

In 1951, Sheen was appointed Auxiliary Bishop of the Archdiocese of New York. That same year, Sheen moved from his weekly radio broadcast to hosting the Catholic television program, Life is Worth Living. This show aired every Tuesday evening at 8pm for six years.

Over the course of the show, Sheen's Life is Worth Living competed for airtime with popular television stars such as Frank Sinatra and Milton Berle. Sheen's show held its own, and in 1953, just two years after its debut, he won an Emmy Award for "Most Outstanding Television Personality." Fulton Sheen credited the Gospel writers - Matthew, Mark, Luke, and John - for their valuable contribution to his success. This television show ran until 1957, boasting as many as 30 million weekly viewers.

In the fall of 1966, Sheen was appointed Bishop of Rochester, New York. During this time, Bishop Sheen hosted another television series, The Fulton Sheen Program; running from 1961 to 1968 that closely modeled the Life is Worth Living series.

After nearly three years as Bishop of Rochester, Fulton Sheen resigned and was appointed the Archbishop of Titular See of Newport Wales by Pope Paul VI. This new appointment allowed Sheen the flexibility to continue preaching.

Sheen was known for his annual Good Friday homilies that he preached for 58 consecutive years in New York and elsewhere. Sheen also led numerous retreats for priests and religious, and preached at conferences all over the world.

When asked by Pope Pius XII how many converts he had made, Sheen responded, “Your Holiness, I have never counted them. I am always afraid if I did count them, I might think I made them, instead of the Lord.”

“If you want people to stay as they are,” he said, “tell them what they want to hear. If you want to improve them, tell them what they should know.” This he did, not only in his preaching but also in the numerous books and articles he wrote. His book entitled ‘Peace of Soul’ was sixth on the New York Times best-seller list.

Three of Sheen’s great loves were for the Missions and the propagation of the faith; the Blessed Mother; and the Eucharist.

He made a daily holy hour before the Blessed Sacrament, from which he drew strength and inspiration to preach the gospel and in the presence of which he prepared his homilies. “I beg [Christ] every day to keep me strong physically and alert mentally in order to preach His gospel and proclaim His Cross and Resurrection,” he said. “I am so happy doing this that I sometimes feel that when I come to the good Lord in Heaven, I will take a few days’ rest and then ask Him to allow me to come back again to this earth to do some more work.”

His contributions to the Catholic Church are numerous and varied, ranging from educating in classrooms, churches, and homes, to preaching over a nationally publicized radio show, and two television programs, as well as penning over 50 written works. Bishop Fulton J. Sheen had a gift for communicating the Word of God in the most pure, simple way. His strong background in philosophy helped him to relate to all of his followers in a highly personalized manner. His timeless messages continue to have great relevance today. He inspires each of us to live a God-centered life with the joy and love that God intended.

On October 2, 1979 Archbishop Sheen received his greatest accolade when Pope John Paul II embraced him at St. Patrick's Cathedral in New York City. The Holy Father said to him, "You have written and spoken well of the Lord Jesus. You are a loyal son of the Church."

The Good Lord called Fulton Sheen home on December 9, 1979. His television broadcasts, now on tape, and his books continue his earthly work of winning souls for Christ. Sheen's cause for canonization was opened in 2002 and in 2012, Pope Benedict XVI declared him "Venerable." In July of 2019, Pope Francis formally approved the miracle that is attributed to the intercession of the Venerable Archbishop Fulton J. Sheen. This announcement allows a beatification ceremony to take place in the future. The time and date for the church to declare Archbishop Fulton J. Sheen a saint is in God's hands.

Fulton J. Sheen Books Used in This Book

(First Meditation) - Fulton J. Sheen, The Seven Last Words – (New York: Century Co. Ltd., 1933)

(Second Meditation) - Fulton J. Sheen, The Fullness of Christ – (Huntington, IN: Our Sunday Visitor, 1935)

(Third Meditation) - Fulton J. Sheen, Calvary And The Mass – (New York: P.J. Kenedy & Sons, 1936)

(Fourth Meditation) - Fulton J. Sheen, The Cross And The Beatitudes, - (New York: P.J. Kenedy & Sons, 1937)

(Fifth Meditation) - Fulton J. Sheen, The Rainbow of Sorrow - (New York: P.J. Kenedy & Sons 1938)

(Sixth Meditation) - Fulton J. Sheen, Victory Over Vice – (New York: P.J. Kenedy & Sons, 1939)

(Seventh Meditation) - Fulton J. Sheen, The Seven Virtues - (New York: P.J. Kenedy & Sons, 1940)

(Eighth Meditation) - Fulton J. Sheen, Seven Words To The Cross – (New York: P.J. Kenedy & Sons, 1944)

(Ninth Meditation) - Fulton J. Sheen, Seven Words of Jesus and Mary - (New York: P.J. Kenedy & Sons, 1945)

Jesus and the Thieves

A Painting by Michael O'Brien (2008)

Artist Commentary: Jesus promises Paradise to the repentant thief. We tend to think that when severe trials come we will suffer with the same courage and love as Jesus did. Or, perhaps as the "good thief" did. Yet we often find ourselves reacting to trials in the manner of the unrepentant thief. Within our hearts is the potential for all three responses. In life's difficulties, we are refined and tested, our hearts are revealed to us, that we might turn and turn again to the One who died for us on the Cross. If we do not succumb to bitterness or despair, or run from what we must learn, we will be with Him "this day in Paradise."

Printed in Great Britain
by Amazon

59429222R00284